POPE PAUL VI

"The most weighty task of *Magisterium* . . . pertains to us by apostolic succession. Its authority and well assured foundation in Christ, our One Supreme Teacher, are quite necessary for the government of the Church . . . defending the People of God from so many and such great errors which are invading the divine deposit of the truth which God has revealed . . . Anyone who rejects or denies this *Magisterium* is in opposition to the One True Church."—*To the International Theological Commission, October 16, 1969.*

CREED AND CATECHETICS

Creed
and Catechetics

a Catechetical Commentary on the
Creed of the People of God

EUGENE KEVANE

Preface by
JOHN CARDINAL WRIGHT

Christian Classics · *Westminster, Maryland*

COPYRIGHT © 1978 by Christian Classics
International Standard Book Number 0-87061-007-4
Library of Congress Catalog Card Number 78-52069
Printed in the United States of America

To St. Thérèse of Lisieux

Whom St. Pius X called "The Greatest Saint of Modern Times," who lived what St. Augustine wrote, that Faith not only has eyes for seeing the truth of God, but also hands for holding on to Someone as we go forward, day after day, in the dark.

Contents

Prefatory Note

by JOHN CARDINAL WRIGHT

OUR LORD told His Apostles that the world would hate *them* because it first hated *Him,* (Jn. 15:18) and certainly the antipathy of the world toward the Church of Christ has diminished little since that solemn prophecy was made. Attacks over the years, however, have seldom been launched without an offer of a measure of immunity in exchange for proper tribute, the extortion varying with the nature of the times. In the first centuries the demand was to deny the faith or lose one's life. Then, one might go free in exchange for a pinch of incense publicly given the gods of paganism, mental reservation being presumably tolerated. Later, the Church was provided a choice between her principles and her patrimony. Today the threat is slightly more subtle: she is offered the option between preaching a message that men will accept and losing her "credibility."

It is somewhat ironic that those who threaten her with the loss of credibility simultaneously attack her Creed. But this paradoxical reaction is not difficult to penetrate. The explanation lies in a brazen distortion of the word "credibility" itself, which to Neo-Modernists does not mean "worthy of belief" but "attractiveness" or "popularity." If the Church's major function is to make men feel good, then her insistence on constant truths tends to make her "incredible" because these can make men uneasy in their conscience.

On the practical level of catechetics, on which the present author writes, we can see how far this "no-Creed" position has influenced recent religious education texts by observing the paucity of doctrine in so many of them. They stimulate; they provoke discussion; they may even seek to make one's conscience uneasy in certain restricted areas '(like social justice, selectively defined), though not in others (like keeping holy the Lord's Day or marital fidelity), but there is scant hint of traditional doctrine, the fact of the Trinity, the Virginity of the Mother of God, or the Last Judgment, to be found in them. Accordingly, children nowadays are beginning their life of faith ignorant of its basic truths.

Pope Paul VI recognized early in his pontificate this drift away from binding statements of doctrinal truths and in 1968 published a modern summary of Catholic belief entitled "Creed of the People of God." It is this Creed that Monsignor Kevane expounds in the present book. The word "modern" when applied to a creed may seem to belie the constancy in doctrine which by definition should characterize every Catholic Creed. But in this case "modern" refers not to content but to emphasis and to doctrinal development. For example, Pope Paul was aware that one of today's central problems is the rejection of the Church's Magisterium, so he amplified the short phrase of the Apostle's Creed; "I believe in the Holy Catholic Church," to read: "We believe in one, holy, catholic and apostolic Church built by Jesus Christ on the rock that is Peter . . . We believe in the infallibility enjoyed by the Successor of Peter when he speaks *ex cathedra* . . ." The two Creeds written centuries apart say the same thing; one is merely a developed statement of the abiding truth.

In fact, it is a thrill for a Catholic to pick up a Creed composed by a contemporary Pope and find that it teaches the same doctrine on the Trinity as St. Irenaeus in the second century. Of course, for those who find doctrinal continuity stultifying and offensive to intellectual freedom, this book will be otiose. But those who believe and who comprehend the role of the theologian and catechist to be that of explaining modern questions in the light of revealed and authentically transmitted truths, and not the other way around, will experience in Monsignor Kevane's presentation the joy of finding ancient truths framed in today's context without distortion of their original meaning.

Grace, the Incarnation, Original Sin are not concepts contrary to human reason, though human reason is incapable of understanding them fully. This is a humiliating situation for men today who are on the verge of bringing forth life in a test tube and are making plans to reach the farthest star. They know so much about the material world and understand so many of its inner secrets that they tend to resent being asked to accept as true propositions that their own minds cannot fully hold. They are in the position of those disciples who heard Christ's prophecy of the Eucharist and thereafter walked with Him no more because "it was a hard saying," that is, they couldn't understand how it could be and were unwilling to take God's word for it. We recall, however, that Our Lord did not retract His teaching because some followers found it "irrelevant" and Him "incredible."

Pope Paul VI in summary form and Monsignor Kevane in developed explanations present to modern Catholics the essential doctrine of the faith. Pope Paul summarizes his brief Creed from the deposit of faith preserved immaculate by the Church over two thousand years. Monsignor Kevane examines in considerable detail what that deposit of faith should mean to man today and how it can best be presented to lead him to God. Some of us were fortunate enough to learn a Creed of faith by heart as youngsters and we still pray it in moments of solitude but present doctrinal confusion may make some of us apprehensive in trying to explain it to younger generations. Careful study of this volume will provide exciting adventure for the reader who knows the experience of tussling within himself to discover what God requires him to believe and to do; it will make the reader more confident when, having clarified his own beliefs, he has the opportunity to transmit them to others, which is the missionary duty of every believer.

JOHN CARDINAL WRIGHT

Vatican City State,
June, 1977.

Introduction

THIS book is divided into five parts. Perhaps a word on the nature of each will clarify the purpose and unity of the whole.

Part One contains the official texts of the chief forms of the Creed, the interrogatory form which is an essential element of the Sacrament of Baptism, and the declaratory forms which since the Apostles have been the substance of the catechesis which prepares for Baptism and helps members of the Church deepen their prayerful conversion to God in faith, hope and charity.

Part Two sketches the historical development of the Creed, the profession of the apostolic faith, from the evangelization and catechesis of Jesus Christ and His Apostles to the present day. There is a direct line of doctrinal development, unchanged in meaning, from the *Nicene Creed* of the fourth century to the *Creed of the People of God* in the present years since Vatican II. There was a similar direct line leading from the initial profession of faith, used by the Apostles and the early Church when baptizing new members, to the Nicene Creed. Whenever in her history the Catholic Church has encountered doctrinal doubt and denial, she always has turned to her original Creed, the profession of the apostolic faith, renewing it and developing it to meet the challenge. So too in the present years since Vatican II. A far-reaching and well-articulated movement of doubt and denial has surfaced in the field of religious education. It was especially visible in the *New Catechism,* the publication which, drawn to the attention of the Holy See, became the immediate occasion of the sequence of events which led to that contemporary and quite fully developed profession of the apostolic faith which is now known everywhere as the *Creed of the People of God.* The Dutch Catechism does not have the vogue at present which it was enjoying ten years ago. But the characteristics of its Neo-Modernist catechetical approach, its ambiguities, its omissions and its outright doctrinal errors, live on in many syllabi and programs of religious education, and in teaching aids which implement them. They have even been visible in the United States in the drafts for a *National Catechetical Directory.* Part Two, then leads across history to this contemporary situation which has had the good effect of occasioning the *Creed of the People of God,* the providential assistance which offers substance and stability of content to catechetical teaching today.

Part Three is divided into two sections which correspond to the actual text of the *Creed of the People of God.* The first section discusses the introductory paragraphs in which the Pope himself relates this profession of faith to the current doctrinal crisis and the resulting contemporary upset in the field of religious education. The second section is a practical commentary on the twelve major headings of Catholic doctrine which the *Creed* professes. It is practical in the sense that the commentary correlates creedal content with the sound teaching method of the *Roman Catechism* and the *General Catechetical Directory,* with brief references to the deficiencies of the Neo-Modernist approach in each case. The *New Catechism* usually offers the best illustration of these characteristic deficiencies. This is so because it not only occasioned the publication of the *Creed* by the Holy See, but also because its catechetical approaches have found the wide and continuing application already mentioned.

Part Four gathers into one convenient presentation several postconciliar documents of the contemporary Holy See which bear upon the Creed, upon Him whom the Creed professes, and upon the problematic of doubt and denial which has arisen since Vatican II. Since the Creed is fundamentally the witness of the Church to Jesus Christ as our Lord, as the Eternal Son of God, as our Creator, Redeemer, and Savior, these documents are all concerned, one way or another, with explaining and defending the profession of the Catholic faith in Him. This means that catechetical teachers need to have them at hand, for, as the *General Catechetical Directory,* No. 40, says, "Catechetics must necessarily be Christocentric."

Part Five is a short conclusion summarizing the relationship between Creed and Catechetics, which the work as a whole attempts to bring into better view by gathering the relevant documentation into one place for practical convenience and for further study.

The general purpose of this book can be illustrated by the idea of a work published a century ago by Father Michael Müller, C.SS.R., entitled *God the Teacher of Mankind: A Plain, Comprehensive Explanation of the Apostles' Creed* (New York: Benziger Brothers, 1877). Circumstances change, but the substance of catechetics abides: the handing on of the same Catholic faith, unchanged in its articles and unchanged in their meaning. And the Creed which summarizes these articles of faith into a brief official statement for the Sacrament of Baptism, for catechetical teaching, and for personal prayer continues to be in every century since the Apostles the instrument by which God is the Teacher of mankind.

How did this present work come to be done? The writer is not a specialized theologian, and has only that training in theology which is common to all priests. His field of study and activity has been catechetical teaching, religious education: the pedagogical principles of formation in the Catholic faith. The purpose of this work is pastoral and catechetical, not theological.[1] It comes out of several years of direct contact by mail with Catholics, especially parents of Catholic children, in anguish about the kind of religious education they were suffering. At the same time, as a part of the effort to help them, to have something to give them, the translation of the *Catechism of Christian Doctrine,* published by order of Pope St. Pius X, was being done. Nothing illustrates better the fact that official catechisms are simply episcopal explanations of the Apostles' Creed than the study of the catechetical documents of St. Pius X. From this it was but a short step to see the significance of the *Creed of the People of God,* given to the Catholic Church by Pope Paul VI, in relationship to the contemporary aberration in the field of catechetics.

For whom has this work been done? For persons of the Catholic faith, especially those who in any way have the responsibility of handing this faith on to the coming generation of Catholics. In the ordination of a bishop, this responsibility is an explicit charge that echoes in the rites which ordain to the priesthood and the diaconate. The principal consecrator asks the bishop-elect: "Do you propose to guard the deposit of faith pure and entire, according to the tradition coming from the Apostles, which has been preserved always and everywhere in the

Church?" And the answer: "I do so will."² But in addition to the bishops, priests, deacons and religious who carry out this responsibility, there are the parents themselves, whom Vatican II calls the principal evangelists and catechists of their own children. This documentation on the Creed has been prepared for them as well, to help them be and feel secure in their knowledge of what the Catholic faith actually professes and teaches, so that they may hand on to their children not only its content but also its mode of supernatural certitude, the fact that it is truth believed on the authority of God revealing and teaching.

It has been our hope, furthermore, to provide some special help for catechetical teachers in the short commentary on the twelve main headings of Christian doctrine which the *Creed of the People of God* professes. Perhaps these twelve headings may assist pastors and parish religious education coordinators in conducting twelve sessions or classes on the content of the Catholic faith, when training their own cadres of parish catechists. In the same context of diocesan and parish catechetical programs, it is hoped that this analytical study of the Creed, always in the light of its relationship to catechetical teaching, may assist in the work of critical evaluation of religion textbooks, programs and teaching aids which all teachers of the Catholic faith today are called upon to do.

In other words, the primary purpose of this work is positive, as the Creed itself is positive. It is intended to serve the apostolate of catechetical teaching in a positive way, by helping this teaching to draw constantly upon the Creed as the living, ever-contemporary source of the revealed truth which is its content.

At the same time, there is an unavoidable negative side. For approximately two centuries a movement of thought in philosophy and theology has been developing and gathering momentum. It has come to be known as "Modernism" in religion. Confined hitherto to priests and bishops, since Vatican II it is being popularized by means of application to religious education, and thus is becoming disseminated widely among teaching sisters, brothers and the laity. It serves no good purpose to pretend that this phenomenon does not exist. The Vicar of Christ, in his introductory paragraphs to the *Creed of the People of God,* it will be noted below, faces it resolutely and lucidly. For this phenomenon does in fact exist as the general cause of the current crisis of faith, and as the particular cause of the upset in Catholic religious education which is being widely experienced. This religious movement is a reality. It has enthusiastic devotees. It is organized. It is driving to consolidate a victory inside the Catholic Church by reaching the children with its approach. Always during these two contemporary centuries the Church has had to face a struggle for the minds and souls of the children. The struggle continues, more subtle and more dangerous in the present crisis of faith than in the times and places when the existence of the Catholic school was the issue as an alternate to a state-imposed secular education.

This is the reason why the *New Catechism* is a part of the present study. For it was the immediate occasion which brought the *Creed of the People of God* into the life of the contemporary Church, and it was to a significant extent the fountainhead of current unsound approaches in Catholic religious education which fail to program and to implement the handing on of the Catholic faith by teaching.[3]

In answering the question—For whom has this work been done?—there is a wider dimension than the field of catechetical teaching, as the Vicar of Christ himself makes clear in his paragraphs which introduce the *Creed of the People of God*. All Catholics everywhere need to renew their personal possession of their baptismal Creed. For God Almighty is permitting a shaking and a sifting of the Catholic Church today which leaves no Catholic untouched.[4] There is a shaking of each Catholic, an awakening and a calling for each to take hold of his Creed personally, to profess it anew, to build it into his personal interior life by an authentic *metanoia,* and thus to follow Him upon whom the Creed centers in a renewed and more personal way.

Sometimes one hears it said that those who profess and defend this Creed "veer off to the right," as if the reasonable center of Christian thought and of ecclesiastical policy were somehow in the present century something other than this apostolic faith, this "Creed of the immortal Tradition of the Holy Church of God," as Paul VI terms it.[5] When this shallow and merely political way of conceiving Catholic Faith and Order is permitted to operate, using the slogans of "right" and "left," "conservative" and "liberal," where the Creed itself is concerned, then conditions develop within the Church which make separatist movements seem plausible to many. The words of Bishop Nestor Adam, the Local Ordinary in which Archbishop Lefebvre's famous seminary is located at Ecône, Switzerland, are relevant to the purpose of the present study. "It cannot be denied," he writes, "that the Ecône affair has sown cockle in this country. That is regrettable in the extreme. But let us not bring here the quarrels that are raging elsewhere. Far be it from us to do so! These difficulties have their good side: they should lead us to reflect seriously and help us to deepen our religious knowledge. As to the hesitations felt by some at this moment in the field of faith, I shall simply say: Take and read the Creed of Paul VI which appeared in 1968. It is a text made for wide publication. It should be found in every family. In this document you have a precise and sure statement of the truths to be believed. It alone is worth infinitely more than all you could read elsewhere. It comes from him who has been appointed by Christ to be the authentic guardian of the Church's faith."[6]

It has been our intention to conduct this study dispassionately, gathering the documentation in the matter so that readers may judge for themselves. The choice of the term "Neo-Modernist" for this phenomenon in contemporary religion and religious education is not a matter of name-calling, but one of objective scholarly communication. This point brings us to an additional category of persons, by no means the least, for whom this work on the Creed is intended. It is the Catholic youth in senior high schools and especially in the various colleges and universities, including the so-called secular ones, together with the young priests and religious who are their counsellors. For the sake of these young people, one cannot participate in the pretense that this phenomenon in religion and religious education does not exist, nor indulge the irenicism that "Neo-Modernist" is a term to avoid. Apart from the fact that neither Pope Paul nor Cardinal Wright are avoiding it,[7] one must be honest with these open and talented younger minds. For they are recognizing frequently today that they are not really acquainted with their own Creed, that they never have been instructed in the articles of its faith, that they are not knowledgeable about things Catholic, that they have never learned to use the prayers of the Catholic way of life, prayers which include this same Apostles' Creed, that there is an entire world of religious heritage in doctrine and worship which they have missed. They are not at fault. Rather, they are victims of this approach which, beguiled into a search for something new, rich, warm and vital (as the phrasing goes), allows religious education to degenerate into something other than the handing on of the articles of the Catholic faith by effective explanatory teaching. When this dawns upon these young people, they are ready for a new kind of personal study of these matters which are connected with the profession of the apostolic faith, the profession which is a part of the Sacrament of Baptism, the profession which is the very substance and meaning of the Catholic name. These young people want to investigate the concept of divine revelation which has been propagated by the Modernist movement in religion, and to analyze the process which eliminates the Creed when that concept is applied in religious education. These young Catholics, wishing to profess Jesus Christ and to be His followers, are not to be denied when with characteristic energy they examine their situation. They were still children when a high Prelate was heard to say wringing his hands, "But what can we do? We cannot go back to the Baltimore Catechism!" Their answer today is clear and direct. "Of course not. But we can go forward with the Creed, always the same in meaning, assisted by the updated episcopal explanations of its articles of faith that used to be called catechisms." One must be forthright with these young Catholics who exist in so special a situation. The present work has them in mind when drawing attention to sources for further study of these matters. And this is why the term "Modernist" has been used for the earlier stage of the phenomenon and "Neo-Modernist" for its contemporary application in religious education. We do not wish to offend anyone of a somewhat older generation by the use of these terms. Quite the contrary. Our purpose is doctrinal, not personal. One hopes in this book to minister to Pope Paul's Document on Reconciliation, in Part Four below. And one hopes that very many who have been beguiled will, on the occasion of this new look at the Creed, take a second look at the dynamic and inescapable interrelationship between the living and practising profession of the Catholic faith and the explanation of its articles by formative catechetical teaching. But in any case there is a sense of loyalty to the young students of the writer's present teaching, who simply want to know the facts, and to call them by their objectively correct names. It was with them primarily in mind that we gave up the idea of a purely positive presentation which would attempt to avoid any mention of the Neo-Modernist phenomenon.

For "Modernism" is the name which this movement of thought has had throughout most of its history.[8] It should also be stated that the phenomenon is far larger than the *New Catechism* of a decade ago, and indeed larger than the field of religious education in general, as we have noted already. This "catechism" was a seminal publication, indeed, as the very existence of the *Creed of the People of God* demonstrates; but its importance for the Church today lies not so much in itself as in the contemporary approaches in religious education that derive from its letter and especially from its spirit. And by the same token, the *Creed of the People of God* abides in the Church as the lasting solution both for the aberrations in catechetics today and for the general crisis of faith troubling the Church today. Whatever these problems may be, one can turn to this post-conciliar profession of faith and find the correct statement of the truth of Christian doctrine. The correspondence between this developed form of the Creed and the need of the contemporary Catholic Church for soundness in catechetical teaching is remarkable to say the least and Providential to say the most.

It may seem to some that the contestation of the position of the Holy See by the advocates of the *New Catechism* and its Neo-Modernist approach has been given short shrift, and that the on-going history of their dissent has not been sufficiently featured in this work. But this is to presume that one studies these matters from a lofty platform of judgment upon both sides, so to speak, as if scholarly study occupied a level above these contending parties, the Holy See, namely, and this movement of thought now at last finding a special and concerted application in the field of religious education. This is not a valid position. On the one hand, it falls victim to the dialectic operating among Catholics which expects a higher religious synthesis out of the conflict in which the Church finds herself in continuing the evangelization and catechesis of the present generation. On the other hand, it fails to see that the Holy See is not simply one group of philosophers and theologians pitted in conflict with another group of the same who have decided upon a different optic, as the French say. The catechist exists in a different dimension. For the authentic catechetical teacher, one of these parties represents the pillar and ground of truth, and is the very voice of the Supreme Being to mankind upon this planet. The profession of the apostolic faith contains the message of God to man, and when the Holy See defends and develops this message in terms of the religious phenomenon under discussion, the catechist without hesitation takes his stand with the Holy See. His contribution is the pedagogical explanation of this message in attractive terms understandable today, using the latest and most effective methodology. By means of his catechetical explanation of the articles of faith which the Creed professes, he shows that the meaning continues unchanged, the same yesterday, today and forever.[9] For the very idea of catechesis is a ministry to the evangelization which the Catholic Church has been carrying on since the Apostles, and which it will continue until the Second Coming.[10]

This is the position which the present study intends to occupy, making available for catechists a comprehensive documentation on the Creed. It has been aided by the learning of many scholars. But if through ignorance the writer should have erred, it is not his intention to depart from the sound doctrine of the Catholic Church. This work is given over without qualification to her light and is submitted to her decisions.

I wish to acknowledge the help of Sisters Mary Sarah, Jessica and Karena, S.N.D., the Staff at the Notre Dame Institute, Middleburg, Virginia: the help of all three for the load of work they carry which has given freedom for this study, and of Sister Mary Karena in particular for her efficient preparation of the typescript. It is a pleasant duty to acknowledge my debt of gratitude for the moral support of St. John's University in New York, and of my colleagues at its Institute for Advanced Studies in Catholic Doctrine.

REV. MSGR. EUGENE KEVANE

Feast of Sts. Peter and Paul
June 29, 1977

PART ONE

The Creed of the Catholic Church in its Official Formulations

"This is the faith imparted to Christian neophytes. They are to make profession of it in the few words contained in the Creed. To believers, these few words are well known. By believing them they are made subject to God, by being subject to God they live a good life, by a good life they obtain purity of heart, and with a pure heart they understand the things they believe."—St. Augustine,
Faith and the Creed,
Chapter 10 (24).

Forma Symboli Interrogativa
seu Baptismalis

PROfESSIO fIÒEI

(*Celebrans, de nomine uniuscuiusque baptizandi tempestive iterum certior factus a patrino (vel a matrina), unumquemque interrogat*):
N, credis in Deum Patrem omnipotentem, creatorem caeli et terrae?

(*Electus*):
Credo.

(*Celebrans*):
Credis in Iesum Christum, Filium eius unicum, Dominum nostrum, natum ex Maria Virgine, passum et sepultum, qui a mortuis resurrexit et sedet ad dexteram Patris?

(*Electus*):
Credo.

(*Celebrans*):
Credis in Spiritum Sanctum, sanctam Ecclesiam catholicam, Sanctorum communionem, remissionem peccatorum, carnis resurrectionem et vitam aeternam?

(*Electus*):
Credo.

(*Post professionem fidei quisque statim immergitur vel abluitur.*)[a]

The Interrogatory or Baptismal Form of the Creed

pROfession of faith

(The celebrant, advised by the godparent of the name of each candidate, asks each one) :

N., do you believe in God, the Father Almighty, Creator of heaven and earth?

(Elect) :

I do.

(Celebrant) :

Do you believe in Jesus Christ, his only Son, our Lord, who was born of the Virgin Mary, was crucified, died, and was buried, rose from the dead, and is now seated at the right hand of the Father?

(Elect) :

I do.

(Celebrant) :

Do you believe in the Holy Spirit, the Holy Catholic Church, the communion of saints, the forgiveness of sins, the resurrection of the body, and life everlasting?

(Elect) :

I do.

(After the profession of faith, each candidate is baptized at once.)[b]

3

Forma Symboli Declarativa
seu Catechetica

tradıtıo symboli

(*Post homiliam diaconus dicit*) :
Accedant electi, ut ab Ecclesia Symbolum fidei recipiant.

(*Tunc celebrans eos alloquitur, his vel similibus verbis*) :
Dilectissimi nobis: Audite verba fidei, per quam iustificationem accipietis. Pauca quidem sunt, sed magna continent mysteria. Corde sincero ea suscipite atque servate.

(*Deinde celebrans incipit Symbolum, dicens*) :
Credo in Deum,

(*et prosequitur vel solus vel una cum communitate fidelium*) :
Patrem omnipotentem,
creatorem caeli et terrae.

Et in Iesum Christum,
Filium eius unicum, Dominum nostrum:
qui conceptus est de Spiritu Sancto,
natus ex Maria Virgine,
passus sub Pontio Pilato,
crucifixus, mortuus et sepultus;
descendit ad inferos;
tertia die resurrexit a mortuis;
ascendit ad caelos,
sedet ad dexteram Dei Patris omnipotentis;
inde venturus est iudicare vivos et mortuos.

Credo in Spiritum Sanctum,
sanctam Ecclesiam catholicam,
Sanctorum communionem,
remissionem peccatorum,
carnis resurrectionem,
vitam aeternam. Amen.[c]

The Declaratory or Catechetical Form of the Creed

pResentation of the pRofession of faith

(*Known popularly in the Roman Rite as the Apostles' Creed*)

(*After the homily the deacon says*):
> Those who have been chosen please come forward to receive the Church's profession of faith.

(*Then the celebrant speaks to them in these or similar words*):
> My dear friends:
> Listen carefully to the words of that faith by which you are to be justified. The words are few, but the mysteries they contain are awe-inspiring. Accept them with a sincere heart and be faithful to them.

(*The celebrant begins the profession of faith*):
> I believe in God,

(*and continues alone or with all the faithful*):
> the Father almighty,
> creator of heaven and earth.

> I believe in Jesus Christ, his only Son, our Lord.
> He was conceived by the power of the Holy Spirit
> and born of the Virgin Mary.
> He suffered under Pontius Pilate,
> was crucified, died, and was buried.
> He descended to the dead.
> On the third day he rose again.
> He ascended into heaven,
> and is seated at the right hand of the Father.
> He will come again to judge the living and the dead.

> I believe in the Holy Spirit,
> the holy catholic Church,
> the communion of saints,
> the forgiveness of sins,
> the resurrection of the body,
> and the life everlasting   Amen.[d]

5

Symbolum Nicaeno-Constantinopolitanum

Credo in unum Deum,
Patrem omnipotentem, factorem caeli et terrae,
visiblium omnium et invisibilium.

Et in unum Dominum Iesum Christum,
Filium Dei unigenitum,
et ex Patre natum ante omnia saecula.
Deum de Deo, lumen de lumine, Deum verum de Deo vero,
genitum, non factum, consubstantialem Patri:
per quem omnia facta sunt.
Qui propter nos homines et propter nostram salutem
descendit de caelis
Et incarnatus est de Spiritu Sancto
ex Maria Virgine, et homo factus est.
Crucifixus etiam pro nobis sub Pontio Pilato;
passus et sepultus est,
et resurrexit tertia die, secundum Scripturas,
et ascendit in caelum, sedet ad dexteram Patris.
Et iterum venturus est cum gloria, iudicare vivos et mortuos,
cuius regni non erit finis.

Et in Spiritum Sanctum, Dominum et vivificantem:
qui ex Patre Filioque procedit.
Qui cum Patre et Filio simul adoratur et conglorificatur:
qui locutus est per prophetas.
Et unam, sanctam, catholicam et apostolicam Ecclesiam.
Confiteor unum baptisma in remissionem peccatorum.
Et exspecto resurrectionem mortuorum,
et vitam venturi saeculi.   Amen.[e]

The Nicene Creed

We believe in one God,
the Father, the Almighty,
maker of heaven and earth,
of all that is seen and unseen.

We believe in one Lord, Jesus Christ,
the only Son of God,
eternally begotten of the Father,
God from God, Light from Light,
true God from true God,
begotten, not made, one in Being with the Father.
Through him all things were made.
For us men and for our salvation
he came down from heaven:
by the power of the Holy Spirit
he was born of the Virgin Mary, and became man.
For our sake he was crucified under Pontius Pilate;
he suffered, died, and was buried.
On the third day he rose again
in fulfillment of the Scriptures;
he ascended into heaven
and is seated at the right hand of the Father.
He will come again in glory to judge the living and the dead,
and his kingdom will have no end.

We believe in the Holy Spirit, the Lord, the giver of life,
who proceeds from the Father and the Son.
With the Father and the Son he is worshiped and glorified.
He has spoken through the Prophets.
We believe in one, holy, catholic and apostolic Church.
We acknowledge one baptism for the forgiveness of sins.

We look for the resurrection of the dead,
and the life of the world to come.   Amen.[r]

Acta Pauli P.P. VI

SOLLEMNIS PROFESSIO FIDEI

A Paulo VI Pont. Max. pronuntiata ante Basilicam Petrianam die XXX mensis Iunii anno MCMLXVIII, anno a fide vocato, et saec. XIX a martyrio SS Petri et Pauli App. completis.

VENERABILES FRATRES AC DILECTI FILII,

1. Sollemni hac Liturgia concludimus sive commemorationem saeculi xix post martyrium a sanctis Petro et Paulo Apostolis factum, sive annum, quem a fide appellavimus. Hunc scilicet annum eo consilio sanctis Apostolis commemorandis dicavimus, non solum, ut constantissimam voluntatem Nostram testaremur incorrupte fidei *depositum custodiendi*,[1] quod nobis ipsi tradiderunt, sed etiam ut propositum nostrum confirmaremus eandem fidem ad vitam hoc tempore referendi, cum Ecclesiae in hoc mundo peregrinandum est.

2. In praesenti Nostrum esse putamus iis christifidelibus publicas persolvere gratias, qui invitationibus Nostris respondentes, id effecerunt ut annus a fide nuncupatum summam ubertatem acciperet, tum ad verbum Dei penitius adhaerentes, tum in multis consortionibus professionem fidei renovantes, tum fidem ipsam perspicuis vitae christianae testimoniis comprobantes. Quare dum praesertim Fratribus Nostris in Episcopatu, omnibusque catholicae Ecclesiae filiis gratissimum declaramus animum Nostrum, ipsis Apostolicam Benedictionem Nostram impertimus.

3. Porro Nostrarum esse partium existimamus mandatum conficere a Christo delatum Petro, cuius Nos, licet meritis longe inferiores, suc-

POPE PAUL VI

The Creed of the People of God

as published in *The Acts of the Apostolic See*, August 10, 1968

THE SOLEMN PROFESSION OF FAITH
pronounced by Pope Paul VI at St. Peter's Basilica,
June 30, 1968, at the end of the "Year of Faith," the
nineteenth centenary anniversary of the martyrdom
of Sts. Peter and Paul.

VENERABLE BROTHERS AND BELOVED SONS:

1. With this solemn liturgy We end the celebration of the nineteenth
centenary of the martyrdom of the holy Apostles Peter and Paul,
and thus close the Year of Faith. We dedicated it to the commemoration of the holy Apostles in order that We might give witness
to our steadfast will to *guard the deposit*[1] of faith from corruption,
that deposit which they transmitted to us, and to demonstrate
again our intention of relating this same faith to life at this time
when the Church must continue her pilgrimage in this world.

2. We feel it our duty to give public thanks to all who responded to
our invitation by bestowing on the Year of Faith a splendid com-
pleteness through the deepening of their personal adhesion to the
Word of God, through the renewal in various gatherings of the
Profession of Faith, and through the testimony of a Christian life.
To our Brothers in the Episcopate especially, and to all the faithful

9

cessores sumus: ut nempe in fide *confirmemus fratres*.[2] Quam ob rem, etsi exiguitatis Nostrae conscii sumus, maxima tamen animi vi, quam a mandato Nobis tradito ducimus, professionem fidei facturi sumus, atque formulam a verbo *credo* incipientem sumus pronuntiaturi, quae, quamvis definitio dogmatica vere proprieque non sit nominanda, tamen formulam Nicaenam, quoad rerum summam, repetit, nonnullis adhibitis explicationibus, quas spirituales nostrae huius aetatis condiciones postulant: formulam dicimus immortalis traditionis Ecclesiae sanctae Dei.

4. Quod dum facimus, probe novimus quibus perturbationibus, ad fidem quod attinet, nunc temporis quidam hominum coetus commoveantur. Qui quidem affectionem mundi sese penitus mutantis non effugerunt, in quo tot veritates vel prorsus negantur, vel in controversiam vocantur. Immo vel nonnullos catholicos homines videmus aut mutandarum, aut novandarum rerum quadam quasi cupiditate capi. Ecclesia sane ad officium suum pertinere putat, nisus non intermittere, ut arcana Dei mysteria, unde in omnes tot salutis fructus manant, etiam atque etiam perspiciat, pariterque secuturae aetatis hominibus aptiore cotidie ratione proponat. Sed simul maximopere cavendum est ne, dum necessarium investigandi officium usurpatur, christianae doctrinae veritates labefactentur. Quod si fiat—videmusque, pro dolor, hodie id reipsa fieri— perturbationem et dubitationem fidelibus multorum animis afferat.

5. Ad hanc rem quod spectat, summi est momenti animadvertere, praeter id quod observabile est, scientiarumque ope recognitum, intellegentiam a Deo nobis datam *id quod est* attingere posse, non vero tantummodo significationes subiectivas structurarum, quas vocant, et evolutionis humanae conscientiae. Ceterum recolendum est, illud ad interpretationem seu ad hermeneuma pertinere, ut, verbo, quod pronuntiatum est, observato, intellegere et discernere studeamus sensum textui cuidam subiectum, non vero hunc sensum ad coniecturae arbitratum quodammodo novare.

6. Attamen ante omnia Spiritui Sancto firmissime confidimus, qui est *anima Ecclesiae,* et theologicae fidei, in qua Corporis mystici vita nititur. Cum profecto non ignoremus homines verba exspectare Christi Vicarii, propterea sermonibus et homiliis, quas Nobis per-

of the Holy Catholic Church, we express our appreciation and we grant our blessing.

3. Likewise we deem that we must fulfill the mandate entrusted by Christ to Peter, whose successor we are, the last in merit; namely, to confirm our brothers in the faith.[2] With the awareness, certainly, of our human weakness, yet with all the strength impressed on our spirit by such a command, we shall accordingly make a Profession of Faith, pronounce a formula which begins with the word *Credo, I believe.* Without being strictly speaking a dogmatic definition, it repeats in substance, with some developments called for by the spiritual condition of our time, the Creed of Nicea, the Creed of the immortal Tradition of the Holy Church of God.

4. In making this Profession, we are aware of the disquiet which agitates certain groups of men at the present time with regard to the faith. They do not escape the influence of a world being profoundly changed, in which so many truths are being denied outright or made objects of controversy. We see even Catholics allowing themselves to be seized by a kind of passion for change and novelty. The Church, most assuredly, has always the duty to carry on the effort to study more deeply and to present in a manner ever better adapted to successive generations the unfathomable mysteries of God, rich for all in fruits of salvation. But at the same time the greatest care must be taken, while fulfilling the indispensable duty of research, to do no injury to the truths of Christian doctrine. For that would be to give rise, as is unfortunately seen in these days, to disturbance and doubt in many faithful souls.

5. It is supremely important in this respect to recall that, beyond what is observable, analyzed by the work of the sciences, the intellect which God has given us reaches *that which is,* and not merely the subjective expression of the structures and development of consciousness. And, on the other hand, it is important to remember that the task of interpretation—of hermeneutics—is to try to understand and extricate, while respecting the word expressed, the sense conveyed by a text, and not to recreate, in some fashion,

6. But above all, we place our unshakeable confidence in the Holy Spirit, the soul of the Church, and in theological faith upon which this sense in accordance with arbitrary hypotheses.

saepe habere placet, eorum exspectationem explemus. Sed hodierno die opportunitas Nobis offertur sollemnius verbum proferendi.

7. Itaque hoc die, a Nobis electo ad concludendum annum a fide appellatum, atque in hac celebratione sanctorum Petri et Pauli Apostolorum, summo Deo viventi obsequium professionis fidei deferre volumus. Atque quemadmodum olim Caesareae Philippi Simon Petrus, duodecim Apostolorum nomine, praeter hominum opiniones, vere Christum Dei viventis Filium professus est, ita hodie tenuis eius Successor, universaeque Ecclesiae Pastor, nomine totius populi Dei, vocem suam intendit, ut firmissimum testimonium divinae Veritati dicat, quae ideo Ecclesiae est credita, ut eam omnibus gentibus nuntiet.

Hanc autem Nostram fidei professionem satis et expletam et expressam esse volumus, ut apta ratione necessitati luminis satisfaciamus, qua tot fideles homines premuntur, iique omnes qui in mundo— ad quemcumque spiritualem coetum pertinent— Veritatem conquirunt.

Ad gloriam igitur omnipotentis Dei et Domini nostri Iesu Christi, fiducia in auxilio Sanctissimae Virginis Mariae et beatorum Petri et Pauli Apostolorum collocata, ad utilitatem spiritualemque progressionem Ecclesiae, nomine omnium sacrorum Pastorum et christifidelium, plenaque vobiscum, Fratres ac Filii dilectissimi, communione, nunc hanc fidei professionem pronuntiamus.

PROFESSIO FIDEI

8. Credimus in unum Deum, Patrem, Filium et Spiritum Sanctum, Creatorem rerum visibilium—cuiusmodi est hic mundus ubi nostram brevem degimus vitam—rerumque invisibilium—cuius generis sunt puri spiritus, quos etiam angelos appellamus[3]— itemque Creatorem, in unoquoque homine, animae spiritualis et immortalis.[4]

9. Credimus hunc unicum Deum ita absolute unum esse in sua sanctissima essentia, ut in ceteris suis perfectionibus: in sua omnipotentia, in sua scientia infinita, in sua providentia, in sua voluntate et caritate. *Ille est qui est,* ut ipse Moysi revelavit,[5] ille est *Amor,* ut nos Ioannes Apostolus docuit:[6] ita ut duo haec nomina, Esse et Amor, ineffabiliter divinam eandem exprimant

rests the life of the Mystical Body. We know that souls await the word of the Vicar of Christ, and we respond to that expectation with the instructions which we regularly give. But today we are given an opportunity to make a more solemn utterance.

7. On this day which is chosen to close the Year of Faith, on this Feast of the Blessed Apostles Peter and Paul, we have wished to offer to the Living God the homage of a Profession of Faith. And as once at Caesarea Philippi the Apostle Peter spoke on behalf of the Twelve to make a true confession, beyond human opinions, of Christ as Son of the Living God, so today his humble Successor, Pastor of the Universal Church, raises his voice to give, on behalf of all the People of God, a firm witness to the divine Truth entrusted to the Church to be announced to all nations.

We have wished our Profession of Faith to be to a high degree complete and explicit, in order that it may respond in a fitting way to the need of light felt by so many faithful souls, and by all those in the world to whatever spiritual family they belong, who are in search of the Truth.

Therefore, to the glory of God Most Holy and of Our Lord Jesus Christ, trusting in the aid of the Blessed Virgin Mary and of the Holy Apostles Peter and Paul, for the profit and edification of the Church, in the name of all the Pastors and all the faithful, we now pronounce this Profession of Faith, in full communion with you all, beloved Brothers and Sons.

PROFESSION OF FAITH

8. We believe in one only God, Father, Son and Holy Spirit, Creator of things visible such as this world in which our brief life passes, of things invisible such as the pure spirits which are also called angels,[3] and Creator in each man of his spiritual and immortal soul.[4]

9. We believe that this only God is absolutely one in His infinitely holy essence as also in all His perfections, in His omnipotence, His infinite knowledge, His providence, His will and His love. He is *He Who Is,* as He revealed to Moses;[5] and He is *Love,* as the Apostle John Teaches us:[6] so that these two names, Being and

Illius essentiam, qui seipsum nobis manifestare voluit, quique *lucem inhabitans inaccessibilem*[7] est in seipso super omne nomen, superque omnes res et intellegentias creatas. Deus unus potest nobis suipsius rectam plenamque impertire cognitionem, seipsum revelans uti Patrem, Filium et Spiritum Sanctum, cuius nos, hisce in terris in obscuritate fidei, et post mortem in sempiterna luce, ad aeternam vitam participandam per gratiam vocamur. Mutua vincula, ex omni aeternitate Tres Personas constituentia, quarum unaquaeque est unum idemque Esse divinum, sanctissimi Dei sunt intima beataque vita, quae infinite omne id superat, quod nos modo humano intellegere possumus.[8] Gratias tamen divinae bonitati agimus, quod quam plurimi credentes coram hominibus nobiscum Unitatem Dei testari possunt, quamvis mysterium sanctissimae Trinitatis non cognoscant.

10. Credimus igitur in Deum, qui in omni aeternitate generat Filium, credimus in Filium, Verbum Dei, qui ab aeterno gignitur, credimus in Spiritum Sanctum, Personam increatam, qui ex Patre Filioque ut sempiternus eorum Amor procedit. Ita in tribus Personis divinis, quae sunt coaeternae sibi et coaequales,[9] vita et beatitudo Dei plane unius quam maxime abundant et consummantur, summa cum excellentia et gloria Essentiae increatae propria; atque *semper unitas in Trinitate et Trinitas in unitate* veneranda est.[10]

11. Credimus in Dominum nostrum Iesum Christum, Dei Filium. Ipse est Verbum aeternum, natus ex Patre ante omnia saecula et consubstantialis Patri, seu *homoousios to Patri;* per quem omnia facta sunt. Et incarnatus est de Spiritu Sancto ex Maria Virgine et homo factus est: aequalis ergo *Patri secundum divinitatem,* minor Patri secundum humanitatem,[11] unus omino *non confusione* (quae fieri non potest) *substantiae, sed unitate personae.*[12]

12. Ipse habitavit in nobis plenus gratiae et veritatis. Annuntiavit et constituit Regnum Dei, in seipso nobis Patrem manifestans. Dedit nobis mandatum suum novum, ut nos invicem diligeremus, sicut ipse dilexit nos. Docuit nos viam Beatitudinum evangelicarum: videlicet esse pauperes in spiritu, et mites, dolores tolerare in patientia, sitire iustitiam, esse misericordes, mundos corde, pacificos, persecutionem pati propter iustitiam. Passus est sub Pontio Pilato, Agnus Dei, portans peccata mundi, mortuus est pro nobis

Love, express ineffably the same divine Reality of Him Who has wished to make Himself known to us, and Who "dwelling in light inaccessible,"[7] is in Himself above every name, above every thing and above every created intellect. God alone can give us right and full knowledge of this Reality by revealing Himself as Father, Son and Holy Spirit, in Whose Eternal Life we are by grace called to share, here below in the obscurity of faith and after death in eternal light. The mutual bonds which eternally constitute the Three Persons, Who are each one and the same Divine Being, are the blessed inmost life of God Thrice Holy, infinitely beyond all that we can conceive in human measure.[8] We give thanks, however, to the Divine Goodness that very many believers can testify with us before men to the Unity of God, even though they know not the Mystery of the Most Holy Trinity.

10. We believe then in God who eternally begets the Son, in the Son, the Word of God, who is eternally begotten, in the Holy Spirit, the uncreated Person, who proceeds from the Father and the Son as their eternal Love. Thus in the Three Divine Persons, *coaeternae sibi et coaequales,*[9] the life and beatitude of God perfectly One superabound and are consummated in the supreme excellence and glory proper to uncreated Being, and always "there should be venerated Unity in the Trinity and Trinity in the Unity."[10]

11. We believe in Our Lord Jesus Christ, Who is the Son of God. He is the Eternal Word, born of the Father before time began, and consubstantial with the Father, *homoousios to Patri,* and through Him all things were made. He was incarnate of the Virgin Mary by the power of the Holy Spirit, and was made man: equal therefore to the Father according to His divinity, and inferior to the Father acording to His humanity,[11] and Himself one, not by some impossible confusion of His natures, but by the unity of His person.[12]

12. He dwelt among us, full of grace and truth. He proclaimed and established the Kingdom of God and made us know in Himself the Father. He gave us His new commandment to love one another as He loved us. He taught us the way of the Beatitudes of the Gospel: poverty in spirit, meekness, suffering borne with patience, thirst after justice, mercy, purity of heart, will for peace, persecu-

Cruci affixus, sanguine redemptionis afferens nobis salutem. Sepultus est, et propria virtute resurrexit tertia die, ad consortium vitae divinae, quae est gratia, Resurrectione sua nos evehens. Ascendit in caelum, unde iterum venturus est tunc cum gloria ad iudicandos vivos et mortuos, unumquemque secundum propria merita: qui Amori et Pietati Dei responderint, ibunt in vitam aeternam, qui vero ea usque ad exitum respuerint, igni addicentur interituro numquam.
Et Regni eius non erit finis.

13. Credimus in Spiritum Sanctum, Dominum et vivificantem, qui cum Patre et Filio simul adoratur et conglorificatur. Qui locutus est per Prophetas; missus est nobis a Christo post eius Resurrectionem et Ascensionem ad Patrem; illuminat, vivificat, tuetur ac regit Ecclesiam, cuius purificat membra, dummodo gratiam ne aversentur. Eius opera, quae ad intimum animum permanat, hominem aptum facit, qui illi Christi praecepto respondeat: *Estote . . . perfecti, sicut et Pater vester caelestis perfectus est.*[13]

14. Credimus Beatam Mariam, quae semper Virgo permansit, Matrem fuisse Verbi Incarnati, Dei et Salvatoris nostri Iesu Christi,[14] eamque, ob singularem suam electionem *intuitu meritorum Filii sui sublimiore modo redemptam,*[15] *ab omni originalis culpae labe praeservatam immunem fuisse,*[16] atque *eximiae gratiae dono omnibus aliis creaturis antecellere.*[17]

15. Arcto et indissolubili vinculo mysterio Incarnationis et Redemptionis coniuncta,[18] Beatissima Virgo Maria, Immaculata, *expleto terrestris vitae cursu, corpore et anima ad caelestem gloriam est assumpta*[19] et Filio suo, qui resurrexit a mortuis, similis reddita, sortem omnium iustorum in antecessum accepit; credimus Sanctissimam Dei Genetricem, novam Hevam, *Matrem Ecclesiae,*[20] *caelitus nunc materno pergere* circa Christi membra *munere fungi, quo ad gignendam augendamque vitam divinam in singulis hominum redemptorum animis opem confert.*[21]

16. Credimus omnes in Adam peccavisse; quod significat originalem culpam ab illo commissam effecisse, ut natura humana, universis hominibus communis, in talem laberetur statum in quo illius culpae consequentias pateretur. Qui status iam ille non est, in quo

tion suffered for justice sake. He suffered under Pontius Pilate, the Lamb of God bearing on Himself the sins of the world, and He died for us on the Cross, saving us by His redeeming Blood. He was buried, and, of His own power, rose the third day, raising us by His Resurrection to that sharing in the divine life which is the life of grace. He ascended to heaven, and He will come again, this time in glory, to judge the living and the dead: each according to his merits—those who have responded to the Love and Piety of God going to eternal life, those who have refused them to the end going to the fire that is not extinguished.
And His Kingdom will have no end.

13. We believe in the Holy Spirit, Who is Lord, and Giver of life, Who is adored and glorified together with the Father and the Son. He spoke to us by the Prophets, He was sent by Christ after His Resurrection and His Ascension to the Father; He illuminates, vivifies, protects and governs the Church; He purifies the Church's members if they do not shun His grace. His action, which penetrates to the inmost of the soul, enables man to respond to the call of Jesus: *Be perfect as your Heavenly Father is perfect.*[13]

14. We believe that Mary is the Mother, who remained ever a Virgin, of the Incarnate Word, our God and Savior Jesus Christ,[14] and that by reason of this singular election, she was, in consideration of the merits of her Son, redeemed in a more eminent manner,[15] preserved from all stain of original sin[16] and filled with the gift of grace more than all other creatures.[17]

15. Joined by a close and indissoluble bond to the Mysteries of the Incarnation and Redemption,[18] the Blessed Virgin, the Immaculate, was at the end of her earthly life raised body and soul to heavenly glory and likened to her risen Son in anticipation of the future lot of all the just;[19] and We believe that the Blessed Mother of God, the New Eve, Mother of the Church,[20]continues, in Heaven her maternal role with regard to Christ's members, cooperating with the birth and growth of divine life in the souls of the redeemed.[21]

16. We believe that in Adam all have sinned, which means that the original offense committed by him caused human nature, com-

natura humana initio in protoparentibus nostris, utpote in sancti-
tate et iustitia constitutis, inveniebatur, et in quo homo expers erat
mali et mortis. Itaque haec humana natura sic lapsa, gratiae
munere destituta, quo antea erat ornata, in ipsis suis naturalibus
viribus sauciata atque mortis imperio subiecta, omnibus hominibus
traditur; qua quidem ratione omnis homo nascitur in peccato.
Tenemus igitur, Concilium Tridentinum secuti, peccatum origi-
nale, una cum natura humana, transfundi *propagatione, non imita-
tione,* idque *inesse unicuique proprium.*[22]

17. Credimus Dominum Nostrum Iesum Christum Crucis Sacrificio
    nos redemisse a peccato originali et ab omnibus peccatis personali-
    bus, ab unoquoque nostrum admissis, ita ut vera exstet Apostoli
    sententia: *Ubi autem abundavit delictum, superabundavit gratia.*[23]

18. Confitemur credentes unum baptisma a Domino Nostro Iesu
    Christo in remissionem peccatorum institutum. Baptismum etiam
    parvulis esse conferendum, *qui nihil peccatorum in semetipsis
    adhuc committere potuerint;* ita ut gratia supernaturali in ortu
    privati, renascantur *ex aqua et Spiritu Sancto* ad vitam divinam
    in Christo Iesu.[24]

19. Credimus in unam, sanctam, catholicam et apostolicam Ecclesiam,
    a Iesu Christo super petram, qui est Petrus, aedificatam. Ea est
    mysticum Christi Corpus, societas aspectabilis, *organis hierarchicis
    instructa* et insimul *communitas spiritualis; Ecclesia terrestris,*
    Populus Dei hic in terris peregrinans, *et Ecclesia caelestibus bonis
    ditata; germen et initium Regni Dei,* quo opus et cruciatus Re-
    demptionis per hominum aetates continuantur, et quod totis viri-
    bus perfectam consummationem exoptat, post finem temporum in
    caelesti gloria assequendam.[25] Temporum decursu, Ecclesiam
    suam Dominus Iesus per Sacramenta, quae ab ipsius plenitudine
    manant, format.[26] His enim Ecclesia facit, ut membra sua my-
    sterium Mortis et Resurrectionis Iesu Christi participent, per
    gratiam Spiritus Sancti, qui illam vivificat et movet.[27] Est igitur
    sancta, licet in sinu suo peccatores complectatur; nam ipsa non
    alia fruitur vita, quam vita gratiae; hac profecto si aluntur, mem-
    bra illius sanctificantur, si ab eadem se removent, peccata sordesque
    animi contrahunt, quae obstant, ne sanctitas eius radians dif-
    fundatur. Quare affligitur et paenitentiam agit pro noxis illis,

mon to all men, to fall to a state in which it bears the consequences
of that offense, and which is not the state in which it was at first
in our first parents, established as they were in holiness and justice,
and in which man knew neither evil nor death. It is human nature so fallen, stripped of the grace that clothed it, injured in its
own natural powers and subjected to the dominion of death, that
is transmitted to all men, and it is in this sense that every man is
born in sin. We therefore hold, with the Council of Trent, that
original sin is transmitted with human nature, "not by imitation,
but by propagation" and that it is thus "in each of us as his own."[22]

17. We believe that Our Lord Jesus Christ, by the Sacrifice of the
Cross redeemed us from original sin and all the personal sins committed by each one of us, so that, in accordance with the word
of the Apostle, "where sin abounded, grace did more abound."[23]

18. We believe in one Baptism instituted by Our Lord Jesus Christ for
the remission of sins. Baptism should be administered even to little
children who have not yet been able to be guilty of any personal
sin, in order that, though born deprived of supernatural grace,
they may be reborn "of water and the Holy Spirit" to the divine
life in Christ Jesus.[24]

19. We believe in one, holy, catholic, and apostolic Church, built by
Jesus Christ on that rock which is Peter. She is the Mystical Body of
Christ; at the same time a visible society instituted with hierarchical
organs, and a spiritual community; the Church on earth, the
pilgrim People of God here below, and the Church filled with
heavenly blessings; the germ and the first fruits of the Kingdom
of God, through which the work and the sufferings of Redemption
are continued throughout human history, and which looks for its
perfect accomplishment beyond time in glory.[25] In the course of
time, the Lord Jesus forms His Church by means of the Sacraments emanating from His Plenitude.[26] By these she makes her
members participants in the Mystery of the Death and Resurrection of Christ, in the grace of the Holy Spirit who gives her life and
movement.[27] She is therefore holy, though she has sinners in her
bosom, because she herself has no other life but that of grace: it
is by living by her life that her members are sanctified; it is by
removing themselves from her life that they fall into sins and dis-

potestatem habens ex his Sanguine Christi et dono Spiritus Sancti filios suos liberandi.

20. Divinarum heres promissionum atque Abrahae filia secundum Spiritum, per illum scilicet Israël, cuius et sacros Libros amanter custodit et Patriarchas Prophetasque pie veneratur; super fundamentum Apostolorum aedificata, quorum per saeculorum decursum sive verbum semper vivax sive proprias Pastorum potestates in Petri Successore et in Episcopis, communionem cum ipso servantibus, fideliter tradens; perpetua denique Sancti Spiritus assistentia fruens, Ecclesia munus obtinet illius custodiendae, docendae, exponendae atque diffundendae veritatis, quam per Prophetas quadamtenus adumbratam Deus per Dominum Iesum plene hominibus revelavit. Nos ea omnia credimus, *quae in verbo Dei scripto vel tradito continentur et ab Ecclesia sive sollemni iudicio sive ordinario et universali magisterio tamquam divinitus revelata credenda proponuntur.*[28] Nos eam credimus infallibilitatem, qua Petri Successor perfruitur, cum omnium christianorum Pastor et Doctor *ex cathedra loquitur,*[29] *quaeque in Corpore Episcoporum etiam inest quando supremum cum eodem magisterium exercet.*[30]

21. Nos credimus Ecclesiam, quam Christus condidit et pro qua preces effudit, unam et fide et cultu et communionis hierarchicae vinculo indeficienter esse.[31] Huiusce in sinu Ecclesiae sive uberrima liturgicorum rituum varietas sive legitima theologici spiritualisque patrimonii peculiariumque disciplinarum differentia, nedum eiusdem *noceant unitati,* eam *potius declarant.*[32]

22. Nos item, hinc agnoscentes *extra* Ecclesiae Christi *compaginem elementa plura sanctificationis et veritatis inveniri, quae ut dona ipsius Ecclesiae propria, ad unitatem catholicam impellunt,*[33] hinc credentes Sancti Spiritus actionem, qui in cunctis Christi discipulis desiderium huiusce unitatis suscitat,[34] id fore speramus, ut christiani, qui nondum plena unicae Ecclesiae communione fruuntur, in uno grege cum uno Pastore tandem uniantur.

23. Nos credimus Ecclesiam *necessariam esse ad salutem. Unus enim Christus est Mediator ac via salutis, qui in Corpore suo, quod est Ecclesia, praesens nobis fit.*[35] Sed divinum propositum salutis universos amplecitur homines: atque illi *qui Evangelium Christi*

orders that prevent the radiation of her sanctity. This is why she suffers and does penance for these offences, of which she has the power to heal her children through the blood of Christ and the Gift of the Holy Spirit.

20. Heiress of the divine promises and daughter of Abraham according to the Spirit, through that Israel whose Scriptures she lovingly guards, and whose Patriarchs and Prophets she venerates; founded upon the Apostles and handing on from century to century their ever-living word and their powers as Pastors in the Successor of Peter and the Bishops in communion with him; perpetually assisted by the Holy Spirit, she has the charge of guarding, teaching, explaining and spreading the Truth which God revealed in a then veiled manner by the Prophets, and fully by the Lord Jesus. We believe *all that is contained in the Word of God written or handed down, and that the Church proposes for belief as divinely revealed, whether by a solemn judgment or by the ordinary and universal magisterium.*[28] We believe in the infallibility enjoyed by the Successor of Peter when he teaches ex cathedra as Pastor and Teacher of all the Faithful,[29] and which is assured also to the Episcopal Body when it exercises with him the supreme magisterium.[30]

21. We believe that the Church founded by Jesus Christ and for which He prayed is indefectibly one in faith, worship and the bond of hierarchical communion.[31] In the bosom of this Church, the rich variety of liturgical rites and the legitimate diversity of theological and spiritual heritages and special disciplines, far from injuring her unity, make it more manifest.[32]

22. Recognizing also the existence, outside the organism of the Church of Christ, of numerous elements of truth and sanctification which belong to her as her own and tend to Catholic unity,[33] and believing in the action of the Holy Spirit who stirs up in the heart of the disciples of Christ love of this unity,[34] we entertain the hope that Christians who are not yet in the full communion of the one only Church will one day be reunited in one Flock with one only Shepherd.

23. We believe that the Church is *necessary for salvation, because Christ who is the sole Mediator and Way of salvation, renders*

eiusque Ecclesiam sine culpa ignorantes, Deus tamen sincero corde quaerunt, eiusque voluntatem per conscientiae dictamen agnitam, operibus adimplere, sub gratiae influxu conantur, ii etiam, numero quidem, quem unus Deus novit, *aeternam salutem consequi possunt.*[36]

24. Nos credimus Missam, quae a sacerdote in persona Christi, vi potestatis per sacramentum Ordinis receptae, celebratur, quaeque ab eo Christi et membrorum eius mystici Corporis nomine offertur, revera esse Calvariae Sacrificium, quod nostris in altaribus sacramentaliter praesens efficitur. Nos credimus, ut panis et vinum a Domino consecrata in ultima Cena in eius Corpus eiusque Sanguinem conversa fuerunt, quae mox pro nobis in Cruce erant offerenda, ita pariter panem et vinum a sacerdote consecrata converti in Corpus et Sanguinem Christi, in caelis gloriose assidentis; credimusque arcanam Domini praesentiam, sub specie illarum rerum, quae nostris sensibus eodem quo antea modo apparere perseverat, veram, realem ac substantialem esse.[37]

25. In hoc igitur Sacramento Christus non aliter praesens fieri potest, quam per conversionem totius substantiae panis in eius Corpus et per conversionem totius substantiae vini in eius Sanguinem, integris manentibus dumtaxat panis et vini proprietatibus, quas nostris sensibus percipimus. Quae arcana conversio convenienter et proprie a sancta Ecclesia *transsubstantiatio* appellatur. Quaevis porro theologorum interpretatio, quae aliquam huiusmodi mysterii intellegentiam quaerit, ut cum catholica fida congruat, id sartum tectum praestare debet, in ipsa rerum natura, a nostro scilicet spiritu disiuncta, panem et vinum, peracta consecratione, esse desiisse, ita ut adorandum Corpus et Sanguis Domini Iesu post ipsam vere coram nobis adsint sub speciebus sacramentalibus panis et vini,[38] quemadmodum ipse Dominus voluit, ut sese nobis alimentum praeberet, nosque mystici Corporis sui unitate sociaret.[39]

26. Una atque individua Christi Domini in caelis gloriosi exsistentia non multiplicatur, sed Sacramento praesens efficitur variis in terrarum orbis locis, ubi Eucharisticum sacrificium peragitur. Eadem autem exsistentia, post celebratum Sacrificium, praesens manet in Sanctissimo Sacramento, quod, in altaris tabernaculo, veluti vivum cor nostrorum templorum est. Quam ob rem suavissimo sane officio

Himself present for us in His Body which is the Church.[35] But the divine Design of salvation embraces all men; and those *who without fault on their part do not know the Gospel of Christ and His Church, but seek God sincerely, and under the influence of grace endeavor to do His will as recognized through the promptings of their conscience,* they, in a number known only to God, *can obtain salvation.*[36]

24. We believe that the Mass, celebrated by the priest representing the person of Christ by virtue of the power received through the Sacrament of Orders, and offered by him in the name of Christ and the members of His Mystical Body, is in true reality the Sacrifice of Calvary, rendered sacramentally present on our altars. We believe that as the bread and wine consecrated by the Lord at the Last Supper were changed into His Body and His Blood which were to be offered for us on the Cross, likewise the bread and wine consecrated by the priest are changed into the Body and Blood of Christ enthroned gloriously in Heaven, and we believe that the mysterious presence of the Lord, under what continues to appear to our sense as before, is a true, real and substantial presence.[37]

25. Christ cannot be thus present in this Sacrament except by the change into His Body of the reality itself of the bread and the change into His Blood of the reality itself of the wine, leaving unchanged only the properties of the bread and wine which our senses perceive. This mysterious change is very appropriately called by the Church *transubstantiation.* Every theological explanation which seeks some understanding of this mystery must, in order to be in accord with Catholic faith, maintain that in the reality itself, independently of our mind, the bread and wine have ceased to exist after the Consecration, so that it is the adorable Body and Blood of the Lord Jesus that from then on are really before us under the sacramental species of bread and wine,[38] as the Lord willed it, in order to give Himself to us as food and to associate us with the unity of His Mystical Body.[39]

26. The unique and indivisible existence of the Lord glorious in Heaven is not multiplied, but is rendered present by the Sacrament in the many places on earth where Mass is celebrated. And

tenemur honore afficiendi atque adorandi in Hostia Sancta, quam
oculi nostri intuentur, Verbum ipsum incarnatum, quod iidem
intueri non possunt, quodque tamen praesens coram nobis effectum
est, quin tamen deseruerit caelos.

27. Confitemur pariter Regnum Dei, quod hic in terris in Christi
Ecclesia primordia habuit, *non esse de hoc mundo,*[40] *cuius figura
praeterit,*[41] itemque eius propria incrementa idem existimari non
posse atque progressionem humanitatis cultus, vel scientiarum, vel
technicarum artium, sed in eo consistere, ut investigabiles divitiae
Christi altius usque cognoscantur, ut spes in aeternis bonis con-
stantius usque ponatur, ut Dei caritati flagrantius usque respon-
deatur, ut denique gratia atque sanctitudo largius usque diffun-
dantur inter homines. At eodem amore Ecclesia impellitur ut etiam
verum hominum bonum temporale continenter cordi habeat. Dum
enim quotquot habet filios monere non cessat, eos *non habere hic
in terris manentem civitatem,*[42] eosdem etiam exstimulat ut, pro
sua quisque vitae condicione atque subsidiis, propriae humanae
civitatis incrementa foveant, iustitiam, pacem atque fraternam
concordiam inter homines promoveant, atque fratribus suis,
praesertim pauperioribus et infelicioribus, largiatur adiumentum.
Quare impensa sollicitudo, qua Ecclesia, Christi Sponsa, hominum
necessitates prosequitur, hoc est eorum gaudia et exspectationes,
dolores et labores, nihil aliud est nisi studium, quo ipsa vehementer
impellitur, ut iis praesens adsit, eo quidem consilio, ut Christi luce
homines illuminet, universosque in Illum, qui ipsorum unus Salva-
tor est, congreget, atque coniungat. Nunquam vero haec sollicitudo
ita accipienda est, quasi Ecclesia ad res huius mundi se conformet,
aut deferveat ardor, quo ipsa Dominum suum Regnumque aeternum exspectat.

28. Credimus vitam aeternam. Credimus animas eorum omnium, qui
in gratia Christi moriuntur—sive quae adhuc Purgatorii igne
expiandae sunt, sive quae statim ac corpore separatae, sicut Bonus
Latro, a Iesu in Paradisum suscipiuntur—Populum Dei constituere
post mortem, quae omnino destruetur Resurrectionis die, quo hae
animae cum suis corporibus coniungentur.

this existence remains present, after the Sacrifice, in the Blessed Sacrament which is, in the tabernacle, the living heart of each of our churches. And it is our very sweet duty to honor and adore in the Blessed Host which our eyes see, the Incarnate Word Whom they cannot see, and Who, without leaving Heaven, is made present before us.

27. We confess that the Kingdom of God begun here below in the Church of Christ *is not of this world*[40] *whose form is passing,*[41] and that its proper growth cannot be confounded with the progress of civilization, of science or of human technology, but that it consists in an ever more profound knowledge of the unfathomable riches of Christ, an ever stronger hope in eternal blessings, an ever more ardent response to the Love of God, and an ever more generous bestowal of grace and holiness among men. But it is this same love which induces the Church to concern herself constantly about the true temporal welfare of men. Without ceasing to recall to her children that *they have not here a lasting dwelling,*[42] she also urges them to contribute, each according to his vocation and his means, to the welfare of their earthly city, to promote justice, peace and brotherhood among men, to give their aid freely to their brothers, especially to the poorest and most unfortunate. The deep solicitude of the Church, the Spouse of Christ, for the needs of men, for their joys and hopes, their griefs and efforts, is therefore nothing other than her great desire to be present to them, in order to illuminate them with the light of Christ and to gather them all in Him, their only Saviour. This solicitude can never mean that the Church conform herself to the things of this world, or that she lessen the ardour of her expectation of her Lord and of the eternal Kingdom.

28. We believe in the life eternal. We believe that the souls of all those who die in the grace of Christ, whether they must still be purified in Purgatory, or whether from the moment they leave their bodies Jesus takes them to Paradise as He did for the Good Thief, are the People of God in the eternity beyond death, which will be finally conquered on the day of the Resurrection when these souls will be reunited with their bodies.

29. Credimus multitudinem earum animarum, quae cum Iesu et
Maria in Paradiso congregantur, Ecclesiam Caelestem efficere,
ubi eaedem, aeterna beatitudine fruentes, Deum vident sicuti est[43]
atque etiam, gradu quidem modoque diverso, una cum sanctis
Angelis partem habent in divina rerum gubernatione, quam
Christus glorificatus exercet, cum pro nobis intercedant suaque
fraterna sollicitudine infirmitatem nostram plurimum iuvent.[44]

30. Credimus communionem omnium Christifidelium, scilicet eorum
qui in terris peregrinantur, qui vita functi purificantur et qui
caelesti beatitudine perfruuntur, universosque in unam Ecclesiam
coalescere; ac pariter credimus in hac communione praesto nobis
esse misericordem Dei eiusque Sanctorum amorem, qui semper
precibus nostris pronas aures praebent, ut Iesu nobis asseveravit:
Petite et accipietis.[45] Hanc fidem profitentes et hac spe suffulti
exspectamus resurrectionem mortuorum et vitam venturi saeculi.
Benedictus Deus sanctus, sanctus, sanctus.   Amen

Pronuntiata ante Basilicam Petrianam, die xxx menis Iunii, anno
MCMLXVIII, Pontificatus Nostri sexto.

PAULUS PP. VI

29. We believe that the multitude of those gathered around Jesus and Mary in Paradise forms the Church of Heaven, where in eternal beatitude they see God as He is,[43] and where they also, in different degrees, are associated with the holy Angels in the divine rule exercised by Christ in glory, interceding for us and helping our weakness by their brotherly care.[44]

30. We believe in the communion of all the faithful of Christ, those who are pilgrims on earth, the dead who are attaining their purification, and the blessed in Heaven, all together forming one Church; and we believe that in this communion the merciful love of God and His Saints is ever listening to our prayers, as Jesus told us: Ask and you will receive.[45] Thus it is with faith and in hope that we look forward to the resurrection of the dead, and the life of the world to come.

Blessed be God Thrice Holy. Amen

Pronounced in front of the Basilica of St. Peter, on June 30, 1968, the sixth year of Our Pontificate.

POPE PAUL VI

PART TWO

The Origin, Nature and Development of the Creed, and its Significance for Catechetical Teaching in the Church

"By the word *kerygma,* message, we mean the Christian teaching is so far as it is intended to be proclaimed, that is, to be realized through pastoral care as the basis of Christian life . . . The message of salvation preached by the early Church found its first systematic summary in the Apostles' Creed . . . Christ must be restored to the center of the faith. The restoration of the *kerygma* to its full power and clarity is, therefore, a principal task of modern pastoral work." Joseph Andreas Jungmann,

Handing on the Faith
(New York: 1959)
387, 389, and 397.

The Origin of the Creed

JESUS CHRIST: ORIGINATOR OF THE CREED

CAN it be true to say that the Apostles' Creed goes back to Jesus, Himself, in person? The early Church was convinced of it. "This, beloved, is the preaching of the truth," writes St. Irenaeus in the second century, concluding his catechetical explanation of what we call the Creed, "this is the manner of our salvation, and this is the way of life, announced by the prophets and ratified by Christ, and handed over by the apostles and handed down by the Church in the whole world to her children."[1] Without doubt this is a question which deserves careful analysis in the light of the recent scholarly studies on the origin and nature of the Apostles' Creed.[2]

When Jesus Christ opened His public life, St. Mark reports that He came before the Jewish people as a herald and raised His voice to deliver a message. "After John had been arrested, Jesus went into Galilee. There He proclaimed the Good News from God. 'The time has come,' He said, 'and the Kingdom of God is close at hand. Repent, and believe the Good News.' " (Mark 1, 14–15). These last words in Greek are: *metanoeîte kai pisteúete én tō evaggelio,* where the verb calling for belief is rooted in *pistis,* meaning "faith." St. Jerome translated this passage into the Latin Vulgate as follows: *poenitemini et credite Evangelio,* where the same verb is *credere,* "to believe."

Believe in the Good News! *Believe* in the Gospel! This is the call of God Himself for an act of faith, a personal response which believes this word or message or Good News from God of which Jesus Christ is the official herald.

The Latin word for *believing,* then, for responding to such a call

30

for faith, is *credere;* "Credo, Domine": "O Lord, I *believe.*" From this Latin word *credo* the English language derives its word *Creed.* Thus simply and in a preliminary way one can say that the Creed originates in the divine call of Jesus Christ to believe in the Gospel.

Let us go further. The early Church obviously could not use the word "creed" to denote this response of faith in the divine message, for the English language was still many centuries in the future; nor did it even use the word "credo," for the Church was not yet using Latin in its writings. But the reality of personal response to this call of Jesus Christ to believe the message He heralded existed from the beginning. Did it have other names, synonyms of our phrase, "The Creed"?

It did indeed. The earliest Church, speaking Greek, called this response simply *pistis,* "The Faith," meaning the act of believing, of personally accepting this message as the truth of God.[3] Bishops at Nicaea, for example, say they signed the *pistis,* meaning what we profess at Sunday Mass to this day and call "The Nicene Creed."[4] St. Athanasius follows the same usage. With the Nicene Creed in mind, he speaks of "the correct *faith* of the Catholic Church," and states that "The *faith* which the Council confessed in writing is that of the Catholic Church," adding that "the *faith* professed by the Council Fathers according to the Scriptures, suffices to overturn all error and to establish the true faith in Christ."[5]

A second way of speaking of this response of faith for which Jesus Christ calls is common in the writings of the Early Church. It is the Greek word *symbolon,* carried into Latin as *symbolum fidei.* It has come into English as well, which uses the word *"symbol"* to mean a short summary of the faith, what Pope Paul VI calls "the Creed of the immortal tradition of the Holy Church of God."[6]

Faith is of course a dominant theme in the teaching of Jesus. "He was amazed at their lack of faith." (Mark 6, 6). "My daughter," He said, "Your faith has restored you to health. Go in peace . . ." (Mark 7, 34).

"And He said to them, 'Go out to the whole world; proclaim the Good News to all creation. He who believes and is baptised will be saved; he who does not believe will be condemned.' " (Mark 16, 16).

"We are always full of confidence . . . ," writes St. Paul, "going as we do by faith and not by sight . . ." (2 Cor. 5, 6). The Apostles knew well what God was asking: "The Apostles said to the Lord, 'Increase our faith.'" (Luke 17, 5). The Epistle to the Hebrews is actually a sustained treatise on faith, a standing testimony to the mind of the Apostolic Church on the matter. "Now it is impossible to please God without faith, since anyone who comes to Him must believe that He exists, and rewards those who try to find Him." (Heb. 11, 6). This is the irreducible minimum of faith and creed on the one hand, and of catechetical teaching on the other.

That the faith was God's truth, revealed truth about God, about His plan for mankind, truth coming from God, is clear in the Scriptures, and nowhere more so than in the Gospel reports on the teaching activity of Jesus. It was perfectly natural, therefore, that His life as a rabbi, a teacher, that is, who taught and formed His own circle of disciples, should culminate in the divine command to build a world-embracing Teaching Church. "Meanwhile the eleven disciples set out for Galilee, to the mountain where Jesus had arranged to meet them. When they saw Him they fell down before Him, though some hesitated. Jesus came up and spoke to them. He said, 'All authority in heaven and on earth has been given to Me. Go, therefore, make disciples of all the nations; baptise them in the name of the Father and of the Son and of the Holy Spirit, and teach them to observe all the commands I gave you. And know that I am with you always; yes, to the end of time.'" (Mt. 28, 16–20).

This divine charter illuminates what we know of the actual life and activity of the earliest Church, the Church of the apostles as reported in the New Testament. It leads directly to the apostolic *kerygma* and catechesis, and to the baptismal act and baptismal Creed.

THE APOSTOLIC KERYGMA

The disciples, carefully trained by Jesus Himself as their *rabbi*, the Hebrew word for "teacher," were now "Apostles," men sent out to accomplish this teaching mission.

"Brothers," St. Paul writes to the Christian community at Corinth, "I want to remind you of the gospel I preached to you, the gospel that you received and in which you are firmly established; because the gospel will save you only if you keep believing exactly what I preached to you—believing anything else will not lead to anything.

"Well then, in the first place I taught you what I had been taught myself, namely that Christ died for our sins, in accordance with the Scriptures; that he was buried; and that he was raised to life on the third day, in accordance with the Scriptures; that he appeared first to Cephas and secondly to the Twelve. Next he appeared to more than five hundred of the brothers at the same time, most of whom are still alive, though some have died . . . And last of all he appeared to me too . . ." (1 Cor. 15, 1–8).

These words of St. Paul give the heart of the original apostolic *kerygma* and throw a ray of light on the origin and nature of what Christians today call the Apostles' Creed. They contain the substance of the second article of the Creed which centers upon the Lord Jesus: His incarnation, His earthly life, His redeeming death and His resurrection from the dead. The apostolic preaching proclaims to the whole world, to every man who has ears to hear, the facts about Jesus Christ. Then the apostolic teaching program explains these facts in terms of the three Divine Persons whom Jesus revealed from within the One Godhead of the Hebrews. The Lord Jesus is the Second Person of this Divine Trinity. Hence everything about Him becomes readily understandable. His first coming, His passion and death, His resurrection, His future second coming in glory to judge the living and the dead: all takes place "according to the Scriptures," that is, in fulfillment of the divine plan for the salvation of mankind. This plan is called "salvation history," and the record of its events, wonderful interventions of God to save and to teach His people, is contained in the Bible.[7]

St. Paul is careful to state that he received this content of the Catholic faith by a process of teaching: "I taught you what I had been taught myself." Scholars conclude that he had been taught by St. Peter and the other apostles at Jerusalem. Then he in turn hands it on by preaching and teaching. This is the process whereby this content of revealed truth comes across the centuries to Catholics of the present day, who continue "to hold and teach the Catholic faith that comes to us from the Apostles," as the first eucharistic prayer of the Mass puts it. It comes to the present by faithful cathechetical teaching across the centuries. In fact, this passage in St. Paul is light from the New Testament itself on the relationship between creed and catechetics. This teaching is done in an official manner by the successors of Peter and the other apostles, by the Pope and by the bishops who are in communion with him. Then it is extended to children and young people by the parents and catechists who are the faithful collaborators of the successors of the apostles. Thus has the faith reached into the twentieth century from the apostles.

How does all this relate to the apostolic *kerygma?* What is this word *kerygma,* and why is it significant? The answer is that it expresses and unveils the meaning of the Apostles' Creed. The reason for this must be analyzed.

Kerygma is one of those meaningful Greek words, like *kyrios,* which reveals to us the mind and reality of the Church of the apostles. For the early Church spoke and wrote in Greek. The word *kerygma* was the ordinary Greek word for an official proclamation or announcement of a piece of news or a message, made by a *keryx,* the Greek word for *herald.* Heralds were important officials in the government of the city-states of antiquity, in all human social life, in fact, before the times of newspapers and electronic media. Homer's works abound with instances of the herald's function in the service of his king.

Always the *keryx* was the authorized spokesman for the supreme ruler of the village or city, who cried out to the people the news, announcements, plans or decisions coming from the king. Always the herald spoke with authority. His function was simply to deliver the message with absolute fidelity. The word *kerygma,* meaning the message, derives from the word *keryx,* the official herald who proclaims with authority the message from the ruler.[8]

Now in the passage above, as in the writings of the New Testament generally, St. Paul uses these words which derive from *keryx* to denote the apostolic preaching. The apostles, in other words, are the authorized spokesmen or "heralds" of God Himself, the Supreme Ruler of the universe.

The apostolic preaching simply continues what the Lord Himself did. "Now after John was arrested," St. Mark writes in the passage given above, "Jesus came into Galilee, preaching the Gospel of God, and saying, 'The time is fulfilled, and the Kingdom of God is at hand; repent and believe in the Gospel.' " The Greek verb commonly translated into English as "preaching" or "proclaiming" is actually a derivative of *keryx,* the verb denoting the function and action of a herald. Jesus came before men in the opening of His public life as the herald mandated to deliver a message, authorized to announce a piece of news, empowered to proclaim a Word of God to man. He prepared and trained His disciples precisely for this same function: to be "apostles," men sent as heralds of this one and same divine message.

St. Paul in the passage just quoted is careful to remind the Corinthians that he himself received the Gospel which he in turn had handed over to them and in which they now stand. From whom, from where did he receive it? Scholars answer by pointing to the "Jerusalem *kerygma*" and the passages of the New Testament which allow us to hear it to this day.[9]

St. Luke describes the birth of the Church on the first Pentecost. "Then Peter stood up with the Eleven, and addressed them in a loud voice . . ." This is precisely the manner of a herald who appears before men authorized to proclaim an official message. Peter *stands,* not as a teacher who sits to teach; he stands as a herald does: and "he lifted up his voice . . ." as heralds have done from time immemorial on the human scene.

What did he proclaim? His words convey to this day the essential content of the original apostolic *kerygma:*

"Men of Judaea," he cried, "and all you who live in Jerusalem, make no mistake about this, but listen carefully to what I say. These men are not drunk, as you imagine . . . On the contrary, this is what the prophet spoke of: 'In the days to come—it is the Lord who speaks—I will pour out my spirit on all mankind . . .' (Joel 3, 1–5). Men of Israel, listen to what I am going to say: Jesus the Nazarene was a man commended to you by God by the miracles and portents and signs that God worked through him when he was among you, as you all know. This man, who was put into your power by the deliberate intention and foreknowledge of God, you took and had crucified by men outside the Law. You killed him, but God raised him to life . . . God raised this man Jesus to life, and all of us are witnesses to that. Now raised to the heights by God's right hand, he has received from the Father the Holy Spirit, who was promised, and what you see and hear is the outpouring of that Spirit . . . For this reason the whole House of Israel can be certain that God has made this Jesus whom you crucified both Lord and Christ." (Acts 2, 14–36).

Baddock in his *History of the Creeds* gives a summary of this original "Jerusalem *kerygma*" or apostolic preaching. "The earliest Apostolic Preaching of which we have record had as its nucleus the

Messiahship and Lordship of Jesus, one or both . . . Correspondingly, the earliest confession of faith demanded [for baptism] was faith in the Messiahship or Lordship of Jesus, and this would run, 'I believe that Jesus is the Christ, or (the) Lord,' 'I believe in Jesus as the Christ or (the) Lord' or 'I believe in Jesus Christ the Lord.' "[10]

"Anyone who welcomes you welcomes me; and those who welcome me welcome the one who sent me." (Mt. 10, 40). The Apostles are the authorized spokesmen or "heralds" of God Himself, the Supreme Ruler of the Universe. "You will be my witnesses not only in Jerusalem but throughout Judaea and Samaria, and indeed to the ends of the earth." (Acts 1, 8). They announce the good news or "Gospel" of the fulfillment of the divine plan regarding mankind, accomplished in the facts about the Lord Jesus. The first coming of Jesus introduces a new age of universal history, the final age, for it will culminate in His Second Coming. Hence the urgency of the message to each and all. The Kingdom of God is at hand! The Judgment will follow soon! The Day of the Lord, so constantly foretold by the prophets of the Old Testament, is approaching! Repent, therefore! Change your lives! Take up the Lord's Way of Life, embrace the Christian Way, for the Kingdom of God is at hand! This is the Gospel "which has been preached in the whole world." (Col. 1, 23, where the Greek verb translated by "preached" is in the root *keryx:* "heralded in the whole world."). St. Paul says the same to the Romans: "Glory to him who is able to give you strength to live according to the Good News I preach, and in which I proclaim Jesus Christ (*kerygma,* the heralded message of Jesus Christ) . . ." (Rom. 16, 25). Hence St. Paul says to Timothy, "I have been named a herald and apostle . . . and a teacher of the faith (in the Greek, *Ego kēryx, kai apóstolos, kai . . . didáskalos*). (1 Tim. 2, 7). And: "Our savior Christ Jesus . . . abolished death, and he has proclaimed life and immortality through the Good News; and I have been named its herald (*keryx* in the Greek), its apostle and its teacher." (2 Tim. 1, 11).

It would be difficult to document more explicitly the relationship between the Apostles' *kerygma* or Creed and catechetical teaching. This is the reason why the bishops, successors of the apostles, are indefectibly both the official heralds of the Gospel and the first catechists of the People of God.[11] The fact that this original apostolic *kerygma* was a content of truth addressed to the minds of men, indeed a didactic pattern or rule or standard in the Trinitarian form of the doctrinal summary which we call the Creed, lays the foundation for the catechetical teaching program which is visible in the New Testament itself.[12]

THE APOSTOLIC CATECHESIS

Jesus Christ appeared before His fellowmen in the social position and function of a *rabbi,* a teacher, and He founded a teaching Church upon His immediate circle of personally-trained disciples. The apostles were teachers, accordingly, as well as heralds of the message. St. Paul was keenly aware of the fact, as we have just noted: "I have been named its (the Gospel's) herald, its apostle and its teacher." (2 Tim. 1, 11). In the Acts of the Apostles Paul is called officially a "teacher" in the church at Antioch, and the fact that "teachers" were a recognized part of the organization and activity of the Apostolic Church is clear in the writings of the New Testament.[13]

What was the nature of this teaching? It was a very practical matter. It prepared for baptism those who declared their faith in the message. It accomplished this by a teaching program which explained the same message or *kerygma.* Since this Word of God is a body of truth addressed to the human intelligence, it is not only proclaimed by authentic heralds and witnesses; it is also taught by all the procedures of natural human communication and pedagogy. Nor does this detract from the unique and divine character of this truth: it is not the result of human research and argumentation. It persuades by a power of its own, by the power of God that inheres in the truth of God.[14] It is revealed truth, essentially a gift from God, and not any learner's own boast. Hence it can be the source of a true interior justification which has value in the sight of God. Nor can any human teacher of this truth guarantee its results simply by the excellence and effectiveness of his natural pedagogy. Certain moral dispositions are required in the learner, a certain pre-existing relationship between the learner and God his creator and redeemer: good faith, good will, openness to the higher order of wisdom and law.[15] And then there are those spiny texts which speak of crisis of faith and even loss of the faith because of some personal failure in the love of truth.[16]

Nevertheless, in the Apostolic Church to which the New Testament writings bear witness, this divine truth was stated and formulated in the propositions of human discourse and was communicated, handed over to others, and explained by a genuine process of teaching. It seems that it was St. Paul who selected the rare and special Greek word, "catechesis," which has denoted this particular and specialized kind of teaching in the Catholic Church to the present day.[17]

Professor J. N. D. Kelly of Oxford summarizes well the research which has identified the elements of both Creed and Catechetics in the New Testament itself. "The early Church," he writes, "was from the start a believing, confessing, preaching Church . . . It is impossible to overlook the emphasis on the transmission of authoritative doctrine which is found everywhere in the New Testament."[18]

Some have tried to maintain that these "references to an inherited corpus of teaching" characterize only the later writings of the New Testament, reflecting a tendency for the faith to assume a hard-and-fast outline only towards the end of the first century.[19] But this is disproved by the other Epistles of St. Paul, who is "a witness to the fact that the process was at work at a much earlier stage."[20] In addition to 1 Cor. 15, 3, noted above, ". . . I taught you what I had been taught myself," there is the doctrine of the eucharistic consecration: "For this is what I received from the Lord, and in turn passed on to you." (1 Cor. 11, 23). The concept of a doctrine handed over to others by a teaching process is clear. St. Paul asks the Galatians, who were being solicited by aberrations in teaching: "Are you people in Galatia mad? Has someone put a spell on you, in spite of the explanation you have had of the crucifixion of Jesus Christ?" (Gal. 3, 1–2).

Writing to the Colossians, St. Paul uses *he pístis,* "The Faith," as the Greek Church has continued to do when referring to what the Latin West calls "The Creed." "You must live your whole life according to the Christ you have received—Jesus the Lord; you must be rooted in him and built on him and held firm by the faith (*tē pístei*) you have been taught." (Col. 2, 6; and see Gal. 1, 23; Eph. 4, 5).

"Stand firm, then, brothers," he urges the Thessalonians, "and keep the traditions that we taught you, whether by word of mouth or by letter." (2 Thess. 2, 15). And he writes to the Romans: "You were once slaves of sin, but thank God you submitted without reservation to the creed you were taught." (Rom. 6, 17). It is interesting to note the use of the word "creed" in the Jerusalem Bible to translate *týpon didachēs,* meaning the standard of teaching or pattern of doctrine which existed already and was operating in the catechesis of the apostolic Church,[21]

"All the evidence goes to prove," the Oxford Professor concludes, "that Paul had a healthy regard for the objective body of teaching authoritatively handed down in the Church . . . Examples could easily be multiplied, and the conclusion is inescapable that, however anachronistic it may be to postulate fixed credal forms for the Apostolic age, the documents themselves testify to the existence of a corpus of distinctively Christian teaching. In this sense at any rate it is legitimate to speak of the creed of the primitive Church. Nor was it something vague and nebulous: its main features were clearly enough defined. The Epistles and Gospels are, of course, rarely if ever concerned to set out the faith in its fulness: they rather presuppose and hint at it. Even so, it is possible to reconstruct, with a fair degree of confidence, what must have been its chief constituents."[22]

In later centuries, a pious legend grew up to the effect that the apostles formulated the Apostles' Creed in the wording used officially in the Western Church today. Each was devoutly imagined to have contributed a statement so that our familiar version of the Apostles' Creed containing twelve articles of faith resulted. From this it is but a step to imagine that the Apostles' Creed, worded as we have it and use it today in the Church, was written down by the apostles and, as it were, distributed on slips of paper.[23] The truth of the matter is quite different. The original "Apostles' Creed" is simply the profession of the apostolic faith made by the living apostles in their *kerygma,* and continued by their living successors, in a living magisterium sustained by an action of Almighty God in the Church of His Incarnate Son across the centuries between His coming in humility and His second coming in glory. This profession of the apostolic faith always has had one and the same doctrinal substance, the confession of Jesus as the Lord, set in a characteristic Trinitarian form because the one who is our Lord is the eternal Son of God. This apostolic profession of faith is a *týpon didachēs,* a pattern of doctrine, a content and norm for catechetical teaching: as the Jerusalem Bible recognizes accurately, it is simply what we today call the Creed.[24]

Jesus Christ, the Divine Teacher, is therefore the founder and initiator of the apostolic teaching program, just as He is the first herald of its content or message—the originator of the apostles' pro-fession or creed. In fact, it was He who gave the first catechism lesson to His two disconsolate followers on the road out of Jerusalem toward Emmaus, on the first Easter Sunday.[25]

"The primitive message," writes Cerfaux, "offered three connected elements, namely Christ's resurrection, His Second Coming, and the Kingdom of God as an actuality. The deciding factor in this concep-tion, as far as facts were concerned, was the early Christians' actual experience of the Resurrection. In a theological framework, however, it was the Second Coming that coloured the whole picture . . . The Resurrection was itself seen as the first of the eschatological resurrec-tions, and the Risen Christ was already enthroned in the glory that He would show to men in His Second Coming."[26] In synthetic summary, Cerfaux points out that St. Paul "connects his teaching to the . . . catechesis which was formulated at Jerusalem . . . , the Apostolic Catechesis to which Paul appeals in 1 Cor. 15, 3–7."[27]

The apostolic catechesis, then, was originally and continues to be a teaching program that is different, unique, for it has a special con-tent to hand on by its teaching. The content is simply the apostolic *kerygma* proclaimed about Jesus in the setting of His revelation of the Three Divine Persons living in the divine nature of Yahweh, the One God of the Hebrew *shema*.[28] It is a teaching of a special kind for two reasons. First, its content comes from God. It is the Word of God delivered by His authorized heralds, the apostles and their successors. Secondly, its motive is the authority of God revealing, and not human scientific discovery or human philosophical doctrine. "For the teach-ing of faith, which God has revealed, has not been proposed as a philosophical discovery to be perfected by human ingenuity, but as a divine deposit handed over to the Spouse of Christ to be guarded faithfully and to be explained infallibly . . . 'that is, with the same dogma, the same meaning, the same sense.' "[29]

Centered upon Jesus Christ as our Lord and Savior, it is a teach-ing that takes place always in living expectation of His second coming, that believes in the resurrection of the body and life everlasting, and that has faith in prayer and the sacraments. For it believes in the real active presence of the Holy Spirit, giving almighty power to the sacraments and guaranteeing the teaching. And it believes in the real presence of Jesus Himself, incarnate, body, soul and divinity, in the

Blessed Eucharist—present risen and glorious just as He is in heaven: Emmanuel, God-with-us, preparing the eschatological resurrections of His members. And thus St. Paul could speak, as Christians do ever since, of His Body, which is the Church.[30]

The apostolic *kerygma* and its explanatory catechesis give the Church abidingly its constitutive note of *apostolicity*.[31] "From its origin," writes the patristic scholar Gustave Bardy, "Christianity has taken the form of an orthodoxy. It has taught a clearly defined doctrine and put its believers on their guard against all possible deviations from that doctrine."[32] "Christianity was a doctrine," he concludes; "it affirmed itself as an orthodoxy and dreaded nothing so much as heresy. Now this doctrine was found identically the same from one end of the world to the other. Those who preached it were not prophets or inspired persons, but witnesses to tradition."[33]

What the Church brought forth from the apostolic age as a treasure in hand after the death of the last apostle, was precisely this apostolic faith which she professed and which she continued to herald, to preach and to teach in her catechetical program. To come to a closer view of the nature of this faith which she professed and taught one must consider that the Church was never simply a "school" like the schools of philosophy.[34] This teaching was a practical one which prepared for sacramental initiation and introduced ever-increasing numbers of persons into the Christian way of life. The sacrament of baptism with its "Interrogatory Creed" provides this closer view, and reveals the true origin of what is called today simply "The Apostles' Creed."

BAPTISMAL ACT AND BAPTISMAL CREED

The fact that the Creed originates with Jesus Christ is illuminated from a new direction when the nature of the Sacrament of Baptism is considered. For He instituted this sacrament as the entrance to His Church and linked it with the apostolic teaching program in the fundamental world-wide missionary command which He gave to the men He had trained.[35] "Meanwhile the eleven disciples set out for Galilee," St. Matthew tells us, "to the mountain where Jesus had arranged to meet them. When they saw him they fell down before him, though some hesitated. Jesus came up and spoke to them. He said, 'All authority in heaven and on earth has been given to me. Go, therefore, make disciples of all the nations; baptize them in the name of the Father and of the Son and of the Holy Spirit, and teach them to observe all the commands I gave you. And know that I am with you always; Yes, to the end of time.' "[36]

In the first instance of the apostolic *kerygma,* St. Peter's pentecostal proclamation of the divine and human facts about Jesus of Nazareth, the response of faith in the message he heralded is striking and explicit. "Hearing this, they were cut to the heart and said to Peter and the Apostles, 'What must we do, brothers?' 'You must repent,' Peter answered, 'and every one of you must be baptized in the name of Jesus Christ for the forgiveness of your sins, and you will receive the gift of the Holy Spirit' . . . He spoke to them for a long time using many arguments, and he urged them, 'Save yourselves from this perverse generation.' They were convinced by his arguments, and they accepted what he said and were baptized. That very day about three thousand were added to their number. These remained faithful to the teaching of the apostles, to the brotherhood, to the breaking of the bread, and to the prayers."[37]

Since these were Jews, elaborate explanation was not needed; they were already familiar with the Scriptures and ready to grasp the concept of their fulfillment. At the same time, "they accepted what he said," which implies some form of profession of faith in the apostolic *kerygma* or message about Jesus. The same procedure is clear elsewhere in the New Testament. The Apostle Philip comes upon the Ethiopian who is reading about the suffering servant in Chapter 53 of the Prophet Isaiah. "Starting, therefore, with this text of Scripture Philip proceeded to explain the Good News of Jesus to him. Further along the road they came to some water, and the eunuch said, 'Look, there is some water here, is there anything to stop me being baptized?' He ordered the chariot to stop . . . , and Philip baptized him."[38] So too in the case of Lydia, the devout woman of Philippi who was in the purple-dye trade. "She listened to us," St. Luke reports, "and the Lord opened her heart to accept what Paul was saying. After she and her household had been baptized she sent us an invitation: 'If you really think me a true believer in the Lord,' she said, 'come and stay with us'; and she would take no refusal."[39] St. Paul judged her to be faithful to the Lord, which implies again some form of profession of faith on her part.

What the form of this profession of faith in the Apostolic *kerygma* about Jesus was, what pattern of words was used, is not stated explicitly in the New Testament. But it is clear that it professed faith in the Three Divine Persons, in the name of whom the Lord Himself had commanded baptism to be given; and that it professed faith in the Divine Sonship and Lordship of Jesus, the essential facts about Him, of which the apostles were the official heralds and witnesses. It is safe to conclude with Prof. Kelly: "A profession of faith of one kind or another must have been demanded . . . A confession of faith was normally expected at baptism . . ."[40]

The nature of this pattern, however, the fact that it was the interrogatory form for professing the apostolic faith, can be seen clearly in the writings of the early Fathers. "All those who have been convinced and who believe that our instruction and our message are true," writes St. Justin Martyr, "and promise that they are able to live according to them, are admonished to pray and with fasting to beseech God for pardon for their past sins; and we pray and fast with them. Then they are conducted to a place where there is water, and are reborn with a form of rebirth such as we have ourselves undergone. For they receive a lustral washing in the water in the name of the Father and Lord God of the universe, and of our Savior Jesus Christ, and of the Holy Spirit . . . The name of the Father and Lord God of the universe is named . . . and only this description of God. The name for this lustral bath is 'Enlightenment,' the idea being that those who receive this teaching are enlightened in their understanding. Moreover, it is in the name of Jesus Christ, who was crucified under Pontius Pilate, and in the name of the Holy Spirit, who through the prophets announced beforehand the things relating to Jesus, that the man who is enlightened is washed."[41]

Approximately a hundred years later, at mid-third century, St. Hippolytus of Rome states the matter with full explicitness in his *Treatise on the Apostolic Tradition:*

"And when he who is to be baptized," he writes, "goes down to the water, let him who baptizes lay hand on him, saying thus:

"*Do you believe in God the Father Almighty?* And he who is being baptized shall say: I believe. Let him forthwith baptize him once, having his hand laid upon his head. And after this let him say:

"*Do you believe in Christ Jesus, the Son of God,*
Who was born of the Holy Spirit and the Virgin Mary,

> *Who was crucified in the days of Pontius Pilate,*
> *And died, and was buried;*
> *And He rose the third day Living from the dead,*
> *And ascended into heaven*
> *And sat down at the right hand of the Father,*
> *And will come to judge the living and the dead?*

"And when he says: I believe, let him baptize the second time. And again let him say:

"*Do you believe in the Holy Spirit, in the Holy Church, And in the resurrection of the flesh?*

"And he who is being baptized shall say: I believe. And so let him baptize him the third time."[42]

Thus from the practice of the living Church carrying out the baptismal command of the Lord Jesus (Mt. 28, 16–20), the interrogatory form of the Apostles' Creed emerges into full view. "It is indisputable," writes Lietzmann, "that the root of all creeds is the formula of belief pronounced by the baptizand, or pronounced in his hearing and assented to by him, before his baptism."[43]

The practice of the Catholic Church has never changed since the Apostles, as the following excerpt from the Rite of Baptism in its renewed, post-Vatican II form, bears witness:

In the baptism of a Catholic baby, the priest asks the parents and godparents, "What do you ask of God's Church for your children?" And all answer: "Baptism." Readings from Scripture follow, with the exorcisms and the anointing with the oil of salvation. Then the group approaches the baptismal font and the Rite of Baptism proceeds with the renunciation of sin and profession of faith. The priest questions the parents and godparents, saying "Do you reject Satan? And all his works? And all his empty promises?" The parents and godparents answer: "I do."

Next the priest asks for the three-fold Profession of Faith from the parents and godparents, saying:

"*Do you believe in God, the Father Almighty, Creator of heaven and earth?*"

And the parents and godparents answer for the baby: "I do."

Then the priest asks:

"*Do you believe in Jesus Christ, His only Son, our Lord, who was born of the Virgin Mary, was crucified, died and was buried, rose from the dead, and is now seated at the right hand of the Father?*"

And the parents and godparents answer for the baby: "I do."

The priest then asks the third question:

"Do you believe in the Holy Spirit, the Holy Catholic Church, the Communion of Saints, the forgiveness of sins, the resurrection of the body, and life everlasting?"

And the parents and godparents answer for the baby: "I do."

Then the priest baptizes the child, saying, "Margaret Elizabeth, I baptize you in the name of the Father, and of the Son, and of the Holy Spirit," pouring water three times at each name of the Divine Trinity.

Without this profession of the apostolic faith, it is impossible to be baptized into the Catholic Church. It is clear that what is recited as the Apostles' Creed and explained in catechetical teaching, is, in the substance of its doctrinal content, simply the declaratory form of this original interrogatory Creed which admits to membership into the Catholic Church.[44]

Research upon the origins of the Creed has established an important insight. "The declaratory creeds . . . belonged rather to the catechetical preparation preceding the sacrament: their recitation logically formed its concluding stage. This comes out clearly in the ritual of the tradition and rendition of the Creed . . . Their roots lie not so much in the Christian's sacramental initiation as in the catechetical training by which it was preceded . . . Declaratory creeds may therefore be regarded as a by-product of the Church's fully developed catechetical system."[45] As Professor Seeberg concluded early in this century, "The primitive Christian creeds are simply and solely the recapitulation, in a formula based upon the Trinitarian ground plan, of the basic catechetical verities."[46] Most important of all, the Declaratory Creed was made out of the phrases of the Interrogatory Creed, linking the ancient baptismal questions together as a continuous statement and stated in the first person for use as a personal profession of faith and as a prayer.[47]

A wealth of evidence on all this has survived from the Fathers of the early Church in connection with the ritual of the *traditio symboli* and the *redditio symboli* in the catechumenate. The word *traditio* means a literal "handing over" of the Apostles' Creed to the Catechumens by means of the official program of catechetical teaching conducted by the local bishop, with the help of his priests and catechetical teachers. It was a moral delivery of the articles of faith by teaching, analogous to the physical delivery of the chalice and paten in the ceremony of priestly ordination. The catechumens who were being prepared for baptism at Easter were instructed intensively during Lent. The heart of these instructions, the "subject matter" or "content," as it would be termed today, was simply the apostolic *symbolum,* the profession of the apostolic faith: the Apostles' Creed, as it is called today. As the catechumenate grew into full bloom in the Golden Age of the Church Fathers, these two striking liturgical ceremonies were developed to give public climax and fulfillment in the Church to this teaching program. The bishop "gave" the class their creed by a synthetic homily upon its articles. And in the *redditio* shortly before Easter they each recited it back to him, making formal profession of the Faith upon which they had been instructed and into which they were to be baptized. "The Creed, then, was presented to the neophyte not primarily as something laboriously passed from mouth to mouth or from book to book, but as a Faith impressively delivered to his keeping by the teaching authority of the living Church."[48]

"My sons and daughters," proclaims St. Augustine in one of these sermons of the *Traditio Symboli,* "receive the rule of Faith which is called the *Symbolum.* And as you receive it, write it on your heart and say it every day within yourselves: before you go to bed, before you go out to your daily work, fortify yourselves with your Creed. No one writes the Creed on paper so that it can be read. But that it be recalled, lest perhaps what has been handed over to you by our pastoral care fall into oblivion, let your memory be the paper upon which it is written. What you are going to hear from us, this you are to believe; and what you believe, you are to give back to us with your tongue. For the Apostle says, If your lips confess that Jesus is Lord and if you believe in your heart that God raised him from the dead, then you will be saved. By believing from the heart you are made righteous; by confessing him with your lips you are saved. (Rom. 10, 10). It is this Creed which you are going to receive and give back to us. These words of the *Symbolum* which you hear are scattered throughout the divine Scripture; but they have been gathered together from the Scriptures and put into this synthesis, lest the matter be too burdensome for the memory of ordinary people, so that every man may hold and profess what he believes. You of course have not begun only recently to hear that God is Almighty, have you? But you are beginning to have

Him now as your Father, through your birth in the Church, your Mother. For it is from her that you have received, that you have meditated upon, and that you have made your own in your prayerful study, what you are now coming to profess: *Credo in Deum Patrem Omnipotentem*, I believe in God, the Father Almighty . . ."[49] And St. Augustine proceeds in this example of the rich patristic literature on the *traditio symboli* to explain in compact doctrinal summary each article of faith summarized in what scholars call today the old Roman formula of the Apostles' Creed.[50]

GNOSTICISM : THE FIRST GREAT CRISIS OF FAITH

Moving into the future by her catechetical teaching programs which reflected the living Ordinary and Universal Magisterium in its concrete operation, adding ever new members to the way of Christian life, the life of conversion to God in the Lord Jesus, the life sustained by prayer and the sacraments, the Church left the age of the apostles behind and turned into the second century. Successors of the apostles, each surrounded by a presbyterium, were in charge at the four great apostolic centers, Jerusalem, Antioch, Rome and Alexandria.

Suddenly a peril from within confronted her, a situation far more dangerous than the external persecutions of the Roman Empire. It was a deceptive *pseudokerygma,* a deviation in the Church's teaching program, carried on by certain bishops and not a few priests who had fallen victims to a crisis of faith.

What was this crisis of faith? It was the adoption of the education and intellectual culture of the day, especially in schools and systems of philosophy, as the criterion of truth. These bishops and priests were teaching an adjustment of Christianity to the prevailing popular philosophical education and culture instead of converting philosophy, education and culture to God in Christ the Divine Teacher. It was a simple introduction of pagan philosophies, as distinct from Christian philosophy and Christian fundamental thinking, into the stream of Christian doctrine and teaching. In the kaleidoscope of ever-changing opinions that these teachers put forth, certain fundamental views recur and emerge as a common pattern in the Gnostic type of teaching.

Under the familiar Christian words coming from the apostles, new meanings were insinuated. This overturned all the Christian values and robbed the moral conversion, the *metanoia,* of its substance: the distinctive Christian way of life was at an end. Above all, the Gnostics rubbed out the distinction between the eternal uncreated Supreme Being and all other beings whatsoever. Pantheism and immanence deviated the profession of the first article of the Creed. Losing the concept of the transcendent personal God who speaks His word to men in His revelation, it was logical for the Gnostics to hold that the Scriptures are merely human literature, not sacred in the Jewish and Christian sense. And Jesus Christ? A great human being indeed, but nothing more. No Gnostic ever really accepted the resurrection. And the Holy Spirit? By this phrase these teachers meant simply their own natural effervescence, their own natural enthusiasm for their own thought-system. The Holy Spirit is reduced to the inspiration that they felt behind their own opinions.

Daniélou sums up the Gnostic doctrinal program as the fruit of unsound philosophies which beget an unsound concept of God. "God is unknown absolutely, both in his essence and in his existence; he is the one of whom, in the strictest sense, nothing is known, and this situation can be overcome only through the *gnosis* . . . The doctrine peculiar to Gnosticism is not that of the hidden God of the Bible nor that of the Platonist God who is hard for men to grasp, but that of a God of whose very existence men are totally ignorant."[51] Hence it is an application of the ancient skepticism clothed now in Christian terminology, leaving each man to be a law unto himself, to think and to act as he pleases, because in practice no higher reality can be known.

It would be difficult to overemphasize the gravity of the crisis which faced the early Church in these post-apostolic times. The Gnostic teachers were everywhere. They wrote tracts and books. They drove for positions of power within the Church. One of them was convinced that he would be elected as the next Successor of St. Peter. So grave was the threat . . .

Gnosticism was a "philosophical faith," not a religious faith.[52] Philosophical faith holds the things of faith, selected according to each one's taste and desire, in a way other than that of faith.[53] The reality of the supernatural order is lost; the concept of a Word from a transcendent personal God is simply dismissed as not credible for educated and cultivated men. It follows logically that the catechumenate ("religious education" we would say today), has no received content to teach. The teachings are reduced to what is intellectually fashionable in the cultural and educational milieu of the time. Thus the divine character of the Christian message is dissipated, for its original essential nature as the Word of God proclaimed and taught through His heralds, the apostles and their successors, is no longer perceived.[54] The Church herself suffers as a result a change in her very constitution at their hands. For the Gnostics, the true Church was never this concrete and visible Church conceived as a social entity divinely authorized to teach, but always a vague, spiritual Church located in the abstract aeons of the Gnostic speculations.[55]

Led by St. Irenaeus, bishop of the then mission-diocese of Lyons in Gaul, spiritually the grandson of St. John the Apostle, for he studied under Bishop Polycarp who in turn had studied under St. John himself, the bishops and priests of the early Church overcame the Gnostic crisis by lucid thought and action in the field of practical catechetics. "To expose the falsity of Gnostic teaching," Quasten writes, "Irenaeus called upon a 'Rule' which he sometimes called 'the Rule of Truth' . . . , or again 'the Rule of Faith' . . . Irenaeus is firmly convinced that the teaching of the apostles continues to live on unaltered. This tradition is the source and the norm of the faith. It is the canon of truth."[56] Irenaeus says that we receive this Rule of Truth in Baptism, a clear indication that he means the interrogatory form of the Apostles' Creed.[57] In his book, *Against the Heresies,* he gives a description of the faith of the Church that follows the doctrinal substance of the Apostles' Creed. "The Church," he writes, "though dispersed throughout the whole world, even to the ends of the earth, has received from the apostles and their disciples this faith: [she believes] in One God, the Father Almighty, maker of heaven and earth, and the sea and all things that are in them; and in one Jesus Christ, the Son of God, who became incarnate for our salvation; and in the Holy Spirit, who proclaimed through the prophets the dispensations of God, and the advent, and the birth from a virgin, and the passion, and the resurrection from the dead, and the ascension into heaven in the flesh of the well-beloved Christ Jesus, our Lord, and His (future) manifestation from heaven in the glory of the Father, to gather all things into one (Eph. 1, 10), and to raise up anew all flesh of the whole human race . . ."[58]

It was the renewal of this apostolic profession of the Trinitarian faith in Jesus as the Lord and divine Redeemer of mankind which conquered the Gnostic heresies and brought the catechetical teaching program of the Church of God safely through the crisis of the Second Century.

"As I have already observed," Irenaeus continues, "the Church, having received this preaching and this faith, although scattered throughout the whole world, yet, as if occupying but one house, carefully preserves it. She also believes these points (of doctrine) just as if she had but one soul, and one and the same heart, and she proclaims them, and teaches them, and hands them down, with perfect harmony, as if she possessed only one mouth. For, although the languages of the world are dissimilar, yet the import of the tradition is one and the same. For the churches which have been planted in Germany do not believe or hand down anything different, nor do those in Spain, nor those in Gaul, nor those in the East . . . But as the sun, that creature of God, is one and the same throughout the whole world, so also the preaching of the truth shineth everywhere, and enlightens all men that are willing to come to a knowledge of the truth."[59]

Irenaeus clinches the matter later in his work. "It is within the power of all, therefore, in every church, who may wish to see the truth, to contemplate clearly the tradition of the apostles manifested throughout the whole world . . ."[60] Noting that it would take too long to trace the apostolic succession in all the churches, Irenaeus turns to the Church of Rome. "Since, however, it would be very tedious, in such a volume as this, to reckon up the successions of all the churches, . . . we indicate that tradition, derived from the Apostles, of the very great, the very ancient, and universally known church, founded and organized at Rome by the two most glorious Apostles Peter and Paul . . . For it is a matter of necessity that every church should agree with this Church, on account of its pre-eminent authority . . ."[61]

The bishops, priests and people of God won the historic victory of the early Church over the humanly cultivated and deceptive unbelief of the Gnostic crisis of faith by a courageous and faithful exercise of what is called today the Ordinary and Universal Magisterium. At that time, this Magisterium was thought of as simply "the catechumenate," the ongoing apostolate of catechetical teaching.[62] Hardly had the victory been won, however, when a new crisis called forth the first intervention of the Extraordinary Magisterium in the life of the Church.

THE NICENE CREED

This victory of the early Church over the heresy of Gnosticism during the second and third centuries, achieved by the faithful use of her baptismal Creed, the profession of the apostolic faith, established a pattern for the centuries to come. This was true not only for the ongoing catechetical teaching program of the Ordinary and Universal Magisterium, but also for the actions of the Extraordinary Magisterium in the ecumenical councils. The crisis of the Arian heresy which filled the fourth century provides the historic illustration.

When Arius, a priest of the diocese of Alexandria in Egypt, caused a stir by his strange opinions delivered from the pulpit, the Arian heresy was born. Essentially it was a denial of the full divinity of the Lord Jesus, considering Him only a creature: an outstanding man, indeed, but fundamentally no more. This implied reduction of the Catholic faith to the level of the modish philosophical thought of the day and its cultural practices found supporters in high places in both the Church and the Empire. A vast new crisis suddenly faced the Church in the fourth century.

Again the Church turned to her baptismal Creed, the profession of the apostles' faith, and developed it accurately to meet the Arian aberrations by means of actions of the Extraordinary Magisterium. These took place in the great ecumenical councils, beginning with that of Nicea in A.D. 325, which produced the Nicene Creed. In its form finalized at the second ecumenical council, at Constantinople later in the same century (381–383), it is professed by the Catholic people every Sunday at Mass to this day.[63] "From the date of this Council," writes Cardinal Newman, "Arianism was formed into a sect exterior to the Catholic Church; and, taking refuge among the barbarian invaders of the empire, is merged among those external enemies of Christianity, whose history cannot be regarded as strictly ecclesiastical. Such is the general course of religious error; which rises within the sacred precincts, but in vain endeavors to take root in a soil uncongenial to it. The domination of heresy, however prolonged, is but one stage in its existence; it ever hastens to an end, and that end is the triumph of the Truth."[64]

In the half-century between the first two ecumenical councils, the Arian heresy did indeed dominate for long periods, and the suffering of Catholics seemed at times endlessly prolonged. It is the time when, with the emperor espousing the Arian cause supporting and promoting the Arian bishops, the whole world awoke one morning, as St. Jerome remarked, to find itself in the grip of the heresy. In a famous page Newman describes the role of the laity in the preservation of the Catholic faith. "The episcopate," he writes, "whose action was so prompt and concordant at Nicea on the rise of Arianism, did not, as a class or order of men, play a good part in the troubles consequent upon the Council; and the laity did . . . In speaking of the laity, I speak inclusively of their parish priests (so to call them), at least in many places; but on the whole, taking a wide view of the history, we are obliged to say that the governing body of the Church came short, and the governed were pre-eminent in faith, zeal, courage, and constancy . . . Of course there were great and illustrious exceptions; first, Athanasius, Hilary, the Latin Eusebius, and Phoebadius; and after them, Basil, the two Gregories, and Ambrose; there are others, too, who suffered . . . [But] it was mainly by the faithful people, under the lead of Athanasius and the Egyptian bishops, and in some places supported by their bishops or priests, that the worst of heresies was withstood and stamped out of the sacred territory."[65]

St. Hilary, bishop of Poitiers in France during this time of troubles, and called in history "The Athanasius of the West," describes the chaos which fell not only upon society in this period but on the Church as well. For the blows of the barbarian invaders were mingled now with the confusions which the Arian heresy generated. "It is a dangerous time for us and a wretched one," he writes; "for now there are as many versions of the faith as there are persons who want to teach; and as many doctrines among us as there are ways of life which people desire; . . . we are falling away from that faith which is always one and the same: for when faiths begin to be several, *plures,* they are entering on the path which will end with no faith at all."[66]

How does St. Hilary solve the problem and lead his flock through the danger? He turns to the original profession of the apostolic faith, the baptismal Creed containing the articles of faith which we now call the

Apostles' Creed, and he renews it among them. "The most secure thing for us," he writes, "is to retain that original and unique Gospel faith, as we understood and professed it in our baptism, without permitting any changes in it, and by continuing to believe firmly that which we received when we were baptized into our Church."[67]

THE ORDINARY AND UNIVERSAL MAGISTERIUM: CREED AND CATECHETICS

It was this fidelity to the Apostles' Creed in catechetical teaching which achieved the victory over the Arian heresy, causing it gradually to wither and at last to die out altogether. Throughout this entire period the Holy See of St. Peter stood firm in the profession of the apostolic faith, like a rock amid and the crosscurrents of a flood. It was the program outlined by St. Hilary which won the day. Everywhere in Christendom this catechetical teaching proceeded, explaining faithfully the Apostles' Creed, in the precisely developed understanding given by the Extraordinary Magisterium in the Nicene Creed. But the teaching itself, in homes, in parishes, in the schools which St. Benedict and his Monks of the West were soon establishing everywhere in Christendom, was nothing else than the Ordinary and Universal Magisterium in its ongoing activity of evangelization and catechesis, a continuing process since the apostles.

This teaching is the explanation of the elements of the Christian message, professed by the Creed, which the apostles and their successors are mandated to proclaim as witnesses to the Lord Jesus. Thus a great fact has come to stand up splendidly and visibly upon the historical and social scene of mankind. It is the fact of the Catholic Church as the ongoing embodiment of the apostolic witness and its corresponding profession of faith. Indeed, this teaching of the Ordinary and Universal Magisterium constitutes the Catholic Church in her very substance and being: it gives to this Church the constitutive note of apostolicity.[68] The Catholic fact manifests a witness and is the work of appointed witnesses: and the baptized members of the Church accept this witness personally by the profession of the apostolic faith.

Thus the faith exists, descending from God to men, and handed on by appointed men from generation to generation, communicated by this catechetical teaching which the successors of the apostles and their helpers carry forward, priests, parents and catechists in the parishes, and catechetical teachers of religion in the schools.

After the Arian crisis, this magnificent teaching program began to fill all the Christian centuries and to reach out to the uttermost bounds of the earth.[69] This is the Magisterium teaching the articles or truths of the faith in its daily or "ordinary" way. It raises up professing Catholics, baptized into the Church and its sacramental life precisely by the personal profession of this same Creed or message. Thus a world of faith exists on earth, the acceptance of the Word of God on the authority of God revealing, and communicated forward among men by the words of human discourse and teaching.

The Word of God is contained of course in the Scriptures. But the ordinary members of the Church need help in making it their own, for it exists there in a diffused state.[70] The People of God need to have the essentials of the divine message gathered into brief compass. We have seen the beginning of this process in the original apostolic *kerygma,* in the preaching of Sts. Peter and Paul.[71] It was the Magisterium itself, put into operation by the apostles, that has given to the Church this summary of the revealed Word of God which we in the English-speaking world have come to call the Apostles' Creed. The essence of the divine message was cast into both the interrogatory form for baptism, and into the declaratory form for catechetical teaching and for personal prayer. It gives the message in a set of brief, simple and clear propositions or formulas, offering it to all Christians for constant meditation and profession. The early Church, as we have seen, called this summary simply "The Faith," as was the custom among the Greeks, or the *symbolum fidei,* as both the Greeks and Latins came to speak of it. We too use the word "symbol" in this sense, but ordinarily we have come to say simply "The Apostles' Creed." The important thing is the doctrinal reality, the proclamation and teaching of the living Magisterium denoted by the various names: the formula received officially in the One, Holy, Catholic and Apostolic Church for professing the apostolic faith.[72]

If this marvellously compact yet comprehensive summary of the Word of God, which authentic catechesis possesses in the set of propositions or formulas of the Creed, required the action of the divine Magisterium of the Catholic Church, so did the explanation of these articles of faith in catechetical teaching require the constant supervision of this same teaching authority. This is the origin of the concept of a "catechism," whether as an oral process or as a written booklet. The concept is simply that basic and official initial explanation of the articles of faith which is destined for all the faithful, that they may know with confidence what it is that they believe. This is a teaching which must be certain and authentic, one and the same for all, because it participates with immediacy in the one and same apostolic faith. This requires the constant action and vigilance of the Magisterium itself, constituted by God to carry on this program of teaching the articles of faith and watching with pastoral care over the fruitfulness in the lives of the faithful of the Word of God thus communicated.

"As one can see," concludes Pègues, "catechetical teaching in the Church, taking place under the authority of the Magisterium, is nothing else than the explanation of the Creed; as the Apostles' Creed itself is nothing else than the declaratory statement of the form for baptismal initiation given to the Church by the apostles."[73]

Thus it has come about that there is a tradition of catechetical teaching in the Church. By means of it the Ordinary and Universal Magisterium reaches everywhere with its witness to the apostolic faith which it proclaims and with the didactic explanation which it supervises. It is assisted by catechetical teachers who cooperate with the successors of the apostles. In its elementary form, adapted therefore by definition to children, this catechetical teaching explains lovingly the formulas of this same Apostles' Creed.[74] Thus Catholic children are helped to deepen their conversion and to mature in professing this one and the same apostolic faith.[75] This heritage of catechetical teaching, centered upon the Creed and therefore upon Him whom the Creed professes, has four chief areas of doctrine: it explains the Creed itself, article by article; it teaches prayer, using the Our Father as its chief guide and text; it expounds the moral way of life proper to Christians; and it teaches the nature of the Sacraments and their power to sustain this Christian life.[76]

THE EXTRAORDINARY MAGISTERIUM: THE ECUMENICAL COUNCILS AND THE CREED

"The Faith is that which the Creed expresses," writes a respected theologian; "it is that of the councils, from Nicea to Vatican II; it is that which the Magisterium of the Church presents."[77] The first Ecumenical Council of Nicea turned to the baptismal profession of the Apostles' Creed as the means for overcoming the Arian heresy. Ecumenical councils continued in this pattern when enacting dogmas to state the correct understanding, explanation and interpretation of the articles of faith professed by the Creed.[78] Some of the councils were concerned primarily with disciplinary decrees to preserve intact the moral life or *metanoia* of the People of God. But when the definition of the truth of the faith against particular errors was uppermost in the mind of the Council Fathers, a profession of faith usually has been made, and more than once it has been the vehicle used, in the pattern of Nicea, to repel the error. But in any case the dogmatic declarations always explain and defend the articles of the apostolic Creed.

Thus the Fourth Lateran Council, twelfth ecumenical in A.D. 1215, enacted a profession of faith which was the historic Creed developed so as to cope accurately with the specific errors of the Waldensians, the Albigensians, and those of Joachim of Flora. It is a development of the original Creed, a profession of the apostolic faith upon the tri-partite form of the Trinitarian interrogatory Creed of baptism, as the following excerpt makes manifest.

"We firmly believe and openly confess that there is only one true God, eternal and immense, omnipotent, unchangeable . . . Father, Son, and Holy Spirit; three Persons indeed but one essence, substance or nature absolutely simple . . . the one principle of the universe, Creator of all things invisible and visible, spiritual and corporeal . . .

"And finally, Jesus Christ, the only begotten Son of God made flesh by the entire Trinity, conceived with the cooperation of the Holy Spirit of Mary ever Virgin, made true man, composed of a rational soul and human flesh, one Person in two natures, pointed out more clearly the way of life. Who . . . suffered on the cross for the salvation of the human race, and being dead descended into hell, rose from the dead and ascended into heaven . . . He will come at the end of the world to judge the living and the dead . . .

"There is one Universal Church of the faithful, outside of which there is absolutely no salvation. In which there is the same priest and sacrifice, Jesus Christ, whose body and blood are truly contained in the sacrament of the altar under the forms of bread and wine; the bread being changed (*transubstantiatis*) by divine power into the body, and the wine into the blood, so that to realize the mystery of unity we may receive of Him what He has received of us. And this sacrament no one can effect except the priest who has been duly ordained in accordance with the keys of the Church, which Jesus Christ Himself gave to the Apostles and their Successors. But the sacrament of baptism . . . leads to salvation. And should anyone after the reception of baptism have fallen into sin, by true repentance he can always be restored. Not only virgins and those practising chastity, but also those united in marriage, through the right faith and through works pleasing to God, can merit eternal salvation."[79]

It is immediately apparent that the development of creedal doctrine is found here primarily in the third article of the Apostles' Creed, on the Holy Spirit and His action in the Church. The reason is that the errors of the time were challenging these doctrines of the faith in a particular way.

The Creed of the Council of Trent illustrates the same principle and pattern perfectly.[80] "I, N., with firm faith believe and profess each and every article contained in the Symbol of Faith which the holy Roman Church uses, namely: I believe in one God, the Father almighty, maker of heaven and earth, and of all things visible and invisible; and in one Lord Jesus Christ, the only-begotten Son of God, born of the Father before all ages; God from God, light from light, true God from true God; begotten not made, of one substance with the Father . . ." And it proceeds to profess anew, *verbatim,* the Nicene Creed. Then it goes on to amplify the profession in the way of Fourth Lateran, adding certain specific developments of doctrine which Protestantism was occasioning, particularly with regard to the work of the Holy Spirit, the Holy Catholic Church, its seven sacraments, especially the Mass, and its divine teaching authority.[81]

The culmination of this conciliar profession of "the Creed of the immortal Tradition of the Holy Church of God," as Pope Paul VI terms it,[82] took place on Jan. 6, 1870, when Pope Pius IX and all the Council Fathers of Vatican I made and subscribed to what is basically the same Tridentine Profession of Faith. The Nicene Creed is repeated at the outset, and then the following points of doctrinal development are added:

"I most firmly admit and cherish the apostolic and ecclesiastical traditions, and the rest of the precepts and regulations of the same

Church. In like manner I accept Sacred Scripture according to the meaning that Holy Mother Church has held and now holds. To her it pertains to pass judgment on the true meaning and interpretation of Sacred Scripture; and I will never accept and interpret it in a manner that is not in accordance with the unanimous consent of the Fathers.

"I profess also that there are truly and properly seven Sacraments of the New Law, instituted by Jesus Christ our Lord; and that these Sacraments are necessary for the salvation of the human race, although not all of them are necessary for each individual. I profess that the seven Sacraments are: Baptism, Confirmation, Eucharist, Penance, Extreme Unction, Holy Orders, and Matrimony. I profess that these Sacraments confer grace; and that, among the seven, Baptism, Confirmation, and Holy Orders cannot be repeated without committing a sacrilege. I accept and admit also the customary and approved rites of the Catholic Church in the solemn administration of all the above-mentioned sacraments.

"I embrace and receive every single statement concerning original sin and justification defined and declared by the holy Council of Trent.

"I profess likewise that in the Mass there is offered to God a true, proper, and propitiatory Sacrifice on behalf of the living and the dead; and that in the holy Sacrament of the Eucharist there is truly, really, and substantially the body and blood together with the soul and divinity of Jesus Christ our Lord; and that there is a change of the entire substance of bread into the body, and of the entire substance of the wine into the blood, a change which the Catholic Church calls transubstantiation. I confess also that the whole and entire Christ, and a true sacrament, is received under each separate species.

"I hold firmly that purgatory exists, and that souls detained there are aided by the prayers of the faithful. Likewise I hold firmly that the saints reigning with Christ should be venerated and invoked; that they offer prayers to God on our behalf; and that the relics of the saints should be venerated. I assert firmly that images of Christ, of the ever Virgin Mother of God, and of the other saints may be possessed and retained; and that due honor and veneration should be given to them. I affirm that Christ left to the Church power to grant indulgences, and that the use of indulgences is very salutary for the Christian people.

"I acknowledge the holy, Catholic, and apostolic Roman Church as the mother and teacher of all churches. And I solemnly promise and swear true obedience to the Roman Pontiff, Vicar of Christ, and Successor of blessed Peter the head of the Apostles.[83]

"I accept and profess as beyond doubt everything handed down, defined, and asserted by the sacred canons, and by the Ecumenical Councils, especially by the holy Council of Trent. At the same time I condemn, reject, and anathematize everything contrary to them, and all heresies whatsoever that have been rejected and anathematized by the Church.

"I, N., solemnly promise, vow, and swear that with God's help I will firmly retain and confess whole and immaculate to my dying breath this true Catholic Faith, which I now profess freely and hold truly, and outside which no one can be saved; and that insofar as I can, I will see to it that my subjects or those entrusted to my care in virtue of my office, hold, teach, and preach this Faith. So help me God and these, His holy Gospels."[84]

The First Vatican Council, accordingly, proceeded full in the context of the Creed which professes the apostolic faith. While its primary purpose was to clarify, explain and defend the first article of the Creed in the face of the rise and spread of modern philosophical atheism, it turned also with unerring insight to the defense of the Creed as a whole from the deceptive ploy of the atheistic movement to continue the use and the terminology of the articles of faith, indeed, but reinterpreted in the light of the so-called "new theology" and its applications in the field of religious education. It is a defined position of the Catholic Church which has new relevance in the present third phase of the Modernist movement, and it reads as follows:

"For the teaching of the Faith which God has revealed," the Council states in chapter 4 of the Constitution *Dei Filius*, "has not been proposed as a philosophical discovery to be perfected by human ingenuity, but as a divine deposit handed over to the Spouse of Christ to be guarded faithfully and to be explained infallibly. Hence that meaning of sacred dogmas must perpetually be retained which Holy Mother Church has once declared; nor is that meaning ever to be abandoned under the pretext and name of a more profound comprehension. 'Let, then, understanding, knowledge and wisdom grow and advance mightily and strongly in individuals as well as in the community, in one man as well as in the Church as a whole, according to the degree proper to each age and each time; but only within their own domain, that is, with the same dogma, the same meaning, the same sense.' "[85] And then its corresponding canon: "If anyone should say that with the progress of knowledge it is sometimes possible that dogmas proposed by the Church can be given a meaning different from the one that the Church has understood and still understands, let him be anathema."[86]

What then of Vatican II? The Council Fathers did not make public profession of this Creed, yet their deliberations and the conciliar documents which they signed and published to the Church proceed in its same context. At least a surface reason for this doubtless may be seen in the opening discourse of Pope John XXIII, on Oct. 11, 1962, which gave the Council a special pastoral orientation. There is little doubt but that a great hope filled the heart of the Pope and a vision animated his mind's eye: he saw the real possibility of genuine and authentic renewal on the human scene. Who is to say it was not possible, at that particular moment of time and of grace? Suppose everyone had cooperated with the pope's call and had obeyed the idea of the Council he was calling? Is not the saying of the German historians perhaps most true of such a moment?—*Jede Zeit steht unmittelbar zu Gott,* each time has its own direct responsibility to God.

"The greatest concern of the Ecumenical Council is this," Pope John XXIII told the assembled Council Fathers, "that the sacred deposit of Christian doctrine should be guarded and taught more efficaciously . . . The salient point of this Council is not, therefore, a discussion of one article or another of the fundamental doctrine of the Church . . . which is presumed to be well known and familiar to all. For this a Council was not necessary . . . [But] it is necessary that this certain and unchangeable doctrine, to which the obedience of Faith must be given, be studied thoroughly and explained in the way for which our times are calling. For the deposit of Faith in itself, namely the truths which form the content of our venerable doctrine, is one thing, and the way in which it is expressed is another thing, *eodem tamen sensa eademque sententia,* but nevertheless with the same meaning and the same sense."[87]

Pope John XXIII is using here the very words of Vatican I, and in turn of St. Vincent of Lerins speaking for the early Church. Vatican II proceeded to make this same fundamental position explicitly its own, establishing thereby the principle of its continuity with Vatican I and with "the Creed of the immortal Tradition of the holy Church of God," in the words of Pope Paul VI, already quoted.[88]

Three years later, on Nov. 18, 1965, Pope Paul VI addressed the assembled Fathers of Vatican II in the allocution "Publica haec sessio," on the arrangements for terminating the Council three weeks later and for carrying on the work of implementation in the years ahead.

"This is the period of the true *aggiornamento*," the Supreme Pontiff states, "proclaimed by our predecessor of venerable memory John XXIII. This word, which described his goal, certainly did not have the meaning for him which some try to give it, as if it allowed for the 'relativization,' according to the spirit of the world, of everything in the Church—dogmas, laws, structures, traditions."[89] The pope had just finished describing that stage during the Council when "in some sectors of public opinion, everything seemed open to discussion and was in fact discussed. Everything was seen as complex and difficult. An attempt was made to subject everything to criticism, with impatience for novelty. There was uneasiness, and currents of opinion made themselves felt." Then he turns to the end of the Council, as one who has come through a great danger, and points to the documents of Vatican II as the guide for the coming period after the council: "Fidelity is their characteristic: *earum propria est fidelitas.*"[90] In other words, the Conciliar Documents have come through the stormy passage unscathed, characterized by the fact that they are true to the Catholic faith, expressing it unchanged in a manner proper to contemporary man and his problems.

This places the present study in the contemporary period after Vatican Council II, when the profession of faith known popularly as the *Creed of the People of God* has become part of the ongoing life of the Church.

CREEDLESSNESS: THE CHALLENGE OF THE DUTCH CATECHISM

The hope which animated the mind and heart of Pope John XXIII was not destined under providence to be fulfilled. The peaceful period of the true *aggiornamento* for which Pope Paul VI hoped, in which

all sons and daughters of the Church would accept in intellectual peace
and unity the documents of Vatican II, unrelativized and in the spirit
of the creedal faith which is their characteristic property, was not to
endure. It lasted, in fact, not even one year. It was shattered by what
Pope Paul VI recognized officially as a "crisis of faith." From the
viewpoint of "Creed and Catechetics," as a negative illustration of
their correlation, the chief outward sign of this crisis was a phenomenon
which appeared first in Holland.

Vatican II closed officially on the Feast of the Immaculate Con-
ception, Dec. 8, 1965. Under the date of March 1, 1966, Cardinal
Alfrink, President of the Dutch Episcopal Conference, gave the *im-
primatur* to a book entitled *The New Catechism*. The Dutch original,
De Nieuwe Katechismus, was published in October of the same year.
Quickly it became a runaway best seller. Immediately Herder and
Herder put translations into the leading languages of the Christian
West and published them in 1968.[91]

Who was the author of this book? None is listed. Was it the Dutch
bishops, themselves personally as the actual writers? It is unlikely. The
Dutch bishops had commissioned the book from the Catechetical Institute at the Catholic University of Nijmegen and its actual author-
ship almost certainly is due to persons connected with the Institute
faculty. In Holland itself, Edward Schillebeeckx, O.P., and Piet
Schoonenberg, S.J. are recognized as "the fathers, if not the authors,
of the *Dutch Catechism.*"[92]

This famous work constitutes a challenge to the faith of the Catholic
Church which it professes by the articles of its historic Apostolic
Creed. This challenge has arisen and deepened on the campuses of
more than a few Catholic institutions of higher education as the years
since Vatican II have gone by. The *Dutch Catechism* was the opening
of a fissure.

Fully in the pattern noted by Newman in the case of the Arian
heresy, it was the Catholic laity of Holland who recognized the issue
and took action by the following letter to Pope Paul VI.

"HOLY FATHER,

"Prostrate at the feet of Your Holiness, we the undersigned write to
you with great sorrow and sadness, as follows.

"For some years now opinions not in accord with Catholic doctrine, and which actually contradict it, have been propagated in our country by Dutch writers and lecturers, both of the laity and of the secular and regular clergy. This way of proceeding has been the origin of great scandal. This scandal is not only continuing, but is increasing day by day, and is the cause of suffering and sorrow for a very great number of the faithful.

"Recently, on October 9, 1966, a 600-page book was published, *The New Catechism,* written by mandate of our bishops. In this book one finds a certain number of opinions that are partly or entirely contrary to the faith, or that interpret the truth in an ambiguous way, so that each is left to understand it his own way, even when this is less than harmonious with the faith.

"Among other things, one finds the following particular points in this book.

"1. Speaking of the mother of Jesus, this book does not affirm her biological virginity, before and after the birth, and seems to deny it indirectly by the use of ambiguous terms. (See p. 89 ff., and 92 ff.). This defect is all the more operative when one takes into account the fact that many Catholics in our ecclesiastical province dare to deny this dogma openly.

"2. With regard to original sin, it is denied that it exists in us as sin that originated by one single first parent and has been transmitted to us by generation.

"3. Speaking of the Eucharist, this book teaches that the bread and wine acquire only a new meaning and a new purpose. (See p. 403 ff.). This contrasts both with the doctrine of the Council of Trent and with the Encyclical *Mysterium fidei.*

"4. The authors assert that Protestantism accepts as true almost all the teaching of the Catholic Church, but that the matter is not yet perfectly reciprocated on our part. (See p. 469).

"5. Regarding birth control, it is clear that this book does not respect the norms stated by the Church on various occasions, among others in the Encyclical *Casti connubii* and in the discourse of Your Holiness on Oct. 29, 1966. (See p. 472 ff.).

"6. When this book speaks of the origin of man, the creation of his immortal soul is not mentioned even once. (See p. 13). Indeed, at the end of the book there is a denial that man has a spiritual and immortal soul. (See p. 554). What takes place after death would not be other than "a sort of resurrection in a new body." (See p. 555).

"7. The existence of the angels is placed in doubt. (p. 565).

"The explanation of various dogmas generally departs from the way in which the Church has understood them and still understands them, and this in the face of the implicit condemnation by Vatican I. (*Denz.* 1818, and 1800).

"The diffusion of this book by means of translations, about which open reference already is being made, will constitute without any doubt a great danger for souls. We humbly beseech Your Holiness to intervene so that in our country, and elsewhere because of us, the faith may not have to suffer even greater dangers."[93]

What happened in Rome? Taking the letter seriously, the Supreme Pontiff launched a series of far-reaching actions with effects that are continuing through the present and on into the future. They provide a helpful illustration, furthermore, of the contemporary relevance of the historic correlation between creed and catechetics, and are therefore central in this present study of the contemporary situation in religious education.

The first of these actions was the Gazzada Conference held in Northern Italy on April 8–10, 1967. The Pope requested that three theologians selected by the Holy See meet with three to be named by the Dutch Episcopal Conference, in order to remedy formulations in the *Dutch Catechism* that offend Catholic doctrine or cause confusion with regard to it.

Desiring to create a favorable atmosphere for the meeting, Pope Paul wrote a kind personal letter to Cardinal Alfrink, President of the Dutch Bishops' Conference, under date of March 30, 1967, thanking him for agreeing to the Gazzada Conference and giving him the names of the three theologians designated by the Holy See. "These theologians have been charged," writes the Pope, "in every word they speak and judgment they make, to take scrupulous account of the Ordinary Magisterium of the Church, of the doctrine contained in the Documents of Vatican Council II, and finally of the Allocutions that We Ourselves make repeatedly, out of the mandate committed to Us, to clarify what our Mother and Teacher the Church has to teach us with certitude . . . We have no doubt that [the outcome of the dialogue] . . . will be certain modifications . . . in the *Catechism,* with more carefully weighed expressions that correspond with the greatest possible exactitude to the faith of the Church, to the truth of reality, and to the sense of the faithful. The intention is far from Us of desiring to determine in advance the course of this projected meeting, which should remain open and completely natural. Nevertheless, We are of the mind that it ought not leave any ambiguity in the matter, for example, of the Virgin Birth of Christ, a dogma of the Catholic faith; nor in that of belief in the real existence of the Angels, rooted as it is in the Gospels and the Tradition of the Church; nor with regard to the nature of the satisfaction and of the sacrifice offered by Christ to the Heavenly Father to cancel our sins and to reconcile men to Him . . .''[94]

The Gazzada Conference accordingly took place. Representing the Holy See were Fathers Edward Dhanis, S.J., John Visser, C.SS.R., and Benedict Lemeer, O.P., all Dutch-speaking priests. The Dutch bishops designated Fathers W. Bless, S.J., Piet Schoonenberg, S.J., and Edward Schillebeeckx, O.P. The agenda, approved by the Sacred Congregation of the Council in Rome, contained 14 principal points and 45 lesser ones. It was requested by the Holy See that the text of the *New (Dutch) Catechism* be corrected on these points so as to eliminate any ambiguity regarding the doctrine of the faith. This was never done. The Gazzada Conference ended in stalement and fruitlessness.[95]

Pope Paul VI quickly took a further step. He named a special commission of Cardinals to examine the *New (Dutch) Catechism* and to produce a judgment upon its text. The commission, composed of Cardinals Frings (chairman), Lefèbvre, Jaeger, Florit, Browne and Journet, truly an international group and distinguished for theological scholarship, held its first meeting on June 27–28, 1967, the eve of the Year of Faith. It organized a group of theologians from seven countries as consultants, and proceeded throughout the summer and fall of 1967 with the work of study and analysis on the text of the *Dutch Catechism.*[96]

In September, 1967, the authors of *The New (Dutch) Catechism* submitted to Rome, by way of the Dutch Bishops' Conference, their own rewritten version of the passages in question. The commission of cardinals examined the material and rejected it as insufficient.[97]

The final meeting of the commission of Cardinals was held on Dec. 12–14, 1967, and its official report bears Dec. 24, 1967 as its date.[98] It identified the doctrinal points and the passages of the *New (Dutch) Catechism* which must be corrected, provided a statement of basic doctrine in each instance, and set up a new mixed committee of four theologians to compose a new corrected textbook version for each of the passages. Fathers Dhanis and Visser were appointed to this committee by Rome, and the Dutch Bishops' Conference designated Father G. Mulders ad Msgr. H. J. Fortmann as their representatives. Mulders, however, subsequently withdrew from the project and refused to attend any of the meetings at which the work was accomplished.[99] Msgr. Fortmann worked harmoniously with Fathers Dhanis and Visser on behalf of the Dutch bishops. Speaking on the Dutch radio, Feb. 15, 1968, Fortmann declared himself in complete accord with the corrections drawn up according to the doctrinal judgments of the commission of Cardinals, and stated that they reflect the opinions of no particular school of theology but simply the teaching of the Magisterium as such.[100]

These official corrections made on behalf of the commission of Cardinals were sent to the authors of the *New Catechism* on March 14, 1968. Then on June 10, 1968, as the Year of Faith of the Catholic Church was in its final month, the authors responded to the Dutch hierarchy from the Catechetical Institute at the Catholic University of Nijmegen, as follows: "We have come to the unequivocal conclusion that the proposed corrections, whether taken singly or as a whole, must be rejected."[101] Later in the same month, Pope Paul VI was to give to the Catholic Church the solemn Profession of Faith known since as the *Creed of the People of God*.[102]

THE CREED OF THE PEOPLE OF GOD

Parallel with these measures taken by the Holy See to meet the specific doctrinal challenge represented by the *New Catechism,* Pope Paul VI launched a positive program designed to renew the Catholic faith throughout the world. In his mind's eye he saw something worldwide taking place, in every diocese and religious community, in every Catholic heart and soul. He called for a special "Year of Faith." It was a hope resting on real possibility, much like that which animated Pope John XXIII when he opened Vatican II. In fact, the two efforts and hopes are interrelated: the renewal of the Catholic faith for which Pope Paul called was exactly the instrument which would have carried out the true meaning and spirit of Vatican II, the authentic renewal for which its documents call and to the nature of which they bear witness.

What was this program of Pope Paul VI? Essentially it was a call to Catholics everywhere to turn to the Apostles' Creed, with manifestations and special convocations led by bishops in their dioceses, by pastors in their parishes, and by superiors in their religious houses, making concerted personal and public use of the Creed as the instrument for renewing the Catholic faith. "We fraternally exhort you all, Venerable Brothers in the Episcopacy," Pope Paul writes on February 22, 1967, in his first call to the Year of Faith, "to explain in your preaching the meaning of the Creed, to honor this Profession of Faith with special religious celebrations and above all to recite it solemnly and repeatedly with your priests and faithful in one or the other of the formulations commonly used in Catholic prayer. We would be very happy if in every cathedral the Creed were recited expressly in honor of SS. Peter and Paul, in the presence of the bishop, the college of priests, the seminarians and the lay Catholics active in promoting the kingdom of God, men and women religious, and as many members as possible of the assembly of the faithful. Similarly every parish and every religious house should do the same in the presence of its assembled community. And so we should like to suggest that on a fixed day this Profession of Faith be made in every single Christian household, in every Catholic association, in every Catholic school, hospital and place of worship, in every group and gathering where the voice of faith can be raised to proclaim and strengthen a sincere adherence to our common Christian calling . . . In this way the year commemorating the centenary of SS. Peter and Paul will be 'The Year of Faith.' To ensure a certain uniformity in its celebration, we will begin the centenary year on the forthcoming feast of the two Apostles, June 29, 1967. Until the same date in the following year, we intend to hold many special commemorative celebrations, all directed toward an interior renewal of our holy faith, a more profound study and a religious profession of our faith and an active witnessing to that faith without which 'it is impossible to please God' (Heb. 11, 6) and by means of which we hope to arrive at the salvation promised to us. (See Mark 16, 16; Eph. 2, 8; etc.). In making this announcement to you, Venerable Brothers and dear Sons, an announcement full of spiritual significance, of encouragement and hope, we are sure of finding you all in agreement and communion with us."[103]

Pope Paul led the way, making the faith which the Creed professes a constantly recurring theme of his own doctrinal actions and allocutions.[104] Not least of these was the Synod of Bishops held at Rome in the fall of 1967, to which the Supreme Pontiff assigned doctrinal fidelity and the protection of the Catholic faith as its first concern. He makes his own the key passage with which Pope John XXIII opened Vatican II: "It is necessary for all the teaching of the Church in its entirety to be accepted with a fresh enthusiasm by all, with serenity and tranquillity, in the precision of language and formulation handed down to us, which is to be seen most clearly in the acts of the Council of Trent and the First Vatican Council . . ."[105]

"The solicitude for doctrinal fidelity," Pope Paul continues, "which was so solemnly declared at the beginning of the recent Council, must therefore direct our post-conciliar times. More watchfulness is required on the part of those who in the Church of God have from Christ the mandate to teach, to spread his message, and to guard the 'deposit of faith,' in proportion as the dangers which today threaten her are more numerous and serious; immense dangers caused by the irreligious orientation of the modern mentality, and insidious dangers which even from within the Church find utterance in the work of teachers and writers, desirous, it is true, of giving new expression to Catholic doctrine but frequently desirous rather of adapting the dogma of the faith to secular thought and language, than of adhering to the norm of the Church's Magisterium.

"Thus they allow free rein to the opinion that one may forget the demands of orthodoxy and select from among the truths of the faith those which instinctive personal preference finds admissible, rejecting the others, as if the rights of moral conscience, free and responsible for its acts, may be claimed in preference to the rights of truth, foremost among which are the rights of divine revelation (See Gal. 1, 6–9), and to the opinion that one may subject to revision the doctrinal heritage of the Church to give Christianity new ideological dimensions, far different from the theological dimensions outlined by genuine tradition with immeasurable respect for God's own thought . . .

"For this reason we considered the safeguarding of the faith so imperative after the close of the Council that we invited the whole Church to celebrate a 'Year of Faith' in honor of the two Apostles, the chief teachers and witnesses of Christ's Gospel. The purpose of this Year is to meditate on the very faith handed down to us, and to assess in the modern context the decisive function this fundamental virtue has for the stability of our religion and the vitality of the Church, for building up God's kingdom in souls, for ecumenical dialogue, and the genuine contact for renewal that Christ's followers intend to make with the world of today. We want in this way to strengthen our own faith as teachers, witnesses and pastors in God's Church, so that Christ her sole and supreme Head, Christ living and invisible, may find it humble, sincere and strong. We want also to strengthen the faith of our children, especially those who pursue the study of theology and religion, so that with a renewed and watchful awareness of the Church's unalterable and certain teaching they may give wise collaboration to furthering the Sacred Sciences and to upholding the sacred aim of Catholic teaching, giving life through light."[106]

The Year of Faith was truly a grand concept. It culminated in a fitting manner on the Feast of Sts. Peter and Paul, June, 1968. At an outdoor evening Mass on the steps of St. Peter's Basilica, surrounded by many cardinals and bishops from various parts of the world and before an immense throng of the faithful who filled St. Peter's Square, Pope Paul VI gave to the Catholic Church, by pronouncing it and making it his own, the Solemn Profession of Faith, "the Creed of the immortal Tradition of the Holy Church of God," as he called it, known now throughout the Church under the familiar name, *The Creed of the People of God*.[107] The Latin version is the official text. But Pope Paul made his own profession of it in the Italian translation, which thereby assumes a special significance. As his voice rose throughout the vast Piazza San Pietro, a hush fell over the crowd, for all seemed to sense that the moment was a uniquely historic one.

It is fascinating to compare the dates connected with the episode of the *New Catechism* with those of the Year of Faith and its renewed profession of faith. It would be idle to claim that the *Dutch Catechism* was exclusively in view on the part of the Holy See, as if it were the only doctrinal aberration of our time. One needs but recall the vast doctrinal phenomenon of Teilhardism. In a very real sense the *Dutch Catechism* is only an application of it in religious education.[108] Yet the fact remains that the Dutch work has had an immense influence, catechizing the whole world, so to speak, by means of the numerous religious education programs and religion textbook series which embody its approach. Furthermore, scholars have been quick to note the correspondence between the points of agenda at the Gazzada Conference and the clarifications of doctrine made by the *Creed of the People of God*. From every point of view, this profession of faith is the answer of the Catholic Church to the creedlessness of the *New Catechism* and of the religious education programs which turn about it as its satellites and continue its approach today.

The significance of the *Creed of the People of God* comes into full view when its relationship to the subterranean volcano of modern philosophical unbelief is considered. The references of the Supreme Pontiff to this situation, and even to the fact of its penetration *within the Church,* have been noted above: "insidious dangers which even from within the Church find utterance in the work of teachers and writers . . ."[108-A] In his call for the Year of Faith he places the Creed explicitly in the context of the modern apostasy from God in philosophical thinking.

"You know also, Venerable Brothers and dear Sons," he writes, "how in its development the modern world reaching out to amazing conquests in the dominion of outward things and proud of its greater degree of self-awareness, is inclined to forget and deny God . . . And while man's religious sense today is in a decline, depriving the faith of its natural foundation, new opinions in exegesis and theology, often borrowed from bold but fluid secular philosophies, have in places found a way into the realm of Catholic teaching. They question or distort the objective sense of truths taught with authority by the Church. Under the pretext of adapting religious thought to the contemporary outlook they prescind from the guidance of the Church's teaching, give the foundation of theological speculation a direction of historicism, dare to rob Holy Scripture's testimony of its sacred and historical character, and try to introduce a so-called 'post conciliar' mentality among the People of God. This neglects the solidity and consistency of the Council's vast and magnificent developments of teaching and legislation, neglects with it the Church's accumulated riches of thought and practice in order to overturn the spirit of traditional fidelity and spread about the illusion of giving Christianity a new interpretation, which is arbitrary and barren. What would remain of the content of our faith, or of the theological virtue that professes it, if these attempts, freed from the support of the Church's teaching authority, were destined to prevail?"[109]

Many have elaborated in detail upon this surprising contemporary phenomenon, the "crisis of faith" after Vatican II, but this papal analysis of the essentials of what is actually a resurrection of the ancient Gnosticism remains unsurpassed.[110] Whether the effort of the Holy See to cause the Catholic Church to make use of the Apostles' Creed as its instrument of defense and renewal in the face of the Neo-Modernist approach in religious education, symbolized and pioneered by the *New Catechism* has been successful in any immediate this-wordly sense, historians of the future no doubt will determine. But the fact remains that pastors and catechetical teachers have at hand in the admonition and request and program of the Holy See an abiding means of personal victory in their care of souls on the battlefield of the present conflict between faith and unbelief. This means of victory is the Apostles' Creed doctrinally developed into this *Creed of the People of God* which professes anew in and for the present day "the Creed of the immortal tradition of the Holy Church of God."[111]

It remains to consider why the Creed is this abiding instrument of spiritual victory for the embattled contemporary Catholic Church. Then we shall proceed to a catechetical commentary upon the articles of faith which the *Creed of the People of God* states and develops with pin-pointed accuracy to meet the barren aberrations of the Neo-Modernist approach in much of modern religious education, and to provide a solid basis for contemporary catechetical teaching.

THE PROFESSION OF JESUS AS LORD AND GOD

The swaying battle-line which engages the Church Militant turns about the Creed. In his own way Goethe saw this clearly when he remarked that the conflict between faith and unbelief rules the course of universal history. He could have used the words creed and creedless-ness instead of faith and unbelief, or he might have noted that the Magisterium is the issue: his meaning would have been the same.

The reason is not difficult to see. It is contained in the fact that the articles of faith professed by the Creed do not terminate in their own verbal statement as mere propositions or formulas. They terminate in the reality of the Person whom the Creed professes.[112] For the New Testament, this bearing of the words of creedal and catechetical dis-course upon Him who is the Word of God Incarnate was self-evidence itself. "Since in Jesus, the Son of God, we have the supreme high priest who has gone through to the highest heaven, we must never let go of the faith that we have professed." (Heb. 4, 14).

The Creed, whether in its interrogatory form at baptism or in its declaratory form used in the catechetical teaching that prepares for the life of prayer and the sacraments, is an official instrument of the Teaching Church. It is an action of the Magisterium, and its written formulations across the centuries since the Apostles are monuments or documents of the Living Church in action.[113] The Creed is a short sustained discourse which expresses in an officially authorized form of human speech the Catholic faith which comes across the centuries from the apostles. It is a web, a fabric, a seamless robe woven with judgments of the mind, in this case the mind of the Catholic Church. Each of these judgments is an "article of faith," expressing a truth of the Catholic faith. "Truth is in the judgment," and judgments are expressed in human communication as sentences, formulas, propositions: human words that formulate in human speech these judgments of the mind.[114]

What is the point? It is a fundamental one, which underlies the contemporary confusion and polarization in religious education. The Creed *is* a set of words and propositions, but it is not *just* words, not *merely* propositions, as if being what it is were to derogate from its relevance for man today. The Creed is also and primarily *meaning*, a meaning which moves from person to person precisely by means of these words and propositions of the Teaching Church. These formulations of judgments are stepping stones for the mind, the will and the heart, for the whole *human* person, by which it becomes possible to know, to love and to serve *another* Person in this life, and to be happy with Him forever in the next.[115]

This is the heart of the matter. The Creed is the profession of faith made in personal response to the apostolic *kerygma* or preaching, the proclamation of the Church that Jesus is the Lord, the Eternal Son, the Second Person of the Divine Trinity, God incarnate. This constitutes and defines the relationship between Creed and catechetics. "Catechesis must necessarily be Christocentric."[116]

Everything in catechesis and religious education turns about the persons of catechetics. The primary concern of this teaching is not with its "methods," with the things of catechetics such as projectors, filmstrips, textbooks with gaily colored pages, not even with the formulas of catechesis, the questions and answers in official books called "catechisms." In its innermost essence catechesis is not anything like these items in the order of means and instruments. Catechesis is a process of introducing Catholic children and young people to the persons of catechetics, getting them to know these persons very well, helping them to know them so well that they will love them daily more and more, and thus desire to imitate and follow them with personal devotion. To accomplish this end, catechesis makes proper use of all these instruments and methods.

This is what catechetics is: it is a process of becoming better acquainted with certain persons.

Who are these persons? Other people sitting beside us, other people whom the students meet in the street or when engaged, laudably, upon social apostolates of various kinds? Other people in general, whether rich or poor, on the horizontal level, as a barren and spiritually bankrupt "horizontalism" believes and programs into syllabi and religious education textbooks?

The answer is a clear and definite "No." Since the Creed is entirely devoted to informing us about our Lord and Savior Jesus Christ, and since catechetics is the explanation of the Creed by teaching, the central Person of catechetics is this same Holy Redeemer and Divine Savior. If catechesis is not centered on Him, it is not authentic. To be centered upon Him, it must be faithful to the Creed which informs us about Him, His doctrine, His saving death, His resurrection and His second coming. Jesus Christ is the primary and the central person of catechetics and religious education.

Immediately we encounter the next two persons associated most closely with Him, and who are by this very fact in the forefront of authentic catechetical teaching. The first is His Virgin Mother, our Lady. Catechetical teaching brings us to know her very well, to become acquainted personally also with her. Such a teaching makes it quite natural for us to take her as a pattern and model, coming to love her and to follow her guidance, forming and modeling ourselves also upon her as an ideal.

In a similar way, again because of the centrality of Jesus Christ, we meet immediately another person of catechetics. It is His Vicar, "blessed Peter on earth," as St. Catherine of Siena termed Peter's successor who was living in her day. For Peter lives today, each today of the Christian era. He teaches, he acts, he governs the Church, and he prays and suffers in the person of the present Pope, just as he did in his own person, or as he did in any of his other successors.

From these persons of catechetics associated with the humanity of our Lord and Savior, we rise immediately to the other persons of catechesis, the other two Divine Persons: God the Father, and God the Holy Spirit whom the Son sends to us in his Church.

Thus, because it explains the Creed, catechetics centers upon God through Jesus Christ who is the eternal Son of God.[117]

Unless the Creed is known and understood well, very well, through effective catechetical teaching, one cannot know and love these persons of the Catholic religion as a Catholic should. But mere memory of formulas that derive from the Creed, important as this is in its proper place, is not what is meant by effective catechetical teaching. There are two other and more important components. The first is a full, well-taught explanation of these truths of the Creed at the age-level and capacity of the one who is catechized. The second is a carefully-cultivated practice of prayer based on the meditation and contemplation of the truths of the Creed. For this develops a formation in personal devotion to the persons of catechesis, known accurately and well, which is the goal of catechetics. And thus the Creed which is professed is made part of the life of each Christian, becoming for each one his personal way of living, as the early Church put it.

The Creed, then, the profession of the apostolic faith, bears and centers upon Him who is the victor over sin and death and who is coming to judge the living and the dead. The Creed is not a mere verbal abstraction. It does not terminate in itself as a set of words and propositions. It opens out upon a concrete Figure, the one and same Jesus of history, of faith and of contemporary presence.[118] This is the inner core of the relationship between the Creed and catechetical teaching. The authentic, objectively real and contemporaneous Jesus Christ whom the Creed professes is the same upon whom authentic catechetical instruction centers all its explanation by teaching.[119]

Pope Paul VI put all of this into luminous synthesis in his call to the Year of Faith which gave to the Church the *Creed of the People of God*. His words may serve here as a summary and conclusion. For he sees the Apostles' Creed, the profession of the apostolic faith, as

"a happy opportunity offered to every son and daughter of Holy
Church . . . of giving to Jesus Christ, the Son of God, the mediator
and accomplisher of revelation, a humble yet exalting 'I believe,' the
full assent of intellect and will to His word, His person, and His mission of salvation."[120]

PART THREE

A Practical Commentary on
The Creed of the People of God

"A Church which does not maintain its Creed
is no longer a Church."

—Dr. C. de Vogel,
Catholic layman and
professor in the
State University of
Utrecht, Holland

The Purpose and Interpretation
of the Creed

1. With this solemn liturgy we end the celebration of the nineteenth centenary of the martyrdom of the holy Apostles Peter and Paul, and thus close the Year of Faith. We dedicated it to the commemoration of the holy Apostles in order that we might give witness to our steadfast will to *guard the deposit* of faith (see 1 Tim. 6, 20) from corruption, that deposit which they transmitted to us, and to demonstrate again our intention of relating this same faith to life at this time when the Church must continue her pilgrimage in this world.

The successor of St. Peter, the Vicar of Christ on earth, prefaces the Solemn Profession of Faith which ended the Year of Faith on June 29, 1968, and which has come to be called universally the *Creed of the People of God,* with seven important paragraphs.[1] They make clear his reasons for giving the Catholic Church this developed form of the Creed: they relate it explicitly to the "crisis of faith" which has arisen inside the Church in the years following Vatican II. This crisis, when reduced to its essentials, arises from the sudden appearance of teachers and teaching programs, whether of theology in Catholic colleges, novitiates, seminaries and universities, or of religious education in Catholic schools and CCD programs, which disregard the articles of faith summarized officially and professed by the Catholic Creed. This fact suffices to indicate the relevance of this *Creed of the People of God* to contemporary post-Conciliar catechetical teaching. The commentary which follows, in addition to references for catechists on content and method, will give details of this relationship between Creed and catechetics. For the positive principles and correct guidelines in catechetical methodology, reference will be made to the *Roman Catechism* and to the *General Catechetical Directory.* For illustrations of unsound content and incorrect method, reference will be made primarily to the *New Catechism.* This cannot be avoided, in the interest of scholarly objectivity, because the Dutch work directly occasioned the *Creed of the People of God.* These negative illustrations, furthermore, have a practical value for contemporary catechetical teachers, because many contemporary works in religious education continue to represent the same basic positions of the Neo-Modernist approach.

The Pope, forthrightly and from the outset, relates his intention in giving the Church this profession of faith to St. Paul in 1 Tim. 6, 20–21: "My dear Timothy, take great care of all that has been entrusted to you. Have nothing to do with the pointless philosophical discussions and antagonistic beliefs of the 'knowledge' which is not knowledge at all; by adopting this, some have gone right away from the faith. Grace be with you."

This English translation of the opening paragraph of the creed is a corrected one, for unfortunately the official version misses not only the force but even the meaning of the Pope's Latin original.[2] More than simply remaining faithful to the deposit, the Vicar of Christ states his inflexible will to preserve that deposit *incorrupte* meaning that he intends to guard it from any adulteration or corruption. Furthermore, he does not merely assert his personal "desire to live by it," as the faulty translation circulating in the United States has it, but rather his intention to bring that unchanged faith into touch with human life today, in the present circumstances of the world. This is a quite different matter. It places the *Creed of the People of God* squarely in the context of the question whether the meaning of the traditional doctrines and dogmas ought to be "reinterpreted" in the light of contemporary life and thought, changing it substantially from the meaning always held in the past, and from the sense in which the dogmas of the faith were defined by ecumenical councils in the past. For some propose such a re-interpretation with a view to making the deposit of faith more vital and relevant, as they say, to modern man. Much of the point and thrust of Pope Paul's *Creed of the People of God* is missed if this strong and clear initial state of the question, so relevant to the present spiritual need of Catholics, is not kept in mind.[3]

2. We feel it our duty to give public thanks to all who responded to our invitation by bestowing on the Year of Faith a splendid completeness through the deepening of their personal adhesion to the Word of God, through the renewal in various gatherings of the Profession of Faith, and through the testimony of a Christian life. To our Brothers in the Episcopate especially, and to all the faithful of the Holy Catholic Church, we express our appreciation and we grant our blessing.

3. Likewise we deem that we must fulfill the mandate entrusted by Christ to Peter, whose successor we are, the last in merit; namely *to confirm our brothers* (Luke 22, 32) in the faith. With the awareness, certainly, of our human weakness, yet with all the strength impressed on our spirit by such a command, we shall accordingly make a Profession of Faith, pronounce a formula which begins with the word *Credo, I believe.* Without being strictly speaking a dogmatic definition, it repeats in substance, with some developments called for by the spiritual condition of our time, the Creed of Nicea, the Creed of the immortal Tradition of the Holy Church of God.

It was the intention and the hope of the Holy See in calling for the Year of Faith that great public manifestations and impressive special gatherings would take place as both cause and effect of a deep and world-wide renewal of the true faith.[4] This was indeed the case in many dioceses, and on the part of entire episcopal conferences in certain parts of the world. In other places, the spiritual opportunity was allowed to pass by in silence and inaction. Several bishops' conferences published pastoral letters more or less in the context of the Year of Faith: the German, on biblical interpretation and the doctrine of the Holy Eucharist; the Belgian, on the doctrine of the incarnation; the United States, on doctrine concerning the Church; the Italian, on the Magisterium, or teaching authority of the Church.

These introductory paragraphs stated by the Pope are indispensable for understanding *The Creed of the People of God* correctly and interpreting it in the right way; for in them the Holy Father himself gives the principles which are to guide this interpretation. A point of primary concern to the teacher and catechist is to know exactly what degree of doctrinal authority this document of the Church's Magisterium possesses. The Holy Father states at the outset that it is not intended to be a definition *ex cathedra*. "A papal definition *ex cathedra* is an act which is infallible by its very nature. In such a doctrinal definition, the Roman Pontiff, 'acting in his office as the pastor and teacher of all Christians, with his supreme apostolic authority, defines a doctrine of faith or morals as a teaching which must be held by the entire Church . . . such doctrinal definitions by the Roman Pontiff are unchangeable and binding in and of themselves, and not by the consent of the Church' . . . In such cases, the Holy Father exercises the highest degree of his teaching authority."[5]

Theologians call this highest degree the "extraordinary magisterium" of the Roman Pontiff. Vatican Council II confirms the same teaching: "This infallibility, however, with which the divine Redeemer wished to endow His Church in defining doctrine pertaining to faith and morals, is co-extensive with the deposit of revelation, which must be religiously guarded and loyally and courageously expounded. The Roman Pontiff, head of the college of bishops, enjoys this infallibility in virtue of his office, when, as supreme pastor and teacher of all the faithful who confirms his brethren in the faith (cf. Luke 22, 32)—he proclaims in an absolute decision a doctrine pertaining to faith or morals. (cf. Vatican Council I, Const. Dogm. *Pastor aeternus, DS* 3074). For that reason his definitions are rightly said to be irreformable by their very nature and not by reason of the assent of the Church, in as much as they were made with the assistance of the Holy Spirit promised to him in the person of blessed Peter himself; and as a consequence they are in no way in need of the approval of others, and do not admit of appeal to any other tribunal. For in such a case the Roman Pontiff does not utter a pronouncement as a private person, but rather does he expound and defend the teaching of the Catholic faith as the supreme teacher of the universal Church, in whom the Church's charism of infallibility is present in a singular way."[6]

In par. no. 3, the Holy Father makes it clear that his profession of faith is an act of his Ordinary Magisterium. It is of an especially solemn type, however, for it simply states again the Nicene Creed with the further developments and explanations of doctrine demanded by "the spiritual condition of the present time." He will specify in the next paragraph what this condition is. He intends that the doctrinal authority of his profession of faith be sufficient to let all souls everywhere know how to be in communion with him, the successor of St. Peter and the Vicar of Christ on earth, and to allay the disquiet which agitates so many since Vatican II with regard to the Catholic faith. It is vital for catechetical teaching, therefore, to recognize with Vatican Council II the doctrinal authority of the Ordinary Magisterium of the Roman Pontiff. "Bishops who teach in communion with the Roman Pontiff are to be revered by all as witnesses of divine and Catholic truth; the faithful, for their part, are obliged to submit to their bishops' decision, made in the name of Christ, in matters of faith and morals, and to adhere to it with a ready and respectful allegiance of mind. This loyal submission of the will and intellect must be given, in a special way, to the authentic teaching authority of the Roman Pontiff, even when he does not speak *ex cathedra,* in such wise, indeed, that his supreme teaching authority be acknowledged with respect, and sincere assent be given to decisions made by him, conformably with his manifest mind and intention, which is made known principally either by the character of the documents in question, or by the frequency with which a certain doctrine is proposed, or by the manner in which the doctrine is formulated."[7]

But with this the last word has not yet been said regarding Pope Paul's *Creed of the People of God* as an infallible teaching. First, the Holy Father presents his *profession of faith* as containing the substance of the Nicene Creed, which Catholics have professed universally for centuries at Sunday Mass, "the Creed" as he says, "of the immortal Tradition of the Holy Church of God." "No one can doubt its infallible character."[8] Secondly, with regard to Pope Paul's amplification of this *Creed* with further statements of doctrine that present conditions call for: many of them reproduce infallible doctrinal definitions made on earlier occasions in the life of the Church. These will be pointed out in the commentary below as they occur. Thirdly, "it is certain that both the College of Bishops in communion with the Pope, and the universal body of the faithful, enjoy the prerogative of infallibility in the faith."[9] Vatican II teaches as follows on this point: "The holy people of God shares also in Christ's prophetic office . . . The whole body of the faithful who have an anointing that comes from the Holy One (cf. John 2, 20 and 27) cannot err in matters of belief. This characteristic is shown in the supernatural appreciation of the faith (*sensus fidei*) of the whole people, when 'from the bishops to the last of the faithful' (St. Augustine) they manifest a universal consent in matters of faith and morals."[10] Pope Paul emphasizes that he utters this profession of faith as "Pastor of the Universal Church," raising his voice to give "on behalf of all the People of God a firm witness to the divine Truth entrusted to the Church to be announced to all nations." And he does so "in the name of all the Pastors and of all the faithful."[11]

Then Pope Paul repeats over twenty times the formula "we believe," establishing the mode of acceptance on the part of the members of the Church in communion with him, which can only be likewise "we believe." Pope Paul saw this acceptance taking place in the months following his own profession of faith. "On the occasion of the Feast of Christ the King, which was celebrated last Sunday," he says in his allocution of Oct. 30, 1968, "the profession of faith that We Ourselves delivered on June 30, in St. Peter's Square, was recited in many churches of the world."[12]

Thus the theologian can establish another aspect of and approach to the infallibility of this *Creed of the People of God,* which is quite unlike the doctrinal confusion which results from unsound opinions of popular writers in the field of philosophy of religion disseminated by a network of manipulators of the communications media. This *Creed* exists in a different dimension. It is a clarification of the contemporary faith of the Church of God, professed by the Holy See to save the Church in the present crisis of faith. Active and conscious communion with the Holy Father, the Successor of Peter and Vicar of Christ on earth, in professing this same *Creed,* is an intrinsically indispensable factor. "The acceptance of this profession of faith by the People of God," concludes Pozo, "confers on it a consequent infallibility."[13] And he points out that a doctrinal definition *ex cathedra* possesses "antecedent infallibility," rooted in the very act of its definition, prior to any acceptance. "This infallibility of which we speak now is consequent upon the acceptance. This is the way several ancient creeds . . . obtained the characteristic of infallibility, . . . for example the Athanasian Creed.

Its actual author is unknown, and its doctrine is infallible on account of its acceptance in the Universal Church as a rule of faith."[14]

This serves to establish the objectively certain and reliable context for authentic catechetics in the post-conciliar Church. The catechist can be conscious of teaching by mandate of the Magisterium of the Church of God, when Pope Paul's *Creed of the People of God* is used for the catechetical apostolate in the crisis of faith since Vatican II. It is intended officially to be the up-to-date and secure "rule of faith" for all who hand on the faith by teaching. The Pope will make this point unequivocably clear in the paragraphs which follow.

4. In making this profession, we are aware of the disquiet which agitates certain groups of men at the present time with regard to the faith. They do not escape the influence of a world being profoundly changed, in which so many truths are being denied outright or made objects of controversy. We see even Catholics allowing themselves to be seized by a kind of passion for change and novelty. The Church, most assuredly, has always the duty to carry on the effort to study more deeply and to present in a manner ever better adapted to successive generations the unfathomable mysteries of God, rich for all in fruits of salvation. But at the same time the greatest care must be taken, while fulfilling the indispensable duty of research, to do no injury to the truths of Christian doctrine. For that would be to give rise, as is unfortunately seen in these days, to disturbance and doubt in many faithful souls.

This paragraph devoted to the post-conciliar theological problem, and the one following on the philosophical problem, are indispensable for the catechist and religious educator, whether parent or teacher. For in them the Holy Father lays down guidelines both for the right approach in teaching the Catholic faith, for discernment in the use of current religious and philosophical literature, and for the evaluation of religion textbooks. Those who ignore or violate these fundamental guidelines will find that Pope Paul's *Creed* does not speak to them and its words will leave them cold.[15]

Parents or teachers can be authentic catechists without having undertaken special studies in philosophy, theology, or religious education. At the same time, it is well that all who teach the Catholic faith should be students of Christian doctrine, in order to improve personal background for more effective work with children and young people. And it is of course good to do specialized and advanced studies in Catholic doctrine if occasion permits. But how to know what to read? How to judge whether programs of studies are authentic in terms of the Catholic faith? The answer is contained in Pope Paul's *Creed of the People of God*. It provides catechists with the indispensable assistance of a clear contemporary criterion for shifting the wheat of communion with the Vicar of Christ from a teaching of chaff, the mere opinions of human theologizers or philosophizers. This always has been the function of the Rule of Faith in the Church of God since the Gnostic crisis in the second century.

Paragraphs 4 and 5 expose with lapidary brevity yet wonderful accuracy the unsound heart of these opinions which beget "disquiet . . . with regard to the faith." As the Holy Father notes, "even Catholics," (sometimes laymen, usually professors or journalists, sometimes priests who enhance the deception by the very fact that they bear the priestly name) attempt to extrapolate from the economic and cultural changes of the day to changes in the truths of the Catholic faith.[16]

These false teachers now active within the Church ("even Catholics") are producing a veritable flood of popular religious literature, and have organized many a program of studies for teachers, in terms of what they call "principles of doctrinal reinterpretation." This creates the confusing and deceptive impression that "a new theological consensus is emerging" which establishes the legitimacy of a different doctrine on the Church, on the sacraments, on the Magisterium, and even a different doctrine on God Himself which actually amounts to a denial of Him in His personal and transcendent reality.

All of this is doubly deceptive because so much of the aberrational teaching proceeds with the deliberate intention of using the words and phrases of "the traditional creeds," as they call them, with more or less subtle shifts in the meaning of these words and phrases. This procedure, coupled with techniques of ambiguity or omission, rends the seamless robe of sacred teaching, brings the doctrine of the faith either to a standstill or places it upon a path of deviation. This phenomenon of widespread unsoundness in teaching, *creedlessness,* to put it in one word, accounts for the fact recognized by the Pope: "the disquiet . . . with regard to the faith."

How then can a catechist discern the spirits in this matter? In earlier times, it was possible for the divinely-authorized teaching authority of the Catholic Church to assist teachers of good will in this problem by compiling a list or "Index" of especially offensive works. In our day, however, the flood of mass-produced publications has made this impractical to attempt. Each parent, teacher and program administrator must take the matter in hand *personally,* therefore, holding fast in personal spiritual life to the eucharistic presence of Christ and teaching the children and the young people in strictest personal communion with His Vicar's Profession of Faith. This means a teaching that avoids the use of literature and of programs for studies in which truths of this faith are either "denied outright" or "made objects of controversy." Only then will it be a teaching that follows the example of the Holy Father, who uttered this profession of faith in fullest supernatural certitude. It is this same supernatural certitude which ought to be the atmosphere wherever religious education of any type takes place; for this is the touchstone of the communion of the teaching with the Holy See, not only in content, but also in method.

In practice, parents and teachers will find the encyclical *Humani generis,* "Concerning some false opinions which threaten to undermine the foundations of Catholic Doctrine" (Aug. 12, 1950), a helpful commentary on this and the following paragraph of Pope Paul's *Creed,* illuminating it with a wealth of detailed explanation on the problem created by contemporary philosophical and theological novelties.[17] The problem, indeed, has antecedents extending back to Pope St. Pius X, whose Encyclical *Pascendi* "On the Doctrine of the Modernists" (Sept. 8, 1908), is likewise helpful to catechists today who seek perspective on this contemporary problem. For, as Pope Paul VI points out in his first encyclical, *Ecclesiam suam,* "The Paths of the Church," the present crisis of faith and the upset which he recognizes in the preamble to this *Creed* result from the phenomenon of Modernism cropping up again. "Was not the phenomenon of Modernism," he asks, ". . . which still crops up in the various attempts at expressing what is foreign to the authentic nature of the Catholic religion, an episode of abuse exercised against the faithful and genuine expression of the doctrine and criterion of the Church of Christ, by psychological and cultural forces of the profane world?"[18]

Most helpful in practice for catechetical teachers of the Catholic Faith are the *Documents of Vatican II,* where the doctrine of the faith summarized and professed in the Creed is explained in detail. For not only are they wonderfully rich in the positive statement of Catholic doctrine in a manner fitted to our times, but, as Pope Paul stated when closing the Council, "they are faithful."[19]

The Holy Father does not deal with the current problem of aberrational and disquieting teaching within the Church with regard to the faith as something hypothetical. It is a fact, a reality. His *Creed of the People of God* is intended to bar the way to an actually existing danger to the Catholic faith, namely the spread of the Neo-Modernist mode in catechizing, an approach in religious education that undermines the supernatural certitude of the Catholic faith, at the same time that it either omits portions of its content or insinuates deviational "interpretations" of the content. This mode or approach in method of teaching, the Holy Father points out explicitly, proceeds either by denying or by questioning the truths of Christian doctrine. This introduces a dialectic, for it reduces the Catholic faith from its supernatural certitude to the merely natural level, making it appear to be simply one more human opinion clashing with other human opinions. This results as a matter of fact in "disturbance and doubt in many faithful souls." This is doubly tragic when these "faithful souls" are the defenseless little ones of Christ, or youths not yet sufficiently educated and intellectually mature to defend themselves.

The Holy Father, concluding this paragraph, amplifies the criterion on theological literature mentioned above. Authentic theological literature theologizes within the Magisterium of the Catholic Church. Its research and its literature "does no injury to the truths of Christian doctrine." Hence it is helpful for catechists and religious educators, whether for their own personal culture or for recommendation to their students. But there is another type of theologizing which proceeds with a false idea of theological research, conceiving it as indulgence of this strange "passion for change and novelty" with regard to the faith itself. Such "theologians" are actually philosophers of religion, and not authentic Catholic theologians at all. Theological research for authentic theologians is not the same as the "research" carried out by philosophers of religion. The touchstone of the difference is that one functions within the Magisterium, the other usually does not. Hence the one deepens the Catholic faith in its readers and ministers by research and publication to the supernatural certitude of the faith, whereas the other engenders "disturbance and doubt." This is a matter of crucial importance in the catechetical methodology of teaching the Catholic faith to children and young people. In the Neo-Modernist approach they will be raised up as questioning sceptics and seekers for a new "synthesis" felt to be coming out of the "creative tension," as some call it, of clashing opposites in opinion. It will be actually a formation unto unbelief. In the other approach, that of the Holy See, teachers will raise up a new generation of Catholic men and women who accept the official teaching of the Catholic Church in full upon the authority of God revealing: Catholic men and women of authentic supernatural faith.

5. It is supremely important in this respect to recall that, beyond what is observable, analyzed by the work of the sciences, the intellect which God has given us reaches *that which is,* and not merely the subjective expression of the structures and development of consciousness. And on the other hand, it is important to remember that the task of interpretation—of hermeneutics—is to try to understand and extricate, while respecting the word expressed, the sense conveyed by a text, and not to recreate, in some fashion, this sense in accordance with arbitrary hypotheses.

Perhaps most immediately pressing for teachers or parents in their catechetical work is the question whether the truths of the Catholic faith are to be taught in the same meaning they always have had since the Apostles. In particular, are the dogmas defined in earlier councils as authentic explanations and interpretations of the Gospel to be taught today, after the Second Vatican Council, in the same meaning which those earlier councils intended when defining them? Or are Catholic children to be taught a different understanding of them, an arbitrary and subjective "re-interpretation," something other than that taught to their Catholic ancestors, including their own fathers and mothers?[20]

Strange as it may seem at first sight, the taproot here, perhaps the deepest cause of the "disquiet" noted by the Holy Father in the previous paragraph, lies in the field of philosophy rather than theology. For theologizing in a way that shifts the meaning of Christian truths, creating "arbitrary hypotheses," is a way of thinking in religion that grows out of poisoned philosophical soil. It is important, therefore, as the Holy Father states, to be clear on this matter.[21]

Hence the Pope turns briefly to the philosophical roots of the theological disturbance and doubt he has just touched upon. Literally volumes are compressed into his carefully-chosen words. For the Holy See has been fostering a vast renewal of Christian philosophy ever since the First Vatican Council, since the encyclical of Pope Leo XIII entitled *Aeterni patris,* "On the Renewal of Christian Philosophy in the Catholic Schools" (Aug. 4, 1879), launching a program to implement the basic doctrinal definitions of Vatican I on atheism, on natural knowledge of God, and on the relationship between faith and reason. This renewal is a fundamental part of the Church's pastoral care of souls, especially youthful souls endangered by the mounting flood of modern doctrinal deviation. It underlies the more popular renewals associated with Vatican II, the biblical, the liturgical and the catechetical renewals, and provides them with their solid foundation. It is concerned with the right kind of "metaphysics," which simply means fundamental thinking that is open to God, the transcendent personal Supreme Being, the God of Abraham, Isaac and Jacob. This transcendent God of Revelation is wholly other, distinct from this cosmos, the Living God both of sound natural human thinking and of supernatural revelation.

To depart from this metaphysics of Christian Philosophy, termed by Pope Paul VI "The Natural Metaphysics of Mankind," even by one step, as Pope St. Pius X put it, is not without serious danger for teachers of Christian doctrine. It is the very heart of this Christian fundamental thinking that man is made to the image and likeness of God because of his God-given intellect. By virtue of this spiritual intelligence, man has two kinds of knowledge, one of the senses and subject to historical relativism, the other intellectual, which can know substantial reality, the very being and truth of realities. Hence it stands above the changing flux of history and human culture and is not subject to historical relativism. As the Holy Father puts it, our intellect "reaches *that which is,*" the abiding reality of truths that are rooted in God Himself, the changeless Eternal Truth.

The reason why the Pope stresses this fundamental philosophical insight is the fact that the Catholic faith, which he is about to profess in his *Creed of the People of God,* is a participation in God's own eternal knowledge, a communication of God's eternal truth "which comes to us from the Apostles," as the Roman canon says. At various times during the life of the Church, usually to protect the purity of this Catholic faith from particular errors, the Magisterium has explained and defined the authentic meaning and interpretation of this revealed truth, often drawing when doing so upon this same intellectual patrimony of the teaching Church, called Christian Philosophy, "the natural metaphysics of mankind." The theological "re-interpretation" which is causing "disquiet," "disturbance and doubt" regarding the truths of the Catholic faith since Vatican II results from using Modern Philosophy, as such, instead of Christian Philosophy in religious thought and in the theological interpretation of Christian doctrine. When this is done in preparing young men for the priesthood, as Cornelio Fabro points out, "Modernism" in the formal sense is born.[22]

It is the hallmark of Modern Philosophy to shut men up within their own subjective selves, closing off the natural openness of their minds to the personal God of Revelation, the God of Abraham, Isaac and Jacob, the Eternal Father of our Lord and Savior Jesus Christ. Men soon consider themselves confined to this world alone, and are taught to see their destiny within its limits. Knowing only "the structures of consciousness," as formed by the evolution of culture (that is, formed chiefly by this same Modern Philosophy), they project from it "arbitrary hypotheses" about religious doctrine, indeed about God Himself. This is why the editor of the *Dossier on the Dutch Catechism* is bold enough to state the principle of this doctrinal relativism in plainest words: "Revelation is not a collection of changeless truths and concepts."[23]

In the second sentence of this paragraph, the Holy Father gives the second of the two factors that are "of supreme importance," *summi momenti,* in removing the causes of the "disquiet . . . with regard to the faith" and the "disturbance and doubt in many faithful souls." This second factor is a technique of methodology used by false teachers of Christian doctrine within the Church. They claim deceptively that "the faith," namely, as they say, "the intention of the faith," abides always the same. Thus they appear to be innocent and in harmony with the Magisterium. But they go on to say or to imply that the *interpretation* of this faith changes with the times. This immediately introduces philosophical and cultural relativism, the idea that the intellectually acceptable twentieth century interpretation, especially since the Second Vatican Council, is a changed one. Hence for them the meaning of the Catholic faith is different now from the meaning contained in the doctrinal definitions and dogmas (and so from the catechetical formulas resting upon them) by which the Catholic faith was taught in the earlier times of the Catholic Church. Having subverted the eternal concept of truth in this manner they replace the sense conveyed by the text of Church teachings with "arbitrary hypotheses," doctrinal innovations that are mere conjectures or guesses, as the Vicar of Christ puts it more forcefully in the Latin original. This subjective procedure derives from admitting unsound forms of Modern Philosophy with their immanentism into the work of catechetics. This is something entirely different from admitting modern scientific progress and technological advances in travel and communication into the work of the Church. Hence the supreme importance of the first factor, the Christian Philosophy sponsored by the Church, which provides clear intellectual vision, open to the personal God of revelation, for the work of interpretation or hermeneutics.

The *New Catechism* which occasioned these words of the Pope is deformed by a characteristic slant toward this philosophical aberration. Specific instances will be documented as this commentary proceeds. Hence the theologians of the Holy See made it a matter of discussion at the Gazzada Conference, calling for a revision of the text so as to "conserve faithfully the deposit of faith while explaining it in a manner adapted to the new problems proper to our times," so as to be truly faithful to the mandate of Pope John XXIII in opening the Second Vatican Council.[24] For the report of the ensuing discussion, with the flat refusal of the theologians representing the Dutch hierarchy to agree, see the "Preliminary Discussion."[25] It is clear from these informative pages that the Neo-Modernist approach in religious education rests on a rationale of man-centrism and philosophical refusal to admit eternal truths. The implications with regard to the existence of God are clear.[26] The Crisis of Faith goes deep indeed. The incisive statement of Pope St. Pius X remains true: "They subvert the eternal concept of truth."[27]

Catechists in faithful communion with the Holy See of St. Peter function in the vertical dimension of prayer and openness to the Word of God that descends from the Father of Lights. This is a different doctrinal world, one that teaches in the context of the communion of saints, united in one and the same truth that comes to us from the apostles, as the first eucharistic prayer says. Thus the teaching of the Catholic faith proceeds unbrokenly in these times after the Second Vatican Council, without any rupture with the past or with the Christian era as a whole. It follows that textbooks in religion which artificially introduce a "generation gap" into today's children, alienating them from the understanding of the Catholic faith held by their parents, are fundamentally unsound. Such productions, however attractively and expensively printed, are simply incapable of serving catechetical teaching programs. The imposition of a philosophical ideology upon children who have a birthright to the Catholic faith is not a work of God. Catechetical evaluators look for this characteristic overall slant in textbooks and programs of religious education perhaps even more than for specific inadequacies regarding particular doctrines of the faith.

The First Vatican Council is very explicit: "For the teaching of faith, which God has revealed, has not been proposed as a philosophical discovery to be perfected by human ingenuity, but as a divine deposit handed over to the Spouse of Christ to be guarded faithfully and to be explained infallibly. Hence that meaning of sacred dogmas must perpetually be retained which holy Mother Church has once declared; nor is that meaning ever to be abandoned under the pretext and name of a more profound comprehension. 'Let, then, understanding, knowledge and wisdom grow . . . ; but only within their own domain, that is, with the same dogma, the same meaning, the same sense.' "[28] This incorporates the rule of St. Vincent of Lerins in the early Church; as we have noted already, Pope John XXIII took it up as programmatic and the Second Vatican Council made it its own in the *Pastoral Constitution on the Church in the Modern World,* no. 62.[29] "From this fact it follows that the Neo-Modernist approach to interpretation cannot appeal on its behalf either to the spirit of Pope John XXIII or to the Second Vatican Council."[30]

6. But above all, we place our unshakeable confidence in the Holy Spirit, the soul of the Church, and in theological faith upon which rests the life of the Mystical Body. We know that souls await the

word of the Vicar of Christ, and we respond to that expectation with the instructions which we regularly give. But today we are given an opportunity to make a more solemn utterance.

In paragraphs 6 and 7 the Holy Father defines the way he will overcome this spiritual malady of "disquiet with regard to the faith" and "disturbance and doubt in many faithful souls." He will not do so by philosophical and theological dialogue or disputation with those who sow this malady by erroneous approaches arising from the misuse of the human intellectual disciplines to which he has just alluded. Fully aware of his position and its special graces, he turns to the assistance of the Holy Spirit. He will come to the aid of these "many faithful souls" by making his profession of *theological* faith. This is a technical term of the science of sacred theology used to denote the supernatural faith which believes all the truths which the Holy Catholic Church teaches because God has revealed them, who can neither deceive nor be deceived, as distinct from the natural faith by which we accept as true the statements of human witnesses to things we ourselves have not seen, as, for example, the statements of nuclear physicists on the nature of matter. In taking this position, the Holy Father demonstrates the right methodological approach in all catechetics and Catholic religious education. For he is the guide and the model for all teachers in the Church, urging them by his example to place their teaching on the same foundation, "the Holy Spirit . . . and theological faith."

There is no question in the mind of Paul VI regarding the identity of the Pope. He is "the Vicar of Christ," "the Supreme Pastor of all the faithful," the "humble successor" of the Apostle Peter.[31] Pastoral charity and concern for souls exposed to the disquieting currents of doctrinal aberration after Vatican II run like a unifying thread through these paragraphs that introduce Pope Paul's profession of faith. Catechetical teaching of the doctrine of the faith has a pattern of method for proceeding in this same atmosphere of recognition of the Vicar of Christ and Successor of St. Peter, using these titles when referring to him. In this way catechetical teaching becomes simultaneously a formation, cultivating a personal devotion to the Supreme Pontiff and his Magisterium among Catholic children and young people.

The reference to "the instructions which we regularly give" has a special significance for teachers of the Catholic faith. These "sermons and homilies," to translate the Latin more fully, are the documents of his on-going Ordinary Magisterium, in particular the allocutions pronounced for example at the regular Wednesday General Audiences in St. Peter's, and the homilies at Masses for feasts and special occasions. Teachers need to have access to these instructions, for they are constantly concerned with the truth of the Catholic Faith in the face of the doctrinal aberrations of the present day. Sometimes the local Catholic press brings only excerpts, or even fails entirely to note important statements of the Vicar of Christ; but Catholic parents and teachers, now since Vatican II, can subscribe to the weekly English Edition of *L'Osservatore Romano,* the journal of the Holy See.[32] There is no better way to renew, to vitalize and above all to authenticate Catholic religious education in this period following upon Vatican II, for all the sermons, homilies, allocutions and instructions of the Vicar of Christ on earth are given accurately and in full.

7. On this day which is chosen to close the Year of Faith, on this Feast of the Blessed Apostles Peter and Paul, we have wished to offer to the Living God the homage of a Profession of Faith. And as once at Caesarea Philippi the Apostle Peter spoke on behalf of the Twelve to make a true confession, beyond human opinions, of Christ as Son of the Living God, so today his humble successor, Pastor of the Universal Church, raises his voice to give, on behalf of all the People of God, a firm witness to the divine Truth entrusted to the Church to be announced to all nations.

We have wished our Profession of Faith to be sufficiently both complete and explicit, in order that it may respond in a fitting way to the need of light felt by so many faithful souls, and by all those in the world to whatever spiritual family they belong, who are in search of the Truth.

Therefore, to the glory of God Most Holy and of Our Lord Jesus Christ, trusting in the aid of the Blessed Virgin Mary and of the Holy Apostles Peter and Paul, for the profit and edification of the Church, in the name of all the Pastors and all the faithful, we now pronounce this Profession of Faith, in full communion with you all, beloved Brothers and Sons.

The meaning of the phrase "profession of faith" and earlier instances of "professions of faith" during the life of the Catholic Church across the centuries have been discussed above.[33] The stress which the Holy Father places on "the living God" should be noted in a day when "the death of God" has become a fadword. "The Living God" recurs constantly in the Old Testament as one of the most important points of present human knowledge about the nature of God. God is alive, a living, personal God, distinct from this material cosmos, to whom therefore person-to-person communication can be made, as in prayer or in this profession of faith on behalf of all the People of God. This attribute of God recurs in the next sentence as equally fundamental in the New Testament: Christ is the Son of the Living God. This concept of God is basic to every aspect of catechesis and religious education.

The Catholic faith is "beyond human opinions." The Vicar of Christ is placing his profession of faith squarely in the line of continuity from the apostolic *kerygma* of the early Church and from St. Vincent of Lerins' rule for distinguishing the true Catholic faith from doctrinal aberration and heresy, to the solemn doctrinal definition of the First Vatican Council: "If any one says that as science progresses it is sometimes possible for dogmas that have been proposed by the Church to receive a different meaning from the one which the Church understood and understands: let him be anathema."[34] It is not difficult to recognize the present relevance of the older Creeds or professions of faith, and the national catechisms by which bishops throughout the world explain the Creed. The *explanations* need to be made in terms of contemporary times and places, of course, and the new electronic media need now to be used in comunicating the doctrines: but the *doctrines themselves* abide.[35]

The Catholic faith is not a doctrine elaborated by theologians or philosophers. Both can help to draw out the implications of the revealed truth or deepen our understanding of them, of course, or defend them against the attacks of unbelievers, provided that they do their work in the right way, namely by theologizing within the Magisterium and philosophizing within the faith. But the Catholic faith in itself is from above. It comes directly from God, "the divine Truth" which the Catholic Church carries across the centuries as a deposit to be proclaimed and to be taught. Pope Paul VI is making his profession of faith explicitly in this perspective. Catechists and religious educators are expected to do exactly the same thing in their own teaching, for catechetical teaching proceeds by mandate from the Magisterium of the Holy See and the bishops in communion with the Holy See. It should be noted that the Holy Father places his pronouncing of this *Creed of the People of God* on the same level as the Apostle Peter's profession of the divinity of Christ.[36]

Pope Paul states here what may be called his method of teaching, namely his concern to make his profession of faith "to be sufficiently both complete and explicit." This is the first obligation of teachers in general and of the religious catechist in particular, to be clear and not confusing regarding the content of their teaching. Thus the Holy Father, the supreme teacher of the Catholic faith, gives in this profession the model and example of catechetical method which all teachers of the faith in the Church ought to use and follow. Succinctly he returns to the pastoral need detailed in paragraph 4, the need for clear teaching on the essentials of the Catholic faith, and the underlying philosophical unsoundness, paragraph 5, which is causing the present disquiet among the faithful. For it is this philosophical subjectivism and anti-intellectualism which causes religious educators, often unwittingly participating in the Neo-Modernist approach, to attempt a separation of "awareness" and "attitudes" from a clear, explicit and complete catechetical teaching of the revealed truth of God. Much of the need for light felt by faithful Catholics today results from this unsound approach by certain teachers, who proceed as if the personal qualities denoted by "awareness" and "attitudes" can exist, let alone be good and wholesome in terms of Catholic Christianity, apart from the Church's divine truth, and as if somehow the values can be "taught" apart from the communication of this divine truth to the intelligences of the children and young people. The opposition to "catechisms published by ecclesiastical authority" which is doing such harm currently to the teaching of the Catholic faith in the United States derives in large part from this philosophical aberration and its characteristic resistance to a teaching that is "complete and explicit."[37] Vatican II likewise rejects this "confusionism" as a "method" in teaching religion. It does so in the context of sound ecumenism, a dimension which Pope Paul includes here in his profession of faith.[38] "Confusionism" in religious education and catechetics leads directly to the unsound form of ecumenism.

In the last sentence the Vicar of Christ reveals the motives and dispositions that fill his mind and heart as he makes this profession of faith for the People of God, "in the name of all the Pastors and all the faithful." He stresses that he is in "full communion with you all." The term "communion" comes from the early Church, when travelers carried letters certifying to the "communion," namely the union of the bearer with the Head of the Church in both truth of doctrine and obedience of Church government. Some English translations of this document gratuitously insert the word "spiritual" with "communion," indicating a failure to perceive the real meaning, which includes the Magisterium with its juridical processes and safeguards.

In handing on the Catholic faith, whether in homes or schools, the teaching should be animated with these same motives and this same consciousness of the twofold unity of doctrine and ecclesiastical government, this "communion" with the Vicar of Christ on earth and the Magisterium of the Catholic Church. The *Creed of the People of God* is the "Rule of Faith" for this kind of catechetical teaching, both in content and in method.

The Profession of Faith

I. THE REALITY OF GOD, OUR CREATOR

8. We believe in One Only God, Father, Son and Holy Spirit, Creator of things such as this world in which our brief life passes, of things invisible such as the pure spirits which are also called angels, (see Vatican Council I, Const. *Dei Filius;* DS 3002) and Creator in each man of his spiritual and immortal soul. (See the Encyclical *Humani generis, AAS* 42(1950) p. 575; Lateran Council V *DS* 1440–1441).

THE fact that the profession of faith opens by stating the mystery of God One and Three as its point of departure constitutes a guideline in method for catechetical teachers. The One Only God, the Lord God of the Old Testament and of the Jewish people to this day, *is* the Father, *is* the Son, *is* the Holy Spirit. "This simultaneity of the Unicity and Trinity in God is the first affirmation of faith made by the profession of Pope Paul VI. This emphasis on the double aspect of the mystery of the Trinity (that God is One and Three) probably was demanded by the present dangers that obscure the truth about this article of faith."[39]

The *New Catechism,* apart from a passing mention of the liturgical feast of the Holy Trinity,[40] places its relatively brief and man-centric discussion of the Trinity at the very end of the book.[41]

The Holy See through its commission of theologians took exception to this approach as follows: "It is desired that the presentation of the mystery of the Trinity . . . not be based uniquely on the biblical sources, but that it take equally into account the Creeds of the Church, her Professions of Faith and her heritage of teaching. It is feared that the *New Catechism* does not give a sufficiently central importance to this mystery, at least in the passages which specifically concern it."[42]

In teaching the Catholic faith, therefore, there is a point of departure and a fundamental orientation in catechetical methodology that harmonizes with the magisterium. This assists catechists to see through the gratuitous view of the Neo-Modernist approach in the teaching of children: "In the religious instruction now given to children, attention is first fixed on the Son and on how he speaks of the Father and how he loves the Father. At Whitsuntide, the Spirit whom they send is spoken of, but it is only years later that the term Holy Trinity is used."[43]

This tactic of forcing Catholic children to wait until "years later" for full catechesis on the doctrine of the Catholic faith has entered widely into the thinking of religious educators and the programs and textbooks which they devise.[44] The *General Catechetical Directory* explicitly states the correct methodology: "Catechesis . . . must take diligent care faithfully to present the entire treasure of the Christian message . . . Catechesis begins, therefore, with a rather simple presentation of the entire structure of the Christian message (using also summary or global formulas), and it presents this in a way appropriate to the various cultural and spiritual conditions of those to be taught. By no means, however, can it stop with this first presentation, but it must be interested in presenting the content in an always more detailed and developed manner . . . This task of catechesis, not an easy one, must be carried out under the guidance of the Magisterium of the Church, whose duty it is to safeguard the truth of the divine message, and to watch that the ministry of the word uses appropriate forms of speaking, and prudently considers the help which theological research and the human sciences can give."[45]

The catechetical teacher who is careful to maintain communion with the Holy See, and with the Catholics homes from which the children come, has a quite different and more realistic approach. The children are not little doubters or questioners. Catholic children have a deep supernatural faith in this same Triune God infused into their minds and souls at baptism, deepened through formation during their pre-school years with their parents, years of prayer in the home, public worship at Mass, years of informal instruction and example in a lifestyle centered upon this same "One Only God, Father, Son and Holy Spirit." Catechists ought to assume this Catholic Faith in the children, else their catechesis cannot be an announcement, communication, teaching and learning of God's revealed truth. To approach these baptised children in the methodology of the Neo-Modernist approach, as if they were "man questioning," is not to teach them the Catholic faith but to impose upon them the post-conciliar aberration called "The Crisis of Faith," the unrest and darkness that the Vicar of Christ has noted in the paragraphs which introduce his profession of faith.

Establishing the teaching firmly upon this foundation of the divine reality as the Holy Father does, prepares for teaching the divinity of Jesus Christ and the divine character of His doctrine and of His actions in constituting the Church and its sacraments. This provides both for soundness in doctrine and for its clear, lucid, and complete communication to the Catholic children.

In the preceding paragraph, no. 7, Pope Paul refers to "Our Lord Jesus Christ." "In the New Testament there are other names (other than Father, Son, Holy Spirit) that are reserved for the Divine Persons. Thus the name of "Lord" (*Kyrios* in Greek) is used as the name which is proper to the Son. The meaning of this name is divine in the strict sense. This is true not only because it is the word used invariably by the Septuagint, the ancient official translation of the Old Testament into Greek, to translate *Yahweh,* Hebrew word for God. There is also the fact that St. Paul, when teaching that God the Father gave Christ the name "Lord" (*Kyrios*) in reward for His humiliation to the death upon the cross, explains that this is 'the name above every other name' (Phil. 2, 9). It is clear that, for a Jew like St. Paul, 'the name above every other name' could be no other than the ineffable name, the divine name of Yahweh."[46]

A catechetical teaching that proceeds in communion with the point of departure and orientation given by the Vicar of Christ immediately becomes sound and authentic. It avoids the current aberration of excessive man-centrism and horizontalism. It begins with God. It knows from the outset that Jesus is this One Only God, God-with-us in the human nature He assumed to Himself. The entire teaching takes on its proper character, accordingly, as the communication of truth that is divine in origin, divine in content, and divine in the motive for our human response of acceptance. Not least among the advantages of Pope Paul's procedure, furthermore, is the fact that it makes no concession to or compromise with that atheism, which, as he wrote in his first encyclical, "is the most serious problem of our time."[47]

The doctrinal development toward deeper and more explicit understanding of the original deposit of Trinitarian faith is visible from the Apostles' Creed through the Nicene Creed and on to the other official professions of faith across the centuries to this contemporary Creed of the People of God.[48]

This lapidary article of Pope Paul's *Creed* contains further guidelines for teaching the Catholic faith today. It eliminates two chief philosophical errors about God that are infecting purity of doctrine in contemporary religious education.

The first is a sort of reborn "Gnosticism" that sees matter, this visible, material world, as somehow independent of God, not created by Him, as if it has always been existing and moving onward and upward, "evolving" and making "progress." This leads quickly to idolatrous attitudes and worshipful approaches toward this world.

The second error is "pantheism." It results from the first, for the mind is impelled to seek a cause for the world's apparent inner dynamism. The mind does this by reducing God to the level of some force or internal vital urge animating what is thought to be the evolution and progress of the visible cosmos. The truth is very different. God is a *personal* reality, the three Divine Persons, not a "thing" or "force" or "vital urge."[49]

Then the Creed professes the truth that God is the Creator of heaven and earth. This means that the Supreme Being is distinct from and infinitely above all other realities. All other things without exception exist solely because He gave them existence by creating them. Furthermore, He takes care of them by His providence, which is simply the all-wise plan He has in mind when creating and sustaining what He has created. This is true of each individual human person. Hence this article lays the foundation for the interior spiritual life of each human person: the humility of spirit that recognizes dependence upon Him; trust in His providence; prayer to Him which recognizes His personality and goodness and omnipotence; obedience to the natural laws of His creation as reflections of His eternal law, the wisdom by which He made things to be as they are and to function as they do; and a reasonable general outlook upon earthly life, namely that it is "brief" and not the true destiny of man. Catechists and religious educators face a new and special challenge to incorporate right concepts of the Creator and hence of creaturehood into their catechetical explanations and the textbooks which they prepare.[50]

In professing the article of faith in the existence of angels, the Pope himself refers to Vatican Council I, the Dogmatic Constitution *Dei filius*.[51] "This expression, 'Creator of all things both visible and invisible,' is full of meaning. . . . It rejects the Gnostic errors that there are two creators, one for spiritual beings, the other for material beings, or that outside of God there can be some form of reality, either matter or spirit, prior to God's creation."[52]

Pope Paul's profession is simply repeating the Nicene Creed as explicitated by the Fourth Lateran Council and the First Vatican Council.[53] By "things invisible," is meant the angels, or pure spirits. The source of this teaching of the councils and creeds on the angels is found throughout the Bible, for example, in St. Paul, Col. 1, 15–16. "Paul VI believed it necessary in our time to insist on this and to give it clear and unambiguous restatement in order to counter a certain tendency to cast doubt upon the existence of the angels . . . (as illustrated by) the doubts of the *New Catechism* on this point."[54]

The Neo-Modernist approach uses the technique of unanswered questions to leave this certitude of the Catholic Faith open to doubt.[55] The Holy See took strong exception to this approach in the *New Catechism* and insisted upon correction. In his letter to Cardinal Alfrink, Pope Paul VI mentions the existence of the angels as a reality that must be taught clearly, with no opening left for ambiguity of any kind.[56] Through its commission of theologians, the Holy See pointed out that "the Dutch Catechism places the existence of both the angels and the devils in doubt," and states that "the majority of theologians would say that this puts a truth of the Catholic faith in doubt. Vatican II (Const. on the Church, nos. 49 and 50), not only refers to the angels who will accompany Christ at His Second Coming, but also reaffirms the cult which the Church always has given to the holy angels."[57] The theologians of the Holy See stated their position as follows: "Our delegation holds that it is difficult to deny that the existence of good and bad angels is a truth of the Faith. We hold that their existence is without any doubt a part of that Catholic doctrine which we must firmly believe. We demand therefore that the existence of the angels be presented as something that Sacred Scripture speaks of very frequently and which Mother Church teaches as matter to be firmly believed."[58] The theologians representing the Dutch Catechism did not rise to this demand. For the outcome, see the judgment made for re-writing these passages by the Commission of Cardinals.[59] This confrontation is helpful in catechetical teaching, for it clarifies what the Catholic faith holds regarding the real and personal existence of angels and how religious education ought to proceed in their regard.

Turning to the doctrine of the Catholic faith on the human soul, the text of the Creed makes reference to the encyclical *Humani generis,* *AAS* 42 (1950), p. 575; and to the Fifth Lateran Council, *Denz.-Sch.* 1440–1441. For some reason, the English translation published by the U.S. Catholic Conference, Washington, D.C., has omitted this reference entirely. Catholic teachers, accordingly, will look into the Encyclical *Humani generis,* "Concerning some False Opinions which Threaten to Undermine the Foundations of Catholic Doctrine" (Aug. 12, 1950), with renewed interest.

"This affirmation of the Creed implies a definite concept of man, as composed of body and soul, that needs special emphasis today when there is no lack of Catholic theologians who put it in doubt as something 'Greek' instead of 'biblical' . . . Such a doubt has grave consequences for our doctrine on eschatology or the last things, for without this definite concept of man's composition of body and soul, . . . the doctrine on the state of souls between death and resurrection becomes impossible."[60] Pope Benedict XII in his Constitution *Benedictus Deus* teaches explicitly that souls after death come either into heaven or into the pains of hell before the resurrection of the body and the General Judgment. Furthermore, the Second Vatican Council teaches the spirituality and immortality of the soul when it treats of the dignity of the human person.[61] Pope Paul himself refers to the Fifth Lateran Council which teaches as follows: "The ancient enemy of the human race has dared to oversow the Lord's field and to give increase to some dangerous errors, which have always been disapproved by the faithful. These errors concern the nature of the rational soul especially, for instance that the soul is mortal or that there is only one soul for all men. Some audacious philosophers have held that this was the truth, at least according to philosophy. Therefore, we desire to use suitable remedies against this error. And with the approval of this Sacred

Council, we condemn and reject all those who claim that the intellectual soul is mortal or that there is a single soul for all men. We
condemn those who raise doubts about this matter. For the soul is not
only truly, of its own nature and essentially the form of the human
body . . . , but it is also immortal. . . ."[62] The reference given by
Pope Paul to the encyclical *Humani generis* of Pope Pius XII reads
as follows: "The Catholic Faith commands us to hold that our souls
are created immediately by God."[63] "This example is helpful for
understanding better (granted the difference in solemnity between an
ordinary encyclical and this *Creed of the People of God*) how one
can have authentic declaration of what the Church believes or the
Magisterium teaches as changeless, in acts of the Magisterium that
are not in themselves a definition *ex cathedra* . . . A spiritual and
immortal soul cannot be the mere product of the generative action of
the human parents. Hence Paul VI, noting certain doctrinal tendencies
of our times, insists that God creates the human soul in each human
being."[64]

The *New Catechism* allows its doctrinal insufficiency on this point
to become quite explicit.[65] The Holy See, through its commission of
theologians, placed this point on the Gazzada agenda, asking whether
the attempt to explain the immediate creation of the human soul in
a new way "does not suppress instead a doctrine which has become
classical in the Church."[66] In the discussion of this item at Gazzada,
the theologians representing the Holy See held that "the *New Catechism* should be more clear in its teaching on the immediate creation
of the human soul. . . . It can give the impression that it is not saying
the same thing with different words, but teaching a different thing.
. . . A spiritual substance, because it is subsistent [i.e., able to exist
by it self and independently of the body], is not the object simply of
mediate creation [like the body], but of immediate creation. In our
judgment, it is necessary to explain the notion of immediate creation
in the *New Catechism,* in a way adapted to educated people who at
the same time are not experts in philosophy or theology. . . . The
human soul, since it exists independently, does not take its existence
from internal causes: it is not the result of an evolutionary or generative process."[67] The Dutch group did not agree.[68]

The Vicar of Christ will return with strong emphasis to the separate
existence and subsistence of the souls of the faithful departed in par.

28 of the *Creed*. This highlights for catechetics the importance of this article of faith in the fact that man is a creature composed of body and separately created soul.

It goes without saying that these articles of faith professed in no. 8 of the *Creed* are the fundamental truths on God and the soul. They ought to illuminate oral catechetical teaching and textbook materials for classes in religion. The principles that determine the Catholic position on abortion, for example, are rooted in this section of the *Creed of the People of God*. These natural foundations on God and the soul, in general, are the truths which make the minds of children and young people "naturally Christian," open and receptive to the Gospel and the following of Christ.[69]

II. THE HOLY TRINITY: GOD REVEALS HIS INNER LIFE

9. We believe that this only God is absolutely one in His infinitely holy essence as also in all His perfections, in His omnipotence, His infinite knowledge, His providence, His will and His love. He is *He Who Is,* as He revealed to Moses (See Exodus 3, 14); and he is *Love,* as the Apostle John teaches us (see 1 John 4, 8): so that these two names, Being and Love, express ineffably the same divine Reality of Him Who has wished to make Himself known to us, and Who "dwelling in light inaccessible" (See 1 Tim. 6, 16), is in Himself above every name, above every thing and above every created intellect. God alone can give us right and full knowledge of this Reality by revealing Himself as Father, Son and Holy Spirit, in Whose Eternal Life we are by grace called to share, here below in the obscurity of faith and after death in eternal light. The mutual bonds which eternally constitute the Three Persons, Who are each one and the same Divine Being, are the blessed inmost life of God Thrice Holy, infinitely beyond all that we can conceive in human measure (See Vatican Council I, Const. *Dei filius, DS* 3016). We give thanks, however, to the Divine Goodness that very many believers can testify with us before men to the Unity of God, even though they know not the Mystery of the Most Holy Trinity.

10. We believe then in God who eternally begets the Son, in the Son, the Word of God, who is eternally begotten, in the Holy Spirit,

the uncreated Person, who proceeds from the Father and the Son as their eternal Love. Thus in the Three Divine Persons, *coaeternae sibi et coaequales* (See the Creed *Quicumque,* DS 75), the life and beatitude of God perfectly One superabound and are consummated in the supreme excellence and glory proper to uncreated Being, and always "there should be venerated Unity in the Trinity and Trinity in the Unity." (See *ibid., DS* 75).

Here again the absolute monotheism of the Catholic faith finds expression, that bond of union and communion with the Jewish people. "Not only is the uniqueness of the Divine nature affirmed, namely that there is only one God, but also the absolute unity of God's nature and all His perfections."[70] In teaching the Catholic faith, catechists have the responsibility of giving full explanations of God's attributes and perfections, especially those named here by the Vicar of Christ, drawing upon the Bible, the best theological and spiritual literature of the Christian heritage, and upon their own prayer and meditation. It is indispensable that this sound idea of God be taught faithfully and carefully. It is a teaching which strives to communicate the conviction that the God of the Catholic faith is an infinitely intelligent personal Being who can communicate His truth and divine knowledge to mankind. Young people today are no different from St. Augustine, who attributed all his early troubles in faith and morals to an unsound concept of God. "I wished to meditate upon my God," he writes, "but I did not know how to think of him except as a vast corporeal mass, for I thought that anything not a body was nothing whatsoever. This was the greatest and almost the sole cause of my inevitable error."[71] Before his conversion, in other words, Augustine was a "materialist." Only faith in God rightly conceived in terms of the heritage summarized by the *Creed of the People of God* overcomes this kind of mental darkness and blindness.

Then the Creed turns to the revealed names of God. " 'I am who am,' I am He Who Exists, Who therefore is to be called *Yahweh,* 'He Who Is,' for this expresses My nature best as *existence itself.* This translation (used by the Vicar of Christ) is the one that fits the text and the context best, and it is the traditional one."[72] "As He does not *have* existence, but *is* existence, so God does not *have* love: 'God *is* love.' The other would imply a composition in God between His nature and His attributes, contrary to His absolute simplicity. It is interesting that these truths about God's nature, which at first sight might seem to be the result of complicated philosophical reflexion, are actually the teaching of the Bible about God."[73] This is the transcendent God of whom St. Paul writes in the passage to which the *Creed* alludes: [1 Tim. 6, 16] ". . . The blessed and only Sovereign, the King of kings and Lord of lords, who alone has immortality and dwells in unapproachable light, whom no man has ever seen or can see. To him be honor and eternal dominion. Amen." (Catholic Edition, Revised Standard Version).

Correct and effective methodology in the teaching approach to this transcendent God is given by the *General Catechetical Directory:* "In catechesis . . . , the meeting with the Triune God occurs first and foremost when the Father, the Son and the Spirit are acknowledged as the authors of the plan of salvation that has its culmination in the death and resurrection of Jesus."[74]

Having given the two Names of God, *Being* and *Love,* that He Himself revealed to us in the Scriptures, the Vicar of Christ stresses in the Creed the transcendence and incomprehensibility of God. These terms mean the fact that His way of existing goes beyond what is given or presented in our human experience, limited earthly organisms as we are. The incomprehensibility of God, in the sense that no created and hence *limited* intelligence can fully comprehend the *unlimited* divine greatness, not even in the light of glory when we shall see Him face to face, was defined by the Fourth Lateran Council and again by the First Vatican Council.[75]

Teachers of the Catholic faith have in this section of the *Creed* the solid position for rejecting an atheistic fallacy that is being propagated widely, to the effect that religious education should stop teaching about "God" and even cease using His name with children. This is sometimes put forth disguised as respect for His greatness, which takes Him beyond our human knowledge. The truth is quite to the contrary. Even our unaided reason can know a very great deal about God, and when God adds a special revelation to mankind concerning His names, His nature, His attributes and perfections, a rich treasure of content about God is at hand to be communicated to children and young people by catechetical teaching. This should be done without any fear or hesitation induced by the Neo-Modernism of the day. And at the same time the "incomprehensibility of God" should be taught in its exact and accurate sense, for this too communicates priceless information concerning God's infinite greatness and transcendence. In sum and substance, it is the transcendence and the intelligent personality of God, distinct from all created things, which the ambient atheism desires not to recognize nor to communicate by teaching. Hence the clear and explicit emphasis in the *Creed of the People of God,* with its implication for teachers to be complete and explicit on both of these preambles of the Catholic faith.

With these articles of faith, the *Creed of the People of God* formulates what we know of the inner life of God, the mystery of the Most Holy Trinity, the central mystery of Christianity. And we know this, as the *Creed* explicitly professes, only by revelation. "Our act of faith corresponds to this divine revelation. It is new knowledge about the interior life of God . . . , even though it lacks full clarity. But God has manifested the mystery of His interior life to us because He wants us to participate in it. He calls us to this participation by His grace, a call which is not due to our nature, but is His gratuitous gift. Insofar as it is already this new knowledge of God, although in an early and imperfect form, it is the beginning of eternal life in us."[76] It follows that the catechetical teaching of the Catholic faith is a cooperation with God in this beginning of everlasting life in the souls of the children and young people. The content of this teaching of course may be broadened and deepened almost endlessly by drawing on the heritage of sacred theology. The *Creed* alludes to this heritage when it professes our faith in "the mutual bonds which eternally constitute the Three Persons, Who are each one and the same divine Being." These bonds are the personal and inter-personal relationships that constitute God's interior life, and form the object of the central and most sublime part of sacred theology, that which treats of the Holy Trinity. "In our opinion, these words *mutual bonds* are practically a synonym for *relations.*"[77]

Alluding to the common consent of mankind regarding the existence of the Supreme Being, the Vicar of Christ lays the foundation for sound ecumenism, the fact that so many men and entire religious bodies the world over profess sincere faith in God. The Second Vatican Council elaborated upon this fact in its *Declaration on the Relation of the Church to Non-Christian Religions,* no. 2.[78]

The *Creed* considers in par. 10 the Three Divine Persons in themselves, professing that each is equally God, and the "processions," as theology terms them, by which the Father begets eternally His Divine

Son, and by which the Holy Spirit proceeds eternally from both the Father and the Son.

Especially significant for catechists and teachers of the faith is the fact that Pope Paul includes the expression "Word of God" for the Eternal Son, which also is found *verbatim* in the Bible, Apoc. 19, 13, and which recurs throughout the prologue of the Gospel according to St. John. "Even from the viewpoint of exegesis it is impossible not to recognize the relationship between the *Logos* (Word) of St. John and Wisdom, that is, the realm of the intellect."[79] This creative Wisdom of God runs like a unifying thread through the Old Testament and its Books of Wisdom to the New Testament with its Good News of Wisdom Incarnate. Catechists and teachers of the faith find here their calling, their reason for being and for working in their apostolate. For this is the source of the intellectual content which they teach. The tendency to deemphasize or suppress content in religious education runs counter to the Word of God.

The *Creed of the People of God* concludes its profession of faith in God One and Three with a glimpse of the eternal life of happiness within the Divine Trinity. For us creatures, there can only be awe, veneration and constant adoration.

To summarize with regard to these articles of the Creed which profess the Catholic faith in the Most Holy Trinity, catechetical explanation recognizes two chief stages or aspects of its teaching about God. The first is the Divine Unity: There is only one God, with the perfections uniquely proper to the Supreme Being. The second is the revealed truth on the interior life of God, that He is One God in Three Divine Persons. Unless this foundation is laid deeply and well in the minds of the learners, they will lack the prerequisites for understanding Christianity: they will lack the preambles of faith. For Christianity has its meaning from the fact that it is the redemptive work and teaching of the eternal Divine Son, made man for our salvation. It is useless to expect the living of a Christian life apart from these basic understandings of Christian doctrine.[80]

III.   JESUS CHRIST: THE MYSTERY OF THE INCARNATION

11. We believe in Our Lord Jesus Christ, Who is the Son of God. He is the Eternal Word, born of the Father before time began, and consubstantial with the Father, *homousios to Patri,* and through

Him all things were made. He was incarnate of the Virgin Mary by the power of the Holy Spirit, and was made man: equal therefore to the Father according to His divinity, and inferior to the Father according to His humanity (see the Creed *Quicumque, DS* 76), and Himself one, not by some impossible confusion of His natures, but by the unity of His person. (See *ibid., DS* 76).

The *Creed of the People of God* proceeds to the second article of the *Apostles' Creed* which professes the Catholic faith in Jesus Christ, Only Son of the Father, our Lord. "The profession of faith in Christ begins with a confession of His divinity by making use of the technical term 'Lord,' traditionally applied to Christ. . . . The meaning of this term is divine in the strict sense. It is obvious from the context that the words which follow, 'who is the Son of God,' mean the natural Son of God in the proper sense, namely the Second Person of the Divine Trinity. It is the same in the Nicene Creed (in the early Church). . . . There the Council Fathers, following in the footsteps of still earlier professions of faith, desired to affirm the divine sonship of Jesus Christ in the strict natural sense, as opposed to the adoptive sonship proper to the justified. . . . This meaning is contained first of all in the New Testament and was maintained explicitly by the tradition of Christian writers prior to the Council of Nicaea (A.D. 325)."[81] For catechetical preparation for this absolutely basic point in teaching the Catholic faith, see Romans 16, 25; Phil. 2, 9–11; Acts 8, 35–37; 2 Cor. 4, 5; Romans 10, 9; Heb. 4, 14; 1 John 4, 15 and 5, 5; Romans 1, 3; 1 Cor. 12, 3; Acts 2, 36 and 10, 36.

Catechists, whether parents or teachers, can consult and meditate upon these texts for themselves. They contain some of the chief original biblical sources of the Apostles' Creed and thence, by living tradition, of all the other creeds and professions of faith across the centuries to this present *Creed of the People of God* which the crisis of faith after Vatican II has evoked. Such are the key insights of proximate preparation for catechetical teaching. Successful catechists maintain in addition a remote preparation for this teaching by systematic daily reading of the New Testament as a whole, with special emphasis on the four Gospels, the record of the apostolic witness to the Lord Jesus.[82]

With the word "consubstantial," the Vicar of Christ as the supreme teacher in the Church develops further the concept of the divinity of

Jesus Christ, the Eternal Son of God, giving an example both of clarity and of procedure for catechetical teachers. For he uses both of the Latin and Greek technical terms elaborated by the great councils of the early Church, "consubstantial" and "homoousios," to make clear that Christianity is firmly monotheistic in its profession of the divinity of Jesus Christ. Jesus Christ is truly and really God, the very same God in Whom the *Creed* has professed faith in the preceding articles.

Some recent translators of the creeds and liturgical texts into the vernacular languages, in an effort to make this basic concept more understandable, have actually become less clear and precise. Sometimes they have translated it into "of the same nature as the Father," which can mean of the same *kind* of nature as the Father; rather than the *same identical nature in number* as the Father, "which is indispensable in order to maintain monotheism."[83] The Holy Father leaves no possible ambiguity in his teaching by linking the clear statement on the Divine Person who Jesus Christ is with the prologue of St. John's Gospel: He is the Eternal Word, through whom all things were made. All of this is a model for the manner in which the truths of the Creed should pass into catechisms and textbooks of religion for fuller elaboration and explanation, always with the purpose of deepening the learner's personal grasp of the clear truth of the Creed.[84]

Then the *Creed of the People of God* passes on to teach the fact of the Incarnation. This "official teaching" (or *dogma*, in Greek) is the "dogma of the Incarnation" which recurs in the catechism question: "Who is Jesus Christ?" and the familiar answer, "Jesus Christ is true God and true man." The Vicar of Christ stresses in a perfectly clear manner the traditional teaching of the Church on the way the Incarnation took place, namely, by the Virgin Birth, without the intervention of a man: "He was incarnate of the Virgin Mary by the power of the Holy Spirit." "There can be no doubt that Pope Paul's words, historically considered, contain that meaning which is called 'biological' in certain circles today."[85]

The *New Catechism* manifests a tendency to exclude the 'biological' aspect of the Dogma of the Incarnation.[86] The Dutch theologians, defending the *Dutch Catechism* at the Gazzada Conference and accepting the philosophical ideology of the "Crisis of Faith" with its doubts and ambiguities as their guide, instead of following the Magisterium as their norm, expressed themselves as follows: "We remain of the opinion out of both exegetical and speculative reasons, that one can question whether the biological aspect of Christ's birth (*'sine semine'*) belongs to the essentials of the faith. Granted that the Ordinary Magisterium expresses itself in this biological sense, the question whether the said biological aspect is or is not an affirmation of faith is not yet clear. In the present actual state of things, whether among simple Christians or serious theologians, from the moment that there is doubt about the matter, it seems illicit to us that consciences should be obliged to accept this biological aspect."[87] But this is simply to make negative and corrosive doubt, planted and spread among the People of God, the norm of "faith," rather than the positive content of the teaching of the Magisterium. It is legitimate to ask, "Have we reached the point of denying within the Church the right to affirm the traditional Catholic faith?"[88] Such, then, is the background for this crucial and fundamental article of the *Creed of the People of God*.

The Holy See, for its part, insisted that the *New Catechism* be re-written so as to be clear in teaching the full truth of the Catholic faith on the Incarnation. This insistence began with the Letter of Pope Paul to Cardinal Alfrink.[89] The Theologians of the Holy See placed this point of doctrine first on the Gazzada Conference agenda, as follows: "The *New Catechism* insists on the symbolic value of the narratives which concern the virginal conception of Jesus. In last analysis, it does not affirm, or at least not clearly, the actual reality of this virginal conception."[90] During the discussion at Gazzada, "the theologian-delegates of the Holy See, taking into consideration Sacred Scripture, Divine Tradition, and the Magisterium, held themselves bound to demand that the virginal conception of Jesus—in the strict sense of conception without the intervention of man (*'conceptus sine semine'*)— be presented in the *New Catechism* in language reverently veiled, yes, but also explicit, as truth lovingly revealed to us by God. We do not say that the *New Catechism* denies this virginal conception of Jesus; what we are pointing out is that it places this truth in such vagueness and ambiguity as to leave the impression that it is a *problem open for discussion,* safeguarding of course the *symbolic meaning* of the reports which the Gospels give us about this event."[91] The final decision of the Commission of Cardinals, ratified by Pope Paul VI, is perfectly clear, explicit and complete.[92]

This confrontation, while it did not obtain a re-writing of the *New Catechism,* at least performs the service of exposing and illustrating the Neo-Modernist approach that gravitates toward the Crisis of Faith, whether in oral teaching or in religion textbooks. More important still, it exemplifies what it is to teach in communion with the Holy See, not only in content, but also in attitude and manner and approach: supernatural certitude, not doubt; and with fullness and clarity, not ambiguity and confusion.

Continuing its lucid clarity and completeness, the *Creed of the People of God* draws upon the Athanasian Creed for its final formulation. "Christ is the subject of a double generation: one is eternal, by which He proceeds from the Father; the other is in time, by which He is born of the Virgin Mary. Each generation terminates in the one and same Person, the Divine Word. Each generation has a corresponding nature which it communicates: the eternal communicates the divine nature, and the temporal generation communicates His human nature. By the first, Christ is equal to His Father, consubstantial with Him; by the second, He is less than His Father, like us in all things except sin (see Hebrews 4, 15). The two natures remain permanently distinct, without confusion, for neither can divinity be changed into something created, nor can a creature be changed into God. But they are united in the unity of the one and only Person in Christ, the Word of God. Thus the definitions of the Council of Ephesus on the unity of Person in Christ and of the Council of Chalcedon on the two natures in Him are gathered into the lapidary phrases of Pope Paul's *Profession of Faith,* inspired by the Athanasian Creed."[93] Here again is the example for teachers and catechists who hand on by their teaching "the Catholic faith which comes to us from the apostles," as the Roman Canon of the Mass says. It has come to us by means of the living divine Tradition of the magisterium, marked by the Councils of the Christian Era.

As to the method of teaching the dogma of the Incarnation, there is "the simple and objective kind of instruction which is appropriate for children."[94] This communicates the facts of Catholic doctrine on behalf of the Ordinary and Universal Magisterium, and is a teaching which is assisted greatly by the official catechisms of the bishops. This helpfulness is the reason why the *General Catechetical Directory* is explicit on this point: "The greatest importance must be attached to catechisms published by ecclesiastical authority. Their purpose is to provide, under a form that is condensed and practical, the witnesses of revelation and of Christian tradition . . . The doctrine of the Church must be presented faithfully. Here the norms set forth in Chapter I of Part Three (of the *General Catechetical Directory*) are to be followed."[95]

When pre-adolescence and adolescence are reached, "it is important not to continue . . . the simple and objective kind of instruction which is appropriate for children."[96] The *General Catechetical Directory* offers sound and challenging guidelines for catechetical teachers, especially in its call to meet the search of these growing youngsters and young adults for the meaning of life, for genuine values, and above all to help them in their intellectual demands. "Catechesis . . . simply cannot neglect the formation of a religious way of thinking, . . . (and) must provide the rational foundations of faith with the greatest care."[97] This simply means to help them know Jesus Christ better, in the fullness of His reality which the Creed professes, and hence to follow Him faithfully, as His baptized members.[98]

IV.   JESUS CHRIST: HIS LIFE AMONG US

12. He dwelt among us, full of grace and truth. He proclaimed and established the Kingdom of God and made us know in Himself the Father. He gave us His new commandment to love one another as He loved us. He taught us the way of the Beatitudes of the Gospel: poverty in spirit, meekness, suffering borne with patience, thirst after justice, mercy, purity of heart, will for peace, persecution suffered for justice' sake. He suffered under Pontius Pilate, the Lamb of God bearing on Himself the sins of the world, and He died for us on the Cross, saving us by His redeeming Blood. He was buried, and, of His own power, rose the third day, raising us by His Resurrection to that sharing in the divine life which is the life of grace. He ascended to heaven, and He will come again, this time in glory, to judge the living and the dead: each according to his merits—those who have responded to the Love and Piety of God going to eternal life, those who have refused them to the end going to the fire that is not extinguished.
And His Kingdom will have no end.

Opening with words from the Gospel according to St. John, 1, 14, the Creed professes that God has come close to us by His Incarnation. He has made Himself *Emmanuel,* God-with-us. (Isaiah 7, 14). By coming to us, dwelling and living with us, God enables us to know Himself in an entirely new way through the truth of the New Testament revelation, and so to turn to Him in a new way of life, the supernatural life of grace.

This opens up a new catechetical teaching program, with a content of learning that has this same Incarnate God, Jesus Christ our Lord, as its principal object. At this point in the *Creed of the People of God,* the Vicar of Christ summarizes in brief articles the life and activity of the Incarnate Word during His First Coming in humility. It should be noted that this implies the historicity of the Gospels as reliable reports on what Christ our Lord said and did. When the documents of the Second Vatican Council are read attentively, it will be recognized that the Council Fathers likewise use the Gospels freely and without artificial inhibitions in their teaching. See, for example, *Dogmatic Constitution on the Church,* nos. 55–58; *Decree on Ecumenism,* no. 2; *Decree on Priestly Training,* no. 8; *Dogmatic Constitution on Divine Revelation, passim,* and esp. nos. 8, 11, 17, 18, 19, 23, 24, 25; *Decree on the Apostolate of the Laity,* no. 8; *Declaration on Religious Freedom,* nos. 1, 11; *Decree on the Mission Activity of the Church,* no. 5. Catechists, whether parents or teachers, who study these passages attentively will see what is the Church's own approach to the Scriptures, especially the Gospels, and how to use them in teaching. The Magisterium presupposes the work of sound human scholarship in establishing the historical character of the Scriptures; it does not constantly repeat this work in its own teaching, which has a different purpose and end in view. So too the catechist who teaches as a delegate of the Magisterium. It has become fashionable in certain circles to say that we "now" recognize that we do not have a "Life of Christ." There is a deception here, as if the Gospels ought to have been written in a "modern" way as "lives" are written in the recent mode about great men in history. This is a lack of clearness that can confuse sacred teaching and even cause it to cease, so that the time for catechetical teaching is actually used some other way. For when catechists think they cannot use the Gospels, they give up their chief instruments of teaching, and the learners begin not to know the primary object of catechetical teaching, namely the Incarnate Word Himself. The Vicar of Christ, summarizing what Jesus taught and did when He lived with us, provides catechesis with its authentic pattern and methodological guideline. There was a real "Life of Christ" with us when He lived among us, and we have authentic records on it for use in catechesis. They do not report everything, as St. John says; but they do tell us the essentials about the Word made flesh and dwelling among us. The authentic catechist believes the Scriptures as a part of his communion with the Magisterium of the Church, and hence his teaching about Him Who dwelt among us, full of grace and truth, proceeds not as a mere exercise in the preliminaries of human science about the records but in the spirit and the content of the Catholic faith itself.

Continuing in his profession of faith, the Vicar of Christ summarizes a vast area of scriptural and theological science, the heritage of teaching about the fact that Jesus Christ personally founded the Kingdom of God on earth and gave it its constitution, its doctrine and its seven sacraments. Pope Paul will elaborate this further in par. 19–23 of his profession of faith. The important point here is the link between this heritage of content in religious education and the personal life and action of Jesus Christ when He lived incarnate on this earth. Convenient and authentic sources for the catechetical teacher's explanations of this article of faith are to be found in the Documents of the Second Vatican Council, esp. the *Dogmatic Constitution on the Church* and the *Dogmatic Constitution on Divine Revelation*.

Jesus by His teaching and example made us know, in Himself, God the Father. Here the Holy Father lays down another major stone in the foundation of religious education. Recalling the earlier articles of the Creed on the right idea of God and the necessity of revelation for us to possess it personally, teachers will recognize here the pedagogical means to the end in view. Knowledge of God the Father on this earth depends on coming to know His Incarnate Son. St. Teresa of Avila admonishes out of her experience against seeking God in any other way than by the meditation and contemplation of the Sacred Humanity of the Word Incarnate. This is the secret also of an effective catechetical teaching, one that binds the soul to God by using Jesus' own method of teaching, so that His followers can say, "Our Father . . ."[99] All catechesis and religious education, whether in home or school, turn upon this fundamental procedure: coming to know Jesus Christ, the Eternal Son Incarnate, and thus to know in Him the Father. In an age ravaged by ignorance of God and mounting atheism, these fundamentals are more necessary than ever. When authentic catechesis is pressed back into the homes, heads of families should see to it that the heritage of *lectio divina,* the daily spiritual reading of the Gospels, and of meditative prayer upon our Lord in the Gospels, is carried forward systematically by family catechetics and family prayer. For it is these two Christian uses of the Gospels that extend to the children and young people of today what He Himself accomplished: "He made us know in Himself the Father."

Then the Creed turns to the essence of the moral teaching of Jesus Christ, again a timely matter for contemporary teachers of the Catholic faith. For the mounting atheism mentioned above is causing a wave of aberration regarding love which makes it increasingly difficult to raise up children and young people in the faith of their forefathers. "The most important point about Christ's moral teaching . . . , His' 'new commandment,' is its newness, determined by its point of reference: 'As He loved us.' No one has ever loved us *as He* did, and this is what constitutes the immense newness of His commandment. And with this let it be said that not all love of neighbor is the love which this new commandment enjoins. Theologically speaking, the new Christian love (*agape*) is not to be confused with merely human love or humanism. Charity exists only when it is the Christian theological virtue: when it loves its neighbor as a brother in Christ or as a son of God."[100]

The *Creed of the People of God* concludes this timely insertion of the "Life of Christ" into the Apostles' Creed by stressing the Beatitudes, the essential marks of the imitation and following of Christ, who said, "I am the way, and the truth, and the life; and no one comes to the Father, but by me." (John 14, 6).

Taken as a whole, these articles which the Vicar of Christ has inserted into the *Creed* reconstitute religious education and renew the integrity and fullness of the content of catechetical teaching. For the primary object of this teaching is Jesus Christ Himself, God Incarnate, who has renewed authentic knowledge of Himself on this earth. This is the renewal program which the Magisterium continues and which those who cooperate with the Magisterium in Catholic homes and schools bring to the young. In doing so, the rich heritage of spiritual literature on the following of Christ and the example of the lives of the Saints ought not to disappear from the scene.

Then the Creed professes the Catholic faith in the Redemption, the culminating work of the Divine Redeemer. "The life-work of Christ culminates in what He did to redeem us. The facts are narrated in the *Creed* with simplicity: 'He suffered under Pontius Pilate, died . . . , was buried, rose again on the third day . . . and ascended into heaven.' The theological meaning is built upon these facts and based upon their reality: Jesus Christ died as 'the Lamb of God, who takes away the sins of the world, saving us by His redeeming Blood . . . elevating us by His resurrection to participation in the divine life which is the life of grace.' It is of supreme importance to note the insistence of the profession of Faith upon the redeeming value of the Passion, Cross and Blood of the Lord."[101]

The *New Catechism* caused the Magisterium to become concerned about this fundamental doctrine of the Catholic faith through the deceptive tenor of its discussion of the Redemption. For its approach seeks to dismiss its very substance as a "medieval notion," reducing it (in a manner veiled by its characteristic ambiguity) to the horizontal level of "Christ's service to His fellowman."[102] Pope Paul requested that the Catechism leave no trace of ambiguity in its presentation of the nature of "the satisfaction and sacrifice offered by Christ to the Eternal Father to take away our sins and reconcile men with God."[103]

The theologians representing the Holy See placed this question on the Gazzada Conference agenda as follows: "Despite two or three good quotations from Scripture, the *New Catechism,* when it expresses its own thinking, dedicates itself quite at length to remove the idea of a satisfaction offered by Jesus to His Father in compensation for the sins of men. . . . It is difficult to admit that (its explanations) are sufficient. . . . The sacrificial offering accomplished by Jesus (His Blood offered to God) is given a secondary place, and is maintained only with reservations. . . . The Father certainly did not demand that Jesus be punished. But He did intend the punishment of mankind insofar as Jesus had not offered His redeeming sacrifice. Does not the text of the *Catechism* perhaps sin by omission?"[104] According to the transcript of the Gazzada Conference, the theologians representing the Holy See maintained that "the *New Catechism* does not safeguard the genuine meaning of the satisfaction offered by Jesus to God the Father, as this meaning comes to us from Sacred Scripture, Divine Tradition and the Magisterium. . . . "[105] After summarizing these truths of the doctrine of the Faith, they continue, "In our judgment, the presentation of these truths in summary cannot be passed over in silence by a catechism, let alone give a distorted notion of satisfaction. The suffering of Christ as a propitiatory reparation for sin is a dimension both profound and essential of the revealed mystery of the Redemption. Little or nothing of it remains in what the *New Catechism* offers, after having abandoned the idea of satisfaction. For its explanation of satisfaction is done in a way which leaves it unacceptable."[106]

To this perceptible hardening on the part of the theologians of the Holy See, the theologians representing the Dutch hierarchy responded with a flat refusal to change the text. "The modification of the text requested by the Roman delegation would lay before the minds of today's faithful a notion of redemption that is incomprehensible to them. . . . Hence we insist that there be no modification whatever along the lines proposed by the Roman delegation, precisely out of fidelity to Christ the Redeemer."[107] The Report concludes the discussion of this article of faith with the observation, "Both of the groups remain therefore in their respective positions."[108] The text of course was not re-written.[109]

It is difficult to exaggerate the importance of this doctrinal phenomenon for teachers and catechists who are concerned to teach in communion with the Holy See and to evaluate correctly the religion textbooks, programs and catechetical aids of the present day, so many of which derive from faulty catechetical texts and which seek to impose this Neo-Modernist mentality upon Catholic children. The Vicar of Christ, for his part, has given a model for accuracy and clarity in teaching the full truth of the Catholic faith, and he will re-emphasize this saving doctrine regarding the Cross of Jesus once more in par. 19 of the *Creed of the People of God,* in connection with original sin: for underneath the aberration under discussion here there is a hidden activator, the denial of all sin, original and personal, as the logical corollary of the growing problem of atheistic infiltration and influence already mentioned.

The *Creed* goes on to profess the Catholic faith in the resurrection of the Lord Jesus. "From the theological point of view this affirma-

tion—and I believe it is something new in the history of the creeds—
of the redeeming dimension of the resurrection of the Lord is of great
interest. . . . The risen Christ is the exemplary cause of our justification, which is accomplished upon Him as the model. For he who possesses this new life, the life of grace, has within himself already something which is a claim upon his own glorious resurrection to the image
and likeness of Christ's resurrection. See John 6, 55. The resurrection
of Christ is thus not an isolated fact: it is the beginning of a process
which involves all his followers. 'But in fact Christ has been raised
from the dead, the first fruits of those who have fallen asleep.' (1 Cor.
15, 20). And the completion of the process: 'Christ the first fruits, then
at His Coming those who belong to Christ. Then comes the end.'
(1 Cor. 15, 23–24)."[110] This personal and contemporary dimension,
it goes without saying, should be developed fully in catechetical explanations, for it lays the foundation for the Christian hope and is a
powerful motive for the Christian life. Christian doctrine is not abstract
and separated from life; it flows directly into life when its full truth
is taught.

Then the article of faith follows in the Ascension of the Lord
Jesus into heaven. "This affirmation, which Pope Paul VI takes from
the Nicene Creed, is not to be understood as a mere synonym for the
glorious life which Jesus possessed by His resurrection, but as the
distinct event reported by Mark 16, 19; Luke 25, 51; and Acts 1, 9."[111]

The *Creed of the People of God* concludes its development of the
second article of the Apostles' Creed by a comprehensive reaffirmation
of the *parousia,* the characteristic doctrine of the apostolic age. This
clear affirmation of the second coming, immediately followed by that
of the general judgment with its eternal and irrevocable consequences,
is again an essential part of the charter of catechetical teachers in the
Catholic Church. It establishes the reality of the moral order, basic
personal responsibility to God, the importance of personal decisions in
this earthly life, and the salvific character of catechetical teaching.
These articles of the Creed are the direct and explicit doctrine of the
New Testament: see Acts 1, 11; 10, 42; 2 Tim. 4, 1; 1 Peter 4, 5;
2 Cor. 5, 10; John 5, 28ff; Mt. 26, 46. "The terms 'eternal life' and
'the fire that is not extinguished' indicate that both states are definitive
and interminable. The eternity of hell is enunciated by stating the
everlasting character of the pain of sense, as the Athanasian Creed
likewise did."[112]

"And His Kingdom will have no end." "This statement originates in Luke 1, 33, and signifies a proclamation that the Messianic Age, the Kingship of the Messiah, constitutes the final and definitive phase of Salvation History. . . . This section of the *Creed of the People of God* describes the life-work of the Incarnate Word up to His Second Coming. And the meaning of this final statement, a paragraph by itself in the section, is that the Incarnation of the Divine Word will have no end even after the *parousia*."[113]

V. THE HOLY SPIRIT

13. We believe in the Holy Spirit, Who is Lord, and Giver of life, Who is adored and glorified together with the Father and the Son. He spoke to us by the prophets, He was sent by Christ after His resurrection and His ascension to the Father; He illuminates, vivifies, protects and governs the Church; He purifies the Church's members if they do not shun His grace. His action, which penetrates to the inmost of the soul, enables man to respond to the call of Jesus: *Be perfect as your Heavenly Father is perfect.* (Matt. 5, 48).

Here the *Creed of the People of God* summarizes the careful definitions of the full and equal divinity of the Third Person of the Most Holy Trinity which have been made at various times by several ecumenical councils of the early Church. "Especially interesting is the term 'Giver of life': the Holy Spirit gives us the supernatural life . . . He is the author of the spiritual life, holiness and virtue. If creatures are made holy, it is by the communication of the Holy Spirit . . . , the fountain and source of holiness. . . . Since the third century the Fathers of the Church have called this process of supernatural life 'our deification.' Speaking of the Holy Spirit, St. Basil writes, 'How could He not be God, who makes gods of the rest of us?'"[114]

The *Creed* offers here once again a timely catechetical guideline. For the teaching of the Catholic faith often must proceed today in the face of the contemporary flood of atheism which infects souls with a spirit of arrogant self-assertion, defended and rationalized by the philosophical aberration called situation ethics. Frequently, each wishes be a god unto himself, determining his own moral law. But truth in doctrine leads directly to genuine Christian life, which is a quite different approach to the human aspiration to be like God, the humble approach of prayer and the sacraments which are the means of grace and supernatural life.

"He spoke to us through the Prophets." The one and same Holy Spirit is the author of both the Old Testament and the New Testament.[115] This article first came into the creeds because of the heresy of Marcion who held that the Holy Spirit spoke through the apostles in the writings of the New Testament, but not through the prophets, the human authors of the Old Testament. The People of God believe in both the unity and the inspiration of the Bible as a whole, accordingly, a fact which is fundamental for catechetical teaching. By this article of faith, the Bible becomes the chief instrument for the explanations which give life, body, attractiveness, motivation, and spiritual power to the catechetical apostolate.

The encyclical of Pope Leo XIII on the Holy Spirit, *Divinum illud munus,* is a helpful commentary for teachers on this article of Pope Paul's *Creed,* for it develops at length its affirmation of the double mission of the Third Person. The first mission is to the Church as an institution, guaranteeing its faith, teaching authority or Magisterium, and indefectibility. The second mission is deep within each soul that enjoys the state of grace, arousing in each one the moral struggle for Christian perfection. "And the *Creed* cites Mt. 5, 48, which in its context and especially in its parallel, Luke 6, 36, places our imitation of the Heavenly Father directly in the realm of mercy. In the Gospels, the idea that we should be merciful is linked with that of our own wretchedness and great need of the mercy of God. Hence, these words of Jesus give not the slightest occasion for presumption; on the contrary, seen in their Gospel context, they are an invitation to humility."[116]

VI.   THE BLESSED VIRGIN MARY

14. We believe that Mary is the Mother, who remained ever a Virgin, of the Incarnate Word, our God and Saviour Jesus Christ (See the Council of Ephesus, DS 251–252), and that by reason of this singular election, she was, in consideration of the merits of her Son, redeemed in a more eminent manner (See Vatican Council II, Const. *Lumen gentium,* No. 53), preserved from all stain of original sin (See Pius IX, *Ineffabilis Deus, Acta,* part One,

Vol. 1, p. 616), and filled with the gift of grace more than all other creatures (See Vatican Council II, Const. *Lumen gentium,* No. 53).

15. Joined by a close and indissoluble bond to the Mysteries of the Incarnation and Redemption (See *Ibid.,* Nos. 53, 58 and 61), the Blessed Virgin, the Immaculate, was at the end of her earthly life raised body and soul to heavenly glory and likened to her risen Son in anticipation of the future lot of all the just (See the Apost. Constitution *Munificentissimus Deus, AAS* 42 (1950), p. 770); and We believe that the Blessed Mother of God, the New Eve, Mother of the Church (See Vatican II *Lumen gentium* Nos. 53, 56, 61, 63; Paul VI at closing of Third Session, Vat. II, *AAS* 56 (1964), p. 1016; and his Apost. Exhortation, *Signum magnum, AAS* 59 (1967), pp. 465 and 467), continues in Heaven her maternal role with regard to Christ's members, cooperating with the birth and growth of divine life in the souls of the redeemed (See Vatican II, *Lumen gentium,* no. 62; Paul VI, Apost. Exhortation *Signum magnum, AAS* (59 [1967], p. 468).

These next two paragraphs of the *Creed of the People of God* represent a striking development of doctrine. "In the history of the Creeds, it is absolutely new to have a special section devoted to the doctrine on the Blessed Virgin Mary. First, the profession of faith affirms that Mary is the Mother of God. This is the mariological dogma of Ephesus . . . This motherhood coexists with the perpetual virginity of Mary. . . . Historically, the dogma of her perpetual virginity has been expressed by saying 'Mary ever Virgin,' or more concretely, 'Mary was a Virgin before, during and after the birth of Jesus.' This later formulation is found in the *Constitution* of Pope Paul IV (Aug. 7, 1555; *Denz.-Sch.* 1880), being included among the truths that are 'the foundation of the faith.' "[117]

The *New Catechism* merely states in its characteristic deceptive manner that it is "highly improbable" that Joseph and Mary had other children.[118] Of its entire approach, conducted in this vein, Pozo writes, "All this is quite far removed from a clear affirmation of the *dogma* of Mary's perpetual virginity *as a truth of the Faith.*"[119] This is the reason for the original objection which the Dutch Catholics sent to Pope Paul,[120] and for the agenda of the theologians representing the Holy See at the Gazzada Conference: "It is to be desired that the *Dutch Catechism* make a more clear declaration that Mary was always a virgin after the birth of Christ."[121] The offensive passage was not re-written and the Supplement in the present English translation says: "Add: the perpetual virginity of Mary is confirmed by the tradition of the Church, and presented by the magisterium to our belief."[122] Catechetical teaching at least obtains once again an illuminating instance of the gulf which separates the two approaches to the Catholic Faith.

Then the *Creed* turns to the privileges of the Mother of God, and first, her fullness of Grace. Pope Pius XII in his Encyclical *Fulgens corona* (8 Sept. 1953) teaches that the Immaculate Conception does not diminish the universality of Christ's redemption, for He redeemed His Mother in a different and more perfect way.[123] All the earlier documents of the Magisterium which teach this privilege of Mary are synthesized by the Second Vatican Council, cited by Pope Paul VI as the direct source of the article in the *Creed of the People of God*.

"This doctrine (of Mary's fullness of Grace) derives from Luke 1, 28 . . . where it is practically her proper name. Let us not forget what a proper name was among the Semites: it denoted what a being or person is in deep interior reality. . . . Her fullness of grace, corresponding to her singular dignity as Mother of God, constitutes her superiority in grace beyond all other creatures."[124]

Paragraph 15 of the *Creed* professes the Catholic faith in the Virgin Mary as mother of the Church. The three official references to Vatican II in the text of Pope Paul's Profession are helpful for teachers and catechists, for they explain how Mary Immaculate is joined and associated with her Divine Son in His work of redemption. "The Virgin Mary's association is not explained as one with the Person of Christ, but with the mysteries of the Incarnation and Redemption. This association is conceived as something active, and has as its first act Mary's answer at the Annunciation, her free decision that the Incarnation take place in her and by her. One should not overlook the fact that the Incarnation, considered also in itself, has a soteriological aspect, and that Mary's 'Be it done to me according to your Word' means also her consent to the plan of Redemption. . . . She lived this consent with greater intensity each day of her life, standing always within her maternal sphere, for it could not be otherwise. She was always the Mother associated with the work of her Son, even to the heroic moment in which this work consisted in immolating Himself for men on the cross. The third Vatican II passage synthesizes this cooperation of Mary and contains a general affirmation of its uniqueness, for it makes Mary also our mother, in the order of grace."[125]

Then the Creed professes the faith of the People of God in the dogma of the Assumption of Mary, solemnly defined by Pope Pius XII by an act of the Extraordinary Magisterium at midpoint of the present century. "Prescinding, as Pope Pius XII likewise did, from the question whether Mary's death is an article of faith, Pope Paul's *Profession* affirms that her condition since the Assumption is that of the glory of the just in their coming final state. (See 1 Cor. 15, 51) . . . In our judgment, there can be other similar exceptional cases 'in anticipation,' as a serious Patristic tradition recognizes . . . from Mt. 27, 52 ff."[126]

Finally, in the profession of faith regarding her spiritual motherhood, the official references given in the *Creed* itself are indispensable for the explanations which catechetical teaching gives to the truths affirmed in Creed and catechism on Mary's intercession for us as "the New Eve" and "the Mother of the Church." "Mary is 'the New Eve' because of her unique association, one of positive cooperation, with 'the New Adam' (as the Second Vatican Council teaches). This cooperation in the objective redemption of mankind is the reality which makes her 'the Mother of the Church.' It is for this reason, again in the words of the Second Vatican Council, that 'the Catholic Church, enlightened by the Holy Spirit, loves her with filial affection as our most loveable Mother.' "[127]

Considering these realities affirmed by the Profession of Faith and reflecting on the passages cited from the Council and the exhortation of the Vicar of Christ, "what the *New (Dutch) Catechism* writes on p. 212 seems impoverished indeed: 'We *can* address her with confidence, *if this helps us* to see Jesus with new eyes and reach him more easily.' "[128] Again the contrast in approach, both in method and in content, is valuable for catechists to see.

The *Creed of the People of God* summarizes the great Mariological events and the relevant documents of the Magisterium that are milestones in the life of the Catholic Church during these contemporary two centuries since the French Revolution, a period frequently called the "Age of Mary." Cathechetical teachers have a wealth of content to draw upon from these sources, a powerful means for helping those who learn the truths of the Catholic faith to practice them in their lives. There is a side to catechetical teaching called "formation," something distinct from "instruction" considered in itself. The presence and influence of Mary is perhaps the most important single factor in this formative function of catechesis.[129]

VII. ORIGINAL SIN

16. We believe that in Adam all have sinned, which means that the original offense committed by him caused human nature, common to all men, to fall to a state in which it bears the consequences of that offense, and which is not the state in which it was at first in our first parents, established as they were in holiness and justice, and in which man knew neither evil nor death. It is human nature so fallen, stripped of the grace that clothed it, injured in its own natural powers and subjected to the dominion of death, that is transmitted to all men, and it is in this sense that every man is born in sin. We therefore hold, with the Council of Trent, that original sin is transmitted with human nature, "not by imitation, but by propagation" and that it is thus "in each of us as his own" (See the Council of Trent, Session V, Decree on Original Sin; DS 1513).

Despite the variety of exegetical explanations of Romans 5, 12, it remains true that all Catholic exegetes recognize with the Council of Trent that St. Paul in Romans 5 is teaching the doctrine of original sin. This is a fundamental matter for catechetical teaching. "The important thing is to maintain the correct way of conceiving this sin in terms of the elements in it that belong to the Catholic faith. This means the following three points: First, . . . that 'our first parents were established in holiness and justice, exempt from evil and death'; secondly, that there existed 'an original sin committed by him, namely Adam'; thirdly, that 'human nature was injured as a consequence,' and 'stripped of the grace that clothed it.' "[130]

The *New Catechism* does not make a clear affirmation of these essentials of the Catholic doctrine on original sin.[131] The original

Dutch edition states, "We should not attach any particular importance to a certain sin at the beginning."[132] At the Gazzada Conference the theologians of the Dutch hierarchy admitted that a better statement could be made by saying, "What the significance of the first sin is merits a more profound meditation." But they defended the general approach: "The *Dutch Catechism* places original sin in the larger context of 'the sin of the world,' which operates ceaselessly across all generations since the origin of mankind."[133] It is interesting to note that the English translation inserted the Dutch emendation evoked at the Gazzada Conference: "The meaning of the first sin needs to be pondered deeply," but as a single sentence, not the fundamental re-writing which the Holy See requested.[134]

When the presentation of this doctrine in the *New Catechism* is reflected upon as a whole, it is no surprise that the theologians of the Holy See placed the matter on the agenda of the Gazzada Conference, calling it "extremely disconcerting" that "original sin is seen as something contracted under the influence of human society, which creates a harmful educative environment."[135] At the Conference, they insisted that "the *Dutch Catechism,* in order to conserve the integrity of the Christian message on original sin, must put in clear light the following three points . . . ," namely those given above as the elements of the doctrine on original sin which pertain to the Catholic faith. They refer to the fact, furthermore, that the *New Catechism's* Neo-Modernist approach is not only out of step with the Council of Trent but also with the Second Vatican Council, citing the Dogmatic Constitution on the Church, no. 56, and the Pastoral Constitution on the Church in the Modern World, no. 18.[136]

Catechetical teaching sometimes finds a thorny problem in the matter of "monogenism" in contrast with "polygenism," the question whether "Adam" was an individual or a group. We shall confine ourselves to Pozo's commentary: "The text of the *Profession of Faith* speaks in monogenist terms. It speaks of Adam, it says that all men sinned in him, that they were all constituted sinners by the original sin he committed. The Council of Trent likewise spoke this way, in the singular. With this we do not mean to say that the *Profession of Faith* is a new insistence on monogenism. Pope Pius XII opposed the acceptance into theology of the polygenist hypothesis (see his Encyclical *Humani generis; Denz.-Sch.* 3897). . . . And Paul VI has insisted that polygenism is a hypothesis that has not been proved. (*AAS* 58 [1966], p. 654) . . . The theologians of the Holy See at Gazzada reproached the *New Catechism* for its confident declaration in so delicate a manner, that nothing has been revealed on the point; greater prudence was requested. (*Dossier*, p. 256) . . . It is clear that science will never be able to demonstrate polygenism if monogenism has been revealed . . . , that is to say, if the revealed doctrine on original sin is demonstrated to be actually irreconcilable with the polygenist hypothesis."[137]

Then the *Creed* turns to the transmission of original sin, reaffirming firmly with the Second Vatican Council, the teaching of the Council of Trent on this basic article of the Catholic faith. "The phrase 'by imitation' is Pelagian. According to Pelagius, Adam introduced a spirit of disobedience into the world. His bad example caused many to imitate him. It is only through this imitation that his sin is in some sense transmitted so that it reaches us."[138]

The Neo-Modernist approach departs even farther than Pelagius from the truth of the Catholic faith. "It is totally inadmissible to substitute personal sins for the concept of transmission by propagation, making original sin a 'Sin of the World,' reducing it to a sinful environment that oppresses us, affirming finally that 'one can say that original sin takes concrete form only in our personal sins.' In this context there would be no true sin until personal sins came into existence."[139] Hence the *Creed of the People of God* will be clear and explicit, in no. 18 below, regarding the baptism of infants not yet able to be guilty of any personal sin.

This matter is fundamental in catechetical methodology, and involves its very heart, the Christocentrism which is called for in *GCD* 40: for the entire doctrine of the Faith regarding "Jesus Christ, Savior and Redeemer of the World," is at stake.[140]

VIII.   JESUS CHRIST, REDEEMER OF MANKIND

17. We believe that Our Lord Jesus Christ, by the Sacrifice of the Cross, redeemed us from original sin and all the personal sins committed by each one of us, so that, in accordance with the word of the Apostle, "where sin abounded, grace did more abound" (Rom. 5, 20).

18. We believe in one Baptism instituted by Our Lord Jesus Christ for the remission of sins. Baptism should be administered even to little children who have not yet been able to be guilty of any personal sin, in order that, though born deprived of supernatural grace, they may be reborn "of water and the Holy Spirit" to the divine life in Christ Jesus (See the Council of Trent, *ibid;* DS 1514).

The *Creed* professes again, with St. Paul, the redeeming power of the passion.[141] "Christ saves us from both original sin and our personal sins. Although the profession of faith does not underline it explicitly, there is a connection between personal sins and original sin. For the latter places us, historically speaking, in a state of rebellion on the part of our instincts which inclines us to personal sins. It is this connection which St. Paul affirms, Ephesians 2, 3."[142]

It has been from the beginning of the Church the heart of the profession of the apostolic faith that Christ died for our sins. One needs but recall St. Paul's allusion to the original pattern of teaching or "Creed" in 1 Cor. 15; 3–5: "I taught you what I had been taught myself, namely that Christ died for our sins, in accordance with the Scriptures; that he was buried; and that he was raised to life on the third day, in accodance with the Scriptures . . ."

Perhaps the best presentation of catechetical methodology is that of the *Roman Catechism:* "How necessary is a knowledge of this Article and how assiduous . . . (catechesis) should be in stirring up in the minds of the faithful the frequent recollection of our Lord's Passion, we learn from the Apostle when he says that he knows nothing but *Jesus Christ and him crucified.* (1 Cor. 2, 2) . . . The greatest care and pains therefore (should be exercised) in giving a thorough explanation of this subject, in order that the faithful, being moved by the remembrance of so great a benefit, may give themselves to the contemplation of the goodness and love of God toward us . . . Furthermore, (catechesis) should not omit the historical part of this Article, which has been so carefully set forth by the holy Evangelists; so that the faithful may be acquainted with at least the principal parts of this mystery, that is to say, such as seem more necessary to confirm the truth of our faith. For it is on this Article, as on their foundation, that the Christian faith and religion rest; and if this truth be firmly established, all the rest is secure.

"Indeed, if one thing more than another presents difficulty to the mind and understanding of man, assuredly it is the mystery of the Cross, which, beyond all doubt, must be considered the most difficult of all; so much so that only with great difficulty can we grasp the fact that our salvation depends on the Cross, and on Him who for us was nailed thereon. In this, however, as the Apostle teaches, we may well admire the wonderful Providence of God; *for, seeing that in the wisdom of God, the world by wisdom knew not God, it pleased God by the foolishness of preaching to save them that believe.* (1 Cor. 1, 21). It is no wonder, then, that the prophets, before the coming of Christ, and the Apostles, after His death and resurrection, labored so strenuously to convince mankind that He was the Redeemer of the world, and to bring them under the power and obedience of the Crucified."[143]

In last analysis, this is why the *General Catechetical Directory* states in no. 40: "Catechesis must necessarily be Christocentric."

In par. 18, the *Creed of the People of God* professes the dogma of faith in the sacraments defined by the Council of Trent: "It seemed fitting to treat here of the holy sacraments of the Church. . . . For all true justification either begins through the sacraments, or once begun, increases through them, or when lost is regained through them. . . . If anyone says that the sacraments of the New Law were not instituted by Jesus Christ our Lord; or that there are more than seven or fewer than seven . . . let him be anathema."[144]

When the *Creed of the People of God* reaffirms the practice of the Church in baptizing infants, it puts the final seal upon the heritage of Catholic doctrine on original sin, and on the reality of the supernatural life of grace.[145]

The *General Catechetical Directory* gives the basic guidelines for sound methodology in teaching the redemption and its application to individual persons, linking, as the *Creed* does, its statements on "Jesus Christ, Savior and Redeemer of the World" with those on "The sacraments, actions of Christ in the Church."[146] "Catechesis will have the duty of presenting the seven sacraments according to their full meaning. First, they must be presented as sacraments of faith . . . Second, the sacraments must be presented, each according to its own nature and end, not only as remedies for sin and its consequences, but especially as sources of grace . . ."[147] Then the *Directory,* under the heading "Catechesis on the Sacraments," gives a pointed and comprehensive definition of each of the seven sacraments.[148]

IX.   THE CATHOLIC CHURCH

19. We believe in one, holy, catholic, and apostolic Church, built by Jesus Christ on that rock which is Peter. She is the Mystical Body of Christ; at the same time a visible society instituted with hierarchical organs, and a spiritual community; the Church on earth, the pilgrim People of God here below, and the Church filled with heavenly blessings; the germ and the first fruits of the Kingdom of God, through which the work and the sufferings of Redemption are continued throughout human history, and which looks for its perfect accomplishment beyond time in glory (See Vatican II, *Lumen gentium*, Nos. 8 and 5). In the course of time, the Lord Jesus forms His Church by means of the sacraments emanating from His plenitude (See *ibid.*, Nos. 7, 11). By these she makes her members participants in the Mystery of the death and resurrection of Christ, in the grace of the Holy Spirit who gives her life and movement. (See Vatican II, Const. *Sacrosanctum concilium*, Nos. 5–6; *Lumen gentium*, Nos. 7, 12, 50). She is therefore holy, though she has sinners in her bosom, because she herself has no other life but that of grace: it is by living by her life that her members are sanctified; it is by removing themselves from her life that they fall into sins and disorders that prevent the radiation of her sanctity. This is why she suffers and does penance for these offences, of which she has the power to heal her children through the Blood of Christ and the Gift of the Holy Spirit.

20. Heiress of the divine promises and daughter of Abraham according to the Spirit, through that Israel whose Scriptures she lovingly guards, and whose Patriarchs and Prophets she venerates; founded upon the Apostles and handing on from century to century their everliving word and their powers as Pastors in the Successor of Peter and the Bishops in communion with him; perpetually assisted by the Holy Spirit, she has the charge of guarding, teaching, explaining and spreading the Truth which God revealed in a then veiled manner by the Prophets, and fully by the Lord Jesus. We believe *all that is contained in the Word of God written or handed down, and that the Church proposes for belief as divinely revealed, whether by a solemn judgment or by the Ordinary and Universal Magisterium* (See Vatican Council I, Const. *Dei filius; DS* 3011). We believe in the infallibility enjoyed by the Successor of Peter

when he teaches *ex cathedra* as Pastor and Teacher of all the faithful (See Vatican I, Const. *Pastor aeternus; DS* 3074), and which is assured also to the Episcopal Body when it exercises with him the supreme Magisterium (See Vatican II, *Lumen gentium,* no. 25).

21. We believe that the Church founded by Jesus Christ and for which He prayed is indefectibly one in faith, worship and the bond of hierarchical communion (See Vatican II, *ibid.,* nos. 8 and 18–23; *Unitatis Redintegratio,* no. 2). In the bosom of this Church, the rich variety of liturgical rites and the legitimate diversity of theological and spiritual heritages and special disciplines, far from injuring her unity, make it more manifest (See Vatican II, *Lumen gentium,* no. 23; Decree *Orientalium ecclesiarum,* nos. 2, 3, 5, 6).

22. Recognizing also the existence, outside the organism of the Church of Christ, of numerous elements of truth and sanctification which belong to her as her own and tend to Catholic unity (See Vatican II, *Lumen gentium,* no. 8), and believing in the action of the Holy Spirit who stirs up in the heart of the disciples of Christ love of this unity (See *ibid.,* no. 15), we entertain the hope that Christians who are not yet in the full communion of the one only Church will one day be reunited in one Flock with one only Shepherd.

23. We believe that the Church is *necessary for salvation, because Christ who is the sole Mediator and Way of salvation, renders Himself present for us in His Body which is the Church* (See *ibid.,* no. 14). But the divine design of salvation embraces all men; and those *who without fault on their part do not know the Gospel of Christ and His Church, but seek God sincerely, and under the influence of grace endeavor to do His will as recognized through the promptings of their conscience,* they, in a number known only to God, *can obtain salvation* (See *ibid.,* no. 16).

The current crisis of faith works out in practice to a massive upset and even loss of faith in the Roman Catholic Church, her Petrine foundation and Magisterium, and her seven sacraments, especially the central one, the Mass and Holy Eucharist. It is both a sign of the times and a providential blessing for catechetical teaching, therefore, that the *Creed of the People of God* devotes to these articles of the Catholic faith its lengthiest and most detailed sections.

It begins with the four marks of the one, true Church of God, in the exact words that the early Christians used.[149] "That the Church is 'one' means in the first place 'unique': Christ founded only one Church, even though this same *Creed* 'recognizes the existence, outside the organism of the Church of Christ, of numerous elements of truth and sanctification which belong to her as her own and tend to Catholic unity.' (par. no. 22, below). Then in the second place it means also the internal unity of the Church. To this unity internal dissensions are opposed, and in it the Church can always become more perfect. Nevertheless this internal unity is secured by God's protection of the 'unity of Church Government' (see *Denz.-Sch.* 3306). This two-fold interior unity of the Church is indestructible, for whoever loses either one of them departs from the Church by heresy or by schism. The Church is 'holy' in the ontological sense for it is the great means . . . by which God communicates His holiness; and also in the moral sense through the higher way of life and even heroic virtue that the Church by its nature produces in its members. (See *DS* 3013). The Church is 'Catholic' because . . . all men are called to form part of this new People of God (see Vat. II, *Constitution on the Church,* no. 13), and because as a matter of fact all nations do contribute members . . . 'Apostolicity,' in its original and traditional meaning, is linked with the idea of the apostolic succession, realized in the hierarchy of the Church. This Church, furthermore, 'is built upon that Rock which is Peter.' This alludes to Matthew 16, 18, and to the function of the Supreme Pontiff in keeping the Church 'one' (and hence of preserving the other three marks which are intimately bound up with the first). But also it determines the practical way of finding the true Church of Christ, for it is equivalent to that additional adjective often added to these four marks, namely the word 'Roman.' "[150] Catechetical teachers, needless to say, must go to the Catholic heritage of catechisms and theological literature when preparing their explanations, tailored to each particular teaching situation, of these condensed articles of the *Creed*.[151]

The official references in par. 19 to the Second Vatican Council's *Dogmatic Constitution on the Church* provide guidelines for teachers, giving the first place to go for the content of teaching on these various aspects of the Church, and for the precise way that the Catholic Church of this concrete history of the Christian era relates to the kingdom of God which Jesus preached, which He began, and which He will fully accomplish "beyond time in glory." It is important in teaching the Catholic faith to explain fully the fact affirmed here once again by the *Creed of the People of God* that the Church established by Jesus upon Peter, the Mystical Body of Christ, and the visible Roman Catholic Church of our ancestors and of today are "one and the same thing."[152] The primary resource material is to be found in the two encyclicals of Pope Pius XII, *Mystici corporis* (1943) and *Humani generis* (1950).

The Vicar of Christ points out the primary source in Vatican II, *Lumen gentium,* nos. 7 and 11, for catechetical teaching on the power and presence of God in the seven sacraments of His Church. Helpful perspectives are offered here to teachers on the right way of organizing and presenting courses on the history of the Church. The Pope alludes to St. Paul's teaching, Romans, Chapter 6 and offers the primary sources for elaborating a full catechesis on what it is to be a Catholic, dead to sin and risen to the new and higher life of union with the risen Christ. "The last words of this article contain a fundamental division in the kinds of grace: habitual or sanctifying grace, which 'gives life'; and actual grace, which is dynamic and 'gives movement.' "[153] This again opens out upon the heritage of Catholic theological literature and spiritual writings which teachers have to draw upon in their explanations of this doctrine of the Creed.

Then the *Creed,* at the end of par. 19, turns to a profession which contains the basis of the loyalty of each Catholic to the Church. These articles are especially helpful to catechists who work with high school youth. For the enemies of the Church see to it that objections abound against the divine character of the Roman Catholic Church, drawn from the human failings, past and present, of her members. "To say that only persons in the state of grace are members of the Church and that sinners are not, is to introduce the division between an invisible Church (declared to be the real Church) and the visible Church (declared to be only apparently the Church). This is the characteristic distinction made by all the Catharist or Puritan movements of history. The real Church, however, possesses the sanctifying life of grace, which it infuses into every member who does not place an obstacle to it. The members of the Church, of course, can refuse to let themselves be penetrated by this life, and as a matter of fact they do refuse. But the Church herself continues to be holy, 'without sin,' as Journet writes, 'but not without sinners'. . . . And she has the power to forgive these sins if her members ask. . . . The words of the *Creed* referring to 'the Gift of the Holy Spirit' are a definite allusion to John 20, 22–23: 'Receive the Holy Spirit. If you forgive the sins of any, they are forgiven; if you retain the sins of any, they are retained.' "[154] The creedal foundation for catechetical teaching on the Sacrament of Reconciliation or Penance is clear to see.

Paragraph 20 turns to the relationship of the Catholic Church to the universal history of mankind. "The 'kerygma' or deposit of revelation proceeds toward us, in one form or the other, from the Apostles. . . . 'This tradition which comes from the Apostles develops in the Church with the help of the Holy Spirit. For there is a growth in the understanding of the realities and the words which have been handed down.' See Vatican II, *Dogmatic Constitution on Divine Revelation,* no. 8, and Hebrews 1, 1ff."[155]

Paragraph 20 is a golden passage of the *Creed* for catechetical teachers. It provides the foundation for catechizing on the framework of salvation history and for using the Bible as St. Augustine directs and exemplifies in the catechetical classic of the early Church, his treatise on *The First Catechetical Instruction.* "At this point we should begin our narration," he writes, "starting out from the fact that God made all things very good (Gen. 1, 31), and continuing down to the present period of Church history, in such a way as to account for and explain the causes and reasons of each of the facts and events that we relate, and thereby refer them to that end of love from which in all our actions and words our eyes should never be turned away."[156] Everything depends on doing this teaching in the right way, not in carping negative criticism and hostility to the past, but in a wholesome manner, bringing into view what great things God has built into our entire human past for the eternal salvation of each human person, and for the earthly social welfare of mankind today. This is to teach biblical history and Church history in the spirit of faith; the principles are provided in the *Creed of the People of God,* particularly in the articles of faith of this and the preceding number.

The remaining statements of par. 20 profess the Catholic faith in the divine teaching authority, or "Magisterium," of the Catholic Church. They are of fundamental catechetical importance, for here the *Creed of the People of God* uses *verbatim* the solemn words of dogmatic definition given by the First Vatican Council.[157] It is difficult to exaggerate the importance and timeliness of this fact for catechetical teaching today. For one of the chief causes of the present unrest and upset, which motivated the Vicar of Christ to profess this *Creed* in communion with the entire People of God, as he states in the introductory paragraphs, is the influence upon catechists and religious educators of "theologians" who say they accept only the solemn definitions of the Extraordinary Magisterium, and proceed to subject the entire much more extensive body of revealed truth proposed so far only by the Ordinary and Universal Magisterium to the technique of unanswered questions, doubt, unbridled speculation, and, perhaps worst of all, omission in religion textbooks. As this article of the *Creed of the People of God* makes clear, such men are really not theologians at all, but only human, all too human "philosophers of religion."

"These two last articles of this number 20 of the *Creed* state who the persons are that exercise the infallible Magisterium of the Church: they are the Pope in his doctrinal definitions *ex cathedra,* as the First Vatican Council defined; and the College of Bishops, when they exercise the supreme Magisterium in communion with the Pope."[158] The words of the Second Vatican Council are clear: "Although the bishops, taken individually, do not enjoy the privilege of infallibility, they do, however, proclaim infallibly the doctrine of Christ on the following conditions: namely, when, even though dispersed throughout the world, but preserving for all that amongst themselves and with Peter's Successor the bond of communion, in their authoritative teaching concerning matters of faith and morals, they are in agreement that a particular teaching is to be held definitively and absolutely. This is still more clearly the case when, assembled in an ecumenical council, they are for the universal Church teachers and judges in matters of faith and morals, whose definitions must be adhered to with the loyal and obedient assent of faith."[159] This paragraph no. 25 of *Lumen gentium* is the primary source for catechetical teaching on the collegiality of the bishops and indeed for all teaching of the truth regarding the Magisterium. In these post-conciliar times particularly, characterized by the upsetting doctrinal irresponsibility that occasioned this *Creed of the People of God,* catechists, whether parents or teachers, have an obligation to follow closely the Ordinary Magisterium of the Roman Pontiff, the Vicar of Christ. This can be done, thanks to the contemporary development of the communications media.[160] For there is no other way to discern whether individual bishops, perhaps even entire conferences of bishops (let alone individual priests and "theological writers") are actually in clear and wholehearted communion with the Vicar of Christ at Rome. For an episcopal body, as the *Creed* states summarizing the Second Vatican Council, must be in communion with the visible head of the Church, the successor of St. Peter, in order to participate in the supreme Magisterium: then and only then does it "exercise with him the supreme Magisterium."

Turning briefly to the negative aspect of the matter, the *New Catechism* offers a prime illustration of the new post-conciliar problem in this area. For in certain of its statements it suggests an excessive dependence of the Pope in his Magisterium upon the ecclesial community.[161] The theologians representing the Holy See at the Gazzada Conference, accordingly, placed the primacy of the Roman Pontiff on the agenda with the following strong words: "The *Dutch Catechism* in treating of the primacy uses expressions that stupefy us. . . . It is true that what the Roman Pontiff teaches on the truth of the faith has already been believed, at least implicitly, by the universal Church. But could he not at some time or other teach what one part of the universal Church were putting in doubt, or what was not yet believed explicitly?"[162] The record of the discussion is illuminating as a revelation of the underlying character of the Neo-Modernist mentality, and hence valuable for a prudent discernment of spirits in the realm of catechetical teaching today. A translation of the substance of the discussion is therefore given here.

"The delegates of the Holy See think that the precise notion of the primacy is not given in the pages devoted to it, and that the primacy is even deemphasized. . . . One cannot say, as the *Dutch Catechism* does, that the Supreme Pontiff receives his faith, that is the body of revealed truth that he is to teach the ecclesial community, from the community itself. He receives it from Revelation by means of Sacred Scripture, which he interprets authentically, and likewise from primitive Tradition. It is true that the People of God, when it walks in the faith under the leadership of the hierarchy and especially the Supreme Pontiff, is also interiorly and directly led by the Spirit of truth toward an ever more full knowledge of Revelation. . . . But this direction by the Spirit is open to interpretation by the faithful in an erroneous way, and hence cannot be considered the only norm of faith. . . . (And they refer to the Papal primacy of jurisdiction over the bishops, defined by Vatican I, *Denz.-Sch.* 3064, as insufficiently recognized by the *Dutch Catechism*). Taking these observations into consideration, we request in all fraternity that the text of the *Dutch Catechism* be subjected to correction."[163]

The theologians representing the Dutch hierarchy showed no sign of yielding, and sought to interpret the *Dogmatic Constitution on Divine Revelation,* no. 10, on behalf of the approach of the *Dutch Catechism* by using what seems to be a very ordinary type of vitalist-existentialist philosophy. Thus the Roman Pontiff would be bound to follow the "vital experiencing" of the faithful in exercising his Magisterium.[164]

In their final word, the delegates of the Holy See stated that "they had weighed attentively the arguments advanced by the delegates of the bishops of Holland, but remain in the conviction that the passages of the *Dutch Catechism* under discussion do not give the exact meaning of the Roman primacy."[165]

"The two delegations therefore remain in their own distinct positions."[166] The text of the *Catechism* was of course not corrected. The final judgment of the commission of Cardinals on this point of doctrine has become a basic resource for use in the preparation of catechetical teaching.[167]

Turning to the unity of the Catholic Church in par. 21, the *Creed of the People of God* in its official text cites the Second Vatican Council, *Dogmatic Constitution on the Church,* no. 8 and nos. 18–23, and the *Decree on Ecumenism,* no. 2. These official references for some reason have been omitted entirely in the official English translation of the *Creed of the People of God* published by the United States Catholic Conference, Washington, D.C. This is regrettable, for these references are an indispensable source for a catechetical teaching which intends to proceed in the spirit of faith, handing on an adequate and comprehensively true concept of the Catholic Church. One could go so far as to say that these are the most timely material among all the references given by the Vicar of Christ officially in the notes which are a part of the *Creed of the People of God*. The catechist who studies them will recognize that they convey the full truth on the fact that God's Church is the concrete Roman Catholic Church of the historical Christian era and of today, a supernatural entity standing as something unique on the human scene, not to be identified with "this developing and evolving world" or with "mankind as a whole." Furthermore, the reference to the *Decree on Ecumenism* gives catechists the solid foundation for teaching true ecumenism, distinguishing it carefully from the false brand that has infiltrated into certain religion textbooks and teaching aids as part of the doctrinal aberration since Vatican II.[168] It is precisely the effort to avoid the positions laid down so clearly in these particular references to the Second Vatican Council that has been chiefly to blame for the rising chaos in contemporary religious education that occasioned this *Creed of the People of God*.

The *Creed* then turns to liturgical diversity in the Catholic Church. It is important for catechetical teaching to recognize that the unity of the Catholic Church is not rightly located in a rigid and frozen monolithic uniformity of liturgical ceremonies, whether backward to some particular period of Church history or laterally across the world from the Latin West to the Catholic Churches of the Eastern Rite. The ceremonies and the language with which the Holy Sacrifice of the Mass is offered have been changed by the legitimate authority of the Church many times since the Apostles as the circumstances of the apostolate have indicated: from Hebrew Aramaic, for example, into Greek and thence into Slavic, Latin and other languages. The important thing in this area of the ceremonies is again communion with Rome in faithful respect for the spirit of the Holy See and for its rubrical laws. For this safeguards respect for the Real Presence of Jesus Christ and for the supernatural purpose and power of the Mass and the Sacraments.[169] It is the Holy See that stands for holiness in the Sacred Liturgy, and this is the unity sought in the Liturgy. The unity of the Church as such, however, is in the realm of faith and Church government: see the *Creed,* par. no. 19.

Having laid the foundation for sound teaching on ecumenism, the *Creed of the People of God* turns in par. no. 22 to the principles regarding ecumenism itself. The first of these is quoted *verbatim* from the Second Vatican Council as indicated, where the desire for unity among all Christians is clearly recognized as a desire for that specific kind and quality of unity which has been identified as one of the four marks of the true Church of Jesus Christ.

The official reference to *Lumen Gentium,* no. 15, gives the wholesome catechetical attitude toward "those who, being baptized, are honored with the name of Christian, though they do not profess the faith in its entirety or do not preserve unity of communion with the Successor of Peter." It is important for catechetical teaching to recognize with the *Creed of the People of God* that it is the action of the Holy Spirit Himself which is leading such souls to desire and to look for the full, authentic unity of the Church. This safeguards catechetics against the pitfalls of the false ecumenism that would approach unity in a merely human way, giving up the full truth and divine constitution of the Catholic Church. Nothing could be more certain to frustrate the action of the Holy Spirit and disillusion the hopes of sincere souls "not yet in the full communion with the one only Church." It is clear that the Vicar of Christ is laying down helpful guidelines in this *Creed* for those who are called upon in any way to teach the Catholic faith.

The Creed concludes the profession of faith in the true ecumenism which is the work of the Holy Spirit by alluding to the words of the Gospel: "And I have other sheep, that are not of this fold; I must bring them also, and they will heed my voice. So there shall be one flock, one shepherd." (John 10, 16). The charter for a catechetical teaching that ministers to this hope is laid down in the same place of Vatican II which was cited in the previous note: "In all of Christ's disciples the Spirit arouses the desire to be peacefully united, in the manner determined by Christ, as one flock under one shepherd, and He prompts them to pursue this end. Mother Church never ceases to pray, hope and work that this may come about. She exhorts her children to purification and renewal so that the sign of Christ may shine more brightly over the face of the earth."

An indispensable prerequisite for this "purification and renewal" is a full and comprehensive catechesis of this "faith in the Roman Catholic Church" which the *Creed of the People of God* professes. For this will raise up the kind of members in this Church whose conversation and mode of life will foster rather than frustrate "the action of the Holy Spirit in . . . Christians who are not yet in the full communion of the one only Church. . . ."

Lastly, the *Creed* turns to the necessity of the Catholic Church for salvation. The profession of faith uses the teaching of Vatican II *verbatim* "in affirming the necessity of the Church for salvation. . . . Naturally, this doctrine must be explained in a way that preserves the divine design of salvation for all men. See 1 Tim. 2, 3ff."[170] The Vicar of Christ himself gives this explanation in the words that follow. He inserts the very words of Vatican II into the *Creed of the People of God*. The heritage of catechetical teaching on "baptism of desire" finds here its continuation and application.

"Although this article of the *Profession of Faith* does not go into detail, one should not forget, when teaching on these matters, the absolute necessity of faith as the factor which accomplishes this adhesion to the Church in order to be saved. Without entering into the further theological explanations, one can note that this doctrine has been defined by the Council of Trent (Session 6, chapter 8; *Denz.-Sch.* 1532) and repeated by Vatican II in the *Decree on the Church's Missionary Activity*, no. 7: 'Though God in ways known to Himself can lead those inculpably ignorant of the Gospel to find that faith without which it is impossible to please Him (Hebrews 11, 6), yet a necessity lies upon the Church (1 Cor. 9, 16), and at the same time a sacred duty, to preach the Gospel. And hence missionary activity today as always retains its power and necessity.' "[171]

X. THE SACRIFICE OF THE MASS AND THE HOLY EUCHARIST

24. We believe that the Mass, celebrated by the priest representing the person of Christ by virtue of the power received through the Sacrament of Orders, and offered by him in the name of Christ and the members of His Mystical Body, is in true reality the Sacrifice of Calvary, rendered sacramentally present on our altars. We believe that as the bread and wine consecrated by the Lord at the Last Supper were changed into His Body and His Blood which were to be offered for us on the Cross, likewise the bread and wine consecrated by the priest are changed into the Body and Blood of Christ enthroned gloriously in Heaven, and we believe that the mysterious presence of the Lord, under what continues to appear to our sense as before, is a true, real and substantial presence (See the Council of Trent, Session XIII, Decree on *The Eucharist; DS* 1651).

25. Christ cannot be thus present in this Sacrament except by the change into His Body of the reality itself of the bread and the change into His Blood of the reality itself of the wine, leaving unchanged only the properties of the bread and wine which our senses perceive. This mysterious change is very appropriately called by the Church *transubstantiation.* Every theological explanation which seeks some understanding of this mystery must, in order to be in accord with Catholic faith, maintain that in the reality itself, independently of our mind, the bread and wine have ceased to exist after the Consecration, so that it is the adorable Body and Blood of the Lord Jesus that from then on are really before us under the sacramental species of bread and wine (See ibid., DS 1642 and 1651; Paul VI, Encyclical *Mysterium fidei, AAS* 97 [1965] p. 766), as the Lord willed it, in order to give Himself to us as food and to associate us with the unity of His Mystical Body (See St. Thomas Aquinas, *S.Th.* III, 73, 3).

26. The unique and indivisible existence of the Lord glorious in Heaven is not multiplied, but is rendered present by the Sacrament in the many places on earth where Mass is celebrated. And this existence remains present, after the Sacrifice, in the Blessed Sacrament which is, in the tabernacle, the living heart of each of our churches. And it is our very sweet duty to honor and adore in the Blessed Host which our eyes see, the Incarnate Word Whom they cannot see, and Who, without leaving Heaven, is made present before us.

The *Creed of the People of God* has professed the Catholic faith in the sacraments in par. 18, for they apply the redemption to souls. The Holy Eucharist is singled out here because it is the central sacrament that contains the Divine Redeemer Himself, and because of the special doctrinal problems in post-conciliar religious education. The *Creed* professes its faith in the Mass and Holy Eucharist in these three carefully and meaningfully worded sections, nos. 24, 25, and 26, which may be considered the very heart of the pastoral action of the Vicar of Christ in the present "Crisis of Faith," especially from the viewpoint of catechetical teaching.

The first section contains four principal statements or formulas of doctrine.

The first doctrinal statement contains the answer of the Catholic faith to the questions, Who is a priest? What is a Catholic priest? What basically does a priest do? The answer is short, clear and pointed: the priest is set apart from the laity, for he represents the person of Christ by virtue of the power received through the Sacrament of Orders. Therefore no priest need have what some call an "identity crisis" and no layman need feel that there is any change in the answers to those questions which the Catholic heritage of teaching always has given. Above all, teachers and catechists have a positive, definite and solid position to stand upon when teaching what the priesthood of Jesus Christ is, what it most basically and fundamentally does, and the fact that the ministerial priesthood has special powers by which it is distinct from the universal priesthood of the laity.

The second doctrinal statement defines concisely and exactly *what the Mass is,* illustrating how the official printed catechism booklets of the Church derive from the formulas or Articles of the Creed. Absolutely basic to this definition is the fact that the Mass is a sacrifice. Then it states clearly what sacrifice it is: "the Mass is actually the Sacrifice of Calvary rendered sacramentally present on our altars."[172] Needless to say, these elements and fundamental formulations can be explained in varying detail, drawing on the Catholic heritage of theological and spiritual literature, as the circumstances of oral catechesis or the writing of religion textbooks may indicate. First among the resources for this teaching in the times after Vatican II is undoubtedly the Encyclical *Mysterium fidei* of this same Pope Paul VI, "On the Holy Eucharist" (Sept. 3, 1965).

On this point of Catholic doctrine the *New Catechism* illustrates once again the contemporary Neo-Modernist problem. "The *New Catechism* was reproached by the delegates of the Holy See at Gazzada because its statements do not recognize in the Mass the existence of a true sacrifice. . . . The words 'offered by the priest' in the *Creed* cannot be reduced to a participation in a banquet or meal. In fact, the communion is the same for both the priest-celebrant and the faithful, and is a participation that is on the same level for both."[173] The theologians of the Holy See placed the Eucharistic Sacrifice on the Gazzada Conference agenda as follows: "The *Dutch Catechism* in its treatment of the Eucharist places the emphasis on the meal-aspect, and speaks of thanksgiving but not of propitiation. Is this not perhaps a one-sided approach?"[174] At the Gazzada Conference itself, they stated their position in these words: "The delegates of the Holy See cannot approve the text of the *New Catechism* in the following points taken almost literally from it: (a) In the celebration of the Mass, strictly speaking, we do not offer a sacrifice; (b) In the celebration we unite ourselves with the Sacrifice of Christ (and this is correct) principally through Holy Communion (and this cannot be approved). . . . See the Encyclical *Mediator Dei* of Pope Pius XII (*AAS* [1947]) and the Second Vatican Council, *Constitution on the Sacred Liturgy,* no. 48, where the act whereby we participate in the sacrificial offering is kept distinct from the act of receiving Communion, in which the adorable Victim of the Sacrifice deigns to unite Himself with us as the source of our Supernatural Life. . . . If the Communion, which the faithful in general receive, is the principal way of our union with the Sacrifice of Christ, then certainly one understands how it can be asserted that in the celebration of the Mass, strictly speaking, we do not offer a sacrifice. . . . It is necessary to insist that this text be fully corrected, and we must say further that this implies a series of other corrections so that the exposition of doctrine on the Eucharist be consistent and homogeneous throughout."[175] This of course was what did not take place, to the on-going detriment of religious education today.

In the preparation of catechetical teaching, the final judgment of the commission of Cardinals on this point of doctrine ought to be given careful consideration.[176] The *New (Dutch) Catechism* in its present text and supplement ought to be studied carefully, for they help catechetical teaching to become more aware of the solemn significance of the *Creed of the People of God* in this matter.[177] Even in the supplement, Catholic catechists will find it difficult to recognize where the *New (Dutch) Catechism* has corrected its teaching really and from the heart; in fact, the doctrine which the Vicar of Christ teaches in *Mysterium fidei,* and which he was to profess more solemnly in no. 25 of this *Creed,* is simply shrugged off as "the way he sees it."[178] In any case, religious educators and textbook evaluators can recognize from this confrontation what the difference is between a clear presentation of the Catholic faith, and a Neo-Modernist approach that verbosely obscures or even deviates from the authentic meaning of the Catholic faith. Furthermore, it reveals a primary source of much current aberration in the field of religious education toward reducing the

Sacrifice of the Mass to the level simply of "a meal," a not insignificant aspect of the confusion and doctrinal upset which made this *Creed of the People of God* a pastoral necessity.[179]

The third doctrinal statement bears upon the consecration at Mass. "With these words, taking the Last Supper as its point of departure, the *Creed of the People of God* begins to treat of the change of the consecrated bread and wine into the body and blood of the Lord, 'under the appearances of these things,' as the consequence of that change. This begins all those great themes which will be developed in no. 25 of the *Creed*. . . . The reference to the Last Supper as something unique is indispensable when speaking of the real presence in the Holy Eucharist, for that was the institution of this sacrament and the first realization of the eucharistic change. See, for example, how the Council of Trent proceeds in its teaching (Session 13, chapter one; *Denz.-Sch.* 1637). On the contrary, it does not contribute to clearness when speaking of the real presence to begin by discussing the Last Supper as if it were simply another among the meals taken by the apostles with Jesus during His earthly life, as some modern texts do. This dilutes the meaning of the Last Supper."[180] No additional commentary appears to be needed. Again, it is the content of the doctrine which catechetical methodology ought to serve, for otherwise catechesis cannot be a true ministry of the word. When methods become too autonomous and undisciplined, they tend to reveal the current "crisis of faith" regarding the creedal content of catechetical teaching.

In the fourth doctrinal statement, the *Creed* makes use of the three words a *"true, real and substantial"* presence, taken *verbatim* from the dogmatic definition of the Council of Trent: "To begin with, the holy Council (of Trent) teaches and openly and straightforwardly professes that in the Blessed Sacrament of the Holy Eucharist, after the consecration of the bread and wine, our Lord Jesus Christ, true God and man, is truly, really and substantially contained under the perceptible species of bread and wine."[181] "These words are repeated in the *Creed of the People of God* to avoid an equivocation: the presence of Christ among the faithful is indeed *real,* and hence can be in this sense also called *true;* but the presence of Christ in the Eucharist is on a different plane (from His other ways of being present) precisely because it is *substantial,* that is to say, because in the Eucharist the entire reality of the Incarnate Word is made present."[182]

The other modes of Christ's presence are discussed, for example, in the Second Vatican Council, *Constitution on the Sacred Liturgy,* no. 7, and in *Mysterium fidei,* the Encyclical of Pope Paul VI on the Holy Eucharist (Sept. 3, 1965), nos. 35–39. Some religious educators today contribute to confusion by treating of the Holy Eucharist as if it were simply one of these other modes of presence, without its own unique and sublime mode, "special" as Vatican II puts it. Catechetical teaching benefits by the fact that the Magisterium in the documents cited exemplifies perfect clarity: "This presence is called 'real' " the Vicar of Christ teaches, "by which it is not intended to exclude all other types of presence as if they were not 'real,' but it is presence par excellence: because it is a substantial presence by which the whole and complete Christ, God and Man, is present. . . . One would therefore falsely explain this manner of presence . . . by restricting it to the limits of symbolism as if this most august sacrament consisted of nothing else than an efficacious sign of the spiritual presence of Christ and of His intimate union with the faithful members of His Mystical Body."[183]

Paragraph no. 25 of The *Creed of the People of God* professes the Catholic Faith in the Real Presence. "What is here expressed in the *Creed of the People of God* as the object of faith is the fact that the Eucharistic Presence, as expressed in the words of institution at the Last Supper and as the Church has understood these words, cannot be explained except by this change of the reality itself."[184] This is the meaning of the dogmatic definition of the Council of Trent on the transubstantiation (Session 13; *Denz.-Sch.* 1642): "Because Christ our Redeemer said that it was truly His body that He was offering under the species of bread (See Mt. 26, 26ff; Mark 14, 22ff.; Luke 22, 19ff; 1 Cor. 11, 24ff.), it has always been the conviction of the Church, and this holy Council now again declares that, by the consecration of the bread and wine, a change takes place in which the whole substance of bread is changed into the substance of the body of Christ our Lord and the whole substance of the wine into the substance of His blood. This change the Holy Catholic Church fittingly and properly names transubstantiation." And the corresponding Canon (*DS* 1652): "If any one says that the substance of bread and wine remain in the holy sacrament of the Eucharist together with the body and blood of our Lord Jesus Christ, and denies that wonderful and extraordinary change of the whole substance of the bread into Christ's body and the whole substance of the wine into his blood while only the species of bread and wine remain, a change which the Catholic Church has most fittingly called transubstantiation: let him be anathema."[185]

Pope Paul VI explains this same doctrine helpfully for teachers and catechists in his encyclical *Mysterium fidei, nos.* 46–55. In teaching, it is good to note the word "reality" used in the *Creed* as an identical alternate to the word "substance" to denote the same thing in the objective extramental being of the bread and the wine. This is in the interest of perhaps better communication with the modern mentality, which sometimes has prejudices against the word "substance" due to the influence of some types of contemporary philosophizing. This use of the alternate word is in the spirit of Pope John XXIII, who when opening Vatican II was concerned that we express the changeless realities of the Catholic faith in a way that communicates in the best and clearest way possible with modern men.

The *Creed of the People of God* uses the word *transubstantiation*. It would be difficult to imagine a more clear and explicit reaffirmation of the teaching of the Council of Trent which was quoted in the preceding note. Catechetical teaching should recognize and respect this insistence by the Magisterium in its living actuality in the times *after* Vatican II that this term "transubstantiation" be preserved in contemporary religious education. For the clear elaboration of this point, see the encyclical of Pope Paul VI, *Mysterium fidei,* nos. 24–25: "The norm, therefore, of speaking which the Church after centuries of toil and under the protection of the Holy Spirit has established and confirmed by the authority of Councils, and which has become more than once the watchword and standard of correct belief, is to be religiously preserved and let no one at his own good pleasure or under the pretext of new science presume to change it. Who indeed would tolerate it that the dogmatic formulae which the ecumenical councils used concerning the mysteries of the Most Blessed Trinity and the Incarnation be declared unsuited to the men of our age and that other formulae be rashly substituted? In like manner we are not to tolerate anyone who on his own authority wishes to downgrade the formulae in which the Council of Trent sets forth the Mystery of the Eucharist for our belief. For by these formulae, as by the rest which the Church uses to express the dogmas of the faith, concepts are expressed which are not tied to one specific form of human civilization, nor definite period of scientific progress, nor one school of theological thought, but they present what the human mind by universal and necessary experience grasps of realities and expresses in suitable and accurate terminology, taken either from the language commonly in use or from polished diction. For this reason, these formulae are suitable to men of all times and all places. The formulae can indeed, and this is highly beneficial, be more clearly and plainly explained, but only in the same meaning they originally had, so that as the knowledge of the Faith increases the truth of the Faith remains unchanged. It is the teaching of the First Vatican Council: 'that meaning of the sacred dogmas must forever be retained which Holy Mother Church has once defined and we may never depart from that meaning under the pretext and in the name of deeper understanding.' "[186]

By these words the *New Catechism* and the Neo-Modernist approach which it illustrates stand revealed as fundamentally unsound. The basic orientation of historical relativism, as if "now" we do indeed have a "deeper understanding," evacuates the original meaning of the sacred dogmas which our Catholic heritage in catechesis since the apostles has taught so precisely and professed so clearly. The approach of the *New Catechism* to this article of the faith is an illuminating example of the approach for it presents this doctrine as a mere explanation belonging to "the Middle Ages," *without even mentioning* the dogmatic definition of the Council of Trent.[187] Furthermore, this approach, in addition to suffering from this widespread and easily recognizable philosophical, historical, and cultural relativism, as if some dialectic had indeed outmoded the Catholic past, is not even scholarly. For, as Pozo points out, the introduction of the terms "substance" and "species" and "change" into eucharistic explanations does not originate in the Middle Ages but is rooted in the early Church, extending back into the times of the Fathers of the Church.[188] Catechetical teaching and textbook evaluation ought to be on guard against what is actually a verbose and subtly confusing form of philosophical propaganda slanted toward a departure from the historic meaning of the sacred dogmas which the Church has defined in the past, under the pretext and in the name of deeper "modern" understanding. This in reality is nothing else than a form of intellectual pride, as noted by Pope Paul VI in his first encyclical, *Ecclesiam suam,* "Paths of the

Church," no. 26. It ought not to be allowed to touch the Catholic children and young people, for they are born with a personal right to be taught carefully, accurately, and precisely the authentic content and meaning of the Catholic faith.

Then the *Creed* states accurately what is to be believed about "transsignification." The official reference is to no. 46 of *Mysterium fidei,* which comes to grips with the contemporary "theological explanations" which use the terms "transsignification" and "transfinalization," sometimes with the intention of avoiding "transubstantiation," the ontological reality of the change and of Christ's Real Presence, "in the reality itself, independently of our mind." Again, therefore, the timeliness of this *Creed of the People of God* is made manifest, together with its helpfulness to catechetics by setting an example of precision and clarity in teaching. There is a tendency today to teach that the reality of the bread has changed because its purpose or meaning is changed by the consecration. "This formulation of doctrine is insufficient. The real presence of Christ in the Eucharist does not consist in a change of signification (meaning) or of finalization (purpose) (in the bread and wine). It is true that His real presence implies a new purpose: Christ makes Himself present 'in order to give Himself to us as food and to associate us with the unity of His Mystical Body' (as the *Creed of the People of God* goes on to say). But, as the encyclical *Mysterium fidei* expressly emphasizes, this new purpose is *consequent upon* the real presence, not prior to it or constitutive of it. (See no. 46) . . . The *Creed* affirms this with strength and clarity. The real presence of the Lord is prior to the change in purpose. The *Creed* insists on the ontological character of the change (in the bread and wine) locating it 'in reality itself, independently of our mind.' These words are of supreme importance, because a mere new purpose for the bread and wine would not be something *independent of our mind.* . . . In fact, after the consecration the consecrated species retain their original earthly power and purpose in the satisfying of bodily hunger. . . . The *Creed* makes the clean-cut affirmation that 'the bread and wine have *ceased to exist* after the Consecration,' with the result that the only aspect of them that remains is the 'sacramental species' that we perceive with our senses. Thus the question is on a much deeper level than a mere change of purpose or 'transfinalization.' "[189]

The *New Catechism* was reproached by the theologians of the

Holy See regarding this point of doctrine. They placed it on the Gazzada Conference agenda as follows: "The exposition in the *Dutch Catechism* is an attempt at presenting the eucharistic 'change' not in the category of 'transubstantiation' (which it attributes to the Middle Ages and without mentioning the Council of Trent), but in the category of a change in destination or purpose without however using the word 'transfinalization.' "[190] After re-stating the Catholic faith in terms that reflect Trent and the encyclical *Mysterium fidei,* the delegates of the Holy See spoke carefully: "Fraternally, but at the same time insistently, we request that the *Dutch Catechism* devote itself to giving this meaning of the doctrine to its readers in a manner that is *clear* and *evident*."[191] "The delegation of the Holy See considers it a duty to request that the explanation which the *Dutch Catechism* gives of *transubstantiation* be corrected."[192] In their replies, the theologian-delegates of the Dutch hierarchy held stubbornly to their different doctrine, that the Holy Spirit through the priest at Mass confers *a new meaning* on the bread and wine, saying that the *Dutch Catechism* simply abstains from 'the Aristotelian interpretation,' as the *Dutch Catechism* theologians term the teaching which has now been professed anew by the *Creed of the People of God.*[193]

At the end the Report states laconically the inherently tragic outcome: "the delegation of the Holy See insists upon its request for correction," and, "The Dutch delegation insists upon its answer."[194] The text of the *New Catechism* was of course not corrected.

Finally, in this essential paragraph, the *Creed* formulates the divine purpose in giving mankind this Holy Sacrament, and refers to St. Thomas Aquinas. As mentioned above, the *Creed of the People of God* professes here its faith in the new purpose which becomes understandable as a *result* of the consecration at Mass, *because of the transubstantiation*. The bread and wine are now the Heavenly Bread, the Bread of Angels, the Bread of Life: see John 6, 48–70, and the official catechisms of Christian doctrine in their answers regarding the purpose of the Holy Eucharist. The reference to the Mystical Body should be linked in catechesis and religious education with the articles of faith in the Roman Catholic Church professed by the *Creed* in nos. 19–23, above.

In paragraph 26, the *Creed of the People of God* turns to the practical consequences of the Roman Catholic faith in the Holy

Eucharist for the actual spiritual life of the Church and her members. This again is timely in view of the post-conciliar crisis of faith and the doctrinal confusion which it causes. It is difficult to exaggerate the present need in catechetical teaching not only to instruct but also to exemplify in practice the fact of the real presence, the continuing existence of the risen Lord Jesus Christ, just as He is in heaven, "in the tabernacle, the living heart of our churches." This is the central factor in catechesis *as formation*. It is especially noteworthy that the Vicar of Christ reaffirms the teaching of the Council of Trent (Session 13 and Canon 6; *Denz.-Sch.* 1656) on the adoration which is due to the Incarnate Word really present in the Blessed Sacrament: "If anyone says that Christ, the only-begotten Son of God, is not to be adored in the holy sacrament of the Eucharist with the worship of latria, including external worship, and that the sacrament, therefore, is not to be honored with extraordinary festive celebrations nor solemnly carried from place to place in processions according to the praiseworthy universal rite and custom of the holy Church; or that the sacrament is not to be publicly exposed for the people's adoration, and that those who adore it are idolators: let him be anathema."[195]

The Neo-Modernist approach, illustrated again in the *New Catechism,* has a characteristically different way of understanding the presence of Christ at Mass and hence of the reservation of the Eucharist. "All that has been said about his presence remains true here. It is a visible sign that the Lord is as personally close to his Church as he was among his Apostles. We should try to remain reverently and thankfully aware of this presence whenever we enter church. It is an excellent custom to genuflect or kneel when we enter or leave."[196] "Is this not something more than an excellent custom . . .?"[197] The *New (Dutch) Catechism* discusses "the duration of the Eucharistic presence" in its wonted verbose and subtly deceptive mode.[198] Catechists and teachers concerned with a teaching that is in wholehearted communion with the Magisterium should compare its approach carefully with that of the Council of Trent, the *Creed of the People of God* and the Encyclical *Mysterium fidei* of Pope Paul VI, nos. 54–76, the rich source for the full explanations needed both in oral catechesis and in the writing of religion textbooks.[199]

This encounter of the *Creed of the People of God* with the creedlessness of the *New Catechism* and its ongoing satellite religious education programs might well be called "Christianity at the Crossroads." The doctrine of the Catholic faith in the real presence is not a mere abstraction or a speculation unrelated to life. It must work out into the habits and practices of authentic Catholic spiritual life, both in the worthy reception of Holy Communion and in the worshipful recognition of the continuing real presence in the tabernacle, else it is mere instruction instead of personal formation. Actions and example speak louder than words. And for a formation of Catholic children and young people in terms of this particular sublime truth which the Catholic faith professes, there must be habitual example regarding "the living heart of each of our churches."

XI. THE CHURCH IN THE MODERN WORLD

27. We confess that the Kingdom of God begun here below in the Church of Christ *is not of this world* (see John 18, 36) *whose form is passing* (see 1 Cor. 1, 31), and that its proper growth cannot be confounded with the progress of civilization, of science or of human technology, but that it consists in an ever more profound knowledge of the unfathomable riches of Christ, an ever stronger hope in eternal blessings, an ever more ardent response to the Love of God, and an ever more generous bestowal of grace and holiness among men. But it is this same love which induces the Church to concern herself constantly about the true temporal welfare of men. Without ceasing to recall to her children that *they have not here a lasting dwelling* (See Hebrews 13, 14), she also urges them to contribute, each according to his vocation and his means, to the welfare of their earthly city, to promote justice, peace and brotherhood among men, to give their aid freely to their brothers, especially to the poorest and most unfortunate. The deep solicitude of the Church, the Spouse of Christ, for the needs of men, for their joys and hopes, their griefs and efforts, is therefore nothing other than her great desire to be present to them, in order to illuminate them with the light of Christ and to gather them all in Him, their only Savior. This solicitude can never mean that the Church conform herself to the things of this world, or that she lessen the ardour of her expectation of her Lord and of the eternal Kingdom.

With two quotations from St. John and St. Paul the *Creed of the People of God* begins to profess the basic truths that govern the relationship between the Catholic Church and this world. These are the truths that guide Catholic social doctrine and social action. These articles of faith are again timely because of the emerging concern and role of the Church in "The Development of the Peoples," the title of Pope Paul's Encyclical *Populorum progressio* (March 26, 1967). For the effect of the "Crisis of Faith" is to induce aberration into this role by attempting to "secularize" the Church and her apostolate, as if she were indeed *of this world* and as if, far from passing away, this world were to go on evolving indefinitely to ever greater development of this its present form.

Catechists and teachers of religion will raise up members of the Church who are authentic Christians in adult life and social action, only if their catechesis and the religion texts they choose or compose are authentic catechetical explanations of the fundamentals laid down in this compressed section of the *Creed of the People of God.*

The *Creed* begins by reaffirming the teaching of the Second Vatican Council, *Dogmatic Constitution on the Church,* no. 5, that the Church on earth is "the seed and the beginning" of the Kingdom of God.[200] Hence it must grow and make progress. It is important for catechetics in the confused aberrations after Vatican II to be clear and explicit regarding the character of this authentic growth and progress of the Church as a whole and of each member personally. "This progress stands on the supernatural level, just as the reality at the end of history is itself supernatural toward which the Church is advancing."[201] The *Creed of the People of God* is explicit: the growth of the Church as a whole, and of each of her members personally, takes place in terms of grace and holiness, in terms of the love of God, the transcendent personal God of this profession of faith.

With the statement from Hebrews 13, 14, holding fast to the truth that man's final destiny is not confined to this world, the *Creed of the People of God* rejects the atheistic view of religion, namely that its otherworldliness "thwarts . . . man's economic and social emancipation . . . by raising man's hopes in a future life, thus both deceiving him and discouraging him from working for a better form of life on earth."[202] The contrary is true, as the Second Vatican Council teaches (*ibid.,* no. 21) and as the Vicar of Christ professes here in the name of the entire Church of God.

The key concept which ought to be communicated clearly in catechetical teaching is the fact that *"it is this same love,"* namely the
theological virtue of charity, the same love of God just mentioned,
which motivates and induces the concern of the Church for the temporal welfare of mankind. "It is clear that the earthly social activities
of the Christian must be born not of a mere humanist love but from a
charity, *agape,* which is always the theological virtue and primarily
God-centered in its orientation. Furthermore, the adjective 'true' as
used here is not without special meaning. 'The *true* temporal welfare
of man' is much more than mere technological progress. This, in and
of itself, is something ambivalent, for progress in one line often provokes regress in another. When technological progress takes place in
isolation, and is proposed as the only factor in development without
all those other factors that a complete concept of man involves, it
arouses those anguished questions that even today many are asking:
'Will not technological progress perhaps make us slaves of technology?'
It behooves us to emphasize that only a temporal social activity born
of charity assures us that we will not be serving such a dehumanizing
process. For when authentic charity guides the problems and processes
of temporal development, it will be a development that cultivates an
integral humanism, one that does not overlook the spiritual and
religious dimensions of man."[203]

Parents and teachers whose catechesis is limited to a simple yet
comprehensive communication of the truths of the Catholic Religion
may not have occasion or opportunity to elaborate fully the social
doctrine of the Church and its Christian humanism. This it is the
privilege of the full-fledged Catholic school to do. But without that
complete and God-centered catechesis of all the earlier articles of this
Creed of the People of God, Christian social doctrine necessarily lacks
its foundation and Christian humanism its substance.

Then the *Creed* turns to Christian concern for true social welfare.
This article professes a vitally important truth of Christian social
doctrine, the fact that Jesus Christ, God Incarnate, is the only Savior
of men, even in their earthly lives and in their social problems of the
temporal order. A catechetical teaching that is clear and explicit on
this point is an external grace which helps to guard the members of
the Church from putting their hope and trust in the promises of any
earthly "savior" who may come in his own name. It is upon this

article of the *Creed of the People of God,* furthermore, that catechetical teaching, in developing programs and textbooks, can build up the wealth of doctrine on the apostolate of the laity: for the Church's concern with the true temporal welfare of men is first and of foremost the preoccupation of the laity, not directly of priests and religious. See the Second Vatican Council, the *Dogmatic Constitution on the Church,* no. 31, and the *Decree on the Apostolate of the Laity* in its entirety.[204]

For contemporary catechetical teaching, the concluding statement of this paragraph is one of the most helpful and illuminating articles professed in the entire *Creed of the People of God.* For it is a forthright rejection of the Modernist approach and its concept of the relationship between the Church and the modern world. The program of this way of thinking impacts heavily upon catechetics, for it alters the meaning of the dogmas of the Catholic faith precisely by conforming them to the contemporary popular thought-patterns of this world, deriving from modern philosophies which are already in apostasy from God.[205]

Nor is the *Creed of the People of God* merely negative regarding the general attitude and approach of the Neomodernists. It offers to catechetical teaching the positive content of doctrine which, if properly explained and emphasized, overcomes the modernist temptation and protects Catholic children and young people from its denaturing, degenerating and deviating effect upon the meaning and substance of the Catholic faith. This is the doctrine of the *parousia,* the second coming of Jesus Christ at the end of history. This has been professed by the *Creed* since the Apostles. The more catechists keep this expectation of the Lord alive in their teaching, the more authentic will be the contemporary renewal of the mind and spirit of the Early Church, including its *Marana tha!*—the greeting and ardent aspiration of that heroic Church of the catacombs and the martyrs: "Our Lord, come!" (1 Cor. 16, 22), "Come, Lord Jesus!" (Revelation 22, 20).[206] It is of interest for a truly contemporary catechesis to note that the Vatican II renewal of the Sacred Liturgy is characterized by a striking emphasis upon this same spirit of the *Marana tha,* "the ardent expectation of the Lord and of the eternal kingdom," as the *Creed of the People of God* expresses it. This becomes especially clear when the new *Roman Missal* of Pope Paul VI (Rome: 1970) is compared with the Tridentine Missal of Pope Paul V (Rome: 1570). When at last the unworthy liturgical aberrations which are a part of the current "Crisis of Faith" subside, and the Catholic heritage of reverence, beauty and dignity in worship is recovered, catechists will enter upon an attractive new era of teaching regarding the true significance of the Second Vatican Council.

XII. THE LAST THINGS

28. We believe in the life eternal. We believe that the souls of all those who die in the grace of Christ, whether they must still be purified in Purgatory, or whether from the moment they leave their bodies Jesus takes them to Paradise as He did for the Good Thief, are the People of God in the eternity beyond death, which will be finally conquered on the day of the Resurrection when these souls will be reunited with their bodies.

29. We believe that the multitude of those gathered around Jesus and Mary in Paradise forms the Church of Heaven, where in eternal beatitude they see God as He is (See 1 John 3, 12; Benedict XII, Const. *Benedictus Deus,* DS 1000), and where they also, in different degrees, are associated with the holy Angels in the divine rule exercised by Christ in glory, interceding for us and helping our weakness by their brotherly care (See Vatican II, *Lumen gentium,* no. 49).

30. We believe in the communion of all the faithful of Christ, those who are pilgrims on earth, the dead who are attaining their purification, and the blessed in Heaven, all together forming one Church; and we believe that in this communion the merciful love of God and His Saints is ever listening to our prayers, as Jesus told us: Ask and you will receive (See Luke 10, 1–10; John 16, 24). Thus it is with faith and in hope that we look forward to the resurrection of the dead, and the life of the world to come. Blessed be God Thrice Holy. Amen.

Finally, the *Creed of the People of God* professes in these paragraphs the truths of the Catholic faith which reveal the Last Things which lie before each human person. "This act of faith in life everlasting proceeds from . . . the Apostles' Creed. The expression 'everlasting life' occurs frequently in the Gospels, both in the Synoptics and in St. John. . . . See Mt. 19, 16; 25, 46; Mark 10, 17; John 5, 24; 6, 47; 6, 55; 1 John 3, 9. . . . 'Everlasting life' . . . is not merely existing endlessly; it is existing in the fullest, most self-fulfilled way, the fullness which means perfect happiness, and which results from the possession of God."[207]

The fact of purgatory is clearly stated. "The *Creed of the People of God* takes this occasion to affirm the existence of purgatory as a state of purification prior to possessing God, for all the just who need to be purified. . . . The entire context of this section of the *Creed* develops the concept of 'everlasting life' in relationship to the intermediate eschatology of the departed souls, the period between death and the resurrection of the body. Without question, the Vicar of Christ is very deliberately emphasizing this eschatology of the departed souls, and affirming their reality."[208]

The *New Catechism,* in both the original text and the authors' Supplement, casts doubt on the distinction between body and soul and hence upon the reality of the departed souls.[209] The theologians of the Holy See placed the matter on the Gazzada Conference agenda: "It is not easy to understand what the *Dutch Catechism* has in mind. . . . The beatific vision is hardly mentioned. . . . But is it not precisely this vision of God that establishes the soul forever in the love of God, thus giving our existence its supreme religious meaning? Is this not a defect to correct in the Catechism?"[210] In the discussion at Gazzada, the theologians representing the Holy See state that the approach of the *Dutch Catechism* "is destined to cause perplexity in the minds of its readers."[211] Again the result was fruitless. Catechetical teaching can only consult the judgment of the commission of Cardinals.[212]

"Death will be finally conquered." This is the Catholic profession of faith in the coming personal victory over death to which each of the faithful looks forward when each soul will be reunited with its own body in the resurrection to come. This article of the Catholic faith in the resurrection was born in the Church on the first Easter morning, was stated with incomparable clarity by St. Paul, 1 Cor. 15, and has been constantly emphasized by the Magisterium across the Christian era to this present *Creed of the People of God.*[213] In the documents of this divine Tradition, there is a recurring stress upon the fact that we are to rise "in this same flesh, with which we now live"; "in the same flesh that I have now"; "a resurrection of this flesh which we have now and not of some other"; "they shall rise with their own bodies which they have now." This is exactly the emphasis of the *Creed of the People of God:* "will be reunited *with their bodies.*" "The numerical identity of the present and the risen body is a truth of Catholic dogma, whatever be the way theologians develop for explaining *how* this is to come about; this is a separate question, and ought not to be confused with the fact professed by the Faith."[214]

The *New Catechism* creates a problem by seeming not to affirm any relationship between our present body and our future resurrected body.[215] It might be noted that the Neo-Modernist approach is in constantly recurring doctrinal difficulty partly because of its hidden substrate of vitalist-existentialist philosophy. Catechetical teaching in the Church needs more than ever to be loyal to the pastoral program of the Holy See in philosophical teaching. When this is done, and the natural metaphysics of mankind is used as the natural foundation in catechetical explanations, the mental blocks to this and other doctrines of the Catholic faith begin to disappear.

Catechetical teaching needs to be clear and not confusing on this particularly vital article of the Catholic faith. For this revealed truth is the basis for conveying a sense of wonder and joy at the things which God has prepared for these who love Him. It generates the Christian hope that in heaven we shall see and know not only God and His Saints but also our own loved ones in the physical characteristics of their individual human personality. Entire families will be together again. True friendships that began in time, but had the substance of the immortal from their beginning, will blossom again in perfected form. It is this unique and priceless value of the Catholic faith as the key of Heaven that parents defend when in their parental love for their children they insist upon its full and unadulterated communication by authentic catechetical teaching.

Just as the "intermediate eschatology of the departed souls" was the primary consideration of the preceding section, so in par. 29 the *Creed of the People of God* considers the Church Triumphant, the Church of Heaven formed by all who are with Jesus and Mary and enjoy the beatific vision. "Seeing God just as He is ought not to be conceived as some sort of cold contemplation of Platonic ideas. It will be an intimate interpersonal communion. . . . It is this idea of intimacy, from which the joy of the blessed flows forth, that is primary in undertsanding what everlasting life will be like."[216]

The angels and the saints in heaven pray and intercede for us. The *Creed* continues the profession of this article of faith in these post-conciliar times. The intercession of Mary ever Virgin and of the saints to help our weakness is a constant reality in the life of prayer that characterizes the Catholic Church in all ages from the apostles through our own times and on to the second coming of Jesus Christ.[217]

This commentary has reported frequently Rome's reproaches and demands for corrections in the text of the *New (Dutch) Catechism*. This has been done in the belief that some good may accrue to catechetical teaching from an insight into precisely how discourse on the things of faith may fail to measure up to the magisterium. The attitudes and positions of the *New Catechism* have been imitated widely in religious education programs and textbooks which are implementing the Neo-Modernist approach.

Putting it positively, a knowledge of the facts regarding this fundamental catechetical confrontation of these post-conciliar years leads to a better understanding of what it is to catechize and to compose religion textbooks in a spirit of communion with the Holy See. A comment may be in order therefore, on the role of prayer in catechesis and religious education in connection with profession of faith in intercessory prayer made by the *Creed of the People of God*. Mere instruction in the knowledge of the Catholic faith is not sufficient for Catholic children and young people, and cannot be acceptable to parents and teachers as their goal. Instruction is indeed necessary as a *part* of the method that leads to the goal of personal conviction and practice of the Catholic faith; but it is only a part. The other and more important part (as St. Augustine pointed out in the early Church) is prayer, prayer on the part of the one who teaches, and prayer fostered and becoming a habit in the young Catholic who is studying and learning his Catholic faith.[218] This is perhaps the chief general objection to the *New Catechism* and to those religion textbooks that follow its lead and seek to communicate its mentality. *Non sapit ibi Jesu,* "There is no taste of Jesus there," as St. Bernard puts it. Such textbooks are filled unto bulging with dry and sterile information. Much of this information is of course true, but the general impact of it is misleading, untrue and inauthentic, when considered from the catechetical viewpoint of clear and helpful communication of the truths of the Catholic faith, as such, just as they are, just as they have been since the apostles, and just as they will be until the second coming of Jesus Christ. This opposed orientation in religious education lacks the spirit of prayer. It wants only the human sciences. This is because it is not clear to itself on the real existence of the personal God of Abraham, Isaac and Jacob, the Eternal Father of Jesus Christ. It is not clear on the reality of the other world, that higher mode of existing that our heritage calls Heaven. Agnostics and atheists do not pray because they cannot pray, and it follows that they cannot bring the spirit of prayer either into their oral catechesis or into the books they write under the title of religious education. "You will know them by their fruits." (Mt. 7, 20). The first fruit, the touchstone which Catholic parents and teachers look for, is prayerful, humble and openly declared communion with the Holy See: for this gives communion with the unbroken heritage of teaching that comes to us from the apostles. This commentary has had no other end in view but to gather documented sources of information and evidence which help to make more visible this supreme fact of a divine teaching that stands in human history, the same yesterday, today and forever, always one and the same in the witness to Jesus as our Lord.

The concluding section of the *Creed of the People of God* is devoted to the dogma of the Communion of the Saints and the resulting life of prayer that binds the faithful of the Church on earth with the departed souls in purgatory and with the saints and angels in heaven. This is that spirit of faith in a personal God and the reality of that other and better world which is the goal of the Christian hope. Catechetical teaching is a formation which raises the mind and heart upwards, toward this transcendent reality. This is the very definition of prayer. It is this which enables catechetical teaching to be a spiritual formation, for it correlates its teaching of the Catholic faith with the habit and practice of prayer. This alone gives entrance into the Communion of the Saints and participation in the happy life of the Blessed.

The *Creed of the People of God* closes with a participation in the life of worship that will take place forever after the resurrection of the dead, in the everlasting life to come. The Bible in several places gives us an insight into this heavenly worship: Isaiah 6, 3; Revelation 5, 12ff, and indeed in the Apocalypse or Book of Revelation as a whole. The sacred liturgy of the Catholic Church on earth is both an anticipation and already an earthly participation in this heavenly liturgy. This is the fundamental reason why an authentic catechesis of the full truth of the Catholic faith leads directly to a personally convinced participation in the liturgical and sacramental life of the Catholic Church.

PART FOUR

Documents of the Magisterium Relating to The Creed of the People of God

"So we can understand why the Catholic Church in the past and today, has given and gives so much importance to the scrupulous presentation of the authentic Revelation. She considers it an invaluable treasure, and is sternly aware of her fundamental duty to defend and transmit the doctrine of the faith in unequivocal terms. Orthodoxy is her first concern. The pastoral Magisterium is her primary and providential function."

—Pope Paul VI,
January 19, 1972

POPE PAUL VI

Apostolic Exhortation
Announcing the year of Faith

FEBRUARY 22, 1967

VENERABLE BROTHERS: GREETINGS AND APOSTOLIC
BENEDICTION

The Apostles Peter and Paul are rightly considered by the faithful to be the principal pillars of this holy Roman See and also of the whole universal Church of the living God. Accordingly we feel it part of our duty to address this exhortation to you, calling on you to unite spiritually with us by promoting in your own territories the devout celebration of the courageous martyrdom in Rome nineteen centuries ago of these two Apostles: Peter, chosen by Christ to be the foundation of His Church and the bishop of this mother City; and Paul, the "Doctor of the Gentiles,"[1] teacher and friend of the first Christian community established in Rome.

The date of this memorable event cannot be fixed with certitude on the basis of historical documents. It is certain that the two Apostles were martyred in Rome during the persecution of Nero, which raged from the year 64 to 68. The martyrdom is recalled by St. Clement, successor of Peter in the government of the Roman Church, in his letter to the Corinthians, to whom he proposes the "noble examples" of the two "heroes," "the greatest and holiest pillars of the Church, who through jealousy and envy, were persecuted and endured to the death."[2]

164

The two Apostles Peter and Paul were joined by a "great multitude,"[3] first fruits of the martyrs of the Roman Church, as Clement also writes: "To these men who lived such holy lives, were added a great number of the elect who suffered many outrages and tortures because of jealousy and became a shining example among us."[4]

Leaving it to the experts to discuss the exact date of the martyrdom of the two Apostles, we have chosen the current year for the centenary celebrations. In so doing we are following the example of our venerated predecessor Pius IX, who wished the solemn commemoration of St. Peter's martyrdom to be held in the year 1867.

And, since the first Christian community of Rome gave joint honor to the martyrdoms of Peter and Paul, and the Church subsequently celebrated the anniversary of both Apostles with a single liturgical feast on June 29, we have decided to join together in this centenary celebration the glorious martyrdom of the Princes of the Apostles.

Moreover, we feel a certain obligation to commemorate this anniversary because of the custom, now universal, of honoring the memory of persons and events which have left their imprint on the course of time, and which, viewed from the distance of past years and given the immediacy of enduring memories, offer to the person who wisely reconsiders and, as it were, relives them, useful lessons on the value of human affairs—something perhaps grasped more clearly today than at the time the events took place, when they were not always or entirely understood. Modern education with its "sense of history" readily inclines us to such a reviewing of the past, while the veneration of sacred traditions—an essential element of Catholic spirituality—stimulates the memory, inflames the spirit, offers suggestions by which a yearly occurrence becomes a happy religious festivity, creates a desire to relive ancient and holy events, and unfolds a panoramic view of time past and future—as if some secret plan united these events and marked them with a seal of their ultimate destiny in the future communion of the saints. This spiritual experience, it seems to us, ought to be verified particularly in the commemoration of these two chief Apostles, Peter and Paul, who with martyrdom for Christ, paid their human tribute of temporal mortality, and who bequeathed to us, and to all future generations the eternal sacrament of Christ's immortality, the Church. Thus winning for themselves "an inheritance, imperishable, undefiled and immutable, reserved in heaven."[5]

What makes us even more happy to commemorate this anniversary with you, venerable brothers and dear sons, is that these blessed Apostles, Peter and Paul, belong not to us alone, but also to you: they are the glory of the entire Church, because to them applies the eulogy of the Second Letter to the Corinthians: "The apostles of the Churches, the glory of Christ,"[6] and from them comes a voice now directed to the whole Church: "We are your glory, and you are ours."[7] It is true that this soil of Rome, marked by woe and blessing, gathered their blood and guarded their tombs as priceless trophies, and that it is to the Church of Rome that belongs the invaluable prerogative of taking up and continuing their specific mission. But these singular privileges are directed, not toward the local church, but rather toward the entire Church, because that mission consists principally in fuctioning as the center of the Church herself and in spreading her visible and mystical circumference to the boundaries of the universe. This means that the unity and catholicity which, thanks to the holy Apostles Peter and Paul, find in the Church of Rome their principal historical and local center, in a distinctive way belong to the entire, true, great family of Christ. This unity and catholicity have been granted as gifts to the entire People of God, for whom the living and loyal Roman tradition guards, defends, dispenses, and augments them.

For this reason our invitation is directed, not only to our beloved diocese of Rome, the heavenly patrons of which are SS. Peter and Paul, but also to all of you, who are successors of the Apostles and pastors of the Universal Church, insofar as you form with us that college of the episcopate which the recent ecumenical council explained with so much richness of doctrine and foreshadowings of future ecclesial growth. Our invitation is also for you faithful Catholics and all the ministers of the holy Church. So, please God, may it also be for all the brethren who, although not in full communion with us, bear nonetheless the distinction of the Christian name, and whom we gladly recognize as devoted to the memory and spirit of the two Princes of the Apostles. It is with deep satisfaction in our heart that we recall in particular that the venerable Oriental Churches solemnly celebrate in their liturgy the two "Coryphei of the Apostles," whose memory they keep fresh among the Christian people. We are happy also to note how the separated Churches and ecclesial Communities of the West cherish the idea of apostolicity, which the present celebration endeavors to make ever more vigorous and effective. This idea was beautifully expressed by St. Paul in the words: "built upon the foundation of the Apostles."[8]

In the practical order, what does our invitation involve? How will we celebrate together this significant anniversary? When this Apostolic See intends to impart solemnity and universality to some outstanding celebration, it is customary for it to grant some spiritual favor—and we shall not fail to do so on this occasion. But this time, rather than give, we prefer to ask something; instead of offering, we wish to request. And our request is both simple and great; we ask you, one and all, our brothers and sons, to desire to mark the memory of the holy Apostles, Peter and Paul, those witnesses by word and blood to their faith in Christ, with an authentic and sincere profession of that very faith which the Church, founded and made ilustrious by them, has jealously acquired and authoritatively formulated. A single profession of faith we wish to offer to the blessed Apostles: one that is individual and collective, free and deliberate, internal and external, humble and frank. We want this profession of faith to arise from the depths of every faithful heart and to resound with the same loving tones throughout the Church.

What better tribute of remembrance, of honor, and of solidarity could we offer Peter and Paul than that of the very faith which we have inherited from them?

You know full well that the heavenly Father Himself revealed to Peter who Jesus was: the Christ, the Son of the living God, the Master and Savior from whom we receive grace and truth,[9] our salvation, the heart of our faith. You know that on the faith of Peter rests the entire structure of holy Church.[10] You know that, when many were abandoning Jesus after the discourse at Capharnaum, it was Peter who, in the name of the apostolic college, proclaimed his faith in Christ, the Son of God.[11] You know that by His personal prayer the same Christ guaranteed the indefectibility of the faith of Peter and entrusted to him the duty of strengthening his brethren in it, in spite of his human weaknesses.[12] And you know that the living Church, after the descent of the Holy Spirit on the day of Pentecost, began with the testimony of the faith of Peter.[13] What could we ask of Peter for our advantage, what could we offer Peter in his honor, if not the faith from which springs our spiritual well-being, and our promise, requested by him, to be "strong in the faith?"[14]

You know equally well what a spokesman for the faith St. Paul was. To him the Church owes the fundamental doctrine of faith as the beginning of our justification, that is, of our salvation, of our supernatural relations with God. To him the Church owes the first formulation of the Christian mystery in theological terms, the first analysis of the act of faith, the affirmation of the relationship that exists between faith, unique and unmistakable, and the firmness of the visible Church with her community and hierarchy. We have every right to pray to him, our master in the faith through the ages; to ask of him the great blessing we long for, the reunion of all Christians in one faith, one hope and one charity in the one mystical body of Christ;[15] we have every reason to pledge ourselves over the tomb of the "apostle and martyr" to our undertaking to profess with the courage and zeal of an apostle and missionary the faith which he taught and passed on to the Church and the world by his words, his writings, his example and his blood.

Hence we find satisfaction in hoping that the commemorative centenary of the martyrdom of SS. Peter and Paul will find its expression chiefly in a great act of faith throughout the Church. We want to see this anniversary as a providential occasion given to the People of God for reawakening a fuller awareness of its faith, giving it fresh life, purifying it, strengthening it and giving testimony to it. We cannot fail to know that the present time shows there is great need of this. And you know also, venerable brothers and dear sons, how in its development the modern world reaching out to amazing conquests in the dominion of outward things, and proud of its greater degree of self-awareness is inclined to forget and deny God and then to be tormented by the logical, moral and social difficulties that accompany a decline in religion; it is resigned to see man made restless by turbulent passions and persistent anxiety. Where God has no place, there is no longer the final explanation for reality, the initial inspiration for thought, the compelling moral sense that human order needs.[16]

And while man's religious sense today is in a decline, depriving the faith of its natural foundation, new opinions in exegesis and theology often borrowed from bold but blind secular philosophies have in places found a way into the realm of Catholic teaching. They question or distort the objective sense of truths taught with authority by the Church; under the pretext of adapting religious thought to the contemporary outlook they prescind from the guidance of the Church's teaching, give the foundations of theological speculation a direction of historicism, dare to rob Holy Scripture's testimony of its sacred and historical character and try to introduce a so-called "post-conciliar" mentality among the People of God; this neglects the solidity and consistency of the Council's vast and magnificent developments of teaching and legislation, neglects with it the Church's accumulated riches of thought and practice in order to overturn the spirit of traditional fidelity and spread about the illusion of giving Christianity a new interpretation, which is arbitrary and barren. What would remain of the content of our faith, or of the theological virtue that professes it, if these attempts, freed from the support of the Church's teaching authority, were destined to prevail?

But here now we have this anniversary of the Apostles, come round again on the wheel of time, to strengthen our faith in the true meaning of that term, to encourage study of the teachings of the recent Ecumenical Council, to sustain the energies of Catholic thought in its search for fresh and original expressions while remaining faithful to the doctrinal "deposit" of the Church, maintaining "the same sense and the same meaning."[17] This anniversary offers to every child of Holy Church the happy opportunity of giving to Jesus Christ, the Son of God, the mediator and accomplisher of revelation, a humble yet exalting "I believe," the full assent of intellect and will to His word, His person and His mission of salvation;[18] it thus offers an opportunity of giving honor to those distinguished witnesses to Christ, Peter and Paul, by renewing the Christian commitment of a sincere and effective profession of the faith, theirs and ours, and by continuing to pray and work for the reestablishment of all Christians in the unity of the same faith.

We do not intend to proclaim a special jubilee for this purpose, so soon after the jubilee we decreed at the close of the ecumenical council. But we fraternally exhort you all, venerable brothers in the episcopacy, to explain in your preaching the meaning of the Creed, to honor this profession of faith with special religious celebrations and above all to recite it solemnly and repeatedly with your priests and faithful, in one or other of the formulations commonly used in Catholic prayer.

We would be very happy if in every cathedral the Creed were recited expressly in honor of SS. Peter and Paul, in the presence of the bishop, the college of priests, the seminarians and the lay Catholics active in promoting the kingdom of God, men and women Religious, and as many members as possible of the assembly of the faithful. Similarly every parish and every religious house should do the same in the presence of its assembled community. And so we should like to suggest that on a fixed day this profession of faith be made in every single Christian household, in every Catholic association, in every Catholic school, hospital and place of worship, in every group and gathering where the voice of faith can be raised to proclaim and strengthen a sincere adherence to our common Christian calling.

We wish to address a special exhortation to those engaged in the study of Sacred Scripture and theology, to collaborate with the hierarchical teaching authority of the Church in defending the true faith from all error and in sounding its unfathomable depths, in correctly expounding its content and in drawing up reasoned norms for its study and spread. This same appeal we make to preachers, to teachers of religion and to catechists.

In this way the year commemorating the centenary of SS. Peter and Paul will be "the year of faith." To ensure a certain uniformity in its celebration, we will begin the centenary year on the forthcoming feast of the two Apostles, June 29. Until the same date in the following year, we intend to hold many special commemorative celebrations, all directed toward an interior renewal of our holy faith, a more profound study and a religious profession of our faith and an active witnessing to that faith without which "it is impossible to please God,"[19] and by means of which we hope to arrive at the salvation promised to us.[20]

In making this announcement to you, venerable brothers and dear sons, an announcement full of spiritual significance, of encouragement and hope, we are sure of finding you all in agreement and communion with us. In the name and with the power of the blessed Apostles and martyrs Peter and Paul, on whose tombs stands and prospers this Church of Rome, heir, disciple and custodian of the unity and catholicity which these Apostles established here forever and caused to spread far and wide, we cordially salute and bless you.

Allocution: The Catholic Faith in Practice

JULY 3, 1968

DEAR SONS AND DAUGHTERS,

You will have heard something, an echo at least, of the profession of faith with which We brought to a formal and solemn conclusion the "Year of Faith"; but a conclusion of this sort could well be called a beginning, not indeed of another year dedicated to the same theme, but rather of the consequences it should produce, and they are innumerable and endless.

THE ORIGIN OF THE APOSTLES' CREED

A profession of faith cannot be other than a summary, a "symbol" as it is called in traditional theological language, a formula, a *"regula fidei"* containing the main truths of faith in terms authoritative yet as far as possible condensed and abbreviated. From the earliest days of the Church there was a synthesis of fundamental dogmas of doctrinal teaching which the candidates for Baptism had to learn and recite from memory. The use of this teaching method probably originated in Rome; we have a record of it at the beginning of the third century in the so-called "apostolic tradition" of Hippolytus which consisted in a kind of interrogation such as is still used in the baptismal liturgy (cf. *DS* 10). It was believed that this text went back to the Apostles, whence our "Apostles Creed," as it is called, and therefore it enjoyed great credit; St. Ambrose saw in it the authentic tradition as being *"quod Ecclesia Romana intemeratum semper custodit et servat"*— what the Roman Church always safeguards and preserves (*Ep.* 42, 5; *P.L.* 16, 1174). The Council of Nicea (A.D. 325) took it up and amplified it in the form in which we recite it in the Mass, with the modification made in the First Council of Constantinople (A.D. 381) and with the addition of the *"Filioque,"* obviously suggested by the Emperor Henry II and approved by Pope Benedict VIII (A.D. 1014); and then it was also accepted by the Greek Church in the second Council of Lyons (A.D. 1274) and in that of Florence (A.D. 1439) (cf. *DS* 125, 150).

St. Augustine, commenting on the Ambrosian formula (later the "Apostles' Creed") concludes: "This is the faith to be held, set down in a few words in the Creed which is given to the new Christians" (*De fide et symb.* n. 25; *P.L.* 40, 196).

FAITH MUST SEEK UNDERSTANDING

All this goes to say that a summary profession of the truths of faith demands study, development, investigation. This is the duty of all believers; and those amongst them who can pass from catechism formulas to the more complete and more organic exposition of the truths of faith, from dry words to doctrinal development and, better still, from verbal expressions to some real understanding of the truths themselves, these experience a joy and at the same time a certain dismay: joy at the richness and beauty of the truths of religion, and dismay at their depth and extent which the mind can perceive but cannot measure. It is the greatest experiment in thinking that we can make. This is likewise the business of the masters, the theologians, the preachers, to whom this present moment in the history of the Church offers a stupendous mission, that namely of examining, purifying, expressing in new terms the declarations of the faith, those beautiful, original, well-tried, comprehensive, ever identical and unchangeable treasures of revelation, "the same doctrine, the same meaning, the same thought" as Vatican Council I has it (cf. Vincent Ler. *Commonitorium,* 28; *P.L.* 50, 668; and Vat. Conc. I *De Fide cath.* IV, in Alberigo, etc. *Conc. Oec. decreta,* p. 785).

SERIOUS STUDY OF OUR RELIGION

There is a work to do, therefore, which, one may say, is a new beginning, following upon the affirmation of faith which the conclusion of the "Year of Faith" gave Us the happy opportunity of making. We must all set ourselves to renewed serious study of our religion; and We hope that in every country there will be a new and original flowering of religious literature.

OUR WAY OF LIFE MUST BE AT ONE WITH OUR FAITH

But there is another consequence deriving from a profession of faith; it is the coherence of life with faith itself. We have never given enough importance to this close relation between believing and living. It is not sufficient to know the Word of God; it has to be lived. To know the faith and not to apply it to life would be gravely illogical, would be a serious responsibility. The faith is a principle of supernatural life, and at the same time it is a principle of moral life. Christian living is born of the faith, enjoys by it the initial communion between us and God which it establishes, makes its own infinite and mysterious thought mingle with our own, disposes us for that vital communion which unites our scarce created existence to the uncreated, infinite Being, God; but at the same time it introduces into our mind and into our activity an obligation, a spiritual and moral criterion, something which qualifies our whole way of life; it makes us Christians. The formula repeated by the Apostle is ever to be remembered: *"Justus ex fide vivit,"* the Christian, we may so translate, lives by faith (*Rom.* 1, 17; *Gal.* 3, 11; *Heb.* 10, 38).

It is this aspect of religious living which now concerns us. How can our everyday life conform to our faith? How can we picture to ourselves the modern type of believer? What is his vocation today when he wishes to take seriously the consequences of his own Creed? We all remember how the recent Council proclaimed that "all the faithful of no matter what rank or status are called to the fulness of the christian life and to the perfection of charity," and adds: "Also by this very holiness a more human manner of living is promoted in this earthly society" (*Lumen Gent.* no. 40). This declaration of the Council with regard to the call of each and all to holiness, corresponding "to the various kinds of life and to the various duties" of each one, is of the highest importance. "Every person," the Council goes on to say, "must walk unhesitatingly, according to his own personal gifts and duties, along the path of living faith, which enkindles hope and operates through charity" (*ib*. n. 41). Therefore there must be no more of the Christian who does not fulfill the requirements of his elevation to sonship of God, to brotherhood with Christ, to membership of the Church. Mediocrity, infidelity, casualness, waywardness, hypocrisy, all these must be removed from the make-up, from the pattern of the modern believer. A generation imbued with holiness ought to be the characteristic of our times. It is not only a matter of looking for singular and exceptional holiness; we must create and promote a holiness of the People, exactly as, from the first dawn of Christianity, St. Peter desired when he wrote the well-known words: "You are a chosen race, a royal priesthood, a holy nation, a purchased people: . . . who in times past were not a people, but are now the People of God" (*1 Pet*. 2, 9–10).

IS HOLINESS POSSIBLE TODAY?

Let us reflect well. Is it possible to attain such an object? Are we not in a land of dreams? How can the common man of our day ever conform his personal life to a true ideal of holiness, so far as it can be accommodated to the honest and legitimate requirements of modern life? How is this possible today, moreover, when everything is in the "melting-pot," when people no longer want to get the standards of guidance for the new generation from tradition, when the change of habits is so impelling and so clear, when social life absorbs and overwhelms the personality of the individual, when everything is secularized and desecrated, when no one knows any more what may be the order of things settled, when everything has become a problem and when the suggestion of reasonable solutions along the lines of proved historical experience by any normal authority is no longer accepted? Is not this a time of confusion in which great and legitimate aspirations are mixed up with excuses for violence and with nihilist and anarchist outbursts?

There is no occasion to close one's eyes to the ideological and social reality which blankets us; on the contrary we shall do well to look it in the face with courage and calm. We can draw from it many conclusions favorable to our principles in regard to humanism deprived of God's light. But now it behooves us to answer the question which we have asked ourselves, and which we should do well to repeat each one in his own inner conscience: Can a man be truly Christian today? And can a Christian be holy (in the biblical meaning of the word)? Can our faith be really and truly a guiding principle of actual modern living? Can a people, a society, a community at least, express itself in authentic Christian fashion?

OUR LORD JESUS CHRIST IS THE ANSWER

Here, dear sons and daughters, is a good opportunity to put our faith immediately into action. We answer: Yes. Nothing must frighten us, nothing stop us. It is St. Teresa who says: *Nada te espante.* Let us repeat to ourselves the words of St. Paul to the Romans: "If thou confess with thy mouth the Lord Jesus and believe in thy heart that God hath raised him up from the dead, thou shalt be saved." That is our compass. In this faithless and tormented sea of the present world let us keep steady to this supreme point: Jesus Christ. He, the light of the world and of our life, at once infuses into our hearts two cardinal certainties, one about God, the other about man; both are to be followed up with a total dedication of love. This being so, we no longer have fear of anything: "Who shall separate us from the love of Christ? shall tribulation? or distress? or famine? or nakedness? or danger? or persecution? or the sword? . . . In all these things we overcome because of him that loved us," says St. Paul again (*Rom.* 8, 35–37).

You begin to see how the faith can have a determining and strengthening influence on our psychology first of all and then on our practical life. But this talk is already long and here We still stop, trusting that you will be able to continue it for yourselves in your own consciences. With Our Apostolic Blessing.

POPE PAUL VI

Allocution: Faith Ever True and Living

JULY 10, 1968

DEAR SONS AND DAUGHTERS,

What shall We speak to you about today? You know that after declaring Our Catholic faith, ancient yet ever new because ever true and living, We are investigating the relation this has to our thinking and our conduct. We aim to find out, that is, what influence it has on our life, what demands it makes, what spurs it offers us, what stamp it puts on our personality. Let us look at the matter from a personal point of view. We have already recalled the great law which establishes faith as a principle of living, whether in the transcendent and mysterious sense of that initial supernatural entrance into us of the presence and operation of God, or in the sense of the moral inspiration which derives from the truths of faith, or again in that of the manner, suggested by faith, in which we weigh up the enormous and complex variety of values, whether these belong to the world within us or to the world without. A modern man, a Christian of our day, one of the faithful ready to listen to the voice of the Council, what account is he to make of his own faith? How does the well-known association of "faith and life" present itself today to our conscience, granted a basic personal sincerity, let us even say a desire for perfection?

176

FAITH GIVES VISION

The answer would require the reply to yet another question: How does one come to believe nowadays? We are not now concerned with the genesis of faith, itself an immense problem but one which, We take it for granted, is to some extent already solved for you who are believers. We will limit Our enquiry to the simpler but always serious question: Is faith a possession of God or is it a search for God? It is first and foremost a possession—the believer is already possessed of some supernatural truths deriving from the Word of God; he is already the guardian of some revelations which enter into his life and dominate it, and he is already happy in his certitude about a number of things, a certitude which gives to his spirit a fullness, a strength, a joy, an urge to express it and make much of it, a certitude which nourishes within him a wonderful interior life. It is for the believer as if in the obscurity and confusion of the inner chamber of his soul a light was turned on. He sees the light, that is to say the divine realities which have come into his soul, and by reason of that light he sees himself, his own conscience; and not this alone—he sees himself in his situation, his place in the world and the world itself. Everything acquires a meaning; everything appears for what it is. Nor can it be denied that this first vision is magnificent, even if it reveals unattainable heights, darksome depths, endless expanses; it also reveals humble things close at hand, things already known but now seen in real and true perspective. The vision is magnificent even if the sense of mystery grows precisely by reason of the initial discovery of the realities whereby we live and in the midst of which our fear-ridden existence is placed.

THE UNENDING SEARCH FOR GOD

But let us take heed. This posession of faith does not exclude but rather calls for further enquiry on our part. Our possession of God in this life is never complete; it is but a beginning, a first spark that beckons us to the greater attainment of a fuller light. This is a very well known normal condition of our religious apprenticeship, even for us Catholics who have the good fortune to base ourselves on fixed and secure articles of faith; these latter do not dispense us from the effort of an ever-advancing research into things divine and a better and better knowledge of them. Those know this well who make a sweet, strong food of their religion and their contemplation. It is a thought to which St. Augustine often returns; for example: *"amore crescente inquisitio crescat inventi"*—with the growth of love, let grow the search for Him we have found (*Ennar. in Ps. 104;* P.L. 37, 1392); and again: *"invenitur ut quaeratur avidius"*—we find God in order to seek Him the more eagerly (*De Trin.* XV, 1; P.L. 42, 1058). The faith is not something static; it is a journeying towards divine truths. The believer is a pilgrim walking along the good road towards God.

TWO ENEMIES FOR FAITH

But today we must take account of a double phenomenon which interrupts this vision of ours of the religious and spiritual sphere, a phenomenon which under either aspect is serious and widespread. The first is atheism which pretends to free man from the so-called bondage of religion. "The denial of God," says the Council, "is presented as a requirement of scientific progress and of a new type of humanism" (*Gaudium et Spes,* n. 7). Here and now We shall not dwell on this sad and oppressive phenomenon; anyone who should wish to know the many forms in which it expresses itself can consult a monumental work of which the first two large volumes have appeared: *"L'Ateismo contemporaneo"* (S.E.I. 1967 and 1968); another two volumes are in preparation principally due to the initiative of the good learned Salesians D. Girardi and D. Maino, with other competent students of the question. Here it suffices to observe that atheism has no place in the make-up of the true, complete, good man that we are describing, notwithstanding that atheism too pretends to establish a morality worthy of serious analysis. (Cf. Cornelio Fabro, *Introduzione all'ateismo moderno.* Rome: Ed. Studium, 1964; English translation, *God in Exile: A Study of the Internal Dynamic of Modern Atheism.* Westminster, Maryland: Newman Press, 1968; pp. xliii, 1230).

THE MODERN MAN-CENTERED RELIGION

We would rather say a word, a single and fleeting one, about the other phenomenon which is to be found in circles claiming to be religious and Christian. It is the phenomenon of man-centered religion, directed, that is to say, towards man as its principle object of interest, whereas religion of its very nature must be God-centered, directed towards God as its beginning and its principal end, and so towards man as considered, sought after, loved in view of his origin from God and of the relationships and duties which spring from this. There is talk of vertical religion and horizontal religion, and it is this latter, philanthropic and social, which tends to prevail today for those who lack the sovereign vision of the ontological order, that is to say of the real and objective order of religion. Does this mean that We want to deny the importance and duty attributed by the Catholic faith to the interest due to man? Not for a moment! Nor do We want to modify this interest, which for us Christians must be of extreme and continual obligation. We remember only too well that we shall be judged by the real love which we have shown towards our neighbor, especially when he is in need, suffering, cast down (cf. Mt. 25, 31 f.). In that matter we set no limit. But we must always remember that the beginning of love of our neighbor is our love of God. He who forgets the reason why we have to call ourselves the brethren of mankind, namely the Fatherhood of God which we have in common, could well at a given moment forget the grave burdens attaching to such brotherhood and see in his own like no longer a brother, but a stranger, a rival, an enemy. To give pride of place in religion to humanitarianism leads to the danger of transforming theology into sociology and of forgetting the basic hierarchy of things and their values: "I am the Lord thy God . . . thou shalt have no other God but me" (cf. Ex. 20, 1 f.); so is it written in the Old Testament; and in the New Testament Christ teaches us: "Love God . . . this is the first and greatest commandment. The second is like unto this: thou shalt love thy neighbor as thyself" (Mt. 27, 37–39).

SOCIOLOGY VERSUS THEOLOGY

Nor must it be forgotten that preference given to sociological interests over the theological properly so-called can bring about another dangerous incongruity, that namely of adapting the teaching of the Church to human standards in the place of the less tangible ones of revelation and of the official teaching authority of the Church. That pastoral zeal should give preference in practice to consideration of human needs, often so grave and so pressing, can be allowed and encouraged, always providing that such consideration does not involve a devaluation and lowering of the pre-eminence and authenticity of theological orthodoxy.

The faith, accepted and put into practice, is not an escape from the duties of charity and from the great and compelling needs of the social order; it is rather the inspiration and driving force of these duties. From another point of view, it is the safeguard against the temptation of falling into 'temporalism,' that is into making a prevailing interest of things temporal, from which today more than ever religion has to be kept clear. It is a safeguard, too, against the even greater danger of wanting to set up a new social order without charity but admitting violence and with the substitution of an overbearing and egoistic superiority in place of what is judged to be improvident and unjust.

A morality without God, a Christianity without Christ and without His Church, a humanism without the true concept of man, these do not lead us to a good end. May our faith preserve us from fatal errors like these and be for us, in our search for personal and social perfection, a light and a teacher.

This is the Apostolic Blessing we wish you.

THE PAPAL COMMISSION OF CARDINALS

Declaration on
"The New Catechism"

OCTOBER 15, 1968

I. HISTORICAL PART

When the "New Catechism" was published in Holland ("De Nieuwe Katechismus," 1966)—a work which on the one hand is marked with exceptional qualities but on the other hand, because of its new opinions, from the very moment of issue disturbed not a few of the faithful—the Apostolic See, in virtue of its office of protecting the faith of the People of God, could not fail to take cognisance of the affair. And so the Holy Father wished that, to begin, a discussion should take place between three theologians named by the Holy See and three theologians named by the Dutch hierarchy concerning the difficulties which the text of the Catechism presented.

In the discussion held from the 8th to 10th April 1967 the theologians chosen by the Holy See, according to an agenda sanctioned by the authority of the Sacred Congregation of the Council and according to the mind of the Holy Father, asked with confidence that certain things be introduced into the Catechism which, in more precise formulation, would beyond doubt correspond to the faith of the Church, to objective truth and to the conviction of the faithful. But the discussion produced very few results; and no change was made with regard to those points which by way of example, the Holy Father himself had indicated: "for example, what pertains to the virginal conception of

181

Jesus Christ, a dogma of the Catholic faith, to the teaching supported
by the Gospel and the Tradition of the Church by which we believe
that angels exist; and to the satisfactorial and sacrificial character of
the redemptive act which Christ offered to His Eternal Father for the
remission of our sins and to reconcile men with the Father."

When he knew of the outcome of this discussion, especially from
the joint report of the theologians designated by the Holy See, and the
theologians of the Dutch hierarchy, the Holy Father ordered that a
Commission of Cardinals (Frings, Lefèbvre, Jaeger, Florit, Browne and
Journet) examine the matter and give their opinion about it. This
Commission meeting for the first time on the 27th and 28th June 1967
with theologians familiar with the Dutch language at hand to assist
them, decided that the New Catechism was to be carefully revised
before new editions and translations were made, and chose another
group of theologians from seven different nations to study the text of
the Catechism and to express their mind about it.

Besides the Catechism itself this group was given the above-
mentioned report of the first discussion between the theologians. In
September a series of emendations presented in the meantime by the
authors of the Catechism was added to this report. After painstaking
work the group of theologians drew up their observations with regard
to the text of the Catechism and with regard to the series of emendations proposed, which on the whole did not seem sufficient. Every
single observation of the group was approved unanimously in its entirety by the members.

When the designated Cardinals had received these observations of
the theologians along with other documents, they met again from the
12th to 14th December 1967. After discussing each of the observations
they definitively decided, by vote on each item, what things had to be
changed in the text of the Catechism and how they were to be
changed; they provided with the help of Cardinal Alfrink that a small
commission be set up consisting of two of their delegates and two
delegates of the Dutch hierarchy to accomplish the task. The Commission completed this assignment in February 1968 and submitted the
results to the Holy See, to the designated Cardinals and to the Dutch
hierarchy.

Previously, however, contrary to the wish of the Dutch hierarchy
and without the prescribed correction, an English translation of the

New Catechism was published; and likewise more recently a German translation has appeared and finally a French translation. Besides, reserved documents of their very nature secret pertaining to this affair, have recently been presented to the public; among them there is even a letter of the Holy Father himself. This was done in a Dutch newspaper and also in a book published in Italy.

In the book just mentioned copious notes and explanations are added to the documents published, and in these not only are there assigned to the theologians named by the Holy See opinions which they never held, but also the very points of the Catechism which needed correction are glossed over time and again in various ways so as to seem harmless enough while they are not so in reality. Often they really are not sufficient to correct the opposite explanations. This is all the more true because very frequently these explanations agree with opinions expressed by the authors of the Catechism in other words. With regard to future editions of the Cathechism, solutions are proposed contrary to those which the Commission of Cardinals, with the approval of the Holy See decreed, and it is suggested that only those corrections of the Catechism which the Holy Father expressly mentioned, be admitted at all; although as is clear from the above quotation from the Holy Father, he himself was only giving examples of the clarification which he wanted.

In that same book a wrong use is made of the opinions of some modern exegetes as to how St. Matthew and St. Luke wanted to present and explain the principal facts about the birth and infancy of Our Lord. Although the particular theologians and authors to whom the book refers hold that the virginal conception of Jesus is to be placed among the principal events which the Gospel of Our Lord's infancy proposed as altogether real, the book itself dares to come to the conclusion, not without violation of the Catholic faith, that the faithful are to be permitted not to believe in the virginal conception of Jesus in its both spiritual and corporeal reality, but only in its certain symbolic signification.

These publications strive in various ways to frustrate the plan of the Holy See to resolve in mutual understanding with the Dutch hierarchy a matter of no small moment for the good of the People of God. For this reason, and because the Catechism in an unemended edition has already appeared in four languages, it seems necessary even before the emended editions and translations of the Catechism are published, to give in this present declaration a compendium of the judgments of the Commission of Cardinals. In this way it will be clear to the faithful how, in full accord with the Church of Christ and the See of Peter, they can think and bear witness without fear of error about the good tidings of salvation.

II. DOCTRINAL PART

1. *Points concerning God the Creator.*—It is necessary that the Catechism teach that God, besides this sensible world in which we live, has created also a realm of pure spirits whom we call Angels. (Cf. v.g. Conc. Vat. I, Const. *Dei Filius,* cap. 1; Const. Vat. II, Const. *Lumen Gentium* n. 49, 50). Furthermore, it should state explicitly that individual human souls since they are spiritual (cf. Conc. Vat. II, Const. *Gaudium et Spes,* n. 14) are created immediately by God (cf. v.g. Encycl. *Humani Generis,* AAS, 42 [1950], p. 575).

2. *The Fall of Man in Adam.* (Cf. Conc. Vat. II, Const. *Lumen Gentium* n. 2). Although questions regarding the origin of the human race and its slow development present today new difficulties, to be faced in connection with the dogma of original sin, nevertheless in the New Catechism the doctrine of the Church is to be faithfully proposed, that man in the beginning of history rebelled against God (cf. Conc. Vat. II, Const. *Gaudium et Spes,* n. 13, 22) and so lost for himself and his offspring that sanctity and justice in which he had been constituted, and handed on a true state of sin to all through propagation of human nature. Certainly those expressions must be avoided which could signify that original sin is only contracted by individual new members of the human family in this sense that from their very coming into the world, they are exposed within themselves to the influence of human society where sin reigns, and so are started initially on the way of sin.

3. *With regard to the conception of Jesus by the Virgin Mary.* The Commission of Cardinals has asked that the Catechism openly profess that the Blessed Mother of the Incarnate Word always enjoyed the honor of virginity, and that the fact itself of the virginal conception of Jesus which is in such great conformity with the mystery of the Incarnation itself, be taught clearly. In consequence the Catechism should offer no excuse for abandoning this factual truth—in face of

the ecclesiastical Tradition founded on Holy Scripture—retaining only a symbolic signification, such as the complete gratuity of the gift which God has given to us in His Son.

4. *The "Satisfaction" made by Christ Our Lord.* The essential elements of the doctrine of the satisfaction of Christ which pertains to our faith are to be proposed without ambiguity. God so loved sinful men as to send His Son into the world to reconcile men to Himself (cf. *2 Cor.* 5, 19). As St. Augustine says: "We were reconciled to a God who loved us even when we were at enmity with Him because of sin" (*In Ioannes Evangelium* Tract. 110, n. 6). Jesus therefore, as the first-born among many brethren (cf. *Rom.* 8, 29) died for our sins (Cf. *1 Cor.* 15, 3). Holy, innocent, immaculate (cf. *Hebr.* 7, 26), he underwent no punishment inflicted on him by God, but freely and with filial love, obedient to His Father (cf. *Phil.* 2, 8) he accepted, for his sinful brethren and as their Mediator (cf. 1 *Tim.* 2, 5), the death, which for them is the wages of sin (cf. *Rom.* 6, 23; Conc. Vat. II, Const. *Gaudium et Spes,* n. 18). By this His most sacred death, which in the eyes of God more than abundantly compensated for the sins of the world, He brought it about that divine grace was restored to the human race as a good which it had merited in its divine Head (cf. v.g. *Hebr.* 10, 5–10; Conc. Trid., sess. VI, Decr. *De justificatione,* cap. 3 and 7, can. 10).

5. *The Sacrifice of the Cross and the Sacrifice of the Mass.* It must be clearly stated that Jesus offered Himself to His Father to repair our wrong-doing as a holy victim in whom God was well pleased. For Christ ". . . loved us, giving himself up in our place as a fragrant offering and a sacrifice to God" (*Eph.* 5, 2).

The sacrifice of the Cross is perpetuated in the Church of God as the eucharistic sacrifice (cf. Conc. Vat. II, Const. *Sacrosanctum Concilium,* n. 47). In the eucharistic sacrifice Jesus as the principal priest offers Himself to God through the consecratory oblation which priests perform and to which the faithful unite themselves. That celebration is both sacrifice and banquet. The sacrificial oblation is completed by communion, in which the victim offered to God is received as food, to unite the faithful to Himself and to join them with one another in charity (cf. *1 Cor.* 10, 17).

6. *The Eucharistic Presence and the Eucharistic Change.* It is necessary that in the text of the Catechism it be brought out beyond

doubt that after the consecration of the bread and wine the very body and blood of Christ is present on the altar and is received sacramentally in Holy Communion, so that those who worthily approach this divine table are spiritually renewed by Christ Our Lord. Furthermore, it must be explained that the bread and wine in their deepest reality (not in appearance or phenomenologically), once the words of consecration have been spoken, are changed into the body and blood of Christ; and so it comes to pass that where the appearance of bread and wine (the phenomenological reality) remain, there, in a way most mysterious, the humanity itself of Christ, lies hidden together with His Divine Person.

Once this marvellous change has taken place, a conversion which in the Church is termed transubstantiation, the appearance of bread and wine,— since they actually contain and present Christ Himself, the fountain of grace and charity to be communicated through the sacred banquet,—take on as a consequence indeed a new signification and a new end. But they take on that new signification and that new end precisely because transubstantiation has taken place (cf. Encycl. Pauli VI *Mysterium Fidei,* AAS, 57 [1965] p. 766; and *Schreiben der Deutschen Bischöfe* an alle die von der Kirche mit der Glaubensverkündigung beauftragt sind, n. 43–47).

7. *The Infallibility of the Church and the Knowledge of Revealed Mysteries.*—It should be more clearly stated that the infallibility of the Church does not give her only a safe course in a continual research, but the truth in maintaining doctrine of faith and in explaining it always in the same sense (cf. Conc. Vat. I, Const. *Dei Filius,* cap. 4, et Conc. Vat. II, Const. *Dei Verbum,* cap. 2). "Faith is not only a seeking of the truth but is above all certain possession of truth" (Paulus VI, Alloc. ad Episcoporum Synodum, *AAS,* 59 [1967] p. 966). Nor is it to be allowed that readers of the Catechism think that the human intellect arrives only at verbal and conceptual expressions of the revealed mystery. Care must be taken rather that they understand that the human intellect is able by those concepts "through a mirror in an obscure way" and "in part," as St. Paul says (*1 Cor.* 13, 12), but in a way that is altogether true, to express and grasp the revealed mysteries.

8. *The Ministerial or Hierarchical Priesthood and the Power of*

Teaching in the Church. Care must be taken not to minimize the excellence of the ministerial priesthood, that in its participation of the priesthood of Christ, differs from the common priesthood of the faithful, not only in degree, but in essence (cf. Conc. Vat. II, Const. *Lumen Gentium,* n. 10); Instructio de cultu mysterii eucharistici, *AAS,* 59 (1967) n. 11, p. 548.

Care should be taken that in describing the priestly ministry there is brought out more clearly the mediation between God and men which they exercise not only in preaching the word of God, in forming the Christian Community and in administering the Sacraments, but also and chiefly in offering the Eucharistic Sacrifice in the name of the whole Church (cf. Conc. Vat. II, Const. *Lumen Gentium,* n. 28; Decr. *Presbyterorum ordinis,* nn. 2, 13).

Furthermore, the Cardinals asked that the new Catechism clearly recognize that the teaching authority and the power of ruling in the Church is given directly to the Holy Father and to the Bishops joined with him in hierarchical communion, and that it is not given first of all to the People of God to be communicated to others. The office of Bishops, therefore, is not a mandate given them by the People of God but is a mandate received from God Himself for the good of the whole Christian community.

It is to be brought out more clearly that the Holy Father and the Bishops in their teaching office do not only assemble and approve what the whole community of the faithful believes. The people of God are so moved and sustained by the spirit of truth that they cling to the word of God with unswerving loyalty and freedom from error under the leadership of the Magisterium to whom it belongs authentically to guard, explain and defend the deposit of faith. Thus it has come about that in understanding the faith that has been handed down, in professing that faith and in manifesting it in deed, there is a unique collaboration between bishops and the faithful (cf. Conc. Vat. II, *Lumen Gentium,* n. 11, and *Dei Verbum,* n. 10). Sacred Tradition and the Sacred Scripture—which constitute the one and only holy deposit of the Word of God—and the Magisterium of the Church are so joined that one cannot stand without the other (cf. Conc. Vat. II, Const. *Dei Verbum,* no. 10).

Finally, that authority by which the Holy Father directs the

Church is to be clearly presented as the full power of ruling, a supreme and universal power which the Pastor of the whole Church can always freely exercise (cf. Conc. Vat. II, Const. *Lumen Gentium,* n. 2).

9. *Various points concerning Dogmatic Theology.* In the presentation of the mystery of the three Persons in God, the Catechism should not seem to deny that Christians do well to contemplate them with faith and love them with filial devotion not only in the economy of salvation where they manifest themselves but also in the eternal life of the Divinity, whose vision we hope for.

The efficacy of the Sacraments should be presented somewhat more exactly. Care must be taken that the Catechism does not seem to say that miracles can only be brought about by divine power insofar as they do not depart from that which the forces of the created world are able to produce.

Finally, let open reference be made to the souls of the just, which, having been thoroughly purified, already rejoice in the immediate vision of God, even while the pilgrim Church still awaits the glorious coming of the Lord and the final resurrection (cf. Conc. Vat. II, Const. *Lumen Gentium,* n. 49 et 51).

10. *Certain points of Moral Theology.* The text of the Catechism is not to make obscure the existence of moral laws which we are able to know and express in such wise that they bind our conscience always and in all circumstances. Solutions of cases of conscience should be avoided which do not sufficiently attend to the indissolubility of marriage. While it is right to attach great moment to the moral habits, still one must be on guard lest that habit be presented without sufficient dependence upon human acts. The presentation of a conjugal morality should be more faithful in presenting the full teaching of Vatican II and of the Holy See.

The above observations, though not few and not insignificant, still leave untouched by far the greater part of the New Catechism with its praiseworthy pastoral, liturgical and biblical character. Neither are they opposed to the laudable purpose of the authors of the Catechism, namely, to present the eternal good tidings of Christ in a way adapted to the understanding and the thinking of the present day man. Indeed the very fine qualities which make this an outstanding work demand that it ever present the true teaching of the Church in no way obscured or overshadowed.

Joseph Card. Frings
Joseph Card. Lefèbvre
Lorenz Card. Jaeger
Ermenegildo Card. Florit
Michael Card. Browne
Charles Card. Journet

October 15th, 1968

Pietro Palazzini, *Secretary*

POPE PAUL VI

Allocution: Integrity of Faith the Foundation of Christian Living

OCTOBER 30, 1968

BELOVED SONS AND DAUGHTERS!

On the occasion of the feast of Christ the King, which was celebrated last Sunday, the profession of faith that We Ourself delivered
on June 30th, in St. Peter's Square, was recited in many churches in
the world. This profession of faith was given at the conclusion of the
centenary commemoration of the martyrdom of the Apostles Peter and
Paul, which was celebrated as the "Year of Faith," and was therefore
concluded with that solemn declaration of faith of Ours that took the
name of "Credo of the People of God." You will remember it; it is a
repetition, amplified with explicit references to some doctrinal points,
of the Nicene Creed, which is, as you know, the celebrated formula
of faith drawn up at the first ecumenical Council, the Council of Nicea,
in the year 325, a few years after Constantine's edict of 313 gave the
Church freedom. This formula became known in the Latin language
mainly in the translation of St. Hilary of Poitiers (cfr. De Synodis, 84;
P.L. 10, 536), and is still substantially repeated by us at Holy Mass,
when the rubrics prescribe the recitation of the Creed.

THE BEGINNING OF HUMAN SALVATION

From being a brief synthesis of the principal truths believed by the Catholic Church, both Latin and Oriental, this Creed has taken on the solemnity of an official act of our faith. To the objective doctrinal value there has thus been added, as is obvious, the subjective value of our personal and community adherence to those same truths, which the Church deems derived from Revelation. Therefore the Creed takes its place with decisive authority and strengthening vigor in the tangle of our confused and agitated consciences, and through these fundamental tenets, it provides light and order with regard to religious questions, which are the most important and difficult of our life. Therefore when we recite the Creed, we should always keep in mind this combination of objective faith (the truths believed) with subjective faith (the virtuous act of assent to those truths).

Why have we drawn the attention of the Church to these combined elements in the profession of faith? This, too, you know. It is for two reasons. Firstly, because, as the Council of Trent says, following with scrupulous fidelity the thought of St. Paul (cfr. Rom 3, 21–28), "fides est humanae salutis initium, fundamentum et radix omnis iustificationis" (Sess. VI, c. 8): "faith is the beginning of human salvation, the foundation and the root of all justification," that is, of our regeneration in Christ, our redemption, and our present and eternal salvation. "Without faith it is impossible to please God" (Heb. 11, 6). Faith is our first duty. Faith is a question of life for us; faith is the irreplaceable principle of Christianity. It is the center of unity; it is the fundamental *raison d'être* of our religion. Secondly, because today, contrary to what should happen with human progress, faith (let us say adherence to faith) has become more difficult. On the philosophical plane, because of the growing attacks on the laws of speculative thought, on natural rationality, on the validity of human certainties; doubt, agnosticism, sophism, the irresponsible spirit of the absurd, the rejection of logic and metaphysics, etc., upset the minds of men today. If thought is no longer respected in its intrinsic rational requirements, faith too (which, it should be remembered, requires reason; it goes beyond it, but requires it) suffers as a result. Faith is not fideism, that is, belief deprived of rational grounds. It is not merely the subconscious search for some religious experience; it is possession of truth, it is certainty. "If your eye is not sound, your whole body will be full of darkness" (Mt. 6, 23).

DEVIATIONS AND ERRORS OF OUR TIMES

We can also add, unfortunately, that today the act of faith has become more difficult also on the psychological plane. Today man apprehends mainly through the senses; we talk of the civilization of the image. All knowledge is translated into figures and signs; reality is measured by what is seen and heard. But faith requires the use of the mind in a sphere of realities which escape the observation of the senses. And let us also say that the difficulties arise, too, from the philological, exegetic, and historical studies applied to that prime source of revealed truth, Holy Scripture. Deprived of its complement found in Tradition and the authoritative assistance of the ecclesiastical Magisterium, even the study of the Bible alone is full of doubts and problems, which are more disconcerting than helpful to faith; and left to individual judgment it generates such a plurality of opinions as to threaten faith in its subjective certainty, and to deprive it of its social authoritativeness. Such a faith thus produces obstacles to the unity of believers, whereas faith should be the basis of ideal and spiritual agreement: there is one faith (Eph. 4, 5).

We speak in sorrow; but this is how things are. Also because the remedies, which people are proposing on so many sides for the modern crises of faith, are often fallacious. There are some who, to restore credit to the content of faith, reduce it to some basic propositions, which they think are the genuine significance of the sources of Christianity and of Holy Scripture itself. It is unnecessary to say how arbitrary, even if elaborated in scientific fashion, and how disastrous such a proceeding is. Others again, with criteria of disconcerting empiricism, arrogate the right to make a selection among the many truths taught by our Creed, in order to reject those that are unpopular, and retain those that are more acceptable. Then there are others who try to adapt the doctrines of faith to modern mentality, often making this mentality, whether secular or spiritualist, the rule and yardstick of religious thought. The effort, in itself worthy of praise and understanding, made by this system to express the truths of faith in terms accessible to the language and the mentality of our times, has sometimes succumbed to the desire for an easier success, by passing over in silence, tempering or altering certain "difficult dogmas." The attempt, though right and proper, is dangerous. It is acceptable only, while making the presentation of the doctrine more accessible, it maintains sincerely its integrity. "Let what you say be simply 'Yes' or 'No' " (Mt. 5, 37; James 5, 12), excluding all false ambiguity.

GUARD THIS WONDERFUL GIFT

This dramatic situation of faith nowadays reminds us of the wise pronouncement of the Council: "Sacred Tradition, Holy Scripture and the Magisterium of the Church are, by the wise disposition of God, so closely connected with one another that they cannot exist independently" (Const. Dei Verbum, n. 10). This is all right for objective faith; that is, to know exactly what we must believe. But for subjective faith, what shall we do, after having listened, studied and meditated honestly and assiduously? Shall we have faith?

We can answer affirmatively, but always keeping in mind a fundamental and, in a certain sense, tremendous aspect of the question—that faith is a grace. "They have not all heeded the Gospel," St. Paul says (Rom. 10, 16). And so, what about us? Shall we be among the fortunate ones to possess the gift of faith? Certainly, but it is a gift that we must treasure, guard, enjoy and practice in our lives. And therefore we must implore it in prayer, like the man in the Gospel: "I believe; help my unbelief" (Mark 9, 24).

Let us pray, beloved sons and daughters, as follows:

PAUL VI'S PRAYER TO OBTAIN FAITH

Lord, I believe; I wish to believe in Thee.

Lord, let my faith be full and unreserved, and let it penetrate my thought, my way of judging divine things and human things.

Lord, let my faith be free; that is, let it have my personal adherence, let it accept the renunciations and duties that this entails and let it express the culminating point of my personality: I believe in Thee, Lord.

Lord, let my faith be certain; certain with the appropriate external proofs and with the interior testimony of the Holy Spirit, with the certainty of its reassuring light, its soothing conclusion, its quiet assimilation.

Lord, let my faith be strong, let it not fear the difficulties of the problems of which the experience of our life, eager for light, is full, let it not fear the hostility of those who question it, attack it, reject it, deny it; but let it be strengthened in the intimate proof of Thy truth, let it resist the attack of criticism, let it be strengthened in continual affirmation overcoming the dialectic and spiritual difficulties of our temporal existence.

Lord, let my faith be joyful and give peace and gladness to my spirit, and dispose it for prayer with God and conversation with men, so that the inner bliss of its fortunate possession may shine forth in sacred and secular conversation.

Lord, let my faith be industrious and give to charity the reasons of its moral expansion so that there may be a continual search of Thee, a continual testimony to Thee, a continuous nourishment of hope in Thee.

Lord, let my faith be humble and not presume to be based on the experience of my thought and of my feeling; but let it surrender to the testimony of the Holy Spirit, and not have any better guarantee than in docility to Tradition and to the authority of the Magisterium of Holy Church.   Amen.

And let the Year of Faith conclude in this way for Us, and for all of you, with Our Apostolic Blessing.

POPE PAUL VI

Apostolic Exhortation
to All the Bishops

DECEMBER 8, 1970

BELOVED BROTHERS,
HEALTH AND OUR APOSTOLIC BLESSING

It is now five full years since, after intense working sessions lived in
prayer, study and fraternal exchange of thought and opinion the
bishops of the whole world returned to their dioceses, resolved to ensure "that nothing would block the great river whose streams of
heavenly graces today 'refresh the city of God.'[21] and that there would
be no lessening of the vital spirit which the Church now possesses."[22]

Thanking God for the work accomplished, each bishop took back
with him from the Council not only the experience he had of collegiality, but also the doctrinal and pastoral texts which had been
painstakingly perfected. These texts were spiritual riches to be shared
with our co-workers in the priesthood, with the religious and with all
the members of the People of God. They were sure guides for proclaiming the Word of God to our age and for internally renewing the
Christian communities.

That fervor has known no slackening. The successors of the apostles
have worked unreservedly to apply the teaching and directives of the
Council to the Church's life, each of them where the Holy Spirit has
placed him to feed the Church of God,[23] and all of them together in

195

many ways, but especially in the episcopal conferences and synods of bishops. In accordance with the hope expressed in our first encyclical "Ecclesiam Suam"[24] the Council deepened the Church's awareness of herself. It shed more light on the demands of her apostolic mission in the world of today. It helped her to engage in the dialogue of salvation with a genuinely ecumenical and missionary spirit.

I

But it is not our intention here to try to draw up a balance sheet of the researches, undertakings and reforms, which have been so numerous since the Council ended. Devoting our attention to reading the signs of the times, we would like, in a fraternal spirit, to make together with you an examination of our fidelity to the commitment we bishops undertook in our message to humanity at the beginning of the Council: "We shall take pains so to present to the men of this age God's truth in its integrity and purity that they may understand it and gladly assent to it."[25]

This commitment was made unambiguously clear by the Pastoral Constitution *Gaudium et Spes,* truly the Council's charter of the presence of the Church in the world: "The Church of Christ takes her stand in the midst of the anxieties of this age, and does not cease to hope with the utmost confidence. She intends to propose to our age over and over again, in season and out of season, the apostolic message."[26]

It is of course true that the shepherds of the Church have always had this duty of handing on the faith in its fulness and in a manner suited to men of their time. That means trying to use a language easily accessible to them, answering their questions, arousing their interest and helping them to discover, through poor human speech, the whole message of salvation brought to us by Jesus Christ. It is in fact the episcopal college which with Peter and under his authority, guarantees the authentic handing on of the deposit of faith, and for that purpose it has received, as Saint Irenaeus expressed it, "a sure charism of truth."[27] The faithfulness of its witness, rooted in Sacred Tradition and Holy Scripture and nourished by the ecclesial life of the whole People of God is what empowers the Church, through the unfailing assistance of the Holy Spirit, to teach without ceasing the Word of God and to make it progressively unfold.

INCREASED EFFORT NEEDED

Nevertheless, the present position of the faith demands of us an increased effort in order that this Word may reach our contemporaries in its fulness and that the works performed by God may be presented to them without falsification and with all the intensity of the love of the truth which can save them.[28] In fact, at the very moment when the reading of God's Word in the liturgy is enjoying a wonderful renewal, thanks to the Council; when use of the Bible is spreading among the Christian people; when advances in catechesis, pursued in accordance with the Council's guidelines, are making possible an evangelization in depth; when biblical, patristic and theological research often makes a precious contribution to a more meaningful expression of the data of revelation—at this very moment many of the faithful are troubled in their faith by an accumulation of ambiguities, uncertainties and doubts about its essentials. Such are the Trinitarian and Christological dogmas, the mystery of the Eucharist and the Real Presence, the Church as the institution of salvation, the priestly ministry in the midst of the People of God, the value of prayer and the sacraments, and the moral requirements concerning, for instance, the indissolubility of marriage or respect for life. Even the divine authority of Scripture is not left unquestioned by a radical demythologization.

BISHOPS ARE AUTHENTIC TEACHERS

While silence gradually obscures certain fundamental mysteries of Christianity, we see manifestations of a tendency to reconstruct from psychological and sociological data a Christianity cut off from the unbroken Tradition which links it to the faith of the apostles, and a tendency to extol a Christian life deprived of religious elements.

All of us, therefore, who through the laying on of hands, have received the responsibility of keeping pure and entire the faith entrusted to us and the mission of proclaiming the Gospel unceasingly, are called upon to witness to the obedience we all give the Lord. It is an inalienable and sacred right of the people in our charge to receive the Word of God, the whole Word of God, of which the Church has not ceased to acquire deeper comprehension. It is a grave and urgent duty for us to proclaim it untiringly, that the people may grow in faith and understanding of the Christian message and may bear witness throughout their lives to salvation in Jesus Christ.

The Council reminded us forcefully of this: "Among the principal duties of bishops, the preaching of the Gospel occupies an eminent place. For bishops are preachers of the faith who lead new disciples to Christ. They are authentic teachers, that is, teachers endowed with the authority of Christ, who preach to the people committed to them the faith they must believe and put into practice. By the light of the Holy Spirit, they make that faith clear, bringing forth from the treasury of revelation new things and old,[29] making faith bear fruit and vigilantly warding off any errors which threaten their flock.[30] Bishops, teaching in communion with the Roman Pontiff, are to be respected by all as witnesses to divine and Catholic truth. In matters of faith and morals, the bishops speak in the name of Christ and the faithful are to accept their teaching and adhere to it with a religious assent . . ."[31]

Certainly, faith is always an assent given because of the authority of God Himself. But the teaching office of the bishops is for the believer the sign and channel which enable him to receive and recognize the Word of God. Each bishop, in his diocese, is united by his office with the episcopal college which, in succession to the apostolic college, has been entrusted with the charge of watching over the purity of faith and the unity of the Church.

II

Let us unhesitatingly recognize that in the present circumstances the urgently needed fulfillment of this preeminent task encounters more difficulties than it has known in past centuries.

In fact, while the exercise of the episcopal teaching office was relatively easy when the Church lived in close association with contemporary society, inspiring its culture and sharing its modes of expression, nowadays a serious effort is required of us to ensure that the teaching of the faith should keep the fullness of its meaning and scope, while expressing itself in a form which allows it to reach the spirit and the heart of all men, to whom it is addressed. No one has better shown the duty laid upon us in this regard than our Predecessor Pope John XXIII in his discourse at the opening of the Council: "In response to the deep desire of all who are sincerely attached to what is Christian, Catholic and apostolic, this teaching must be more widely and more deeply known, and minds must be more fully permeated and shaped by it. While this sure and unchangeable teaching must command faithful respect, it should be studied and presented in a way demanded by our age. The deposit of faith itself—that is to say the truths contained in our venerable teaching—is one thing; the way in which these truths are presented is another, although they must keep the same sense and signification. The manner of presentation is to be regarded as of great importance and, if necessary, patient work must be devoted to perfecting it. In other words there must be introduced methods of presentation more in keeping with a Magisterium which is predominantly pastoral in character."[32]

SAFEGUARD THE TRUTH

In the present crisis of language and thought, each bishop in his diocese, each synod and each episcopal conference must be attentive lest this necessary effort should ever betray the truth and continuity of the teaching of the faith. We must beware, in particular, lest an arbitrary selection should reduce God's design to the limits of our human views and restrict the proclaiming of His Word to what our ears like to hear, excluding on purely natural criteria what does not please contemporary taste. "If anyone," Saint Paul warns us, "preaches a version of the Good News different from the one we have already preached to you, whether it be ourselves or an angel from heaven, he is to be condemned."[33]

In fact it is not we who are judges of the Word of God. It is His Word which judges us and exposes our habit of conforming to this world. "The weakness and insufficiency of Christians, even of those who have the function of preaching, will never be a reason for the Church to water down the absolute nature of the Word. The edge of the sword[34] can never be dulled thereby. The Church can never speak otherwise than as Christ did of holiness, virginity, poverty and obedience."[35]

In passing, let us remember this: if sociological surveys are useful for better discovering the thought-patterns of the people of a particular place, the anxieties and needs of those to whom we proclaim the Word of God, and also the opposition made to it by modern reasoning through the widespread notion that outside science there exists no legitimate form of knowledge, still the conclusions drawn from such surveys could not of themselves constitute a determining criterion of truth.

All the same, we must not be deaf to the questions which today face a believer rightly anxious to acquire a more profound understanding of his faith. We must lend an ear to these questions, not in order to cast suspicion on what is well-founded, nor to deny their postulates, but so that we may do justice to their legitimate demands within our own proper field which is that of faith. This holds true for modern man's great questions concerning his origins, the meaning of life, the happiness to which he aspires and the destiny of the human family. But it is no less true of the questions posed today by scholars, historians, psychologists and sociologists; these questions are so many invitations to us to proclaim better, in its incarnate transcendence, the Good News of Christ the Savior, a message which in no way contradicts the discoveries of the human mind but which rather raises that mind to the level of divine realities, to the point of allowing it to share, in a still inarticulate and incipient yet very real way, in that mystery of love which the Apostle tells us "is beyond all knowledge."[36]

ENCOURAGE THEOLOGIANS, EXEGETES

To those in the Church who undertake the responsible task of studying more deeply the unfathomable riches of this mystery, namely theologians and in particular exegetes, we shall manifest encouragement and support in order to help them to pursue their work in fidelity to the great stream of Christian Tradition.[37] In the recent past it has quite rightly been said: "Theology, being the science of the faith, can only find its norm in the Church, the community of the believers. When theology rejects its postulates and understands its norm in a different way, it loses its basis and its object. The religious freedom affirmed by the Council and which rests upon freedom of conscience is valid for the personal decision in relation to faith, but it has nothing to do with determining the content and scope of divine revelation."[38] In like manner, the utilization of human scientific knowledge in research in hermeneutics is a way of investigating the revealed data, but these data cannot be reduced to the analyses thus provided, because they transcend them both in origin and content.

In this period which follows a Council which was prepared by the rich attainments of biblical and theological knowledge, a considerable amount of work remains to be done, particularly in the field of developing the theology of the Church and working out a Christian anthropology taking into account progress made in human sciences and the questions the latter pose to the mind of the believer. We all recognize, not only how important this work is, but also that it makes particular demands; we understand the inevitable waverings. But in face of the ravages being inflicted upon the Christian people by the diffusion of venturesome hypotheses and of opinions that disturb faith, we have the duty to recall, with the Council, that true theology "rests upon the written Word of God, together with sacred Tradition, as its perpetual foundation."[39]

Dearly beloved brothers, let us not be reduced to silence for fear of criticism, which is always possible and may at times be well-founded. However necessary the function of theologians, it is not to the learned that God has confided the duty of authentically interpreting the faith of the Church: that faith is borne by the life of the people whose bishops are responsible for them before God. It is for the bishops to tell the people what God asks them to believe.

This demands much courage of each one of us; for, even though we are assisted by exercising this responsibility in community, within the framework of the synods of bishops and the episcopal conferences, it is none the less a question of a personal and absolutely inalienable responsibility for us to meet the immediate daily needs of the People of God. This is not the time to ask ourselves, as some would have us do, whether it is really useful, opportune and necessary to speak; rather it is the time for us to take the means to make ourselves heard. For it is to us bishops that Saint Paul's exhortation to Timothy is addressed: "Before God and before Christ Jesus who is to be judge of the living and the dead, I put this duty to you, in the name of his Appearing and of his kingdom: proclaim the message and, welcome or unwelcome, insist on it. Refute falsehood, correct error, call to obedience—but do all with patience and with the intention of teaching. The time is sure to come when, far from being content with sound teaching, people will be avid for the latest novelty and collect themselves a whole series of teachers according to their own tastes; and then, instead of listening to the truth, they will turn to myths. Be careful always to choose the right course; be brave under trails; make the preaching of the Good News your life's work in thorough-going service."[40]

III

Therefore, dearly beloved brothers, let each of us examine himself on the way in which he carries out this sacred duty: it demands from us assiduous study of the revealed Word and constant attention to the life of men.

How in fact shall we be able to proclaim fruitfully the Word of God, if it is not familiar to us through being the subject of our daily meditation and prayer? And how can it be received unless it is supported by a life of deep faith, active charity, total obedience, fervent prayer and humble penance? Having insisted, as is our duty, on teaching the doctrine of the faith, we must add that what is often most needed is not so much an abundance of words as speech in harmony with a more evangelical life. Yes, it is the witness of saints that the world needs, for, as the Council reminds us, God "speaks to us in them, and gives us a sign of his kingdom, to which we are powerfully drawn."[41]

TEACH THEM JESUS CHRIST

Let us be attentive to the questions that are expressed through the life of men, especially of the young: "What father among you," Jesus says to us, "would hand his son a stone when he asked for bread?"[42] Let us listen willingly to the questionings that come to disturb our peace and quiet. Let us bear patiently the hesitations of those who are groping for the light. Let us know how to walk in brotherly friendship with all those who, lacking the light we ourselves enjoy, are nevertheless seeking through the mists of doubt to reach their Father's house. But, if we share in their distress, let it be in order to try to heal it. If we hold up to them Christ Jesus, let it be as the Son of God made man to save us and to make us sharers in his life and not as a merely human figure, however wonderful and attractive.[43]

In being thus faithful to God and to the men to whom he sends us, we shall then be able, with prudence and tact, but also with clear vision and firmness, to make a correct assessment of opinions. This is, beyond any doubt, one of the most difficult tasks for the episcopate,

but also one of the most necessary today. In fact, in the clash of con-
flicting ideas, the greatest generosity runs the risk of going hand-in-
hand with the most questionable statements. "Even from your own
ranks," as in the time of Saint Paul, "there will be men coming forward with a travesty of the truth on their lips to induce the disciples
to follow them";[44] and those who speak in this way are often convinced
of doing so in the name of God, deluding themselves about the spirit
that animates them. In the matter of discerning the word of faith, do
we take sufficient note of the fruits that it brings? Could God be the
source of a word that would make Christians lose the sense of evangelical self-denial or which would proclaim justice while forgetting to be
the herald of meekness, mercy and purity? Could God be the source
of a word which would set brothers against brothers? Jesus warns us
of this: "You will be able to tell them by their fruits."[45]

Let us demand the same from those co-workers who share with
us the task of proclaiming the Word of God. Let their witness always
be that of the Gospel; let their word always be that of the Word who
stirs up faith and, together with faith, love of our brothers, bringing all
the disciples of Christ to imbue with His spirit the mentality, the man-
ners and the life of the terrestrial city.[46] It is in this way that, to quote
the admirable expression of Saint Augustine, "God, not men, brought
you this; thus even through the ministry of timid men God speaks in
full freedom."[47]

Dearly beloved brothers, these are some of the thoughts suggested
to us by the anniversary of the Council, that "providential instrument
for the true renewal of the Church."[48] In joining with you in all fraternal simplicity to examine our fidelity to this fundamental mission of
proclaiming the Word of God, we have been aware of responding to
an imperative duty. Someone perhaps will be surprised, may even
protest. In the serenity of our soul we call upon you to witness to the
necessity that urges us on to be faithful to our charge as shepherd; we
call upon you likewise to witness to our desire to join with you in
taking the means most adapted to our days and at the same time most
in conformity with the Council's teaching, the better to ensure its
fruitfulness. As we join you in entrusting ourselves to the sweet motherly
care of the Virgin Mary, we invoke with all our heart upon you and
your pastoral mission the abundant graces of "him whose power,
working in us, can do infinitely more than we ask or imagine; glory

be to him from generation to generation in the Church and in Christ Jesus for ever and ever.   Amen."[49]

May these wishes be supported by our Apostolic Blessing, which we impart to you with affection.

Given in Rome, at Saint Peter's, on the eighth day of December, the solemnity of the Immaculate Conception of the Blessed Virgin Mary, in the year nineteen hundred and seventy, the eighth of our pontificate.

Paulus PP. VI

Allocution: The Church Is the Transmitter and Interpreter of the Faith

JANUARY 19, 1972

BELOVED SONS AND DAUGHTERS!

Consider the many great questions concerning the origin of the universe, the meaning of life, the longing to know the destiny of mankind, the religious phenomenon, which seeks to answer these problems, assimilating and transcending what science and philosophy can tell us about them. Then set the Christian fact in the face of these questions, which recognized in their boundless demands we call darkness, but which confronted with the Christian fact itself, light up and give us a glimpse of their mysterious depths and at the same time of a certain marvelous beauty. Do this and you will feel echoing within you, as if they had been uttered that very moment, the well-known words of John's Gospel: "the light shines in the darkness" (Jn. 1, 5). The panorama of the cosmos is lit up as if the sun had risen from the night; things show a delightful order, which can still be explored; and man, almost laughing and trembling with joy, gets to know himself.

He discovers himself as the privileged wayfarer advancing, tiny and supreme, over the world stage. At the same time he is aware that he has the right and the capacity to dominate it, and both the duty and the possibility of transcending it in the fascination of a new relationship that is superior to him—the dialogue with God: a dialogue that opens in this way: "Our Father, who art in heaven. . . ."

It is not a dream, or imagination, or an hallucination. It is simply the first and normal effect of the Gospel, of its light shining on a soul, which has opened to its rays. What do we call this projection of light? It is Revelation. And what is this opening of the soul? It is called faith.

A DIVINE INTERVENTION

We learn these stupendous things from that sublime book of theology and mysticism, which is called the catechism, that is, the religious book of fundamental truths. But today this introduction aims at interesting those who hear it in a further question, which we consider of the utmost importance with regard to the ideological condition in which thinking man finds himself on the religious plane. The question is this. Is contact with God, resulting from the Gospel, a moment of a natural evolution of the human spirit, an evolution that still continues, transforming and surpassing itself? Or is it a single, definitive moment, on which we must nourish ourselves endlessly, but always recognizing its essential content as unchangeable?

The answer is clear: it is a single and definitive moment. Revelation is inserted in time, in history, at a precise date, on the occasion of a specific event, and it must be regarded as concluded and complete for us with the death of the Apostles (cfr. *DS* 3421). Revelation is a fact, an event, and at the same time a mystery, which did not have its origin in the human spirit, but came from a divine intervention. It had many progressive manifestations, spread out over a long history, the Old Testament; and it culminated in Jesus Christ (cfr. Heb. 1, 1; 1 Jn. 2-3; Conciliar Constitution, *Dei Verbum,* n. 1). Thus for us eventually the Word of God is the Word Incarnate, the historical Christ, who continues to live in the community united with him through faith and the Holy Spirit, in the Church which is his Mystical Body.

This is how things are, beloved Sons; and in this way our doctrine is separated from the errors which have circulated and still crop up in the culture of our times, and which might ruin completely our

Christian conception of life and history. Modernism was the characteristic expression of these errors, and it still exists today, under other names (cfr. Decr. *Lamentabili* of St. Pius X, 1907, and his Encyclical *Pascendi; DS* 3401, ss.). So we can understand why the Catholic Church, in the past and today, has given and gives so much importance to the scrupulous preservation of the authentic Revelation. She considers it an inviolable treasure, and is sternly aware of her fundamental duty to defend and transmit the doctrine of the faith in unequivocal terms. Orthodoxy is her first concern; the pastoral Magisterium is her primary and providential function. The apostolic teaching fixed the canons of her preaching. The Apostle Paul's order: *Depositum custodi,* "guard the deposit" (1 Tim. 6, 20; 2 Tim. 1, 14), is for her such a commitment that it would be a betrayal to violate it. The teaching Church does not invent her doctrine; she is a witness, a custodian, an interpreter, a transmitter. As regards the truths of the Christian message, she can be called conservative, uncompromising. To those who urge her to make her faith easier, more in keeping with the tastes of the changing mentality of the times, we answer with the Apostles: *Non possumus,* "we cannot" (Acts 4, 20).

This too brief lesson does not end here. It still remains to be explained how this original Revelation is transmitted through words, study, interpretation, application; that is, how it gives rise to a Tradition, which the Magisterium of the Church receives and verifies, sometimes with decisive and infallible authority. It should also be recalled how the knowledge of the faith and the teaching that sets it forth, namely theology, can be expressed in different measure, language and form. In other words, a theological "pluralism" is legitimate when it is contained within the limits of the faith and the Magisterium entrusted by Christ to the Apostles and their successors.

FRUITFUL AND ALIVE

It would also be necessary to explain that the Word of God, preserved in its authenticity, is not for that reason dry and sterile, but fruitful and alive, and meant to be listened to not merely passively, but to be lived, always renewed and ever embodied in individual souls, in individual communities, in individual Churches, according to human gifts and according to the charisms of the Holy Spirit which are at the disposal of all those who become faithful disciples of the living and penetrating Word of God (cfr. Heb. 4, 12).

We will speak about this again, perhaps, God willing. But in the meantime may these fragments of Catholic doctrine suffice to make you fervent and happy, and give you food for thought. With our Apostolic Blessing.

Declaration for Safeguarding the Doctrine of the Incarnation and the Trinity

FEBRUARY 21, 1972

1. The mystery of the Son of God, who was made man, and the mystery of the Most Holy Trinity, both pertaining to the innermost substance of Revelation, must be in their authentic truth the source of light for the lives of Christ's faithful. But because some recent errors undermine these mysteries, the Sacred Congregation for the Doctrine of the Faith has determined to reaffirm and to safeguard the belief in them that has been handed down to us.

2. *Catholic belief in the Son of God who was made man.* Jesus Christ, while dwelling on this earth, manifested in various ways, by word and by deed, the adorable mystery of His Person. After being made "obedient unto death."[50] He was divinely exalted in His glorious resurrection, as was fitting for the Son "through whom all things"[51] were made by the Father. Of Him St. John solemnly proclaimed: "In the beginning was the Word and the Word was with God and the Word was God . . . And the Word was made flesh."[52] The Church reverently preserved the mystery of the Son of God, who was made man, and "in the course of the ages and of the centuries"[53] has propounded it for belief in a more explicit way. In the Creed of Con-

209

stantinople, which is still recited today during Mass, the Church proclaims her faith in "Jesus Christ, the only-begotten Son of God and born of the Father before all the ages . . . true God from true God . . . consubstantial with the Father . . . who for us men and for our salvation . . . was made man."[54] The Council of Chalcedon laid down to be believed that the Son of God according to His divinity was begotten of the Father before all the ages, and according to His humanity was begotten in time of the Virgin Mary.[55] Further, this Council called one and the same Christ the Son of God a 'person' (hypostasis), but used the term 'nature' to describe His divinity and His humanity, and using these terms it taught that both His natures, divine and human, together belong, without confusion, unalterably, undividedly and inseparably to the one person of our Redeemer.[56] In the same way, the Fourth Lateran Council taught for belief and profession that the Son of God, coeternal with the Father, was made true man and is one person in two natures.[57] This is the Catholic belief which the recent Vatican Council II, holding to the constant tradition of the whole Church, clearly expressed in many passages.[58]

3. *Recent errors in regard to belief in the Son of God.* The opinions according to which it has not been revealed and made known to us that the Son of God subsists from all eternity in the mystery of the Godhead, distinct from the Father and the Holy Spirit, are in open conflict with this belief; likewise the opinions according to which one must abandon the notion of the one person of Jesus Christ begotten in His divinity of the Father before all the ages and begotten in His humanity of the Virgin Mary in time; and lastly, the assertion that the humanity of Christ existed not as being assumed into the eternal person of the Son of God but existed rather in itself as a person, and therefore, that the mystery of Jesus Christ consists only in the fact that God, in revealing Himself, was present in the highest degree in the human person Jesus.

Those who think in this way are far removed from the true belief in Christ, even when they maintain that the special presence of God in Jesus results in His being the supreme and final expression of divine Revelation. Nor do they come back to the true belief in the divinity of Christ by adding that Jesus can be called God by reason of the fact that, in what they call His human person, God is supremely present.

4. *Catholic belief in the Most Holy Trinity, and especially in the*

Holy Spirit. Once the mystery of the divine and eternal person of Christ the Son of God is abandoned, the truth respecting the Most Holy Trinity is also undermined, and with it the truth regarding the Holy Spirit who proceeds eternally from the Father and the Son, or from the Father through the Son.[59] Therefore, in view of recent errors, some points concerning belief in the Most Holy Trinity, and especially in the Holy Spirit, are to be reaffirmed.

The Second Epistle to the Corinthians concludes with this admirable expression: "The grace of our Lord Jesus Christ, and the love of God, and the fellowship of the Holy Spirit be with you all."[60] The commission to baptize, recorded in St. Matthew's Gospel, names the Father, and the Son, and the Holy Spirit as the three pertaining to the mystery of God and it is in their name that converts must be reborn.[61] Lastly, in St. John's Gospel, Jesus speaks of the coming of the Holy Spirit: "When the Paraclete comes whom I will send you from the Father, the Spirit of truth who proceeds from the Father, He will give testimony of me."[62]

On the basis of the indications of divine Revelation, the Magisterium of the Church, to which alone is entrusted "the office of authentic interpretation of the Word of God, written or handed down,"[63] acclaims in the Creed of Constantinople "the Holy Spirit, Lord and giver of life . . . who together with the Father and the Son is adored and glorified."[64] In like manner the Fourth Lateran Council taught that it is to be believed and professed "that there is only one true God . . . Father and Son and Holy Spirit: three Persons indeed, but one essence . . . : the Father proceeding from none, the Son from the Father alone and the Holy Spirit equally from both, without beginning, always, and without end."[65]

5. *Recent errors concerning the Most Holy Trinity, and especially concerning the Holy Spirit.* The opinion that Revelation has left us uncertain about the eternity of the Trinity, and in particular about the eternal existence of the Holy Spirit as a Person in God distinct from the Father and the Son, is out of line with the faith. It is true that the mystery of the most Holy Trinity was revealed to us in the economy of salvation, and most of all in Christ Himself who was sent into the world by the Father and together with the Father sends to the People of God the life-giving Spirit. But by this Revelation there is also given to those who believe some knowledge of God's intimate life, in which

"the Father who generates, the Son who is generated, and the Holy Spirit who proceeds" are "consubstantial and coequal, alike omnipotent and co-eternal."[66]

6. *The Mysteries of the Incarnation and of the Trinity are to be faithfully preserved and expounded.* What is expressed in the documents of the Councils referred to above, concerning the one and the same Christ the Son of God, begotten before the ages in His divine nature and in time in His human nature, and also concerning the eternal persons of the Most Holy Trinity, belongs to the immutable truth of the Catholic faith.

This certainty does not prevent the Church in her awareness of the progress of human thought from considering that it is her duty to take steps to have these mysteries continually examined by contemplation and by theological examination and to have them more fully expounded in up-to-date terminology. But while the necessary duty of investigation is being pursued, diligent care must be taken that these profound mysteries not be given a meaning other than that with which "the Church has understood and understands them."[67]

The unimpaired truth of these mysteries is of the greatest importance for the whole Revelation of Christ, because they pertain to its very core, in such a way indeed that if they are undermined, the rest of the treasure of Revelation is falsified. The truth of these same mysteries is of no less concern to the Christian way of life both because nothing so effectively manifests the charity of God, to which the whole of Christian life should be a response, as does the Incarnation of the Son of God, our Redeemer,[68] and also because "through Christ, the Word made flesh, men have access to the Father in the Holy Spirit and are made partakers of the divine nature."[69]

7. With regard to the truths which the present Declaration is safeguarding, it pertains to the Pastors of the Church to see that there is unity in professing the faith on the part of their people, and especially on the part of those who by mandate received from the Magisterium teach the sacred sciences or preach the word of God. This function of the Bishops belongs to the office divinely committed to them "of keeping pure and whole" . . . "the deposit of faith" together with the Successor of Peter and "of proclaiming the Gospel without ceasing"[70] and by reason of this same office they are bound not to permit that ministers of the Word of God, deviating from the way of sound doctrine, should

pass it on corrupted or incomplete.[71] The people, committed as they are to the care of the Bishops who "have to render account to God"[72] for them, enjoy "the sacred and inalienable right of receiving the Word of God, the whole Word of God, into which the Church does not cease to penetrate ever more profoundly."[73]

The faithful, then, and above all the theologians because of their important office and necessary function in the Church, must make faithful profession of the mysteries which this Declaration reaffirms. In like manner, under the guidance and illumination of the Holy Spirit, the sons of the Church must hold fast to the whole teaching of the faith under the leadership of their Pastors and of the Pastor of the universal Church[74] "so that, in holding, practising and professing the faith that has been handed down, a common effort results on the part of the Bishops and faithful."[75]

The Supreme Pontiff by divine Providence, Pope Paul VI, in an audience granted on February 21, 1972 to the undersigned Prefect of the Sacred Congregation for the Doctrine of the Faith, ratified and confirmed this Declaration for safeguarding from certain recent errors the belief in the mysteries of the Incarnation and of the Most Holy Trinity, and ordered it to be published.

Given at Rome, from the offices of the Sacred Congregation for the Doctrine of the Faith, on the 21st day of February, feast of St. Peter Damian, in the year of our Lord 1972.

Francis Cardinal Seper, *Prefect*

Paul Philippe, Titular Archbp. of Heracleopolis, *Secretary*

THE SACRED CONGREGATION FOR THE
DOCTRINE OF THE FAITH

Declaration for Safeguarding
The Catholic Doctrine
on the Church

JUNE 24, 1973

The mystery of the Church, upon which the Second Vatican
Council shed fresh light, has been repeatedly dealt with in numerous
writings of theologians. While not a few of these studies have served
to make this mystery more understandable, others, through the use
of ambiguous or even erroneous language, have obscured Catholic
doctrine, and at times have gone so far as to be opposed to Catholic
faith even in fundamental matters.

To meet this situation, the bishops of several nations, conscious
both of their duty of "keeping pure and intact the deposit of faith"
and of their task of "proclaiming the Gospel unceasingly"[76] have,
through concurring declarations, sought to protect the faithful entrusted to their care from the danger of error. In addition, the second
General Assembly of the Synod of Bishops, in dealing with the ministerial priesthood, expounded a number of important points of doctrine regarding the constitution of the Church.

Likewise, the Sacred Congregation for the Doctrine of the Faith,
whose task it is to "preserve the doctrine of faith and morals in the
whole Catholic world"[77] intends to gather together and explain a num-

214

ber of truths concerning the mystery of the Church which at the present time are being either denied or endangered. In this it will follow above all the lines laid down by the two Vatican Councils.

THE ONENESS OF CHRIST'S CHURCH

One is the Church, which "after His Resurrection our Savior handed over to Peter as Shepherd" (cf. Jn. 21, 17), commissioning him and the other Apostles to propagate and govern her (cf. Mt. 18, 18 ff.) (and which) He erected for all ages as "the pillar and mainstay of the truth" (cf. 1 Tim. 3, 15). And this Church of Christ, "constituted and organized in this world as a society, subsists in the Catholic Church which is goverened by the Successor of Peter and the bishops in union with that Successor."[78] This declaration of the Second Vatican Council is illustrated by the same Council's statement that "it is through Christ's Catholic Church alone, which is the general means of salvation, that the fullness of the means of salvation can be obtained,"[79] and that same Catholic Church "has been endowed with all divinely revealed truth and with all the means of grace"[80] with which Christ wished to enhance His messianic community. This is no obstacle to the fact that during her earthly pilgrimage the Church, "embracing sinners in her bosom, is at the same time holy and always in need of being purified,"[81] nor to the fact that "outside her visible structure," namely in Churches and ecclesial communities which are joined to the Catholic Church by an imperfect communion, there are to be found "many elements of sanctification and truth (which), as gifts properly belonging to the Church of Christ, possess an inner dynamism towards Catholic unity."[82]

For these reasons, "Catholics must joyfully acknowledge and esteem the truly Christian endownments derived from our common heritage, which are to be found among our separated brethren,"[83] and they must strive for the reestablishment of unity among all Christians, by making a common effort of purification and renewal,[84] so that the will of Christ may be fulfilled and the division of Christians may cease to be an obstacle to the proclamation of the Gospel throughout the world.[85] But at the same time Catholics are bound to profess that through the gift of God's mercy they belong to that Church which Christ founded and which is governed by the successors of Peter and

the other Apostles, who are the depositaries of the original apostolic
tradition, living and intact, which is the permanent heritage of doctrine
and holiness of that same Church.[86] The followers of Christ are therefore not permitted to imagine that Christ's Church is nothing more
than a collection (divided, but still possessing a certain unity) of
Churches and ecclesial communities. Nor are they free to hold that
Christ's Church nowhere really exists today and that it is to be considered only as an end which all Churches and ecclesial communities
must strive to reach.

THE INFALLIBILITY OF THE UNIVERSAL CHURCH

"In His gracious goodness, God has seen to it that what He had
revealed for the salvation of all nations would abide perpetually in its
full integrity."[87] For this reason He entrusted to the Church the treasury of God's Word, so that the pastors and the holy people might
strive together to preserve it, study it and apply it to life.[88]

God, who is absolutely infallible, thus deigned to bestow upon His
new people, which is the Church, a certain shared infallibility, which is
restricted to matters of faith and morals, which is present when the
whole People of God unhesitatingly holds a point of doctrine pertaining to these matters, and finally which always depends upon the wise
providence and anointing of the grace of the Holy Spirit, who leads
the Church into all truth until the glorious coming of her Lord.[89] Concerning this infallibility of the People of God the Second Vatican
Council speaks as follows: "The body of the faithful as a whole,
anointed as they are by the Holy One (cf. 1 Jn. 2, 20.27), cannot err
in matters of belief. Thanks to a supernatural instinct of faith which
characterizes the people as a whole, it manifests this unerring quality
when, 'from the bishops down to the last member of the laity' (St.
Augustine, *De Praed. Sanct.*, 14, 27), it shows universal agreement
in matters of faith and morals."[90]

The Holy Spirit enlightens and assists the People of God inasmuch
as it is the Body of Christ united in a hierarchical communion. The
Second Vatican Council indicates this fact by adding to the words
quoted above: "For, by this instinct of faith which is aroused and
sustained by the Spirit of truth, God's People accepts not the word of
men but the very Word of God (cf. 1 Thes. 2, 13). It clings without

fail to the faith once delivered to the saints (cf. Jude 3), penetrates it more deeply by accurate insights, and applies it more thoroughly to life. All this it does under the lead of a sacred teaching authority to which it loyally defers."[91]

Without doubt the faithful, who in their own manner share in Christ's prophetic office,[92] in many ways contribute towards increasing the understanding of faith in the Church. "For," as the Second Vatican Council says, "there is a growth in the understanding of the realities and the words which have been handed down. This happens through the contemplation and study made by believers, who treasure these things in their hearts (cf. Lk. 2, 19, 51), through the preaching of those who have received through episcopal succession the sure charism of truth."[93] And the Supreme Pontiff Paul VI observes that the witness the pastors of the Church offer is "rooted in sacred Tradition and holy Scripture and nourished by the ecclesial life of the whole People of God."[94]

But by divine institution it is the exclusive task of these Pastors alone, the successors of Peter and the other Apostles, to teach the faithful authentically, that is with the authority of Christ shared in different ways; so that the faithful, who may not simply listen to them as experts in Catholic doctrine, must accept their teaching given in Christ's name, with an assent that is proportionate to the authority that they possess and that they mean to exercise.[95] For this reason the Second Vatican Council, in harmony with the First Vatican Council, teaches that Christ made Peter "a perpetual and visible principle and foundation of the unity of faith and of communion";[96] and the Supreme Pontiff Paul VI has declared: "The teaching office of the bishops is for the believer the sign and channel which enable him to receive and recognize the Word of God."[97] Thus, however much the sacred Magisterium avails itself of the contemplation, life and study of the faithful, its office is not reduced merely to ratifying the assent already expressed by the latter; indeed, in the interpretation and explanation of the written or transmitted Word of God, the Magisterium can anticipate or demand their assent.[98] The People of God has particular need of the intervention and assistance of the Magisterium when internal disagreements arise and spread concerning a doctrine that must be believed or held, lest it lose the communion of the one faith in the one Body of the Lord (cf. Eph. 4, 5).

THE INFALLIBILITY OF THE CHURCH'S MAGISTERIUM

Jesus Christ from whom derives the task proper to the pastors of teaching the Gospel to all His people and to the entire human family, wished to endow the pastors' Magisterium with a fitting charism of infallibility in matters regarding faith and morals. Since this charism does not come from new revelations enjoyed by the Successor of Peter and the College of Bishops,[99] it does not dispense them from studying with appropriate means the treasure of divine Revelation contained both in Sacred Scripture which teaches us intact the truth that God willed to be written down for our salvation[100] and in the living Tradition that comes from the Apostles.[101] In carrying out their task, the pastors of the Church enjoy the assistance of the Holy Spirit; this assistance reaches its highest point when they teach the People of God in such a manner that, through the promises of Christ made to Peter and the other Apostles, the doctrine they propose is necessarily immune from error.

This occurs when the bishops scattered throughout the world but teaching in communion with the Successor of Peter present a doctrine to be held irrevocably.[102] It occurs even more clearly both when the bishops by a collegial act (as in Ecumenical Councils), together with their visible Head, define a doctrine to be held,[103] and when the Roman Pontiff "speaks *ex cathedra,* that is, when, exercising the office of Pastor and Teacher of all Christians, through his supreme apostolic authority, he defines a doctrine concerning faith or morals to be held by the universal Church."[104]

According to Catholic doctrine, the infallibility of the Church's Magisterium extends not only to the deposit of faith but also to those matters without which that deposit cannot be rightly preserved and expounded.[105] The extension however of this infallibility to the deposit of faith itself is a truth that the Church has held from the beginning as having been certainly revealed in Christ's promises. The First Vatican Council, basing itself upon this truth, defined as follows the matter of Catholic faith: "All those things are to be believed by divine and Catholic faith which are contained in the written or transmitted Word of God and which are proposed by the Church, either by a solemn judgment or by the Ordinary and Universal Magisterium, to be believed as having been divinely revealed."[106] Therefore the objects of Catholic faith—which are called dogmas—necessarily are, and always have been, the unalterable norm both for faith and for theological science.

THE CHURCH'S GIFT OF INFALLIBILITY NOT TO BE DIMINISHED

From what has been said about the extent of and conditions governing the infallibility of the People of God and of the Church's Magisterium, it follows that the faithful are in no way permitted to see in the Church merely a fundamental permanence in truth which, as some assert, could be reconciled with errors contained here and there in the propositions that the Church's Magisterium teaches to be held irrevocably, as also in the unhesitating assent of the People of God concerning matters of faith and morals.

It is of course true that through the faith that leads to salvation men are converted to God,[107] who reveals Himself in His Son Jesus Christ; but it would be wrong to deduce from this that the Church's dogmas can be belittled or even denied. Indeed the conversion to God which we should realize through faith is a form of obedience (cf. Rom. 16, 26), which should correspond to the nature of divine Revelation and its demands. Now this Revelation, in the whole plan of salvation, reveals the mystery of God who sent His Son into the world (cf. 1 Jn. 4, 14) and teaches its application to Christian conduct. Moreover, it demands that, in full obedience of the intellect and will to God who reveals,[108] we accept the proclamation of the Good News of salvation as it is infallibly taught by the pastors of the Church. The faithful, therefore, through faith are converted as they should be to God, who reveals Himself in Christ, when they adhere to Him in the integral doctrine of the Catholic faith.

It is true that there exists an order and as it were a hierarchy of the Church's dogmas, as a result of their varying relationship to the foundation of the faith.[109] This hierarchy means that some dogmas are founded on other dogmas which are the principal ones, and are illuminated by these latter. But all dogmas, since they are revealed, must be believed with the same divine faith.[110]

THE NOTION OF THE CHURCH'S INFALLIBILITY NOT TO BE FALSIFIED

The transmission of divine Revelation by the Church encounters difficulties of various kinds. These arise from the fact that the hidden mysteries of God "by their nature so far transcend the human intellect that even if they are revealed to us and accepted by faith, they remain concealed by the veil of faith itself and are as it were wrapped in darkness."[111] Difficulties arise also from the historical condition that affects the expression of Revelation.

With regard to this historical condition, it must first be observed that the meaning of the pronouncements of faith depends partly upon the expressive power of the language used at a certain point in time and in particular circumstances. Moreover, it sometimes happens that some dogmatic truth is first expressed incompletely (but not falsely), and at a later date, when considered in a broader context of faith or human knowledge, it receives a fuller and more perfect expression. In addition, when the Church makes new pronouncements she intends to confirm or clarify what is in some way contained in Sacred Scripture or in previous expressions of Tradition; but at the same time she usually has the intention of solving questions or removing certain errors. All these things have to be taken into account in order that these pronouncements may be properly interpreted. Finally, even though the truths which the Church intends to teach through her dogmatic formulas are distinct from the changeable conceptions of a given epoch and can be expressed without them, nevertheless it can sometimes happen that these truths may be enunciated by the sacred Magisterium in terms that bear traces of such conceptions.

In view of the above, it must be stated that the dogmatic formulas of the Church's Magisterium were from the very beginning suitable for communicating revealed truth, and that as they are they remain forever suitable for communicating this truth to those who interpret them correctly.[112] It does not follow, however, that every one of these formulas has always been or will always be so to the same extent. For this reason theologians seek to define exactly the intention of teaching proper to the various formulas, and in carrying out this work they are of considerable assistance to the living Magisterium of the Church, to which they remain subordinated. For this reason also it often happens that ancient dogmatic formulas and others closely connected with them remain living and fruitful in the habitual usage of the Church, but with suitable expository and explanatory additions that maintain and clarify their original meaning. In addition, it has sometimes happened that in this habitual usage of the Church certain of these formulas gave way to new expressions which, proposed and approved by the sacred Magisterium, presented more clearly or more completely the same meaning.

As for the *meaning* of dogmatic formulas, this remains ever true and constant in the Church, even when it is expressed with greater clarity or more developed. The faithful therefore must shun the opinion, first, that dogmatic formulas (or some category of them) cannot signify truth in a determinate way, but can only offer changeable approximations to it, which to a certain extent distort or alter it; secondly, that these formulas signify the truth only in an indeterminate way, this truth being like a goal that is constantly being sought by means of such approximations. Those who hold such an opinion do not avoid dogmatic relativism and they corrupt the concept of the Church's infallibility relative to the truth to be taught or held in a determinate way.

Such an opinion clearly is in disagreement with the declarations of the First Vatican Council, which, while fully aware of the progress of the Church in her knowledge of revealed truth,[113] nevertheless taught as follows: "That meaning of sacred dogmas . . . must always be maintained which Holy Mother Church declared once and for all, nor should one ever depart from that meaning under the guise of or in the name of a more advanced understanding."[114] The Council moreover condemned the opinion that "dogmas once proposed by the Church must with the progress of science be given a meaning other than that which was understood by the Church, or which she understands."[115] There is no doubt that, according to these texts of the Council, the meaning of dogmas which is declared by the Church is determinate and unalterable.

Such an opinion is likewise in contrast with Pope John's assertion regarding Christian doctrine at the opening of the Second Vatican Council: "This certain and unchangeable doctrine, to which faithful obedience is due, has to be explored and presented in a way that is demanded by our times. One thing is the deposit of faith, which consists of the truths contained in sacred doctrine, another thing is the manner of presentation, always however with the same meaning and signification."[116] Since the Successor of Peter is here speaking about certain and unchangeable Christian doctrine, about the deposit of faith which is the same as the truths contained in that doctrine and about the truths which have to be presented with the same meaning, it is clear that he admits that we can know the true and unchanging meaning of dogmas. What is new and what he recommends in view of the needs of the times pertains only to the modes of studying, expounding and presenting that doctrine while keeping its permanent meaning. In a similar way the Supreme Pontiff Paul VI exhorted the pastors of the Church in the following words: "Nowadays a serious effort is required of us to ensure that the teaching of the faith should keep the fullness of its meaning and force, while expressing itself in a form which allows it to reach the spirit and heart of the people to whom it is addressed."[117]

THE CHURCH ASSOCIATED WITH THE PRIESTHOOD OF CHRIST

Christ the Lord, the High Priest of the new and everlasting covenant, wished to associate with His perfect priesthood and to form in its likeness the people He had bought with His own blood (cf. Heb. 7, 20–22.26–28; 10, 14.21). He therefore granted His Church a share in His priesthood, which consists of the common priesthood of the faithful and the ministerial or hierarchical priesthood. These differ from each other not only in degree but also in essence; yet they are mutually complementary within the communion of the Church.[118]

The common priesthood of the laity, which is also rightly called a royal priesthood (cf. 1 Pt. 2, 9; Rv. 1, 6; 5–9ff.) since through it the faithful are united as members of the messianic people with their heavenly King, is conferred by the sacrament of baptism. By this sacrament "the faithful are incorporated into the Church and are empowered to take part in the worship of the Christian religion" in virtue of a permanent sign known as a character; "reborn as children of God they are obliged to profess before men the faith which they have received from God through the Church."[119] Thus those who are reborn in Baptism "join in the offering of the Eucharist by virtue of their royal priesthood. They likewise exercise that priesthood by receiving the sacraments, by prayer and thanksgiving, by the witness of a holy life, and by self-denial and active charity."[120]

Moreover, Christ, the Head of the Church, which is His Mystical Body, appointed as ministers of His priesthood His Apostles and through them their successors the bishops, that they might act in His person within the Church[121] and also in turn legitmately hand over to priests in a subordinate degree the sacred ministry which they had received.[122] Thus there arose in the Church the apostolic succession of the ministerial priesthood for the glory of God and for the service of His people and of the entire human family, which must be converted to God.

By means of this priesthood bishops and priests are "indeed set apart in a certain sense in the midst of God's people. But this is so, not that they may be separated from this people or from any man, but that they may be totally dedicated to the work for which the Lord has raised them up":[123] namely, the work of sanctifying, teaching and ruling, the actual execution of which is more precisely specified by the hierarchical communion.[124] This manysided work has as its basis and foundation the continuous preaching of the Gospel,[125] and as the summit and source of the entire Christian life, the Eucharistic Sacrifice.[126] Priests, acting in the person of Christ the Head, offer this Sacrifice in the Holy Spirit to God the Father in the name of Christ and in the name of the members of His Mystical Body.[127] This sacrifice is completed in the Holy Supper by which the faithful, partaking of the one body of Christ, are all made into one body (cf. 1 Cor. 10, 16ff.).

The Church has ever more closely examined the nature of the ministerial priesthood, which can be shown to have been invariably conferred from apostolic times by a sacred rite (cf. 1 Tim. 4, 15; 2 Tim. 1, 6). By the assistance of the Holy Spirit, she recognized more clearly as time went on that God wished her to understand that this rite conferred upon priests not only an increase of grace for carrying out ecclesiastical duties in a holy way, but also a permanent designation by Christ, or character, by virtue of which they are equipped for their work and endowed with the necessary power that is derived from the supreme power of Christ. The permanent existence of this character, the nature of which is explained in different ways by theologians, is taught by the Council of Florence[128] and reaffirmed by two decrees of the Council of Trent.[129] In recent times the Second Vatican Council more than once mentioned it,[130] and the second General Assembly of the Synod of Bishops rightly considered the enduring nature of the priestly character throughout life as pertaining to the teaching of faith.[131] This stable existence of a priestly character must be recognized by the faithful and has to be taken into account in order to judge properly about the nature of the priestly ministry and the appropriate ways of exercising it.

Faithful to sacred Tradition and to many documents of the Magisterium, the Second Vatican Council taught the following concerning the power belonging to the ministerial priesthood: "Though everyone can baptize the faithful, the priest alone can complete the building up of the Body in the Eucharistic Sacrifice."[132] And again: "The same Lord, in order that the faithful might form one body in which 'all the members have not the same function' (Rom. 12, 4), appointed some ministers within the society of believers who by the power of Orders would be capable of offering the Sacrifice and of forgiving sins."[133]

In the same way the second General Assembly of the Synod of Bishops rightly affirmed that only the priest can act in the person of Christ and preside over and perform the sacrificial banquet in which the People of God are united with the oblation of Christ.[134] Passing over at this point questions regarding the ministers of the various sacraments, the evidence of sacred tradition and of the sacred Magisterium make it clear that the faithful who have not received priestly ordination and who take upon themselves the office of performing the Eucharist attempt to do so not only in a completely illicit way but also invalidly. Such an abuse, wherever it may occur, must clearly be eliminated by the pastors of the Church.

***

It was not the intention of this Declaration, nor was it within its scope, to prove by way of a study of the foundations of our faith that divine Revelation was entrusted to the Church so that she might thereafter preserve it unaltered in the world. But this dogma, from which the Catholic faith takes its beginning, has been recalled, together with other truths related to the mystery of the Church, so that in the uncertainty of the present day the faith and doctrine the faithful must hold might clearly emerge.

The Sacred Congregation for the Doctrine of the Faith rejoices that theologians are by intense study exploring more and more the mystery of the Church. It recognizes also that in their work they touch on many questions which can only be clarified by complementary studies and by various efforts and conjectures. However, the due freedom of theologians must always be limited by the Word of God as it is faithfully preserved and expounded in the Church and taught and explained by the living Magisterium of the Pastors and especially of the Pastor of the entire People of God.[135]

The Sacred Congregation entrusts this Declaration to the diligent attention of the bishops and of all those who in any way share the task of guarding the patrimony of truth which Christ and His Apostles committed to the Church. It also confidently addresses the Declaration to the faithful and particularly, in view of the important office which they hold in the Church, to priests and theologians, so that all may be of one mind in the faith and may be in sincere harmony with the Church.

Pope Paul VI, by divine providence Supreme Pontiff, in the audience granted to the undersigned Prefect of the Sacred Congregation for the Doctrine of the Faith on 11 May 1973, has ratified and confirmed this Declaration in defence of the Catholic doctrine on the Church against certain errors of the present day and has ordered its publication.

Given in Rome, at the Sacred Congregation for the Doctrine of the Faith, on 24 June 1973, the feast of Saint John the Baptist.

FRANJO CARDINAL SEPER, *Prefect*
+JEROME HAMER, *Secretary*
Tit. Archbishop of Lorium

POPE PAUL VI

Apostolic Exhortation on Reconciliation within the Church

DECEMBER 8, 1974

VENERABLE BROTHERS
AND DEAR SONS AND DAUGHTERS,
HEALTH AND THE APOSTOLIC BLESSING!

With affection, confidence and hope we turn to all of you, our brothers in the episcopate, the beloved members of the clergy, religious families, and the Catholic laity. We do so just before the celebration of the Holy Year in Rome at the Basilicas of the Apostles, now that you have already celebrated the Jubilee in the local Churches with piety and with harmony of sentiments and resolutions.

It is a moment of great importance for the entire world, which is looking to the Church. But principally so for the sons and daughters of the Church herself—those who are aware of the riches of her mystery of holiness and grace, which the recent Council has opportunely shed light upon. And therefore we address ourself to them with a cordial invitation to charity and to mutual union in the spirit of reconciliation proper to the Holy Year, in the bond of the one love of Christ.

In fact, from the moment in which on 9 May 1973 we manifested our decision to celebrate the Holy Year in 1975, we likewise manifested the primary goal of this spiritual and penitential celebration. This goal was to be reconciliation, founded on conversion to God and the interior of man, and which would heal the rifts and disorders which mankind, and the very ecclesial community itself, are suffering from today.[136]

Since the beginning of the jubilee celebrations which began by our decision in the local Churches at Pentecost 1973, we have neglected no opportunity of accompanying those celebrations with our doctrinal and pastoral interventions and with pressing reminders of the goal to be reached—a goal which we consider to be in perfect harmony with the most authentic spirit of the Gospel and with the guidelines of renewal formulated by the Second Vatican Council for the entire Church.

This Church, established by Christ as a permanent sign of the reconciliation accomplished by Him in accordance with the will of the Father,[137] has the task "under the guidance of the Holy Spirit, who renews and purifies her ceaselessly, to make God the Father and His Incarnate Son present and in a sense visible."[138] In order that this task may be even better fulfilled, it has therefore seemed to us necessary to underline the urgency for everyone in the Church to promote "the unity of the Spirit in the bond of peace." (Eph. 4, 3).

With the Solemnity of Christmas imminent—the date which we established for the opening of the universal Jubilee in Rome[139]—we present this Exhortation to the Pastors and faithful of the Church, that they may all become agents and promoters of reconciliation with God and with their brethren, and that this coming Christmas of the Holy Year may truly be for the world the "Birth of Peace,"[140] as was the birth of the Savior.

I. THE CHURCH : RECONCILED AND RECONCILING WORLD

From the very beginning of the transformation wrought by Christ's redeeming action the Church has been aware and has joyfully proclaimed that through that action the world has become a radically new reality (cf. 2 Cor. 5, 17)—a reality in which men have rediscovered God and hope (cf. Eph. 2, 12) and even here and now have been made sharers in the glory of God "through our Lord Jesus Christ, through whom we have already gained our reconciliation." (Rom. 5, 11).

This newness is owed exclusively to the merciful initiative of God (cf. 2 Cor. 5, 18–20; Col. 1, 20–22)—an initiative that comes to meet man who, having withdrawn from God by his own fault, was no longer able to find peace once more with his Creator.

This initiative of God was then actualized through a direct divine intervention. God in fact has not simply pardoned us, nor has He made use of a mere man as an intermediary between us and Himself: He has established His "only begotten Son an intercessor of peace."[141] "For our sake God made the sinless one into sin so that in Him we might become the goodness of God." (2 Cor. 5, 21). In reality, Christ, by dying for us, has cancelled out "every record of the debt that we had to pay; He has done away with it by nailing it to the Cross." (Col. 2, 14). And by means of the Cross He has reconciled us with God: "In His own person he has killed the hostility. " (Eph. 2, 16).

Reconciliation, effected by God in Christ crucified, is inscribed in the history of the world. That history now includes among its irreversible elements the event of God having become man and having died to save man. But reconciliation finds a permanent historical expression in the Body of Christ, which is the Church, in which the Son of God calls together "His brethren from all peoples"[142] and, as her Head (cf. Col. 1, 18), is her principle of authority and of action that constitutes her on earth as a "reconciled world."[143]

Since the Church is the Body of Christ and Christ is the "Savior of His body," (Eph. 5, 23), in order to be worthy members of this Body all must in fidelity to the Christian commitment contribute to preserving it in its original nature as the community of those who have been reconciled—a community having its origin in Christ, who is our peace (cf. Eph. 2, 15) and who "makes us reconciled."[144] In fact, once reconciliation has been received, it is, like grace and like life, an impulse and a current that transforms their beneficiaries into agents and transmitters of the same reconciliation. For every Christian the credential of his authenticity in the Church and in the world is this: "First make peace with yourself, so that when you have become peaceful you may bring peace to others."[145]

The duty of making peace extends personally to each and every member of the faithful. If it is not fulfilled, even the sacrifice of worship which they intend to offer (Mt. 5, 23ff.) remains ineffective. Mutual reconciliation, in fact, shares in the very value of the sacrifice itself, and together with it constitutes a single offering pleasing to God.[146] In order that this duty may be effectively fulfilled and that reconciliation which takes place in the depths of the heart may have a public character just like the death of Christ that brings it about, the Lord has conferred on the Apostles and on the Church's Pastors, their successors, the "ministry of reconciliation" (2 Cor. 5, 18). "Taking on as it were the Person of Christ,"[147] they are permanently deputed "to build up their flock in truth and holiness."[148]

The Church therefore, because she is a "reconciled world," is also a reality that is by nature permanently reconciling. As such she is the presence and the action of God, who "in Christ was reconciling the world to himself." (2 Cor. 5, 19). This action and presence are expressed primarily in Baptism, in the forgiveness of sins and in the Eucharistic celebration, which is the renewal of the redeeming Sacrifice of Christ and the effective sign of the unity of the People of God.[149]

II. THE CHURCH: THE SACRAMENT OF UNITY

Reconciliation, in its double aspect of peace restored between God and men and between man and man, is the first fruit of the Redemption, and like the Redemption has dimensions that are universal both in extent and in intensity. The whole of creation therefore is involved in reconciliation "till the universal restoration comes" (Acts 3, 21), when all creatures will again meet Christ, the "first to be born from the dead" (Col. 1, 18).

And since this reconciliation finds a privileged expression and greater concentration in the Church, the latter is "a kind of sacrament or sign of intimate union with God, and of the unity of all mankind."[150] It is the source from which radiate union of men with God and unity of men among themselves, which, through progressive affirmation in time, will find completion at the end of time.

In order to be able to express fully this sacramentality of hers, with which is bound up the very reason for her existence, the Church must be a meaningful sign, as is demanded of every sacrament. That is, there must be realized and verified in her that harmony and consistency of doctrine, life and worship which marked the first days of her existence (cf. Acts 2, 42) and which ever remain her essential element (cf. Eph. 4, 4–6; 1 Cor. 1, 10). This harmony, in contrast to any division that might attack the solidity of her structure, cannot but increase the force of her witness, reveal the reasons for her existence and throw clearer light upon her credibility.

In order to cooperate with God's plans in the world, all the faithful must persevere in fidelity to the Holy Spirit, who unifies the Church in "fellowship and service" and "by the power of the Gospel . . . makes the Church grow, perpetually renews her, and leads her to perfect union with her Spouse."[151] This fidelity cannot fail to have happy ecumenical effects upon the quest for the visible unity of all Christians, in the manner laid down by Christ, in one and the same Church; and this Church will thus be a more effective leaven of fraternal oneness in the community of the peoples.

III. OBSCURING THE SACRAMENTALITY OF THE CHURCH

However, "although by the power of the Holy Spirit the Church has remained the faithful spouse of her Lord and has never ceased to be the sign of salvation on earth, still she is very well aware that among her members, both clerical and lay, some have been unfaithful to the Spirit of God during the course of many centuries."[152]

In reality, "from her very beginnings there arose in this one and only Church of God certain rifts, which the Apostle strongly condemns."[153] Therefore when there occurred the well-known breaches that no one knew how to heal, the Church overcame the situation of internal dissension by clearly reaffirming as the irreplaceable condition of communion the principles that make it possible to preserve intact her constitutive unity and to manifest that unity "in the confession of one faith, in the common celebration of divine worship, and in the fraternal harmony of the family of God."[154]

But there appear equally dangerous, and such as to warrant this clarification and call to unity, the ferments of infidelity to the Holy Spirit existing here and there in the Church today and unfortunately attempting to undermine her from within. The promoters and the victims of this process, who are in fact small in number by comparison with the vast majority of the faithful, claim to remain in the Church, with the same rights and opportunities of expression and action as the rest of the faithful, in order to attack ecclesial unity. Not wishing to recognize in the Church one single reality resulting from a double element both human and divine, analogous to the mystery of the

Incarnate Word, which constitutes her "here on earth . . . the community of faith, hope and charity, as a visible structure" through which Christ "communicates truth and grace to all"[155] they set themselves up in opposition to the hierarchy, as though every act of that opposition were a constitutive aspect of the truth of the Church that has to be rediscovered as Christ instituted her. They question the duty of obedience to the authority willed by Christ; they put on trial the Pastors of the Church, not so much for what they do or how they do it but simply because, so it is claimed, they are custodians of an ecclesiastical system or structure that competes with what was instituted by Christ. In this way they cause bewilderment to the whole community, introducing into it the fruits of dialectical theories alien to the spirit of Christ. While making use of the words of the Gospel they change their meaning. We observe this state of things with regret, even though, as we have said, it is very small in comparison with the great mass of the Christian faithful. But we cannot but inveigh with the same vigor as Saint Paul against this lack of loyalty and justice. We appeal to all Christians of good will not to let themselves be impressed or disorientated by the undue pressures of brethren who are unfortunately misguided, and yet who are always in our prayers and close to our heart.

As for ourself, we reaffirm that the one Church of Christ "constituted and organized in the world as a society, subsists in the Catholic Church, which is governed by the successor of Peter and by the bishops in union with that successor, although many elements of sanctification and truth can be found outside her visible structure."[156] We likewise reaffirm that these Pastors of the Church, who preside over the People of God in His name, with the humility of servants but also with the frankness of the Apostles (cf. Acts 4, 31) of whom they are the successors, have the right and the duty to proclaim: "For as long as . . . we occupy this see, for as long as we preside, we have both authority and power, even though we may be unworthy."[157]

IV. SECTORS WHICH OBSCURE THE SACRAMENTALITY OF THE CHURCH

The process that we have described takes the form of doctrinal dissension, which claims the patronage of theological pluralism and is not infrequently taken to the point of dogmatic relativism, which in various ways breaks up the integrity of faith. And even when it is not taken as far as dogmatic relativism, this pluralism is at times regarded as a legitimate theological stand that permits the taking up of positions contrary to the authentic Magisterium of the Roman Pontiff himself and of the hierarchy of bishops, who are the sole authoritative interpreters of divine Revelation contained in sacred Tradition and sacred Scripture.[158]

We recognize that pluralism of research and thought which in various ways investigates and expounds dogma, but without disintegrating its identical objective meaning, has a legitimate right of citizenship in the Church, as a natural component part of her catholicity, and as a sign of the cultural richness and personal commitment of all who belong to her. We recognize also the inestimable values contributed by pluralism to the sphere of Christian spirituality, to ecclesial and religious institutions and to the spheres of liturgical expression and dispilinary norms. These are values which blend together into that "one common aspiration" that "is particularly splendid evidence of the catholicity of the undivided Church."[159]

Indeed we admit that a certain theological pluralism finds its roots in the very mystery of Christ, the inscrutable riches whereof (cf. Eph. 3, 8) transcend the capacities of expression of all ages and all cultures. Thus the doctrine of the faith which necessarily derives from that mystery—since, in the order of salvation, "the mystery of God is none other than Christ"[160]—calls for constant fresh research. In reality the dimensions of the Word of God are so many, and so many are the viewpoints of the faithful who explore them,[161] that harmony in the same faith is never immune from personal characteristics in the assent of each individual. Nevertheless, the different emphases in the understanding of the same faith do not prejudice the essential content of that faith, since these emphases are unified in common assent to the Chuch's Magisterium. This Magisterium, which is the proximate norm determining the faith of all, is also a guarantee for all against the subjective judgment of every varied interpretation of the faith.

But what is to be said of that pluralism that considers the faith and its expression not as a common and therefore ecclesial heritage but as an individual discovery made by the free criticism and free examination of the Word of God? In fact, without the mediation of the Church's Magisterium, to which the Apostles entrusted their own

Magisterium[162] and which therefore teaches "only what has been handed on,"[163] the sure union with Christ through the Apostles who are the ones who hand on "what they themselves had received,"[164] is compromised. And once perserverance in the doctrine transmitted by the Apostles is compromised, what happens is that, perhaps in a desire to avoid the difficulties of mystery, there is a quest for formulas deceptively easy to understand but which dissolve the real content of mystery. Thus there are built up teachings that do not hold fast to the objectivity of the faith or are plainly contrary to it and, what is more, become crystallized side-by-side with concepts that are even mutually contradictory.

Furthermore, we must not shut our eyes to the fact that every concession in the matter of identity of faith also involves a lessening of mutual love.

In fact, those who have lost the joy that derives from the faith (cf. Phil. 1, 25) are driven, to the detriment of fraternal communion, to seek glory from one another and not to seek that glory which comes only from God (cf. Jn. 5, 44).

It is impossible to substitute the spirit of faction, which leads to discriminating choices, for the sense of the Church, which recognizes in all the same dignity and freedom of the children of God,[165] and in this way also to deprive charity of its natural support, which is justice. It would be vain to try to improve ecclesial communion in accordance with the type shared at the level of factions.

Must not we all, on the contrary, make ourselves perfect through the Gospel? And where does the Gospel manifest fully operative its divinely begotten power if not in the Church, with the contribution of all believers without distinction?

Finally, this spirit of faction reflects negatively also upon the necessary harmony of worship and of prayer, and it manifests itself in an isolation dictated by a spirit of presumption which is certainly not in accordance with the Gospel and which precludes justification before God (cf. Lk. 18, 10–14).

We try hard to understand the root of this situation, and we compare it to the analogous situation in which contemporary civil society is living, a society which is divided by the splintering up into groups opposed one to another. Unfortunately, the Church too seems to be in some degree experiencing the repercussions of this condition. But she ought not to assimilate what is rather a pathological state. The Church must preserve her original character as a family unified in the diversity of her members. Indeed, she must be the leaven that will help society to react, as was said of the first Christians: "See how much they love one another."[166] It is with this picture of the first community before our eyes—a picture that is certainly not idyllic, but one that was matured through trails and suffering—that we call upon all to overcome the illicit and dangerous differences and to recognize one another as brethren united by the love of Christ.

V. POLARIZATION OF DISSENT

When the internal oppositions affecting the various sectors of ecclesial life become crystallized into a state of dissension, they reach the point of setting up in opposition to the single institution and community of salvation a plurality of "dissenting institutions of communities." These are not in accordance with the nature of the Church which, with the creation of opposing factions fixed in irreconcilable positions, would lose her very constitutional fabric. There then occurs the "polarization of dissent," by virtue of which all interest is concentrated on the respective groups, in practice autonomous, each one claiming to be giving honor to God. This situation bears within it and, as far as it can, introduces into the ecclesial community the seeds of disintegration.

It is our lively hope that the voice of conscience will lead individuals to a process of reflection which will bring them to a wise choice. We exhort each and every one of them: "Search out the innermost secrets of your heart and diligently explore all the pathways of your soul."[167] And in each one we would like to reawaken the longing for what he has lost: "Think where you were before you fell: repent, and do as you used to at first." (Rev. 2, 5). And we should like to exhort each one to reconsider the wonderful things which God has achieved in him and to draw his attention to what this calls for before the Lord: "For there is nothing that a Christian should fear so much as being separated from the Body of Christ. For if he is separated from the Body of Christ, he is not one of his members, if he is not one of his members, he is not nourished by Christ's spirit. Whosoever does not have the spirit of Christ, says the Apostle, does not belong to Christ."[168]

VI. ETHIC AND DYNAMIC OF RECONCILIATION

It is therefore vitally necessary that everyone in the Church—bishops, priests, religious and lay people—should take an active share in a common effort for full reconciliation, so that in and between them all there may be reestablished that peace which is "the nursing mother of love and the begetter of unity."[169] Let all then show themselves to be ever more docile disciples of the Lord, who makes reconciliation between us the condition for being forgiven by the Father (cf. Mk. 11, 26) and mutual charity the condition for being recognized as His disciples (cf. Jn. 13, 35). Whoever therefore feels that he is in any way implicated in this state of division, let him return and listen to his own voice irresistibly insisting, even when he is about to pray: "Go and be reconciled with your brother first." (Mt. 5, 24).

In different degrees and ways according to the position and standing of each individual, and pondering anew God's salvific work for us, let all in unison commit themselves to creating a climate in which reconciliation can become effective. Since we have been reconciled with God through the exclusive initiative of His love, let our conduct be marked by good will and mercy, forgiving one another as God in Christ has forgiven us (cf. Eph. 4, 31–32). And since our reconciliation springs from the sacrifice of Christ who freely died for us, may the Cross, set up as a main mast in the Church to guide her in her voyage through the world,[170] inspire our mutual relations so that they may all be truly Christian. Let none of these relations ever lack some personal renunciation. From this there will follow a fraternal openness to others such as will allow willing recognition of each one's abilities and will permit all to make their proper contribution to the enrichment of the one ecclesial communion: "Thus through the common sharing of gifts and through the common effort to attain fullness in unity, the whole and each of the parts receive increase."[171] In this sense, one can agree on the fact that unity, properly understood, permits each individual to develop his own personality.

* * *

This openness to others, sustained by the willingness to understand and the capacity to make sacrifices, will give stability and order to the performance of that act of charity commanded by the Lord: fraternal correction (cf. Mt. 18, 15).

Given that this can be done by any one of the faithful to every brother in the faith, it can be the normal means of healing many dissensions or of preventing them from arising.[172] In its turn this impels the one who corrects his brother to take the plank out of his eye (cf. Mt. 7, 5), lest the order of correction be perverted.[173] Thus the practice of fraternal correction becomes the beginning of encouragement towards holiness, which alone can confer upon reconciliation its fullness. This fullness consists not in an opportunist making of peace which would conceal the worst of enmities[174] but in interior conversion and in the unifying love in Christ which flows therefrom, such as is effected principally in the sacrament of reconciliation, Penance, whereby the faithful "obtain pardon from the mercy of God for offences committed against him. They are at the same time reconciled with the Church, which they have wounded by their sins,"[175] provided that "this sacrament of salvation . . . is, as it were, rooted in their whole life and is an impulse towards more fervent service of God and fellowmen."[176]

It is still the case, however, that "in the building up of the Body of Christ there is a variety of members and functions,"[177] and that this diversity provokes inevitable tensions. These can be met with even in the saints, but "not such as would kill harmony, not such as would destroy charity."[178] How can these tensions be prevented from degenerating into divisions? It is from that very diversity of persons and of functions that there derives the sure principle of ecclesial oneness. In fact the primary and irreplaceable element of that diversity is the Pastors of the Church, constituted by Christ as His ambassadors to the rest of the faithful and for this purpose endowed with an authority which, transcending the individuals' positions and choices, unifies these last in the integrity of the Gospel, which is precisely the "Word of reconciliation" (cf. 2 Cor. 5, 18–20). The authority with which the Church's Pastors set forth this Word is binding not through acceptance on the part of men but because of its conferral by Christ (cf. Mt. 28, 18; Mk. 15, 15–16; Acts 16, 17ff.). Since therefore whoever hears them or rejects them hears or rejects Christ and Him who sent Him (cf. Lk. 10, 16), the duty of the faithful to obey the authority of the Pastors is an essential requirement of the very nature of Christianity.

The Pastors of the Church, moreover, by nature form a single undivided body with the successor of Peter and in dependence upon him; hence from the harmonious fulfillment and faithful acceptance of their ministry there depend the oneness of faith and communion of all believers,[179] a manifestation to the world of the reconciliation brought about by God in his Church. Let a gracious hearing then be granted to the common invocation to the Savior: "Be ever present in the College of Bishops united with our Pope, and grant them the gifts of unity, charity and peace."[180] Let the sacred Pastors, as they represent Christ Himself and take His place in an eminent and visible way,[181] thus imitate and infuse into the People of God the love with which He was immolated who "loved the Church and sacrificed Himself for her." (Eph. 5, 25). And may this their renewed love be an effective example to the faithful, in the first place to those priests and religious who may not have lived up to the demands of their own ministry and vocation, so that all in the Church, "united, heart and soul" (cf. Acts 4, 32), may return to a commitment "to spread the gospel of peace." (Eph. 6, 15).

Like a mother, the Church looks with sorrow on the departure of some of her sons on whom the priestly ministry has been conferred or who have been consecrated to the service of God and their brethren by some other special title. Nevertheless she finds consolation and joy in the generous perseverance of all those who have remained faithful to their commitments to Christ and to her. Being supported and comforted by the merits of this great number, she wishes to change also the sorrow which has been visited upon her into a love that can understand everything and in Christ pardon everything.

CONCLUSION

We who, as the Successor of Peter, certainly not through our personal merit but in virtue of the apostolic mandate transmitted to us, are, in the Church, the visible principle and foundation of the unity of the sacred Pastors as also of the multitude of the faithful,[182] make our appeal for the full reestablishment of that supreme good of reconciliation with God, within us and among us, so that the Church may be an effective sign in the world of union with God and of unity among all His creatures. This is a demand of our faith in the Church herself, "which in the Creed we recognize as one, holy, catholic and apostolic."[183] To love her, to follow her, to build her up we earnestly exhort all men, making our own the words of Saint Augustine: "Love this Church, remain in such a Church, be such a Church."[184]

This is the invitation that we extend with this Exhortation to all our sons and daughters, especially those who have the responsibility of guiding the brethren. We have wished it to be pastoral and full of confidence, dictated by a spirit of peace. To some perhaps it may seem severe. But it has arisen from a detailed study of the situation of the Church on the one hand, and of the unrenounceable demands of the Gospel on the other. But it has sprung especially from our heart: we have the duty to love the Church with the same spirit of the allegory of the branch that must be pruned in order to bear more fruit. (Cf. Jn. 15, 2). This Exhortation, finally, is backed by a great hope, a hope that the heavy burden of our apostolic mandate has never altered. We are grateful for the fidelity of God. We hope that the Holy Spirit will stir up an irresistible echo to our words: He is already present and working in the inmost heart of each member of the faithful, and He will lead all, in humility and peace, along the paths of truth and love. It is He who is our strength. We know that the vast majority of the Church's sons and daughters has been awaiting such a call and is prepared to receive it profitably. We trust that the entire People of God—this is our ardent wish—will set out with us, as on the Biblical journey, undertake with us the stages of sanctification of the Jubilee, and be one with us, so that the world may believe. And we trust that they will allow themselves to be guided by the grace of our Lord Jesus Christ, by the love of God the Father and by the fellowship of the Holy Spirit.

We entrust these wishes to the intercession of the Immaculate Virgin "who shines forth to the whole community of the elect as a model of the virtues . . . and by her profound sharing in the history of salvation unites in a certain way and mirrors within herself the central truths of the faith."[185] And to strengthen the common desire for sanctification and reconciliation we cordially impart our Apostolic Blessing.

Given at Saint Peter's in Rome, on the Solemnity of the Immaculate Conception of the Blessed Virgin Mary, on the eighth day of December in the year 1974, the twelfth of our Pontificate.

PAUL pp. VI

THE SACRED CONGREGATION FOR THE
DOCTRINE OF THE FAITH

Declaration on Two Books of
Professor Hans Küng

FEBRUARY 15, 1975

The Sacred Congregation for the Doctrine of the Faith, in fulfillment of its duty to foster and defend the doctrine of faith and morals
in the universal Church, has examined two works by Professor Hans
Küng, *Die Kirche* (The Church) and *Unfehlbar? Eine Anfrage* (Infallibility? An Inquiry), which have been published in several languages. In two separate letters, dated respectively 6 May 1971, and
12 July 1971, the Congregation notified the author of the difficulties
it found in his opinions and requested that he show in writing how
these opinions were not in contradiction with Catholic doctrine. In a
letter of 4 July 1973, the Congregation offered Professor Küng further
opportunity to explain his ideas orally. Finally, Professor Küng, in his
letter of 4 September 1974, omitted any mention of this possibility. On
the other hand, he offered no proof in this reply that certain opinions
of his regarding the Church were not in contradiction with Catholic
doctrine, but continued to maintain them even after the publication of
the Declaration "Mysterium Ecclesiae."

Therefore, so that there may be no doubt concerning the doctrine
which the Catholic Church holds and that the belief of Christ's faithful
may be in no way obscured, this Sacred Congregation, recalling the

239

teaching of the Magisterium of the Church set forth in the Declaration "Mysterium Ecclesiae," states:

The two works of Prof. Hans Küng mentioned above contain certain opinions which, in varying degree, are opposed to the doctrine of the Catholic Church that must be professed by all the faithful. The following opinions are only selected for mention, as being of greater importance, prescinding for the time being from a judgment on certain other opinions held by Professor Küng.

The opinion which at least casts doubt on the dogma of the faith concerning infallibility in the Church or reduces it to a kind of basic indefectibility in truth on the part of the Church, together with the possibility of error in the doctrines that the Magisterium of the Church definitively teaches as necessary to be believed, contradicts the doctrine defined by Vatican Council I and confirmed by Vatican Council II.

Another error that seriously compromises the teaching of Professor Küng concerns his opinion with regard to the Magisterium of the Church. In fact, he does not present a true concept of the authentic Magisterium, according to which the Bishops in the Church are "authentic teachers, that is, teachers endowed with the authority of Christ, who preach to the people committed to them the faith they must believe and put into practice" (*Lumen Gentium*, 25); for "the task of authentically interpreting the word of God, whether written or handed down, has been entrusted *exclusively* to the living teaching office of the Church" (*Dei Verbum*, 10).

Again, the opinion suggested by Professor Küng in his book *Die Kirche* (The Church), according to which the Eucharist can be validly consecrated, at least in cases of necessity, by baptized persons not in priestly Orders, cannot be reconciled with the teaching of the Fourth Lateran Council and of the Second Vatican Council.

Nevertheless, notwithstanding the serious character of these opinions, since Professor Küng, in his letter of 4 September 1974, did not at all exclude the possibility that after an adequate period of deeper study, he might bring his opinions into harmony with the doctrine of the authentic Magisterium of the Church, this Sacred Congregation, by order of the Supreme Pontiff Paul VI, for the present admonishes Professor Hans Küng not to continue teaching these opinions and reminds him that ecclesiastical authority has granted him permission to teach sacred theology in the spirit of the doctrine of the Church, but not opinions that subvert this doctrine or call it into question.

The Bishops of Germany and those in other places where particular necessity requires it, especially where the aforesaid opinions are maintained in theological faculties, in seminaries and other institutions for Catholic or clerical instruction, are asked to see to it that the faithful are suitably instructed in the doctrine of the Church and in the Declaration "Mysterium Ecclesiae," as well as in this present declaration.

Priests, preachers of the gospel, teachers of Catholic doctrine and catechists are *ex officio* bound to profess faithfully the doctrine of the Church in these questions and so to present it to others.

Finally, theologians are asked once more to study and expound the mystery of the Church and the other mysteries of faith in the obedience of faith and for the genuine edification of the Church.

In an audience granted to the undersigned Prefect of the Sacred Congregation for the Doctrine of the Faith on 14 February 1975, Pope Paul VI approved and ordered to be published this Declaration, which for the present completes the action taken by the aforesaid Congregation.

Given at Rome, at the Sacred Congregation for the Doctrine of the Faith, the 15th day of February 1975.

Franjo Cardinal Seper, *Prefect*
Archbishop Jérôme Hamer, O.P., *Secretary*

POPE PAUL VI

Allocution: The Apostolicity
of the Church

AUGUST 10, 1977

You also are certainly interested in knowing, among the many religious manifestations in history and in the contemporary world, how to distinguish the true religion. And if the Christian religion appears as the one that merits our preference, and therefore our choice for so many reasons (which I presume to be present in your souls), there still remains in the mind another question. Among the many Christian professions, is there one which is not alone prevalent, but unique and exclusive?

If we are accustomed to recite the "Credo" of the Holy Mass we will find the answer already springing to our lips: "I believe . . . the holy Church, one, holy, catholic and apostolic." We believe that these titles are intrinsic qualities of this great and singular institution which is called the Church, because this is what was desired by Christ, her founder. And so we know that these properties normally emerge also externally in the historical and human life of this "mystical body" of Christ which is precisely the Church. These properties serve as a guarantee for us that, remaining faithful to the Church, we are by God's grace on the right road.

CHRIST FOUNDED ONLY ONE CHURCH

Christ founded one single and unique Church. Christ did not set limits to her universality, he wanted her to be holy, like a pure and inexhaustible fountain—even though not all those who drink at this fountain are equally pure and clear—even if not all advert to their need to be purified, that is, sanctified by the grace that flows from the Church.

Finally, we believe in an apostolic Church; not one invented by a man of genius, or arising from some social movement. We want an "apostolic" Church, that is, derived from the Apostles, in so far as they, and they alone, were directly and exclusively charged by Christ to be the authentic witnesses to His word and His work. This means that Christ Jesus chose the ministers who are the guardians, transmitters and defenders of the work of redemption carried out by Him.

Jesus wished to found an organized Church. The entire Gospel points to this. Jesus did not write. He spoke, and turning to the disciples, he proclaimed: "He who hears you, hears me, and he who rejects you, rejects me . . . and rejects him who sent me" (Lk. 10, 16). Jesus did not say, "The text of Scripture is enough." Because the very text of Scripture comes from a teaching authority which gave it its origin. Furthermore, Jesus did not authorize anyone to set himself up as legislator between men and God in order to found a new form of religion, which is something which Jesus alone can establish (cf. 1 Tim. 2, 4–7; Mt. 10, 40; Jn. 20, 21; etc.).

This mark of apostolicity regards, practically speaking, the transmission of the message of the faith, which is a demanding and binding truth. It is a transmission which demands absolute fidelity and prohibits any arbitrariness, precisely there where it confers hierarchical power on the Apostles who are invested with it. To cut oneself off from apostolicity is to wish to cut oneself off from Christ, and to expose oneself to contestability in faith and barrenness in religion.

But this is how the love of God for His Church is shown—and it is good to reflect on this—that she might be the teacher of truth and charity. This is what we believe when we proclaim the apostolicity of the Church.

Allocution: Fidelity to True Doctrine

SEPTEMBER 7, 1977

Our reflection is still about the Church, considered in her operational aspect, rather than in the mystery of her being. This method of study offers an experimental apologia of our faith, which was sustained by Christ himself in favor of his divine Person and of his messianic mission: "even though you do not believe me, believe the works," the Lord affirmed in the polemical heat of the controversy with his adversaries the Jews (cf. John 10, 38). It is a controversy still open with regard to the Church and to our religion in times such as ours, in which the evidence of rational and tangible proofs prevails in public opinion over that of the Spirit and of faith.

GOSPEL TRUTH

We remember that it was Christ the Lord himself, who, on taking leave of the scene of this world engraved in the famous last words of his Gospel the synthesis of the Church's operational programme, a programme to which we now give a moment of attention. Jesus said in fact, to the disciples, already constitutionally erected in an apostolic and ecclesiastical hierarchy: "Go and teach" (Mt. 28, 19). Teach what? "All that I have commanded you" the Lord concluded. This teaching investiture is supremely important: the disciples, chosen as apostles (Lk. 6, 13), are raised to the rank of "witnesses" (Acts 1, 8; 1, 22; 2, 32; 3, 15; etc.). They vouch for a truth, which will be called the Gospel, and which will be interiorly confirmed in them by the Paraclete, that is, the counsellor, the Holy Spirit (John 14, 26). They are the future "martyrs," that is, those who bear witness to the Word with their blood. They are the Pastors, the specialized guides of the People of God. They are the Church in the teaching and also in the understanding and expression of the supernatural knowledge of God, faith.

NEED OF LIGHT

Moreover, in our days, as always in the course of the centuries, we hear repeated: The Church, why? What does it do? What use is it? Well, let us make the supposition, fortunately, after Christ, an unreal one, that the apostolic Church was no longer on earth. What would happen? What would happen would be what happens in a dark night, in a closed room where the light has gone out: a great confusion about the prospect of vital space, an interminable, irrational struggle, a time without hope. "I am the light of the world," Christ said; "he who follows me will not walk in darkness, but will have the light of life" (John 8, 12).

TRUTH AND FIDELITY

Here endless questions arise, especially on two problems which are like two open windows: on the fixity of the truths, that is, of the dogmas, which the Church teaches as teacher of men, and first of all as a disciple of Christ, of the one and only Teacher of the supreme truths, unattainable for us (Mt. 23, 8), of God the Revealer. On this we well know the attitude of the Church. It is that of faith, it is fidelity, according to an expression of a fifth century saint, Vincent of Lerins: the truths of faith can be studied, explained and illustrated, but always keeping the identical substantial meaning (cf. Denz.-Schoen. 2803, 3020). The other dogma, or teaching, is that of Cardinal Newman. It is that of the development of doctrine, as a tree from the same, fruitful root, where the growth of the doctrine is not dissipated in the misinterpretations of a certain modern pluralism, judge and arbiter of itself, free to model the mysteries of the faith according to the limits of personal conceptions (cf. Denz.-Schoen. 3806). The Church as we know, is severe about consistency to this fidelity. She may even seem lacking in understanding with regard to certain religious and pietistic systems and attitudes. These, freeing themselves from the univocal, perennial and authentic teaching of the Revelation defended by the Church, first slacken, then break the bonds with the one apostolic Truth, which alone ensures the identity of religious doctrine with that of Christ, exacting lover of the unity of his message of salvation, sealed in his Word to the Apostles: "He who hears you, hears me" (Lk. 10, 16).

So may it be for us and for you, with our apostolic blessing.

POPE PAUL VI

Discourse Closing the Synod of Bishops

OCTOBER 29, 1977

Pope Paul VI delivered the following address at the close of the Synod of Bishops.

Venerable Brothers and beloved Sons,

At the end of this fifth Assembly of the Synod of Bishops you have wished to express your greeting to us, through Cardinal Ribeiro, Patriarch of Lisbon, and to manifest the sentiments that animate you in the hour of leave-taking.

On our side we thank you heartily and express to you in return our brotherly greeting. After a month of intense consultations on a very important subject for the future life of the Church such as catechesis, you are now preparing to return to your Sees and resume your occupations, with the intention of promoting a renewed catechetical action in your countries.

During this period each of you has sought to communicate his own experience to his Brothers and to offer the results of his own competence—results reached in the concrete reality of life—with the intention of promoting catechesis in the Church in such a way as "to make men's faith become living, conscious and active" (cf. *Christus Dominus,* 14). You have done this not with theoretical and historical investigations—which are useful in other fields—but rather with a pre-eminently pastoral concern, guided by your experience as Pastors of souls who daily share the anxieties and difficulties, among which the men of today are struggling. Precisely because of this pastoral approach, this synodal assembly has a joyous and happy outcome.

***

Aware of the importance that must be attributed to this form of proclamation of the Word of God to the men of today, we had summoned you to Rome, to the tomb of St. Peter, for the two specific purposes of every Assembly, such as they are indicated in the *Motu proprio* "Apostolica Sollicitudo": "the mutual exchange of seasonable information and the indication of suggestions regarding the problems for which the Synod is convened on each occasion" (*A.A.S.,* LVII, 1965, p. 777).

Now the exchange of experiences on the part of individuals has been abundant for the benefit of all; and many proposals have been made in order that catechetical activity may become more and more effective in the whole Church, at every level.

INVITATION TO ACTION

The conclusions reached at the end of the work will have to be communicated by you to your Brothers in the episcopate, when you have returned to your dioceses and your duties. For you will hand on—we are quite sure—the fire with which you are aflame to those united with you in the pastoral office. In this way the Synod will have the beneficial function of stimulating a renewed commitment for catechesis, with new programmes of action, with a more intense formation of catechists, with a more careful search for suitable aids, always observing the wisdom of canon law in this area as well as those norms laid down in the General Catechetical Directory, published by the Sacred Congregation for the Clergy and approved and confirmed by us.

A good many among you, Venerable Brothers and beloved Sons, have opportunely endeavoured to clarify the causes of the catechetical crisis during the last few years. We consider it unnecessary, therefore, to dwell on these difficulties, but we intend rather to call upon you to look to the future and, through you, to make an appeal to all those who feel their responsibility as Christians to commit themselves in order that a renewed catechetical action may spread throughout the Church as a result of this Synod.

In successive concentric waves, this impulse will be propagated from the Synod to the episcopal assemblies of both East and West, and from these to parishes, families, schools, and communities that meet in Christ's name, under the guidance of the legitimate Pastors. Thus Bishops living in different parts of the world, united with the Vicar of Christ, will initiate, direct and sustain this on-going renewal of catechesis. They will be joined closely with those priests, religious men and women, and laity who perceive the importance and beauty of this apostolate. Indeed, this is the meaning and impact of your Message to the People of God, issued today from the city of Rome to the entire Church as this meeting of the Synod of Bishops comes to an end.

Considering the work carried out, we express our joy that the members of the Synod have found themselves in agreement on the principal aspects of catechesis, and that at the conclusion of their work, they have submitted to us very useful suggestions contained in thirty-four propositions. On our side, we will examine them carefully, together with all the material that has been presented to us. Subsequently—acceding to the desire expressed by you—we will be happy to make known to the universal Church the points we consider most opportune.

INTEGRITY OF THE DOCTRINE

In the first place, we rejoice over the emphasis placed on the Bishops' responsibility to be vigilant and to see to it that full fidelity to the Word of God, as it has been manifested to us by divine Revelation and transmitted in the course of the centuries by the Magisterium of the Church, be always preserved in catechesis. Certainly, this same duty of vigilance also concerns other forms of presentation of the Word of God, from that of its announcement in general, or evangelization, to its proclamation in the liturgy or preaching, and to its thorough study in theology. But vigilance over catechesis is certainly one of the aspects of this duty on the part of those who have been constituted Pastors and Teachers by Christ in his Church. We do not intend to repeat now how dear to us is the activity of defending and promoting wholesome doctrine. In fact, as regards this concern of ours, the message we addressed to all the Bishops, at the end of the first five years after the conclusion of the Second Vatican Council, retains all its value (cf. Apostolic Exhortation *Quinque iam anni: A.A.S.* LXIII, pp. 97–106). Faithfulness to the deposit of Revelation clearly demands also that no essential truth of faith should be passed over in silence. "The people entrusted to our care has the sacred and inalienable right to receive the Word of God, the entire Word of God" (*ibid.,* pp. 99–100).

NECESSITY OF A SYSTEMATIC CATECHESIS

In the second place, it was a great comfort for us to see how everyone noted the extreme necessity of a systematic catechesis, precisely because this orderly study of the Christian mystery is what distinguishes catechesis itself from all other forms of presentation of the Word of God. You yourselves have stressed this, in the conviction that no one can arrive at the whole truth on the basis solely of some simple experience, that is, without an adequate explanation of the message of Christ, who is "the Way, the Truth and the Life" (Jn. 14, 6), Alpha and Omega, the beginning and end of all things (cf. Apoc. 22, 13). The complete presentation of the Christian message obviously comprises also the explanation of its moral principles both with regard to individuals and with regard to the whole of society. To educate to the faith also the children and young people of our Christian communities will mean, therefore, educating them to "follow Christ," as you well indicated in the twelfth proposition you transmitted to us. This is, moreover, the meaning of the doctrine of the Apostle St. John, when he admonishes: "He who says 'I know him (God),' but disobeys his commandments is a liar" (I Jn. 2, 4).

USEFULNESS OF FORMULAS

In the third place we fully agree with you when you authoritatively recall the necessity of some fundamental formulas which will make it possible to express more easily, in a suitable and accurate way, the truths of the faith and of Christian moral doctrine.

These formulas, if learnt by heart, greatly aid the stable possession of these truths, as you too pointed out in the nineteenth proposition which was presented to us and in the Message itself to the People of God, sent today to the whole Church. Among these formulas, you have rightly included the most important biblical texts, especially in the New Testament, and the liturgical texts that serve to express common prayer and make the profession of the faith easier.

APPEAL FOR THE FREEDOM OF THE CHURCH

Finally, we recognize more than ever the influence and the necessity of the appeal for the freedom of the Church, in order that the latter may carry out her task of instructing her members in the Christian faith. Unfortunately, there are not a few nations in which the right of individuals to religious freedom, the right of families to the education of their children, the right of religious communities to the education of their own members, are trampled upon or at least unjustly limited. At this particularly solemn hour, we once more beseech the rulers of peoples to respect—for the very good of their nations—the right of individuals and of religious communities to social and political freedom in religious matters. In fact, "the protection and promotion of the inviolable rights of man ranks among the essential duties of government" (*Dignitatis Humanae*, n. 6).

THE POPE'S THANKS

After having conveyed to you some thoughts of ours on the most striking aspects of the subject dealt with at this brotherly assembly, we consider it opportune, before concluding to thank all those who contributed to the preparation and orderly development of this fifth Synodal Assembly.

Our thanks go in the first place to the Presidents Delegate, the Rapporteur and the Secretary General, to the Special Secretary and his assistants, and to all those who, with competence and generosity, have given in every form their precious service to the Roman Pontiff and to this select representation of the world Episcopate.

Venerable Brothers and beloved Sons, taking leave of you, we beg you to take the greeting and the blessing of the Common Father to your confreres in the Episcopate, to the priests your collaborators, to the religious men and women, as well as to all the laity who work in the catechetical field. May the Holy Spirit comfort us, gladden us and vivify us all and prepare us for a renewed and concordant commitment "that the Word of the Lord may speed on and triumph" (2 Thess. 3, 1). And for this purpose, we willingly impart our Apostolic Blessing to all of you present here.

PART FIVE

Conclusion: The Relationship Between the Creed and Catechetics

"It seems to us, however, that in a period in which the world is in crisis, as formerly, and in which most values, even the most sacred ones, are rashly questioned in the name of freedom, so that many people have no longer any point of reference, in a period in which danger comes certainly not from an excess of dogmatism but rather from the dissolution of doctrine and the nebulousness of thought, it seems to us that an additional effort should be courageously undertaken to give the Christian people, who are waiting for it more than is thought, a solid, exact catechetical basis, easy to remember."—Pope Paul VI, April 27, 1975.

The relationship between the Creed and catechetical teaching has been implicit throughout the foregoing study. These short concluding considerations may serve to bring it more explicitly into view.

Catechesis is an essential part of the pastoral ministry or care of souls. "The ministry of the word," states the *General Catechetical Directory,* "takes many forms . . . There is the form called evangelization, or missionary preaching. This has as its purpose the arousing of the beginnings of faith . . . Then there is the catechetical form, 'which is intended to make men's faith become living, conscious and active, *through the light of instruction.*' (C.D. 14). And then there is the liturgical form . . . (and) finally, there is the theological form, that is, the systematic treatment and the scientific investigation of the truths of faith . . . Catechesis proper presupposes a global adherence to Christ's Gospel as presented by the Church. Often, however, it is directed to men who, though they belong to the Church, have in fact never given a true personal adherence to the message of revelation. This shows that, according to circumstances, evangelization can precede or accompany the work of catechesis proper. In every case, however, one must keep in mind that the element of conversion is always present in the dynamism of faith, and for that reason any form of catechesis must also perform the role of evangelization."[1]

Catechesis, the *Directory* continues, "forms the minds of the faithful for prayer, for thanksgiving, for repentance, for praying with confidence, for a community spirit, and for understanding correctly the meaning of the creeds. All these things are necessary for a true liturgical life."[2] "Catechesis performs the function of disposing men to receive the action of the Holy Spirit and to deepen their conversion. It does this through the word, to which are joined the witness of life and prayer."[3]

Finally, the relationship is declared in the most definite way possible when the *Directory* states, "Catechesis must necessarily be Christocentric."[4] Since the Creed is the officially formulated profession of the apostolic faith in Jesus as our Lord, as the Son of God, and as our Divine Creator, Savior and Holy Redeemer, catechesis must necessarily be a teaching of the articles of faith. By explaining these articles of faith which are summarized in the Creed, catechesis helps to deepen the conversion of those who are taught to God in Jesus Christ. Through the light of instruction, instruction about Him who is the light of the world, it helps make men's faith living, conscious and active. There can be no authentic and effective pastoral care of souls without the truth about Him whom the Creed professes, the same truth which catechesis exists to hand on by teaching.

This catechetical teaching, therefore, has a truth or content of doctrine. It is a content which contains the apostolic witness to Jesus as the Word. The insight expressed by Yves Congar is needed in catechetics today more than ever before. "An adequate theory of revelation," he writes, "shows that all its weight bears on the vital covenant relationship that God wants to establish with men. This relationship is perfect and definitive in Jesus Christ, but we know Jesus Christ through the apostolic witness, and through that alone."[5] Pope Paul VI gives the support of his authority to this same ecclesiastical reality. In his General Audience of January 15, 1975, he stated: "Let us recall the great statement of a famous German Catholic thinker, John Adam Moehler, (1796–1838), a forerunner of the ecumenical movement, on the necessity of the mediation of the Church to know Christ and live by His life."[6] This mediation is constituted primarily by the catechetical teaching program of the Church which implements her Ordinary and Universal Magisterium at the level of the on-coming generation by explaining her Creed.

Thus Jesus Christ is Himself the relationship between the Creed and catechetics. Without this content of teaching which the Creed provides, and which gives substance to religion textbooks and programs, catechetics must necessarily suffer a change in its character. It may still be some kind of "religious education," indeed, but it can no longer qualify as the authentic catechetical teaching which preserves the constitutive note of apostolicity in the Catholic Church.

This is precisely the tragedy of that creedlessness in religious education which is the hallmark of the Neo-Modernist approach. It cannot preserve knowledge, love, service and imitation of Jesus Christ. It cannot but contribute to that dimming of Christ which is coming more and more to characterize religious education and religious life. Whether it is the *New Catechism* or the approaches which are continuing in its wake, the motive of this creedlessness is always the thought that "the Church ought to adapt herself somewhat, not only with regard to the rule of life but also to the doctrines in which the *deposit of faith* is contained."[7] The result is always the same: the omission or the reinterpre-

tation of the content of the divine truth which the Creed professes:
". . . to pass over certain heads of doctrines, as if of lesser moment,
or to so soften them that they may not have the same meaning which
the Church has invariably held."[8]

The internal logic of creedlessness leads quickly away from the
Lord Jesus whom the apostolic faith professes. It seems to be approaching its full development in "The New Christianity" which has raised
its head in the years after Vatican II. An editorial in *La civiltá cattolica*
has described it with great accuracy and intellectual honesty: "The
final characteristic of this new 'Christianity' is a passionate devotion
to and faith in Christ; not Christ the Son of God who was made man
(the Christ of Catholic theology), but rather the Christ-man, the
Christ for others, the Christ who was the friend and defender of the
poor, the liberating Christ seen as a revolutionary . . . As a result,
Christianity becomes a 'religion of man': in effect atheistic, even
though the name of God is retained . . . If this is the new 'Christianity', we have cause to ask ourselves whether we have come face to
face with a new form of Modernism which, in its efforts to make
Christianity more 'meaningful' for man today, has emptied it of its
true substance. It is certainly true that the new 'Christianity' does not
deny any of the great Christian realities—God, Christ, the Church,
eternal life, the Kingdom of God, sin, salvation; but while giving
nominal acceptance to these fundamental realities, it reinterprets them,
and dilutes them to such an extent that little, if anything, remains of
their true and authentic Christian meaning. We are forced to the conclusion that this new 'Christianity' . . . is not only irreconcilable with
traditional Christianity, but is in radical opposition to it."[9]

This, then, is a further aspect of the relationship between the Creed
and catechetics, one for which the *New Catechism* provides a comprehensive illustration. For creedlessness ministers to the advent of this
new atheistic religion. Without the Creed, in the thought-world of creedlessness, catechetics changes its character. It becomes a mere program
of naturalistic religious education in the context of Karl Jaspers'
"philosophical faith." A pantheistic and naturalistic religious education may give the children a thin veneer of vague religiosity and a
residue of incorrectly understood Christian terminology, but it cannot
produce professing Catholic Christians devoted to Jesus Christ, their
Divine Savior and Holy Redeemer. The reason is obvious: the Creed

which makes this profession, and the Catechesis which deepens knowledge of it and love for Him, have both been eliminated. It cannot but be a different kind of religious education, more in harmony with the mind of Spinoza than with the mind of Christ.

Due chiefly to the *New Catechism,* the word "catechism" has been recurring throughout this study. What is a "catechism"? How does it enter into this matter of the relationship between the Creed and catechetics? To answer such questions comprehensively a separate work would be required. Here only the principles can be noted, following the *General Catechetical Directory.* "Catechisms," it states, "are among the chief working tools for catechesis."[10] The Catechism is a tool which came into existence with the invention of printing. In the five centuries of the early Church, catechesis was an oral explanation of the Creed, as the works of the Fathers bear witness. During the next thousand years, when adults were for the most part members of the Church and catechesis was primarily concerned with children born into Catholic homes, the same thing continued to be the case. Catechesis was an oral explanation of the Creed, upon which, as a foundation, oral teaching on the Commandments, the Sacraments and the Prayers was built.

Martin Luther was the first to use the new invention of printing for religious instruction. His two printed booklets, called "catechisms," one for teachers, the other intended for direct use by children, simply incorporated this heritage of oral questioning and answering in explanation of the articles of faith professed by the Creed.[11] These works were immediately successful, and were reprinted in thousands of copies. It is not too much to say that this use of the printing press spearheaded the Protestant movement. The Catholic Church could not, of course, stand aloof from this new invention and its usefulness for raising up Catholic Christians: similar Catholic booklets, likewise called "catechisms," were soon in print. Like Luther's catechism, they were simple extensions of the Interrogatory Creed, incorporating in printed form the heritage of oral instruction on the articles of the baptismal faith. National catechisms were drawn up and made official by the Catholic bishops of the various countries, such as the Penny Catechism of Britain and the Baltimore Catechism of the United States. To this day Luther's original Catechism and the Italian national Catechism, improved and made more universal through the publication of a special edition by order of Pope St. Pius X, reflect perhaps best the basic nature of this instrument of catechetical teaching, that of an elementary explanation of the articles of faith summarized in the Apostles' Creed.

This brings into clear view the manner in which a "catechism" relates to the Creed and catechetical teaching. This is the reason why the *General Catechetical Directory* states, again with perfect accuracy: "The greatest importance must be attached to catechisms published by ecclesiastical authority . . . , (for) they provide, under a form that is condensed and practical, the witnesses of revelation. . . ."[12] One cannot ponder too much the fact that the rejection of such catechisms "published by ecclesiastical authority" implies the creedless approach in religious education, which by definition cannot raise up professing Catholic Christians, and which by a tragic internal logic works toward the atheistic religion described above. "The great cop-out of this era," Kelly observes incisively, "is not to answer questions at all. This explains the great decline of catechisms. They provide answers which some of us do not like."[13]

Faced by the nihilism of the current wave of creedlessness, Catholics are sometimes heard to say that the solution is to "return to the Baltimore Catechism." This is ambiguous, because an instrument or a tool operates in the mode of an instrumental cause: it can do *nothing* by itself. When it operates, like the carpenter's hammer or the surgeon's scalpel, it does so in complete dependence on the mode and the action of the principal cause. In the case of Catechetics, the principal cause is the person, the catechist who does the catechetical teaching. He may use the catechism wrongly, and this produces one form of extremism, the mere mechanical memorization of the propositions and formulas which express the articles of faith and their immediate explanations in human discourse. He may refuse to use it at all, and this produces the opposed extremism, the creedlessness illustrated by the *New Catechism* and its satellite religious education programs which are following its pattern. Or he may use it rightly, drawing from it the substantial content which he illuminates and communicates with all the pedagogical artistry and methodology of which he is capable. This helps to make faith living, conscious and active, and it does so through the light of instruction. This is the ministry of the word, to which are joined the witness of life and prayer. The catechism is indeed only a tool.

But it is not an unimportant one for the living catechist, the minister of the word, precisely because it is the Church's official instrument for communicating the Creed and explaining it accurately.[14]

There is another aspect of the relationship between the Creed and catechetical teaching which deserves much additional research and study. It is the ecumenical one brought before Christians of today by the mention of the nature and format of Luther's Catechism. Here again, the creedlessness of the Neo-Modernist approach stands revealed in its intrinsic nihilism. For it takes the heart out of the Ecumenical Movement, just as it stills the voice of the Catholic Church and stops its action. On August 3, 1927, 500 delegates from the various Protestant Churches opened a pioneer ecumenical conference at Lausanne by the recitation of the Apostles' Creed, held in common by them all.[15] Only a catechesis sincere in its relationship to the Creed ministers to this sincerity of desire for Christian unity.

But whatever be the aspect of the relationship between the Creed and catechetical teaching which is considered, the mind is forced always to return to one central fact. Both Creed and catechesis move beyond their propositional expression in human discourse to Him who is professed and upon whom the teaching is centered, Jesus Christ, the same yesterday, today and forever. Catechetics is not subject to modes and styles, nor to the findings of the sciences, nor to any form of historical and cultural relativism, precisely because of its relationship to the Creed. When a time of confusion and chaos arises in religious education, when the Catholic faith is menaced in its very heart, and indeed from within the Church, it is a sure sign that the Creed must be grasped anew, and by means of it the Catholic faith professed anew. It is this profession of the apostolic faith which will bring to catechetics that authentic renewal which continues to be the message and the hope of the Second Vatican Council.

References

Footnotes—Introduction

¹ The order in which the faith and its communication exist and function is distinct from that in which theology exists and functions. St. Irenaeus made the point in the early Church, and Cardinal John Wright is making it today, for example in his opening discourse for the Second International Catechetical Congress: "The plain fact is that theology is not the faith. There are a hundred theologies, good, bad and indifferent. There is only one faith." Cf. "Prolusione del Card. Wright" in *Atti, II Congresso Catechistico* (Rome: Editrice Studium, 1971), p. 32. The English translation of this discourse is re-printed in John Cardinal Wright, *The Church the Hope of the World* (Kenosha: Prow Books, 1972), Chap. IV, "The Point of Contemporary Catechetics," pp. 50–68. In illustration of his point, Cardinal Wright raised a question regarding the approach of Bishop William E. McManus. "One wonders," he writes, "if, while being correct in asking that Christian Doctrine not begin with sociology, Bishop McManus has not attached a little too much importance to the 'professionals' of a discipline which, in the last analysis, also seeks to be, like sociology, an autonomous science, namely theology. I wonder if it would not be more exact and more proper to say that the study of religion, certainly of Christian Doctrine, should begin with the *faith* . . . , not theology nor sociology." (*Ibid.*) One wonders further whether these words do not perhaps reveal the tip of an iceberg. In any case, there are those who would prefer that the present book not be published, apparently because, in keeping the Creed before the mind and in the heart of the People of God, it represents the catechetical order as something distinct from that of the theologies, especially the modern philosophical ones.

² Sacra Congregatio Rituum, *Pontificale Romanum: De ordinatione Diaconi, Presbyteri, et Episcopi.* Rome: Typis Polyglottis Vaticanis, 1968; p. 108. The Latin reads: *Vultis depositum fidei, secundum traditionem inde ab Apostolis in Ecclesia semper et ubique servatam, purum et integrum custodire?* And the answer: *Volo.*

³ In his book, *On Being a Christian* (New York: Doubleday, 1976), pp. 605–606, Hans Küng lists a group of titles under the interesting heading "Introductions to Christianity or to the Apostles' Creed," and includes *The New Catechism* among them. While one must question his accuracy, it points up the continuing significance of the Dutch catechetical publication which was the immediate occasion for the *Creed of the People of God.* On Professor Küng, cf. the document in Part

Four pp. 239–241, below, and Joseph Ratzinger, "On Hans Küng's 'Being a Christian,'" *Doctrine and Life* (May, 1977) 3–17.

⁴ The tragic side of this situation is the fact that so many Catholics are becoming separated from the living dynamism of their own baptismal Creed, no longer thinking within its articles of faith, no longer in personal communion with the living and divine teaching authority of their Roman Catholic Church which is the Body of Christ. For them, when Rome speaks, as Rome is doing at present in this *Creed of the People of God* and the documents that relate to it, the case is not finished. They consider everything still open for discussion. It is only an ongoing merely human debate. The formulated truths of the Catholic faith, proposed, explained and interpreted by the Teaching Church, are no longer a vital personal concern to them. But this attitude is the very definition of the "crisis of faith" for a Catholic. For the Rule of Faith in the Catholic Church is this living and divine Teaching Authority which proposes the creedal articles of faith in the Lordship of Jesus to the members of the Church and which explains and interprets the correct meaning of these articles as occasions arise. It is a basic purpose and hope of the present work, in the spirit of Pope Paul's Year of Faith, to help wavering Catholics recover their baptismal profession. For their situation is far more dangerous spiritually than that of those who have been born and raised in Christian ecclesial bodies separated long ago from the Catholic Church. Often these Christians manifest today a wonderful strength of personal devotion to the living God of the first article, and to Jesus Christ, His only Son, our Lord, according to the second article of the Creed. It is this fact which offers to professing Catholics the foundation for sound ecumenism. The official teaching of the Church on this matter (see DS 3014; *Vatican I*, p. 45) is more relevant today than ever; "The situation of those who have adhered to Catholic truth by the heavenly gift of faith is not at all equivalent to the situation of those who have been led by human opinions into following a false religion. For those who have received the faith under the Magisterium of the Church can never have a just cause for changing the same faith or for calling it into question. This being so, 'giving thanks to God the Father, who has made us worthy to share the lot of the saints in light' (Col. 1, 12), let us not neglect so great a salvation. Rather, 'looking toward the author and finisher of faith, Jesus' (Heb. 12, 2) 'let us hold fast the confession of our hope without wavering' (Heb. 10, 23)." See the Document of Pope Paul VI on "Reconciliation Within the Church" (Dec. 8, 1974), pp. 226–238, above. The Catholic faith has a twofold object simultaneously: within us, the articles of faith which the Catholic Creed professes; and outside, transcendent above us, Him whom the Creed professes. This is the issue and the drama today: for souls cannot give up the illumination of the doctrine without departing from Him to whom the doctrine witnesses. Cf. Charles Journet, *What is Dogma?* (New York: Hawthorn, 1964), pp. 11–14; 45–60; 100–105.

⁵ Cf. The *Creed of the People of God*, No. 3; above, pp. 9–10.

⁶ Adam, Most Rev. Nestor, "Declaration on the Ecône Affair," *L'Oss. Rom. English Edition* (Sept. 9, 1976), p. 12.

⁷ See p. 207, and the "Prefatory Note," p. xi above.

⁸ There is a need for research on the three phases or moments of this history, into which it has been broken by actions of the teaching authority of the Catholic Church. The first moment was the genesis of the movement among German priests which furnished the immediate occasion of Vatican I over a century ago. The

second moment was the better known set of events from the encyclical of Leo XIII *Providentissimus Deus* on the Bible (1893) to the actions of Pope St. Pius X regarding Fathers Tyrrell and Loisy, leaders of the second phase. The movement then seemed to disappear. But the third phase of the phenomenon has become visible in the "crisis of faith" after Vatican II, with its application in religious education. This research needs to analyze the philosophical identity of these three moments or phases. For the principles which are being popularized in this third moment and applied in religious education at present were stated and developed in the first two moments. The distinguishing feature of the movement, as Charles Journet points out in the passage quoted on p. 283, is the fact that it eliminates the Creed as a whole, whereas similar phenomena earlier in the life of the Church moved against only this or that particular article of the Creed.

[9] It is beyond the scope of this book to study the philosophical dimensions of historical and cultural relativism, the pattern of thought which considers the phrase of Vincent of Lerins ambiguous, when he summarizes the teaching of the early Church: "We must hold that faith which has been believed everywhere, always, and by all." For the catechist, it suffices to receive the teaching proposed by the Church today in the same meaning which the Church has understood and still understands, knowing that the principle stated by the early Church is a part of the ordination of bishops, the chief catechists of the Church, to this day. See footnote 2, above. Perhaps such a philosophical study may be part of a subsequent work.

[10] Some may wish that a chapter had been included on the relationship between the Magisterium of the Catholic Church and the *Creed of the People of God*. But the writer considers this a point proper to the theologian as such. For the catechist, the matter actually is not complicated. Jesus Christ, the eternal Son of God, continues His life among us in His Body, which is the Church. He continues to teach by means of the authority to teach which He gave to this same Church. This living teaching of the Church (called technically the "Magisterium") is not concerned with physics or chemistry or ancient history, but with the articles of faith of which the Creed is the official summary for baptism, for prayer, for witnessing and for catechetical teaching. The Magisterium itself professes this Creed, this apostolic faith, explaining and defending it as occasions arise. Hence, the documents in Part Four of the present work. Catholics accept this teaching as proposed by the living Church, believing with divine faith that it is the Word of God, Teacher of mankind by means of this voice of His Church. The catechist knows that he participates at a humble level in this very same teaching authority of the Church itself, and it suffices for him to know what the Church teaches by means of her official documents, especially those which bear upon evangelization and catechesis. This is the central idea of the present study. The catechist says in his heart with the Church herself, in Vatican I (Denz. 3011): "All those matters must be believed with divine and Catholic faith that are contained in the Word of God, whether in Scripture or Tradition, and that are proposed by the Church, either by a solemn decision or by the Ordinary and Universal Magisterium, to be believed as divinely revealed." For the present-day catechist it is sufficient to know that the Vicar of Christ gave this profession of faith called the *Creed of the People of God* to the Church of God, to see that it is included among these matters which Catholics believe by divine faith. And it is simply a part of the ministry of the word to want to help in proclaiming and teaching the articles of faith which it professes. There is also the related question of the concept of divine Revelation which the very nature of the Creed presupposes. The treatment of this central issue

which the Modernist movement raises in religion and applies in religious education would involve separate works in theology and philosophy. For the study of the forms which the teaching authority of the Catholic Church uses for various purposes and in different circumstances, cf. for example, the bibliographies in J. P. Mackey, *The Modern Theology of Tradition* (New York: Herder and Herder, 1963); E. Doronzo, *The Channels of Revelation* (Middleburg, Virginia: Notre Dame Institute Press, 1974); Yves M.-J. Congar, *Tradition and Traditions* (New York: Macmillan, 1967). For the role of the Teaching Magisterium, especially the Ordinary and Universal Magisterium, in begetting the unity of the Church's communion, cf. Jerome Hamer, *The Church is a Communion* (New York: Sheed and Ward, 1964). For a short introduction to the concept of divine revelation which the Creed presupposes, cf. Charles Journet, *What is Dogma?* (New York: Hawthorn, 1964). For the comprehensive and classic study, cf. F. Marin-Sola, O.P., *L'évolution homogène du dogme catholique,* Vols. I–II (Fribourg, Suisse: Librairie de Saint-Paul, 1924); for the fundamental state of the question that bears upon the confrontation between the *Creed of the People of God* and the Neo-Modernist approach in religious education, cf. Vol. I, pp. 19–24, "L'évolution homogène et l'evolution transformiste en général." The former "represents a development in formulation without any change in meaning," while the latter "conceives a development in formulation that is accompanied by a change in meaning." *Ibid.,* p. 21, with reference to Vatican I citing Vincent of Lerins: "crescat igitur . . . , sed *in eodem sensu.*" Cf. p. 60, on Pope John XXIII in the Discourse which opened the Second Vatican Council.

Footnotes—Creed of the Catholic Church in its Official Formulations

ᵃ Rituale Romanum, auctoritate Pauli VI promulgatum. *Ordo initiationis christianae adultorum* (Romae: Typis Polyglottis Vaticanis, 1972), pp. 91–92. This text of the Interrogatory Creed, currently used in the Catholic Church as the profession of the apostolic faith for the Sacrament of Baptism, dates in unbroken history from the earliest times of the Church. Cf. the text of Hippolytus, page 43 above. St. Ambrose states explicitly that it was given to the Church by Jesus Christ Himself, through His Apostles. "You confessed the Father—recall to mind what you did—you confessed the Son, you confessed the Spirit. Reflect upon these realities, one after the other. In this faith, you died to the world, you rose again unto God . . . , dead to sin, you rose unto everlasting life . . . Believe, therefore, that these are not mere empty waters . . . Peter and Paul handed this mystery down to us, having received it from the Lord Jesus." St. Ambrose, *De mysteriis,* in *Sources Chrétiennes,* No. 25 bis (Paris: Cerf, 1961), pp. 164–170. Joseph Ratzinger teaches today the unchanged understanding of the early Church. "This baptismal questioning with its Interrogatory Creed," he writes, ". . . is the very heart of the Roman Rite of Baptism, and corresponds to the very essence of the baptismal event as witnessed by the oldest formulas of the Sacrament which have been handed down . . . (Hippolytus, Ambrose, Augustine, and the Oriental Church before Gregory of Nyssa) . . . The sacramental formula, itself based on Mt. 28, 9, is the original 'Short formulation of the Faith,' a concentrated statement of the basic structure and substantial content of the Faith which the Creed professes." J. Ratzinger, "Taufe und Formulierung des Glaubens," *Ephemerides Theologicae Lovanienses* (May 1973), 81. Ratzinger takes issue with Karl Rahner's view of "Kurzformeln des Glaubens" in *Schriften zur Theologie,* VIII, 153–164. **For**

Rahner, a "Creed" is a mere abstract summary of a theology, a doctrinal structure
contrived out of mere human thinking of today. This, Ratzinger points out, "is to
lose all perceptiveness regarding the original meaning of the Profession of Faith by
means of the Symbol or Creed," p. 82. The relationship to Christian life, Ratzinger
concludes, tends to be missing from this contemporary discussion, and thus the way
is barred to the renewal of the Sacraments and of catechetical teaching. "The
contemporary discussion is confined to summaries of this or that theology, and not
the short summary of the Faith." *Ibid.,* p. 82. Ratzinger goes on to link this
baptismal Creed with the content of catechetical instruction, the very heart of early
Church catechetical practice, and the pattern for the renewal of contemporary
catechetics for which Vatican II has called.

ᵇ Executive Committee, NCCB. *Rite of Christian Initiation of Adults: Provisional Text.* (Washington: USCC, 1974), p. 69.

ᶜ Rituale Romanum, *ibid.,* p. 76. This is the form known as the Apostles'
Creed in the prayerbooks and catechetical teaching of the Catholic Church.

ᵈ Executive Committee, NCCB, *Rite of Christian Initiation of Adults, ibid.,*
pp. 56–57. This text of the Apostles' Creed occurs in the Rite of the Catechumenate
Received in Stages. It is the "Presentation of the Profession of Faith," which takes
place in the Second Stage, the Rite of Electing. The rubric states: "First comes the
profession of faith or Creed, which the elect are to memorize and then render in
public before they profess their faith in accordance with that Creed on the day of
their baptism . . ." *Ibid.,* p. 55.

ᵉ Rituale Romanum, *ibid.,* p. 77. In the renewed form of the Rite of Baptism
after Vatican II, this form, the Nicene Creed which Catholics of the Roman or
Latin Rite always have profesed at Sunday Mass, can be used instead of the
Apostles' Creed in the *traditio symboli.*

ᶠ Executive Committee, NCCB, *Rite of Christian Initiation of Adults, ibid.,*
p. 57. It will be noted that this "Provisional Text" does not translate the *credo,* "I
believe," of the Latin, but offers "we believe" in the English, instead.

[1] Cfr. *1 Tim.* 6, 20. (This and the following notes for this Part One are the
official references given in the text of the *Creed of the People of God* as published
in the *Acta Apostolicae Sedis* (August 10, 1968)—E.K.)

[2] *Luc.* 22, 32.

[3] Cfr. Conc. Vat. I, Const. dogm. *Dei Filius, DS.* 3002.

[4] Cfr. Litt. Enc. *Humani Generis,* A. A. S. 42 (1950), p. 575; Conc. Lateran.
V, *DS.* 1440–1441.

[5] Cfr. *Ex.* 3, 14.

[6] Cfr. *1 Io.* 4, 8.

[7] Cfr. *1 Tim.* 6, 16.

[8] Cfr. Conc. Vat. I, Const, dogm. *Dei Filius, DS* 3016.

[9] Symbolum *Quicumque, DS* 75.

[10] *Ibid.*

[11] *Ibid.,* n. 76.

[12] *Ibid.*

[13] Cfr. *Matth.* 5, 48.

[14] Cfr. Conc. Ephes., *DS* 251–252.

[15] Cfr. Conc. Vat. II, Const. dogm. *Lumen Gentium,* n. 53.

[16] Cfr. Pius IX, *Ineffabilis Deus, Acta,* pars. I, vol. I, p. 616.

[17] Cfr. *Lumen Gentium,* n. 53.

[18] Cfr. *Ibid.,* nn. 53, 58, 61.

¹⁹ Cfr. Const. Ap. *Munificentissimus Deus, A. A. S.* 42 (1950), p. 770.
²⁰ *Lumen Gentium,* nn. 53, 56, 61, 63; Paulus VI, Alloc in conclusione III Sessionis Concilii Vat. II, *A. A. S.,* 56 (1964), p. 1016; Exhort. Apost. *Signum Magnum, A. A. S.,* 59 (1967), pp. 465 et 467.
²¹ Cfr. *Lumen Gentium,* n. 62; Paulus VI, Exhort. Apost. *Signum Magnum, A. A. S.,* 59 (1967), p. 468.
²² Cfr. Conc. Trid. Sess. V, Decret. *De pecc. orig., DS* 1513.
²³ *Rom.* 5, 20.
²⁴ Cfr. Conc. Trid., *ibid., DS* 1514.
²⁵ Cfr. *Lumen Gentium,* nn. 8 et 5.
²⁶ Cfr. *ibid.,* nn. 7, 11.
²⁷ Cfr. Conc. Vat. II, Const. *Sacrosanctum Concilium,* nn. 5, 6; *Lumen Gentium,* nn. 7, 12, 50.
²⁸ Cfr. Conc. Vat. I, Const. *Dei Filius, DS* 3011.
²⁹ Cfr. *ibid.,* Const. *Pastor Aeternus, DS* 3074.
³⁰ Cfr. *Lumen Gentium,* n. 25.
³¹ Cfr. *ibid.,* nn. 8, 18–23; Decret. *Unitatis Redintegratio,* n. 2.
³² Cfr. *Lumen Gentium,* n. 23; Decret. *Orientalium Ecclesiarum,* nn. 2, 3, 5, 6.
³³ Cfr. *Lumen Gentium,* n. 8.
³⁴ Cfr. *ibid.,* n. 15.
³⁵ Cfr. *ibid.,* n. 14.
³⁶ Cfr. *ibid.,* n. 16.
³⁷ Cfr. Conc. Trid., Sess. XIII, Decret. *De Eucharistia, DS* 1651.
³⁸ Cfr. *ibid., DS* 1642, 1651; Paulus VI, Litt. Enc. *Mysterium Fidei, A. A. S.,* 57 (1965), p. 766.
³⁹ Cfr. *S. Th.,* III, 73, 3.
⁴⁰ Cfr. *Io.* 18, 36.
⁴¹ Cfr. 1 Cor., 1, 31.
⁴² Cfr. *Hebr.,* 13, 14.
⁴³ *1 Io.* 3, 2; Benedictus XII, Const. *Benedictus Deus, DS* 1000.
⁴⁴ Cfr. *Lumen Gentium,* n. 49.
⁴⁵ Cfr. *Luc.* 10, 9–10; *Io.* 16, 24.

Footnotes—The Origin and Development of the Creed and its Significance for Catechetical Teaching in the Church

¹ Joseph P. Smith (Transl.), *St. Irenaeus: Proof of the Apostolic Preaching.* Westminster, Maryland: The Newman Press, 1952 (ACW no. 20); p. 108. Cf. Tertullian, *Apol.* 47 (*Corpus Christianorum,* Series Latina, Vol. I, p. 164), where he says that "there is one rule of truth which proceeds from Christ and has been transmitted through His companions." Cf. Arbesmann-Daly-Quain (Transl.) *Tertullian: Apologetical Works.* New York: Fathers of the Church, Inc., 1950; p. 116. This does not mean, of course, that Jesus Christ composed the set of words which we today call the Apostles' Creed and handed it to His Apostles, any more than He wrote any portion of the New Testament. He taught and trained His Apostles and sent them to exercise a living and authoritative Magisterium, Trinitarian in its pattern, and centering upon the meaning of His own death and resurrection for all men everywhere. It is this substance of the Creed, including its Trinitarian pattern, that goes back to Jesus. Cf. Mt. 28, 16–20; and St. Ambrose

and Joseph Ratzinger in footnote a, p. 263, above. For the research which has identified the substance of the Apostles' Creed in the writing of the New Testament, cf. Th. Camelot, O.P., "Le Symbole des Apôtres: origines, développement, signification," *Lumiere et Vie* (1952) 61–80; Pierre Benoit, O.P., "Les origines du Symbole dans le Nouveau Testament," in *Exégèse et Théologie* (Paris: Cerf, 1961), Vol. II, pp. 193–211; and especially Paul Feine, *Die Gestalt des apostolischen Glaubensbekenntnisses in der Zeit des Neuen Testaments* (Leipzig: Dörffling und Francke, 1925). Feine's research did much to reveal the insecure foundations of the Liberal Protestantism which had become dominant in Germany in the late 19th and early 20th centuries.

 [2] There has been an immense amount of scholarly research on the origin and nature of the Apostles' Creed during the last hundred years or so. Protestant scholars of Germany have led the way with their *Symbolforschung,* producing a series of works which represent German university research at its best. It took the entire first volume of Joseph de Ghellinck's *Patristique et Moyen Age* to summarize and evaluate this labor and its publications. Cf. *Les recherches sur les origines du Symbole des Apôtres.* Paris: Desclée de Brouwer, 1949. For a compressed synthesis, cf. Johannes Quasten, "Symbolforschung," *LTK* 9, 1210–1212; and see the literature given in his *Patrology* (Westminster: The Newman Press, 1950) 29–36. The impact of this century of research can be studied in Denzinger-Schönmetzer, *Enchiridion Symbolorum.* Freiburg: Herder, 1973 (Ed. 35ᵃ emendata); Sectio I, "Symbola fidei liturgica antiqua," pp. 17–42 (Nos. 1–76), especially when contrasted with the earlier editions of Denziger, e.g. Denziger-Umberg, *Enchiridion Symbolorum.* Freiburg: Herder, 1932 (Ed. 18–20). For the standard comprehensive presentation in English of modern research on the Creed, cf. J.N.D. Kelly, *Early Christian Creeds.* London: Longman, 1972 (3rd edition; first published in 1950). As a statement formulated by the Church in the past, summarizing the articles of faith, the Apostles' Creed is of course one of the official documents of the living Magisterium and its Tradition. There are other ways of looking at it: as "active tradition" in Billot's sense, as the officially-expressed Profession of Faith continually heralded and taught by the living Magisterium, as the correlative of the pouring of water in the Sacrament of Baptism, as the original and enduring pattern, standard, rule or syllabus for catechetical teaching, and the like. Obviously, these are aspects that need to be distinguished in order to unite them in a fully conprehensive understanding of what the Apostles' Creed is in the indefectible life of the Church. There are of course many theological problems and questions in this area, the theory of Tradition, or the doctrine of the Magisterium, to mention only immediate examples. The present study intends to prescind from such problems, confining its purpose to the practical one of studying the Creed in itself, in its origin, nature, development and relationship to Catechetics as background for the contemporary significance and catechetical use of the *Creed of the People of God.* For an introduction to the theological questions and the literature, cf. Yves M.-J. Congar, *Tradition and Traditions: An Historical and a Theological Essay.* New York: Macmillan, 1967; *passim,* and esp. Chapter 6, "The Monuments of Tradition," pp. 425–458; and Etienne Menard, O.P., *La Tradition: Révélation, Écriture, Église selon Saint Thomas d'Aquin.* Paris: Desclée de Brouwer, 1964; esp. the discussion of "tradere-docere, traditio-doctrina," pp. 29–46. Perhaps the most comprehensive treatment of this entire question, which has been agitating Catholic thought one way or another throughout the Twentieth Century, is to be found in the works of Louis Billot, S.J., especially his treatise *De Ecclesia,* and the *ex professo* study,

De immutabilitate traditionis contra modernam haeresim Evolutionismi. Rome: Gregorian University Press, 1929 (4th ed.). For a short summary of the matter, see his *De virtitutibus infusis.* Rome: Gregorian University Press, 1928; "Epilogus," pp. 423–430. That the Creed involves the Magisterium, or better, is an act of the living Magisterium, living and active today as it has been since St. Peter stood with the rest of the Apostles proclaiming its substance, has never been more apparent than at the present time of the Church. This is due to the contemporary *Creed of the People of God,* which is the focal point of the contemporary burning question of the Magisterium in its relationship to catechetics and religious education.

3 For the Greek word *pistis,* "faith," cf. G. Kittel, *TDNT,* Vol. 6, pp. 174–228, esp. "Specifically Christian Usage," pp. 208–228. *"Pistis* (is) acceptance of the *Kerygma"* (208); *"Kerygma* and faith always go together" (209). This article is by Bultmann, and a certain caution regarding his Heideggerian Existentialism with its over-emphasis on the act of faith at the expense of the content of faith, is in order; but the scholarship regarding the meaning of *pistis* in Greek is comprehensive and valuable. Cf. p. 214: "The orthodox doctrine handed down by the Church is also *pistis* in Jude 3, 20 and 2 Pet. 1, 1," reviewing the fact that "the message itself can be called *pistis."*

4 Cf. Migne, P.G. 67, 973, where Bishop Eusebius of Nicomedia and Bishop Theognis of Nicaea say they signed the *pistis:* ". . . fidei, *te pistei,* quidem subscripsisse, anathematismo vero noluisse subscribere." The editor wonders in a footnote how these bishops could sign the *fides,* the *pistis,* without signing the anathema joined to the *formula fidei.* What is clear is the fact that what we today call the "Nicene Creed" professed at Mass on Sundays they in their day called simply *pistis,* "The Faith."

5 Cf. Migne, P.G. 25, 428; 27, 458; 26, 1042. See Pierre Thomas Camelot, O.P., " 'Symbole de Nicée' ou 'Foi de Nicée'?" *Orientalia Christiana Periodica* 13 (1947) 425–433. As Camelot points out, the Latins followed the same usage, saying simply *fides,* "The Faith," where we say "The Creed." In Migne, P.L. 10, 654, St. Hilary, for example, writes: *Incipit fides apud Nicaeam conscripta,* . . . and he proceeds to give the text of what we call the Creed: *"Credimus in unum Deum patrem omnipotentem . . . Et in unum Dominum Jesum Christum Filium Dei . . . Et in Spiritum Sanctum . . ."*

6 Pope Paul VI, "Sollemnis Professio Fidei," *A. A. S.* 60(10 Aug. 1968), 434; the *Creed of the People of God,* No. 4, above, pp. 9–10. It seems that the term *Symbolum* came to mean the profession of the apostolic faith made in short summary at the reception of the Sacrament of Baptism. Cf. Pierre Thomas Camelot, O.P., as cited in the previous footnote, p. 432: "Le 'symbole', c'est la profession de foi exigée au catéchumène à la prédication évangélique." See Joseph de Ghellinck, *op. cit.,* index, p. 317, s.v. "symbole, *sýmbolon,* le nom lui-même"; also *JNDK,* pp. 52–61. For the general use of the word "symbol" in classical antiquity, see the monograph of W. Müri, *Symbolon: Wort und Sachgeschichtliche Studie* (Bern, 1931); and H. J. Carpenter, " 'Symbolum' as a title of the Creed," *Journal of Theological Studies* (1942) 1–11.

7 Cf. C.H. Dodd, *The Apostolic Preaching and Its Developments.* London: Hodder and Stoughton, 1972 (1936); and his *According to the Scriptures: The Sub-structure of New Testament Theology.* London: Collins, 1962 (1952).

8 For the Greek word *Keryx,* "herald," cf. G. Kittel, *TDNT,* Vol. III, 683–718, in which Prof. Gerhard Friedrich discusses the dignity, social position and religious significance of the Herald in the Greek world; the Herald in the Jewish world;

and the *Keryx* in the New Testament. Cf. Johannes Hofinger, S.J., and Reedy,
W.J., *The ABC's of Modern Catechetics*. New York: Sadlier, 1962, Chap. 2, "The
Kerygma and Catechesis," pp. 14–23; "The verb *keryssein* . . . , used sixty-one
times in the New Testament . . . , denotes the action of a herald: one who
announces a message and calls his hearers to action . . . Historically, the word
kerygma is the term used in the writings of the Church to refer to that body of
essential truths which God meant to be specifically and emphatically proclaimed.
It is the substance of the Christian Good News upon which detailed doctrine is
built. . . . The Gospels and Epistles took shape from a nucleus of primitive
preaching common to all the Apostles. This primitive preaching took on the name
Kerygma. It is found throughout the New Testament as its unifying element." p.
15. One can add the conclusion of modern *Symbolforschung*: This nucleus of
primitive preaching common to all the Apostles is the "Apostles' Creed," not in
the exact wording which we use today, but in its pattern and substance of doctrine.
Hofinger, in fact, puts the same insight another way: "It is out of these *kerygma*
truths that the Creed has grown." (*Ibid.*)

⁹ Cf. *The Jerusalem Bible: The New Testament*. New York: Doubleday, 1966,
p. 203 (note on Acts 2,22): "The content of the earliest apostolic preaching (the
'Kerygma') is here summarized for the first time; cf. the five discourses of Peter,
Acts 2, 14–39; 3, 12–26; 4, 8–12, 5, 29–32; 10, 34–43; and the discourse of Paul,
13, 16–41. The kerygma is a witness to Christ's death and resurrection . . . ,
to his exaltation . . . , it provides certain details of Christ's ministry . . . (It)
appeals to the past, adducing the O.T. Prophecies, and it surveys the future, the
advent of the messianic era, inviting Jews and pagans to repentance . . . , so
that Christ's glorious return come the sooner. The gospels, which are developments
of the primitive preaching, adopt the same scheme." And cf. Lucien Cerfaux,
Christ in the Theology of St. Paul. New York: Herder and Herder, 1966, pp.
15–30.

¹⁰ F. J. Badcock, *The History of the Creeds*, London: S.P.C.K., 1938; p. 123.
Cerfaux concurs: "Paul speaks of his 'Gospel' . . . , and in 1 Cor. 15, 11, he
calls it his 'kerygma' . . . ; 1 Cor. 15, 3–8 is a summary of doctrine which is
already seen as a kind of 'symbol' or creed, judging by the concise style and the
exact phraseology, at least in verses 3–5. We are not here talking about a confession of faith in the strict sense, but rather of a summary account, which sets out
the fundamental event of Christian history . . . From the Acts of the Apostles
we can obtain a rough idea of the prehistory of this 'tradition.' " Cerfaux adds:
"Paul speaks of it as a *parádosis*, a 'tradition' received from the community at
Jerusalem." See his *Christ in the Theology of St. Paul, op. cit.*, pp. 21–22. And
Yves M.-J. Congar, *Tradition and Traditions, op. cit.*, p. 25: "The Early Church
was conscious of embodying in its daily life the reality conveyed in these words of
our Lord: 'As the Father has sent me, even so I send you.' " Cf. John 10, 14–15;
17, 18; 17, 26; 20, 21; 1 John 1, 1–3; Luke 22, 29–32; Rom. 1, 1–6; 1 Cor. 3,
23; 1 Cor. 11, 3.

¹¹ Cf. *Christus Dominus*, the Decree on the Pastoral Office of Bishops in the
Church, *Vatican II*, pp. 564–590; esp. nos. 11–21; and *Dei Verbum*, the Dogmatic
Constitution on Divine Revelation, *ibid.*, esp. Chap. 2, "The Transmission of
Divine Revelation," Vatican II, pp. 753–756.

¹² Cf. Rom. 6, 17; and footnote 24 below. The *wording* of the Apostles' Creed

as used commonly throughout the Roman Rite of the Catholic Church and among most Protestant Churches today is not the point, as superficial mentalities since Lorenzo Valla have erroneously supposed. The point under discussion is rather in the order of *meaning* and the *pattern* of its expression, and not in this or that fixed formulation of the expression. Fixed verbal formulations seem impossible for scholarly research to determine in Apostolic times, and probably did not exist until later in the life of the early Church. Cf. *JNDK,* "The Original Pattern," pp. 23–29, and Chapter III, "The Movement Towards Fixity," pp. 62–99. Johannes Quasten puts the matter succinctly when he speaks of the transition *von festen Typen zu festen Formeln,* "from fixed types of patterns to fixed formulas." Cf. "Symbolforschung" in *LTK,* Vol. 9, 1212. St. Paul's reference to the *týpon didachēs,* Rom. 6, 17, is the abiding witness of the Church of the Apostles to the functioning substance and pattern of what we today call the Apostles' Creed.

¹³ Cf. Acts 13, 1; also I Cor. 12, 27–30; Eph. 4, 11–13; James 3, 1; and in fact the three Pastoral Epistles to Timothy and Titus as a whole, of which St. Augustine in his *De doctrina Christiana,* 4, 16, 33, says: ". . . a teacher in the Church should have these three Apostolic Epistles before his eyes." Professor Kelly summarizes accurately: ". . . in the Pastoral Epistles such phrases as 'model of sound words' (2 Tim. 1, 13), 'the healthy doctrine' (2 Tim. 4, 3; Tit. 1, 9), 'the deposit' . . . and 'the noble deposit' (1 Tim. 6, 20; 2 Tim. 1, 14), 'the faith' in its concrete acceptation (1 Tim. 1, 19; Tit. 1, 13), and 'the splendid teaching' (1 Tim. 4, 6) form a constant refrain;" cf. *JNDK,* p. 8. In general, Rengstorf in *TDNT,* Vol. II, pp. 135–165, and esp. 157–159, "The *didáskaloi* of the Early Christian Community," who correlate with what we today call parish catechists or CCD teachers.

¹⁴ See, for example, 1 Cor. 2, 4; 2 Cor. 2, 17; 2 Cor. 5, 11; Col. 2, 4; 1 Thess. 2, 5; Gal. 1, 10; 1 Pet. 1, 3–9; 2 Pet. 1, 12–21.

¹⁵ See Rom. 9, 32 ff; Rom. 11, 7–10; 1 Tim. 1, 13–16. Also, *GCD,* No. 71: "The importance and magnitude of the work to be done by catechists does not prevent the necessary establishing of boundaries around the role of catechists . . . For adherence on the part of those to be taught is a fruit of grace and freedom, and does not ultimately depend on the catechist; and catechetical action, therefore, should be accompanied by prayer."

¹⁶ See 2 Cor. 2, 15–16; 2 Cor. 4, 4–5; 2 Thess. 2, 10–12.

¹⁷ For examples in the New Testament of the use of the Greek root for the English word "Catechetics," cf. Luke 1, 1; Acts 21, 24; Acts 21, 28; Rom. 2, 18; 1 Cor. 14, 19; Gal. 6, 6. The ordinary Greek word for teaching, instruction and doctrine, with the entirely different root in *didask-,* is also commonly used in the New Testament: *didachē* appears regularly for "doctrine," and Jesus is addressed constantly as *Didáskalos,* the Greek word for "Rabbi" or "Teacher." See *TDNT,* Vol. II, 135–165. Apparently it was St. Paul who introduced into Christian circles the use of the comparatively rare Greek word *katechéo,* meaning a simple oral instruction. Perhaps he wished this teaching *with a difference* to have its own distinctive name, if one may venture a speculation, separate from the common Greek words denoting secular instruction. Cf. *TDNT,* Vol. III, 638–639; "*Katechéo* . . . is a late and rare word in secular Greek . . . Paul himself uses *katechéo* exclusively in the sense (of) 'to give instruction concerning the content of the faith' . . . Galatians 6, 6 draws a contrast between the *katechon,* the

catechist who gives instruction in Christian doctrine, and the *katechoúmenos,* the catechumen who receives this instruction . . . " Cf. *JNDK,* pp. 49–52, "The Catechetical Setting of the Creeds."

[18] *JNDK,* pp. 7–8.

[19] Cf. *JNDK,* p. 8, where he cites the three Pastoral Epistles, the First Epistle of St. John, and the Epistle to the Hebrews.

[20] *Ibid.,* p. 9.

[21] See below, footnote 24.

[22] *JNDK,* pp. 10–11. And Kelly refers to the German *Symbolforschung* of the last hundred years, particularly the works of A. Seeberg, *Der Katechismus der Urchristenheit.* Leipzig: 1903; and P. Feine, *Die Gestalt des apostolischen Glaubensbekenntnisses in der Zeit des Neuen Testaments.* Leipzig: 1925. See Joseph de Ghellinck, *Patristique et Moyen Age,* Vol. I: *Les recherches sur les origines du Symbole des Apôtres.* Paris: Desclée de Brouwer, 1949; esp. "Le symbole et le Nouveau Testament," pp. 191–203; and Pierre Benoit, O.P., *Exégèse Théologie,* Paris: Cerf. 1961; Vol. II, pp. 193–211, "Les origines du Symbole des Apôtres dans le Nouveau Testament."

[23] Quite understandably, granted their predisposition to place the Rule of Faith in something written rather than in the living teaching of a body of men sent by God with authority from God and sustained in their trans-secular witness by a special action of His almighty grace and power, there has been a tendency among German Protestant scholars in the *Symbolforschung* to seek the *wording* of the present Apostles' Creed in the documents of the Early Church. Something like this seems to have animated the work of Seeberg cited in the previous footnote. The hope has been in vain, however, for the truth of the matter lies in a closely-related yet quite different perspective, that of the Living Teaching or Magisterium or *Kerygma* of the Apostles and their Successors. It is the doctrinal substance and Trinitarian pattern of the profession of the Apostolic Faith which comes from the Apostles, and not any one given fixed verbal formulation of it. On this entire question, cf. Yves M.-J. Congar, O.P. *Tradition and Traditions: An Historical and a Theological Essay.* New York: Macmillan, 1967. The verbal *formulation* of the Apostles' Creed which is official in the Latin Church in recent centuries varies slightly from the Old Roman formula, which scholars identify in ancient Christian writings of the second and third centuries. For the history of wording of the Apostles' Creed in use today, *cf. JNDK,* Chap. 12, "The Apostles' Creed," pp. 368–397. The earliest form of all seems to have been the Interrogatory Creed, as one would naturally expect, the baptismal Creed associated with the baptismal act. See above, pp. 43–44, with footnote 41.

[24] Cf. Romans 6, 17: *Týpon didachēs* in the Greek. The Latin Vulgate translates: *in eam forman doctrinae in quam traditi estis.* The Revised Standard renders the passage into English as follows: "But thanks be to God, that you who were once slaves of sin have become obedient from the heart to *the standard of teaching* to which you were committed . . . " The New American: ". . . though once you were slaves of sin, you sincerely obeyed *that rule of teaching* which was imparted to you . . . " The Jerusalem Bible: "You were once slaves of sin, but thank God you submitted without reservation to *the Creed* you were taught."

[25] Cf. Luke 24, 13–35. Cf. C.H. Dodd, *According to the Scriptures.* London: Collins, 1965; pp. 109–110: "This is a piece of genuinely creative thinking . . . Whose was the originating mind here? . . . The New Testament itself avers that

it was Jesus Christ Himself who first directed the minds of His followers to certain parts of the Scriptures as those in which they might find illumination on the meaning of His mission and destiny." Cf. Cardinal John Wright, *The Church: Hope of the World.* Kenosha: Prow Books, 1972; p. 66: "The catechesis needed today is that which is set forth in St. Luke's Gospel, chapter 24, where is described the two melancholy, discouraged, confused disciples in flight from Jerusalem to Emmaus. Suddenly Jesus stood beside them and said: 'What are these conversations you are having among you, and are sad?' They replied: "We expected so many wonderful *changes* and now we are sad!' *Sperabamus! Sperabamus!* They were precisely like some—but by no means *all*—post-Council Catholics! We had hope . . . but no longer! What did Jesus do? He did not give a course in theology . . . *He gave them a lesson in catechetics.* He recalled not theories, not speculations—but *facts of doctrine, dogmas of faith.*"

²⁶ Lucien Cerfaux, *Christ in the Theology of St. Paul.* New York: Herder and Herder, 1966; p. 31.

²⁷ *Ibid.,* p. 180.

²⁸ See Deut. 6, 4–9; cf. Louis Jacobs, *Principles of the Jewish Faith: An Analytical Study.* New York: Basic Books, 1964; for Maimonides' summary of "The Jewish Creed" into its thirteen articles, cf. pp. 14–15.

²⁹ *Vatican I,* p. 48, citing the *Commonitorium* of St. Vincent of Lerins; P.L. 50, 668. See for the Latin, *DS* 3020: "Crescat igitur . . . sed in suo dumtaxat genere, in eodem scilicet dogmate, eodem sensu eademque sententia," the famous words from the Church of the Fathers which will recur in the Pontificates of John XXIII and Paul VI.

³⁰ Cf. *Vatican II,* pp. 66–67 and 355–356.

³¹ Cf. Charles Journet, *The Church of the Word Incarnate.* London: Sheed and Ward. 1955; Vol. I, pp. 526–559 (and below, footnote 68).

³² Bardy, Gustave. *The Church at the End of the First Century.* London: Sands, 1938; p. 109.

³³ *Ibid.,* p. 152.

³⁴ This *pistis* or Faith is not correctly called "The Apostles' Creed" in the sense of the set form of words that came into use later in the life of the Church, familiar to us today in the Roman Rite. But the substance of the Faith which the Apostles professed and handed on to their Successors, the bishops, was the same as the doctrine we profess in our present "Apostles' Creed." Cf. *JNDK,* p. 95: "Admittedly great stress is laid on orthodox belief by many of [early Christian] writers we have consulted, and they are all convinced that there is one, universally accepted system of dogma, or rule of faith, in the Catholic Church. But this is never unambiguously connected, even by theologians like St. Irenaeus and Tertullian, with any set form of words." The *pattern* in which this doctrine of the Faith was taught and professed was the Trinitarian one, which will become clear in connection with the baptismal act. Cf. *JNDK,* p. 60: "The questions and answers [at baptism] were a sign, an expressive and portentous symbol, of the Triune God in Whose name the baptism was being enacted and with Whom the Christian catechumen was being united."

³⁵ Cf. Yves M.-J.Congar, *Tradition and Traditions.* New York: Macmillan, 1967; p. 249: "Faith, Creed and Sacrament are all *received.* Orthodoxy, true belief and true praise, is what has been communicated to us by those who have taught us the true faith and baptized us into its profession . . . Baptismal faith is the faith

of the Church, in continuity with the apostles . . . St. Thomas Aquinas still had a strong sense of this when, in the treatise on baptism in the *Summa,* he made more than twenty references to the classical formula, 'Baptismus est fidei sacramentum' . . . What is implied is a spiritual and corporeal entry into the one reality, whose origin is Christ and the apostles, the reality of saving faith." This throws additional light on Jesus Christ as the originator of the Creed and on the correlation between Creed and Catechetics.

[36] Mt. 28, 16–20.

[37] Acts 2, 37–42; for Peter's first sermon, Acts 2, 14–36.

[38] Acts 8, 26–40.

[39] Acts 16, 11–15.

[40] *JNDK,* pp. 41–42. It is beyond the scope of the present study to go into the more recent research on the two-fold formulation of the earliest profession of the Faith, the Trinitarian and the Christological, and the process of their combination into the formula we know today as the Apostles' Creed. Cf. J. deGhellinck, *op. cit.,* Vol. I, pp. 117–178, "La double formule et l'Antiquissima." It must be kept in mind, of course, that the research and discussion bear upon the "prehistory" of the verbal *formulation* of the Apostles' Creed, as the specialists in this field term it, and not upon its *content.* As Ghellinck points out lucidly in his "Conclusion," pp. 239–250, the *content* originates from the Apostles. The *Symbolforschung* has confirmed this fact: "Loin de mettre en doute l'origine apostolique du contenu du symbole . . . " (p. 240). And since the Apostles were only simple fishermen until Jesus Christ, the Divine Teacher, called them to His school and trained them in it, we have suggested that Jesus Himself is the actual originator of the Apostles' Creed.

[41] St. Justin Martyr, *Apol.* 1, 61, 3–10; P.G. 6, 420–421. See also *Apol.* 1, 6, 2; 1, 65, 3; 1, 67, 2. "It is remarkable" Kelly writes, "how deeply . . . the familiar three-clause pattern was imprinted on his mind." *Op. cit.,* p. 71. "Plainly St. Justin's Church has orderly arrangements for instructing converts in Christian doctrine and for satisfying itself that they had properly absorbed it." p. 43. "In St. Justin we for the first time come across what can plausibly be taken to be quotations from semi-formal creeds." p. 71. "He provides the earliest direct evidence we possess for the emergence of relatively fixed credal questions at baptism . . . A fact which deserves notice is the fidelity with which these reproduce the primitive *kerygma,* without bending it to any appreciable extent to polemical or apologetic needs or colouring it with St. Justin's own philosophical theology." p. 75.

[42] Johannes Quasten, *Patrology.* Westminster: Newman, 1953; Vol. II, p. 191. "The description of baptism given here," Quasten comments, "is invaluable because it provides us with the first Roman Creed."

[43] Hans Lietzmann, *Die Anfänge der Glaubensbekenntnisse* (Tübingen: 1921), 226; quoted by J.N.D. Kelly, *op. cit.,* p. 30. "Who is unaware," asks St. Augustine, "that it is no true baptism if the evangelical words of which the Symbol consists are missing?" *De bapt. contra Donatistas* 6, 47; P.L. 43, 214. It would be difficult to state more succinctly the nature of the Symbol or Creed and its origin in the Apostolic *Kerygma.*

[44] For the official Latin of this "Triplex professio fidei," see the new *Ordo Baptismi Parvulorum.* Rome: Typis Polyglottis Vaticanis, 1973; p. 31. The same Profession of Faith recurs in the *Ordo Initiationis Christianae Adultorum.* Rome: Typis Polyglottis Vaticanis, 1972; p. 91; see the text, pp. 2–3, above.

[45] *JNDK,* pp. 40 and 50–51.

46 Alfred Seeberg, *Der Katechismus der Urchristenheit.* Munich: Chr. Kaiser Verlag, 1966 (Photostatic re-print of the 1903 edition); p. 271; and the whole of Part II, "Die Glaubensformel," pp. 45–171.

47 Cf. *JNDK,* p. 52–61. The name "Symbol," *sýmbolon,* seems to have referred originally and primarily to the baptismal interrogatory form of the Creed. See Pierre Thomas Camelot, O.P., " 'Symbole de Nicée' ou 'Foi de Nicée'?" *Orientalia Christiana Periodica* 13(1947), pp. 428–429: "Therefore one concludes that in the Fourth Century, the Nicene Faith (Creed) is not a symbol. The Symbol is the profession of baptismal faith . . . This baptismal profession is the *pisteos didaskalia* . . . , or, quite simply, the *pistis* . . . , the profession of faith in the Trinity to which baptism in the name of the Father, and of the Son and of the Holy Spirit corresponds." See D. Van den Eynde, *Les normes de l'enseignement chrétien dans da littérature patristique des trois premiers siècles.* Paris: Gabalda, 1933; p. 245, his summary on Cyprian: "It follows that the unanimous faith of the bishops and their churches is the criterion which serves to judge between heresy and truth. The division between heretics and true Christians takes place by means of the faith or 'Symbol' which is communicated at baptism." See above, footnotes 5 and 6.

48 G. L. Prestige, *Fathers and Heretics: Six Studies in Dogmatic Faith.* (London: SPCK, 1958), 7. These Studies were the Bampton Lectures for 1940. For the ecumenical significance of the Creed, which can be seen in the opening of the first Lausanne Conference when all the delegates recited together the Apostles' Creed, and in the career of Karl Barth, it is interesting to note the terms of foundation laid down by the Anglican divine, Rev. John Bampton (1690–1751): "I direct and appoint that . . . a Lecturer may be chosen by the Heads of Colleges only, and by no others . . . , to preach eight Divinity Lecture Sermons . . . at St. Mary's in Oxford . . . , upon either of the following subjects: upon the divine authority of the holy Scriptures, upon the authority of the writings of the primitive Fathers as to the faith and practice of the primitive Church, upon the Divinity of our Lord and Saviour Jesus Christ, upon the Divinity of the Holy Ghost, [or] upon the Articles of the Christian Faith as comprehended in the Apostles' and Nicene Creed." *ibid.,* flyleaf, p. v.

49 St. Augustine, *De Symbolo sermo ad catechumenos;* M.L. 40, 627–628. For a convenient collection of fifteen of these catechetical discourses on the Creed by St. Augustine, see Suzanne Poque, *Augustin d'Hippone: Sermons pour la* Pâque. Paris: Cerf, 1966. (*Sources Chrétiennes* No. 116). And C. Eichenseer, *Das Symbolum Apostolicum beim hl. Augustinus.* St. Ottilien, 1960. Also F. Van der Meer, *Augustine the Bishop.* London: Sheed and Ward, 1961; Chap. 12, "Becoming a Christian," pp. 347–387. "The lapidary formula," Van der Meer writes, "which was accounted apostolic and which they were supposed to learn by heart at the beginning of the Easter Vigil had never been heard by them before. It was a formula that was nowhere set down in writing but had been orally handed down. It came under the discipline of secrecy . . ." (p. 359). For an eye-witness description of the Fourth Century catechumenate in Jerusalem, see John Wilkinson (transl.) *Egeria's Travels.* London: SPCK, 1971; p. 144: "During forty days . . . the bishop goes through the whole Bible . . . He also teaches them at this time all about the resurrection and the faith. And this is called *catechesis.* After five weeks' teaching they receive the Creed, whose content he explains article by article . . ."

⁵⁰ The propositions of the Apostles' Creed which state the basic articles of faith can be gathered readily from such writings of the Fathers of the Church, which manifest the baptismal Creed in the living baptismal acts of the Church. The same on-going Ordinary Magisterium of the Church can be studied in the Catechetical Discourses of St. Cyril of Jerusalem. See for example the Fifth Discourse (P.G. 33, 519–523): "In learning your Faith and professing it, be careful to embrace and preserve in your heart only that Faith which is being handed over to you now by the Church, put together firmly out of all the Scriptures . . . For since not all can read and many lack leisure, we summarize in the few propositions of the Symbol the entire dogmatic teaching of the Faith, lest souls perish through ignorance . . . I command you, therefore, to have this Faith as your constant companion in whatever way you go in the whole time of your life, and never to accept any other in its place . . . And as you hear it now in its bare words, keep this Faith fast in your memory . . . For this Summary of the Faith was not composed according to mere human opinions; it consists of the basic articles selected from all the Scriptures, so that is completes and perfects one single teaching of the Faith . . ." For a convenient translation of these *Catechetical Discourses,* see Leo P. McCauley (transl.) *The Works of St. Cyril of Jerusalem* (Washington: CUA Press, 1969). See also Hugh M. Riley, *Christian Initiation: A Comparative Study of the Interpretation of the Baptismal Liturgy in the Mystagogical Writings of Cyril of Jerusalem, John Chrysostom, Theodore of Mopsuestia and Ambrose of Milan* (Washington: CUA Press, 1974). And see J.N.D. Kelly (Transl.) *Rufinus: A Commentary on the Apostles' Creed.* Westminster: The Newman Press, 1955 (ACW no. 20); p. 9: "The particular literary *genre* to which Rufinus' essay belongs was by no means unfamiliar to his contemporaries," and Kelly gives a summary of the more notable Patristic commentaries on the Apostles' Creed, pp. 9–10. For a short synthesis illustrating this entire topic, see Johannes Quasten, "Baptismal Creed and Bâptismal Act in St. Ambrose's *De Mysteriis* and *De Sacramentis,*" in *Mélanges Joseph de Ghellinck* (Gembloux: Duculot, 1951), Vol. I, pp. 223–234.

⁵¹ Jean Daniélou, *Gospel Message and Hellenistic Culture.* London: Darton, Longman and Todd, 1973; 336–337.

⁵² Karl Jaspers has elaborated the concept. See, for example, his *Philosophical Faith and Revelation.* New York: Harper and Row, 1967.

⁵³ St. Thomas Aquinas, *Summa Theologiae,* 2–2, q. 5, art. 3: "ea quae sunt fidei alio modo tenet quam per fidem."

⁵⁴ Cf. Claudio Morino, "Catechizzare con gioia," in *Studi e Ricerche* (1971), p. 158: "The temptation to reduce God and His Creative Word to a purely human and a merely temporal dimension exercised among the Gnostics a terrifying fascination. The fascination continues throughout history and is operating today: and so it will be until the end of time."

⁵⁵ It is not difficult to recognize the parallel with a certain type of philosophical theologizing in the aftermath of Vatican II, which places the Church-of-Law and the Church-of-Love in opposition, which no longer has eyes to see that the concrete social entity called the Roman Catholic Church is the Mystical Body of Christ, and which, giving up the Church which comes from the Apostles, puts its philosophical faith in an emerging Church-of-the-Future. See, below, p. 278 and fn. 85. Pope Paul VI in an Allocution to bishops of the Church on Nov. 15, 1975, makes the point explicitly: "The first and principal duty of us Bishops . . . is to be firm

in the faith, to guarantee the continuity and the purity of the message entrusted
to us . . . so that the People of God may be able to distinguish clearly the truth,
which is light and strength, from its nebulous expressions which, according to a
fashion that we would call gnostic, as it actually is, would like to confuse its
outline and veil its integrity." See *L'Osservatore Romano-English Edition* (Nov.
27, 1975), p. 11. For a comprehensive treatment of the matter, cf. Jerome Hamer,
The Church is a Communion (New York: Sheed and Ward, 1964), esp. Chap. I,
"The Meaning and Implications of the Encyclical 'Mystici corporis'," pp. 13–34.

⁵⁶ Johannes Quasten, *Patrology*. Westminster, Maryland: The Newman Press,
1950, Vol. I, p. 300.

⁵⁷ Cf. St. Irenaeus, *Against Heresies*, 1, 9, 4; *The Ante-Nicene Fathers*. Grand
Rapids: Eerdmans, 1973, Vol. I, p. 330: "[Keeping] unchangeable in his heart
the rule of the truth which he received by means of baptism . . ." And see
Quasten, *ibid.*, p. 300: "For Irenaeus this canon of truth seems to be the baptismal
creed, for he says that we receive it in baptism (*Adv. Haer.* 1, 9, 4). He gives a
description of the faith of the Church which follows exactly the Apostolic Symbol."
For the same understanding, cf. St. Hilary, above, p. 52, with the reference to
P.L. 10, 566 and 568.

⁵⁸ *Ibid.*, 1, 10, 1; *The Ante-Nicene Fathers, ibid.*, p. 330.

⁵⁹ *Ibid.*, 1, 10, 2; p. 331.

⁶⁰ *Ibid.* 3, 3, 1; p. 415.

⁶¹ *Ibid.*, 3, 3, 2; p. 415. Since this passage plainly appears to support the
Primacy of the Bishop of Rome in the Universal Church, Protestant and Catholic
scholars quite naturally take opposing views in interpreting it. For a short summary of the chief Protestant references, cf. R.P.C. Hanson, *Tradition in the
Early Church*. London: SCM Press, 1962; p. 265: "Appendix B: Irenaeus, *Adversus Haereses* 3.3.1. For the standard Catholic treatment of the passage, see D.
Van den Eynde, *Les normes de l'enseignement* chrétien. Paris: Gabalda, 1933;
pp. 170–180.

⁶² Vatican II has called for the renewal of the Catechumenate in our day;
cf. *Sacrosacrum concilium*, Nos. 64–66; *Lumen gentium*, n. 14; *Ad gentes*, n. 14;
and *Christus Dominus*, n. 14. One of the primary reasons is no doubt the contemporary need for the Ordinary and Universal Magisterium to continue its
teaching of the articles of faith professed by the Creed. The entire matter of this
Vatican II renewal is illumined by and rests upon the solemn definition in Chapter
3, "Faith," of the Constitution *Dei Filius* of Vatican I: "Moreover, all those
matters must be believed with divine and Catholic faith that are continued in the
word of God, whether in Scripture or tradition, and that are proposed by the
Church, either by a solemn decision or by the Ordinary and Universal Magisterium,
to be believed as divinely revealed". James F. Broderick, S.J., *Documents of
Vatican Council I* (Collegeville, Minnesota: The Liturgical Press, 1971), p. 44
(cited henceforth as *Vatican I*); for the Latin original, Denz. 3011. The "solemn
decision" is of course an action of the "Extraordinary Magisterium" as distinct
from "the Ordinary and Universal Magisterium." Cf. J. M.A. Vacant. *Études
théologiques sur les constitutions du Concile du Vatican*. Paris: Delhomme et
Briguet, 1895; Vol. II, Chap. 3, "De la foi," and esp. pp. 89–95, "Qu'est-ce que
le magistère ordinaire et universel de l'Église?"

⁶³ See J. H. Card. Newman, *The Arians of the Fourth Century* (London:
Longmans, Green, 1901), esp. pp. 133–150, "On the Principle of the Formation

276 *Creed and Catechetics*

and Imposition of Creeds." And see Newman's translation, *Select Treatises of St. Athanasius in Controversy with the Arians* (London: Longmans, Green, 1900), 2 Vols. For a recent comprehensive study, see Ephrem Boularand, S.J. *L' Hérésie d'Arius et la 'Foi' de Nicée* (Paris: Letouzey, 1972), 2 vols.

[64] Newman, *The Arians of the Fourth Century, op. cit.,* pp. 392–393.

[65] Newman, *ibid.,* pp. 445–446.

[66] P.L. 10, 566: ". . . Et facta est fides temporum potius quam Evangeliorum, dum et secundum annos describitur, et secundum confessionem baptismi non tenetur. Periculosum nobis admodum atque etiam miserabile est, tot nunc fides existere, quot voluntates; et tot nobis doctrinas, quot mores . . . et cum, secundum unum Deum et unum Dominum et unum baptisma, etiam fides una sit, excedimus ab ea fide quae sola est: et dum plures fiunt, ad id coeperunt esse, ne ulla sit." Cf. *Hardon,* pp. 126–141 for a summary of this period of crisis and the action of the Catholic Church through the great Ecumenical Councils, especially Ephesus and Chalcedon, to maintain the original purity of the apostolic kerygma or witness concerning Jesus as our Lord, Son of God incarnate and Savior; pp. 129–130: "Immediately after Nicea there was an outcropping of Arian-sponsored councils, at Sirmium, Arles, Milan, Beziers, Rimini and Seleucia, where the anti-Nicene party triumphed through pressure (including physical violence) from imperial authority dominated by Arian bishops from the East."

[67] P.L. 10, 568: "Quod hieme undoso mari observari a navigantibus maxime tutum est, ut naufraugio desaeviente, in portum ex quo solverant revertantur . . . ita inter haec fidei naufragia, coelestis patrimonii iam pene profligata haereditate, tutissimum nobis est, primam et solam evangelicam fidem confessam in baptismo, intellectamque retinere."

[68] Cf. Charles Journet, *The Church of the Word Incarnate.* London: Sheed and Ward, 1951; Chapter X, "Apostolicity, Property and Note of the True Church," pp. 526–559; in particular p. 526: "For all their grandeur, the names 'Roman Church,' and 'Sacramental Church,' are still inadequate. They designate the true Church by the two divine powers without which she could neither propagate nor maintain herself. But the adequate name, naming the Church in the fullness of her reality, naming her by her efficient and conserving cause, is Apostolic." Cf. pp. 528–529, "The Property of Apostolicity considered as in the Church at once Believing and Teaching"; and pp. 543–544, "Modernism and the Argument from Prescription."

[69] "On Sundays," St. Francis Xavier writes from his mission in India to St. Ignatius Loyola, "I assemble all the people, men and women, young and old, and get them to repeat the prayers in their language. They take much pleasure in doing so and come to the meetings gladly. We begin with a profession of faith in the unity and trinity of God, I first saying the Creed in stentorian tones and they all together in a mighty chorus. That done, I go through the Creed article by article . . . As they confess themselves to be Christians, I require them to tell me whether they firmly believe each and every one of the articles, and they reply in loud chorus, with their arms folded in their breasts in the form of a cross, that they do. I make them repeat the Creed more often than anything else because only a man who believes in the twelve articles has a right to call himself a Christian." Quoted by Josef Andreas Jungmann, *Handing on the Faith.* New York: Herder and Herder, 1959; p. 252.

[70] Cf. St. Cyril of Jerusalem, above, footnote 50.

⁷¹ See "The Apostolic Kerygma," above, pp. 32–37.

⁷² Again, it is important to note that it is not the verbal formula as such which is the proximate rule of faith for Catholics, but the substance of the apostolic profession given or "channelled" to souls by the living Magisterium. The Magisterium proclaims and teaches, elaborates upon and defends, the Faith or Creed of the Apostles, in St. Peter's day and across the centuries to the day of his present successor. This will be the significance of the *Creed of the People of God;* see above, pp. 253–259. Cf. Emmanuel Doronzo, *The Channels of Revolution.* Middleburg: Notre Dame Institute Press, 1974; esp. Chap. 3, "The Magisterium, Organ of Revelation," pp. 33–37.

⁷³ Pègues, Thomas, O.P. *Aperçus de philosophie thomiste et de propédeutique* (Paris: Blot, 1927), p. 430.

⁷⁴ Cf. *GCD,* No. 83: ". . . the simple and objective kind of instruction which is appropriate for children." It is this that Modernist and Neo-Gnostic religious education omits.

⁷⁵ Cf. *GCD,* No. 22: "Catechesis performs the function of disposing men to receive the action of the Holy Spirit and to deepen their conversion. It does this through the word, to which are joined the witness of life and prayer." This "word" is "the catechetical form" of the ministry of the word, "which is intended to make men's faith become living, conscious and active, through the light of instruction." (*ibid.,* no. 17).

⁷⁶ It is the great merit of *The Roman Catechism* that it preserves this fourfold division of catechetical content; cf. McHugh and Callan (transl.) *Catechism of the Council of Trent for Parish Priests.* New York: Wagner, 1934. The same fidelity to this heritage is reflected in the *Catechism of Christian Doctrine* published by order of Pope St. Pius X. Middleburg: Notre Dame Institute Press, 1974.

⁷⁷ Charles Boyer, S.J. "Un appello: fare di più," *L'Osservatore Romano* (Oct. 1, 1974), p. 1. Cf. Th. Camelot, O.P., "Le magistère et les symboles," *Divinitas* (1961), pp. 607–622; and the comment of Yves Congar, *Tradition . . . , op. cit.,* p. 336: "The Councils and the Fathers made painstaking reference to objective tradition and the received Creeds."

⁷⁸ Cf. Charles Journet, *What is Dogma?* New York: Hawthorn Books, 1964; esp. Chap. I, "Are Dogmas an Object of Faith," pp. 11–14; Chap. VI, "The Life of Dogma: Preservation and Explanation of the Revealed Deposit," pp. 53–60; and Chap. IX, "The Truth Value of Revealed Statements," pp. 81–91. This work of Journet, actually a treatise on Fundamental Catechetics, is helpful for the catechetical teacher in the situation which has developed in the aftermath of Vatican II. See also his introduction to theology, *The Wisdom of Faith.* Westminster, Maryland: The Newman Press, 1952; esp. chap. 2, "The Wisdom of Faith and the Use of Concepts," pp. 14–32. It is well known that the Modernist movement throughout its three eruptions in these two contemporary centuries has resisted consistently the idea of a divine use of the concepts and propositions of human discourse in order to communicate among men the articles or abiding truths of the Catholic Faith. For further study of this fundamental matter, upon which basic approach in catechetics and religious education must necessarily depend, cf. R. Garrigou-Lagrange, *Le Sens Commun: La philosophie de l'être et les formules dogmatiques.* Paris: Declée, 1922 (3rd ed.). Part III of this work, pp. 263–377, on "Common Sense and the Understanding of the Dogmatic Formulas of the Church" is more relevant than ever in the "Crisis of Faith" situation that

has followed upon Vatican II. Likewise A. Gardeil, *Le donné révélé et la theologie.* Paris: J. Gabalda, 1910; catechesis is concerned with this *donné révélé,* this revealed truth as given to us by the Teaching Church, and not directly with theology. See Cardinal John Wright, footnote 25 above. One of the great exegetes of the twentieth century, the German convert Heinrich Schlier, addresses himself to this point constantly in his writings. See for example *Das Ende der Zeit.* Freiburg: Herder, 1971; "Das bleibend Katholische: Ein Versuch über ein Prinzip des Katholischen," pp. 297–320; *Wort Gottes: Eine Neutestamentliche Besinnung.* Würzburg: Werkbund Verlag, 1962; and *Die Zeit der Kirche.* Frieburg: Herder, 1956; esp. Chap. 15, "Kerygma und Sophia: zur neutestamentlichen Grundlegung des Dogmas," pp. 206–232. The dogmas stated and defined by the councils turn about the articles of faith professed by the Creed, and develop them with deepened understanding. These articles of faith are the facts of the Catholic Religion, the abiding truths of God, the Word of God revealed to man through the ministry of the word in His Church. This is what Newman was saying in the nineteenth century. The more recent defenders of the Faith are saying the same thing, each in his own way, in response to the Nietzschean nihilism of twentieth century creedlessness. Cf. below, footnote 85.

[79] Schroeder, H.J., O.P. *Disciplinary Decrees of the General Councils: Text, Translation and Commentary* (St. Louis: B. Herder, 1937), pp. 237–239.

[80] The First President of the Council of Trent, Cardinal del Monte, addressed the Council on Feb. 12, 1546, in these words: "Your Paternities know how all our Faith is given to Divine Revelation. The Church has transmitted this Revelation to us partly out of the Scriptures which are in the Old and New Testament, partly also out of a simple transmission by hand. Thus, to proceed with order, we must first make a profession of Faith, then we must receive the Sacred Scriptures, and, finally, deal with the ecclesiastical traditions." Quoted by Yves M.-J. Congar, *Tradition and Traditions.* New York: Macmillan, 1966; p. 287.

[81] For the English translation see John F. Clarkson, S.J. *et al, The Church Teaches: Documents of the Church in English Translation* (St. Louis: B. Herder, 1955), pp. 6–9. This "Creed of the Council of Trent" was published by Pope Pius IV on Nov. 13, 1564.

[82] The *Creed of the People of God,* no. 4; AAS (Aug. 10, 1968), p. 434.

[83] Pope Pius IX omitted this sentence when the Act of Profession took place by the bishops of the Catholic Church assembled in St. Peter's Church at Rome.

[84] *Vatican I,* pp. 34–36.

[85] *Vatican I,* p. 48. Vatican Council I is quoting St. Vincent of Lerins, *Commonitorium,* c. 23 (P.L. 50, 688). For the Latin original, see *DS* 3020: ". . . sed in suo dumtaxat genere, in eodem scilicet dogmate, eodem sensu eademque sententia." For a clear expression of the movement of thought which Vatican I has in mind, a movement extending in three moments or waves from the early decades of the nineteenth century to the present concluding decades of the twentieth, see George Tyrrell, *Through Scylla and Charybdis, or, The Old Theology and the New* (London: Longmans, Green, 1907), pp. 216–217: "Secular knowledge moves on by a process of true development and transformation, the old ever dying away and dissolving into the new. Dogmatic revealed theology professes to stand still; to say, to mean, the same today as two thousand years ago; to be as exactly and finally true . . . But, in proportion as . . . repressive effort proves impossible, as science marches forward heedless of anathemas . . . , the substantial sense of the

'form of sound words' is quietly transformed into something different. He would
be a bold theologian who should affirm that such articles of belief as the Creation,
or as Christ's ascent into Heaven, His descent into Hell, His coming to judge the
living and the dead, and many others, are held today in substantially the same
theological sense as formerly." Those who suffer from the delusion that "The
New Theology" has emerged from "research" consequent upon Vatican II should
ponder the subtitle of Tyrrell's work. Much research is needed on the Loisy-Tyrrell
phenomenon as a whole. Scholars of the future have a fertile field for further
research on the underlying unity of the three "moments" of the Modernist phenomenon in the Catholic Church: that of Günther and other German priests prior
to Vatican I; that of Loisy and Tyrrell, leaders of a group of Italian, French and
English priests after Vatican I; and that of the "Crisis of Faith" which has
emerged after Vatican II, of which *The New (Dutch) Catechism* is its typical
application to the field of religious education.

86 *Vatican I*, p. 51; for the Latin original, cf. *DS* 3043.

87 Pope John XXIII, "Gaudet Mater Ecclesia," the Allocution of Oct. 11,
1962, which opened Vatican Council II; for the Latin original, the actual words
spoken by John XXIII, cf. *A.A.S.* 54 (26 Nov. 1962) 792. The Abbott-Gallagher
translation, *The Documents of Vatican II* (New York: America Press, 1966) p.
715, is incredibly falsified at this point, for the key phrase, *eodem tamen sensu
eademque sententia,* which binds the mind of the Supreme Pontiff to the dogmatic
definition of Vatican I and to the Rule of Faith in the early Church, in his very
act of opening Vatican II and giving it its orientation, *is simply omitted.* Abbott-
Gallagher fails to translate the adjectives *certa et immutabilis,* "Certain and unchangeable," referring to the *doctrina;* and it says this doctrine is to be "studied
and expounded through the methods of research and through the literary forms
of modern thought," concepts not to be found in the original Latin spoken by
Pope John XXIII when he opened Vatican II. When one pauses to consider how
many English-speaking Catholics, especially those of the United States, have im-
bibed this fictitious "spirit of Vatican II" from what can only be called unscholarly and dishonest falsifications at such key points, the immense measure of
the harm already done comes home. For the question is whether the substantial
sense, as Tyrrell put it, of the 'form of sound words' is to be quietly transformed
into something different. Pope John XXIII was perfectly clear on the point.

88 Pastoral Constitution on the Church in the Modern World, no. 62; see
Austin Flannery, *Vatican II,* p. 966: "Furthermore, theologians are now being
asked, within the methods and limits of the science of theology, to seek out more
efficient ways—*provided the meaning and understanding of them is safeguarded*—
of presenting their teaching to modern man; for the deposit and the truths of
Faith are one thing, the manner of expressing them is quite another." And
reference is made to John XXIII, "Speech delivered at the opening of the
Council": *AAS* 54 (1962) 792. As the words emphasized (our emphasis) make
clear, the intention of this translation is honest. But it does not make clearly
visible the fact that Vatican II is using again the very words of both Vatican I
and of St. Vincent of Lerins who first uttered them, speaking for the Church of
the Fathers. For this explicitness, see the Latin original of *Gaudium et Spes,* no.
62: Praeterea theologi, servatis propriis scientiae theologicae methodis et exigentiis,
invitantur ut aptiorem modum doctrinam cum hominibus sui temporis com-
municandi semper inquirant, quia aliud est ipsum depositum Fidei seu veritates,

aliud modus secundum quem enuntiantur, *eodem tamen sensu eademque sententia.*"
(Our emphasis). See *AAS* 58 (Dec. 7, 1966) 1083, with official reference to the
Allocution of John XXIII on Oct. 11, 1962.

[89] See *L'Osservatore Romano* (Nov. 19, 1965) p. 1 (NCWC translation); in
the Pope's Latin original: *Quasi accommodatione illa liceret secundum "relativismi"
placita.* The program of this doctrinal relativism is the same movement of thought,
two centuries old, to which allusion is made in note 85 above. It will be of interest
in connection with the *Creed of the People of God* to note that the Pope was
already thinking of a special post-conciliar concern coming in 1967, "when we
shall have to commemorate in a suitable manner the centenary of the martyrdom
of the Apostle Peter, an observance which was already instituted in the last century
by our predecessor of revered memory, Pius IX." (*Ibid.*).

[90] Pope Paul VI, *ibid.*

[91] Cf. Manuel Alcalá, S.J. *El "Cisma" de Holanda.* Madrid: Editorial PPC,
1971; p. 73: ". . . In June and July, 1968, the German and French translations
of the work were published, becoming 'best sellers' in both countries. Since the
German Episcopate, through the Bishop of Freiburg, had at the request of the
Roman Congregation for the Doctrine of the Faith, refused the ecclesiastical
permission to publish, Herder of Freiburg transferred its rights over the translations
to the publisher of the Dutch original in Nijmegen, Holland, so that juridically a
new ecclesiastical *imprimatur* would not be needed. The French translation appeared without the *nihil obstat* and *imprimatur*. Each of these actions evoked
strong protests from the two Episcopal Conferences." In the United States, it is
well known that the *imprimatur* was given for the English translation, then revoked.
The further vicissitudes, resulting finally in a new *imprimatur* for the English
translation with "corrections" printed as a Supplement at the end, are summarized
below.

[92] See E. Dhanis, J. Visser and H.J. Fortmann (Eds.) *Las correcciones al
Catecismo Holandés* (Madrid: Biblioteca de Autores Cristianos, 1969), "Intro-
duccion," pp. xxiii–xxiv, citing F.M. William, "Der holländische Katechismus" in
Orientierung 32 (1968), 209. (Cited henceforth as *Dhanis*).

[93] This letter is translated from the text published in Italian. See *Il dossier
del Catechismo olandese,* texts collected by Aldo Chiruttini, with introduction and
historical and theological notes by Leo Alting von Geusau, Secretary General of
I-DOC, and by Fernando Vittorino Joannes. Verona: Arnoldo Mondadori Editore,
1968; pp. 98–99. This book will be cited henceforth under the abbreviation *Dossier*.
The text of the letter is published without its date and without the names of
those who signed it. The date was between Oct. 9, 1966 and Nov. 23, 1966, the
date of the Dutch periodical *De Volkskrant* in which Father Edward Schillebeeckx,
O.P. published an attack upon this letter to the Pope in an article entitled "A
new Outburst of Integralism: A Dangerous Letter to Rome," concluding with
the words, ". . . A recourse to Rome is always suspect." The text of Schillebeeckx'
rather surprising article is given in full in *Dossier,* pp. 101–106.

[94] *Dossier, op. cit.,* pp. 146–147; the text of the Pope's letter is given in full,
pp. 146–148.

[95] For the text of the two sets of points on the agenda, see *Dossier,* pp. 149–156
for the 14 major doctrinal problems with the *Dutch Catechism* and pp. 253–259
for the 45 lesser ones. For the record of the discussion, see *ibid.,* pp. 157–249.
Interspersed with this record published in *Dossier* are the "historical and theological

notes" done in the characteristic I-DOC slant. The tenor of the discussion can be followed throughout the commentary on the *Creed of the People of God*, pp. 77–161, above. It bears out the "Conclusion of the Delegates of the Holy See," *Dossier*, p. 248: "After this colloquium on The *New Catechism*, the theologians of both sides regret that sincere and prolonged discussion has failed almost completely to reach a common consent on the points which have been examined. The union of hearts has not been diminished, but for the most part there has been no agreement of minds. But the work of this Conference ought not to be judged useless on account of this, because the present report can serve to make the thinking of each side, on each of these doctrinal points, known to the authorities who mandated the theologians, namely the Holy See and the Dutch bishops. The theologians delegated by the Holy See hope that these same authorities will know how to find a solution of benefit to the Church of Christ, and declare themselves ready to accept religiously the decision which their shepherds will make, and in the first place, the Universal Pastor of the Church."

[96] Apologists for the slanted philosophy of the *New (Dutch) Catechism* in theology and religious education frequently cast all of this in a false light, speaking of "Roman theologians" who are able only to indulge the "bias" of one particular kind of "theology." The truth is quite different, as the composition of the Gazzada Conference and the Commission of Cardinals makes clear. Furthermore, as the letter of Pope Paul VI to Cardinal Alfrink gives everyone to understand, "theology" is not the context of this work of analysis at all, but rather the teaching of the Ordinary and Universal Magisterium of the Catholic Church. What is at stake, in other words, is precisely the set of articles of faith professed by the Creed and explained by authentic catechetical teaching.

[97] See the *Declaration* of the Commission of Cardinals, *AAS* 60(1968) 686 and *Dhanis*, p. xv. There is at least one instance, that of the Spanish translation of the *New (Dutch) Catechism*, in which these "corrections" made by the *authors* were reprinted as an Appendix to the original text, without informing the reader that they had been rejected officially by the Church. In fact, the Foreword referred to them as "Notes and explanations from a trustworthy source." See Dhanis, p. xvi.

[98] For the text of this Report, see above, pp. 181–189.

[99] See *Dhanis*, p. xvi–xvii. The commission of Cardinals, proceeding in the same spirit as Pope Paul, clearly wished to arrange the work of correction so that it would come jointly from Holland and the Holy See, and be accepted also in Holland. Always the Holy See, it should be noted, expected that the expressed wish of the Supreme Pontiff for a new edition of the Dutch Catechism, with the offending passages eliminated and replaced by these completely re-written ones, would be respected. This, of course, is what has never been done; the *New (Dutch) Catechism* has continued to circulate, and to be used in its various translations, in the original form of its text, with the corrected passages printed at best as an appendix. The refusal of Father Mulders has more than personal significance, for he belonged to the Catechetical Institute of the Catholic University of Nijmegen. This gave the University its apparently desired occasion to dissociate itself from the correction of the text. In fact, Fathers Bless and Mulders protested publicly against the corrections: see *Dhanis*, p. xvii, note 11; and cf. the *White Book on the New Catechism*, edited by W. Bless, S.J. (Utrecht: 1969), which carried the explanation on its cover, "Why the corrections for the Catechism prescribed by Rome are unacceptable." (*Ibid.* xxi).

[100] See *Dhanis,* p. xvii. The Dutch press, Catholic and secular, orchestrated the protests of Mulders and Bless, but passed over Fortmann's declaration in silence. See G. deRosa, S.J., in *La Civiltà Cattolica* 120 (1969) 260.

[101] *Dhanis,* p. xviii, quoting W. Bless, S.J., *White Book on the New Catechism* (Utrecht: 1969), p. 231.

[102] For the official Latin text of the *Creed of the People of God,* the "Sollemnis Professio Fidei," cf. *AAS* (August 10, 1968), pp. 433–445, the document itself is dated June 30, 1968. For the original Authorized Edition of the Dutch Catechism, see *A New Catechism: Catholic Faith for Adults.* New York: Herder and Herder, 1967. No *imprimatur* for the English edition appears: that of Cardinal Alfrink, March 1, 1966, for the original Dutch edition is re-stated. The second edition, *A New Catechism: Catholic Faith for Adults, with Supplement.* New York: Herder and Herder, 1969, carries the *imprimatur* of Robert F. Joyce, Bishop of Burlington, Sept. 29, 1969. The *Supplement* by E. Dhanis, S.J. and J. Visser, C.SS.R., "On Behalf of the Commission of Cardinals appointed to examine *A New Catechism,* occupies pp. 511–574, at the end of the volume, which in itself is a verbatim reprint of the uncorrected original. "The text of this Supplement follows *in essentials* (our emphasis) the modifications of the text . . . prepared under the direction of the commission of Cardinals who were charged with the examination of the book. The modifications were then intended to be inserted into the text of the Catechism. But they are now presented separately." (Preface, p. 515).

[103] Pope Paul VI, "Apostolic Exhortation: Petrum et Paulum Apostolos, Feb. 22, 1967." *AAS* (March 31, 1967), pp. 193–200; translation published by the U.S.C.C., Washington, D.C. See above, pp. 164–170 for the text in full.

[104] See above, pp. 171–180.

[105] See the Allocution with which Pope Paul VI opened the Synod of Bishops, *AAS* (November 20, 1967), pp. 963–969.

[106] Pope Paul VI, *ibid.*

[107] See note 102 above for the reference to the official Latin text. The Italian translation was published in *L'Osservatore Romano* on the following day.

[108] To document this statement, cf. *passim* in the *Dossier,* the editorial explanations in italic type by Leo Alting von Geusau, Secretary General of I-DOC; for example, pp. 139–145, his description of the underlying philosophical contrast between the representatives of the Holy See at Gazzada, and the worldview of Schillebeeckx and Schoonenberg. If vitalism and existentialism are validly substituted in Christian teaching for the renewal of Christian Philosophy sponsored by the Catholic Church consistently since Vatican I, then the I-DOC view of the matter does indeed become a self-evidence.

[108-A] See the Allocution of Paul VI to the 1967 Synod of Bishops; footnote 105, above.

[109] Pope Paul VI, "Petrum et Paulum Apostolos," *AAS* (March 31, 1967), pp. 198–199.

[110] One of the earliest and still helpful analyses of the phenomenon is the work of Andreas Heinrich Maltha, O.P., *Die Neue Theologie.* Munich: Manz Verlag, 1960. More recent examples include Karl Straeter, S.J., *Die neue Theologie in Holland.* Regensburg: Verlag Josef Habbel, 1970; Louis Bouyer, *The Decomposition of Catholicism.* Chicago: Franciscan Herald Press, 1969; Marcel de Corte, *La Grande Eresia.* Rome: Volpe, 1970; Oskar Köhler, *Bewusstseinsstörungen im Katholizismus.* Frankfurt: Josef Knecht, 1973; and the short study by the Bishop

of Regensburg, Rudolph Graber, *Athanasius and the Church of our Time*. London: Van Duren, 1974.

[111] "Solemnis Professio Fidei," no. 4; *AAS* (Aug. 10, 1968), p. 434.

[112] Cf. John 20, 24–29. When the Risen Jesus said to the doubting Apostle, "Doubt no longer, but believe," Thomas replied, "My Lord and my God!" This continues to be the meaning and the bearing of the Creed in all its developments. See Cerfaux, *op. cit.*, p. 467: "The faith was first formulated in the words, 'Jesus is Lord' . . . , [and] Paul's letters echo the original faith." Across the centuries, the essential act of faith, the essential meaning of the Creed, is always one and the same: it is a personal act addressed to Jesus: "You are my Lord and my God."

[113] See Yves M.-J. Congar, O.P. *Tradition and Traditions: An Historical and a Theological Essay* (New York: Macmillan, 1967), "The Monuments of Tradition," pp. 425–458, especially "The Relation between Tradition and its Monuments," pp. 451–458. And the reference to Charles Journet, footnote 78 above.

[114] "Truth is in the judgment," an act of spiritual insight and understanding on the part of the human intellect, and not in the apprehensions and experiencings of the organism: cf. St. Thomas Aquinas, *Summa Theologica*, I, q. 16, art. 2: "When the intellect judges that a thing corresponds to the form which it apprehends about that thing, then first it knows and expresses truth." Cf. *Quaest. Disp. de Veritate*, q. 1, art. 3, "Utrum in intellectu componente et dividente sit veritas." This is the fundamental issue between the Catholic Church and the Modernist or Neo-Gnostic "Church-of-the-Future." The Catholic Church guards the deposit of faith which comes from the apostles, preserving it and handing it on by its teaching approach in catechetics. The articles of faith, as formulated and understood by the Church, are handed on by teaching. Neo-Modernism removes the deposit of faith by eliminating the entire Creed. It then substitutes what it itself calls the experiential approach in religious education. Cf. Charles Journet, *The Church of the Word Incarnate*. London: Sheed and Ward, 1951; Vol. I, p. 543: "It is not to be believed, say the Modernists, that God has revealed through Christ and the apostles any definitive truth to be received by the intelligence and preserved intact forever. All that God did—insofar as it is possible to speak about God at all—was to move the souls of the apostles, and these then attempted to translate their experience into more or less happy conceptual formulas, not in the least to be taken for a 'divine law' or as binding on later generations. A genuine apostolicity therefore does not consist of the handing down of an unaltered doctrine; it consists in a reliving by each one of us of that experience of divine things which Christ and the apostles lived so admirably, and in translating it perhaps for ourselves into a new conceptual synthesis better adapted to a changing world. The mark of apostolicity will be rather innovation than tradition, doctrinal fluidity rather than the immobility of the *Credo*." For the bearing of this on the relationship between creed and catechetics, see the conclusion, pp. 253–259, above. For the implications of a refusal to use Creed and catechism because of an aversion to formulated creedal content or doctrine, cf. Yves M.-L. Congar, O.P., *Tradition and Traditions, op. cit.*, p. 21: "An adequate theory of revelation shows that all its weight bears on the vital covenant relationship that God wants to establish with men. This relationship is perfect and definitive in Jesus Christ, but we know Jesus Christ through the apostolic witness, and through that alone. The collection of events, truths and realities, which constitute or form the basis of this relationship between men and God in Christ, has been given once and for

all by the apostles, and no one can substantially add to it." The doctrine handed on in catechesis *is* this apostolic witness. This is why Pope St. Pius X pointed out accurately in *Pascendi* the central trust of the Modernist movement in each of its three historical moments: it proceeds against Jesus Christ, while pretending always to be His friend and to further His cause. "Even while he was speaking, Judas, one of the Twelve, came up with a number of men . . . Now the traitor had arranged a signal with them. 'The one I kiss,' he had said, 'he is the man. Take him in charge, and see he is well guarded when you lead him away.' " (Mark 14, 43–44).

115 When the *Creed of the People of God* was published to the Catholic Church, a well-known American religious educator whom we shall not name was quoted widely in the press as protesting that it said nothing to him. Considering the meaning of "the Creed of the immortal Tradition of the Holy Church of God," recalling who it is upon whom it centers, whom it professes, such a nihilistic Nietzschean declaration is simply a profession of bankruptcy in the order of the interior and spiritual life. The Holy See decades ago saw this unhappy phenomenon coming in the United States of America, as anyone who re-reads the documents of Leo XIII, *Longinqua oceani* (Jan. 6, 1895) and *Testem benevolentiae* (Jan. 22, 1899), will recognize. If religious education is becoming barren and unproductive, then this entire matter urgently needs to be studied anew and in depth. Catechetics as a field of university study is open to many fruitful research projects.

116 *GCD*, No. 40. This is the briefest possible definition of the relationship between Creed and Catechetics. It is also the reason why no "neutralism" is possible for a Catholic in the face of creedlessness in religious education programs and the doctrinal omissions and aberrations to which creedlessness always opens the door. Such "neutralism" leads logically (and quickly in point of fact) to a betrayal of the Lord Jesus in His Church, as contemporary exponents of "The-Church-of-the-Future" make manifest. The *Apostolic Exhortation* of Pope Paul VI dated Dec. 8, 1970 ought to be studied carefully from this point of view; see the text, above, pp. 195–204. See also M. Ajassa, "La tentazione della neutralità," *L'osservatore Romano* (May 18, 1974), p. 3 (Italian edition). For a discussion of the manner in which the Hegelian dialectic, especially in the hands of Marxist mentalities, moves against Jesus Christ by attempting to place the Creed which professes Him in an outmoded past, see E. Kevane, "The Significance of the Creed of the People of God," *L'Osservatore Romano-English* (June 26, 1975), pp. 6–8. St. Augustine's *Sermo 46* (P.L. 38, 270–295) is a penetrating discussion on "neutralism" on the part of persons holding authority in the Church; it is of interest to note that this Sermon has been included in the readings of the Vatican II revision of the Divine Office, prayed by all bishops and priests. Cf. *Liturgia Horarum*, Vol. IV, pp. 181–225. The failure to remain loyal to Jesus Christ as the Creed professes Him to be is the central characteristic of the aberrational theologizing which has become stylish after Vatican II. This kind of theologizing is perhaps the most manifest cause (and effect) of the crisis of faith which occasioned the *Creed of the People of God*. Cf. Battista Mondin, *Le Christologie Moderne*. Rome: Editrice Apes, 1973. Mondin identifies the Catholic theological position and states that it is represented at the present time by Pietro Parente, Romano Guardini, M.D. Chenu and the Greek Orthodox theologian, George Florovski, who maintain the Creed as developed by the ecumenical councils, especially Nicea, Constantinople, Ephesus and Chalcedon, as the foundation of

theological Christology. Then Mondin gathers the evidence that there are six other kinds of "Christology" represented in current theological literature, each including certain well-known contemporary *Catholic* writers: for example, Mondin lists Karl Rahner with Bultmann under the heading "Existentialist Orientation"; Piet Schoonenberg and Teilhard de Chardin under "Secularist Orientation"; Edward Schillebeeckx with Moltmann under "eschatological orientation" (a Kingdom of God of this world), and Metz and Gutierrez under the heading, "political orientation." *Cf.* pp. 9–10. Each orientation is discussed in a chapter of Mondin's treatise. Obviously these "orientations" tend to overlap and to coalesce into a broad current of theological aberration from the reality of the Lord Jesus Christ whom the Creed professes. The implications for catechetical teaching are readily visible: this is a literature of aberration which offers no hope for a Christocentric catechesis (*GCD,* No. 40), and no help in the preparation of authentic catechists. See the two works of Cornelio Fabro, *La svolta antropologica di Karl Rahner,* and *L'avventura della teologia progressista,* both published at Milan, Rusconi, 1974. The work on Rahner's turning of theology down and in upon man, changing its orientation toward the transcendent Supreme Being, quickly became a best seller in Italy and went into its second edition in three months. Among other things, it documents thoroughly Rahner's unscholarly way of citing texts of St. Thomas Aquinas out of context, making him seem to support an alien philosophical position. One can hope that these studies will not be delayed in English translation. For a comprehensive introduction to the work of the early Church in preserving the Christ of the Gospels for the faith of posterity, see Aloys Grillmeier, S.J., *Christ in Christian Tradition: From the Apostolic Age to Chalcedon* (451). New York: Sheed and Ward, 1965. "On a closer inspection," Grillmeier writes on p. 493, "the christological heresies turn out to be a compromise between the original message of the Bible and the understanding of it in Hellenism and paganism. It is here that we have the real Hellenization of Christianity. The formulas of the Church, whether they are the *homoousios* of Nicaea or the Chalcedonian Definition . . . clarify only one, albeit the decisive point of belief in Christ: that in Jesus Christ God really entered into human history and thus achieved our salvation." The christological aberrations of unsound philosophical theologizing today do more than a "Hellenization" of Christianity; they secularize it and deviate it into the channel of modern philosophical atheism. It is clear that catechetical teaching which follows these aberrational "Christologies" will lose its authenticity and its communion with the *General Catechetical Directory* of the Holy See. It may seem superficially to follow *GCD,* No. 40, but will be actually some other kind of religious education. The deception can be unmasked through fidelity to the Creed, the Rule of Faith in discerning catechetical authenticity. This was true at the time of Irenaeus; it has been true in the centuries since; it continues to be true today. The *Creed of the People of God,* coming as it does after Vatican II, removes any possible foundation for an approach in religious education that seeks to relegate the works of Hardon and Lawler, for example, to some point "thirty or forty years ago."

117 Cf. *GCD,* No. 40, "Christocentrism of Catechesis," together with No. 41, "Trinitarian Theocentrism of Catechesis." This is the heart of catechetical methodology. The fundamental aberration of the *New (Dutch) Catechism,* and of the Neo-Modernist programs and textbooks which continue its approach today, is man-centrism, the failure to lead children and youth to God through

the Divine Savior whom the Creed professes. It is an approach in religious
education which applies the aberrational theologizing touched upon in the previous
footnote. Cf. *Dhanis,* pp. xxvii–xxviii, where it is stated accurately that the man-
centrism of the Dutch Catechism is the constituting principle of its creedlessness.
The post-conciliar actions of the Magisterium have been intended to guard this
basic theistic orientation in Christian doctrine; see the documents above, pp.
163–252.

[118] In Question 94, marked for use with small children, the *Catechism of
Christian Doctrine* published by order of Pope St. Pius X asks, "At the present
time is Jesus Christ only in heaven?" And it answers, "At the present time, Jesus
Christ is not only in heaven, but as God he is in every place, and as God-man,
he is both in heaven and in the Most Holy Sacrament of the Altar." Such synthetic
formulations of doctrine obviously need analysis and inductive presentation by
good catechetical teaching; cf. *GCD,* Nos. 71–74, for the prinicples of catechetical
methodology which are involved.

[119] Enemies of the Catholic Faith wish to brand adherence to the articles of
faith professed by the Creed, and hence fidelity to the teaching approach in
Catechetics which explains them, even when open to the most up-to-date didactic
media and methods in doing so, as a form of "extremism." This is why the *Symbolforschung,* the wealth of recent research on the origin and nature of the Creed,
has providential significance. For the articles of faith summarized in the Creed
state the divine Word of God entrusted to the apostles and their successors. These
articles or divine truths occupy the central position, and stand elevated above all
forms of error to the right and to the left, all varieties of "conservative" and
"liberal" attitudes, and similar slogans drawn from the political and social
arena. The fact of the matter is that the Neo-Modernist creedlessness in religious
education, with its "experiential approach," is a form of extremism. It stands
at the opposite pole from the other form of extremism, the mere mechanical
memorization of catechetical formulas. Neither of these extremisms can qualify
as catechetics in the Catholic Church, for neither one of them is an authentic
teaching that explains the articles of faith professed by the Creed, helping to
deepen conversion "through the light of instruction." (*GCD,* No. 17).

[120] Pope Paul VI, "Petrum et Paulum Apostolos," *AAS* (March 31, 1967),
p. 199.

Footnotes—A Practical Commentary on The Creed of the People of God

[1] See pages 61–71 above for "The Year of Faith," and the section on the
Documents of the Magisterium regarding it, pages 164–180, above.

[2] The official "translation," (Washington: United States Catholic Conference,
1968), p. 1 reads as follows: "With this solemn liturgy We end the celebration
of the nineteenth centenary of the Martyrdom of the holy Apostles Peter and
Paul, and thus close the Year of Faith. We dedicated it to the commemoration
of the holy Apostles in order that We might give witness to our steadfast will to
be faithful to the Deposit of the Faith which they transmitted to us, and that we
might strengthen our desire to live by it in the historical circumstances in which
the Church find herself in her pilgrimage in the midst of the world." When this
is compared with the Latin original, (see p. 8, above), it appears to have a
tendentious character. The key omission is the failure to translate *incorrupte fidei
depositum custodiendi.*

[3] All of this needs to be placed against the general background of the Neo-Modernist resistance to the *eodem dogmate, eademque sententia* of the Constitution *Dei filius;* cf. *Vatican I*, p. 48 and p. 51; *DS* 3020; 3043, together with Pope Paul VI in the Document of Feb. 22, 1967 which established the Year of Faith: ". . . sed cum deposito doctrinae Ecclesiae plane consentientes *eodem sensu aedemque sententia* . . . ," together with his reference to the same dogmatic definition of Vatican I, *DS* 3020. For the English translation of Pope Paul's document, see above, pp. 164–170. In general, cf. the actions regarding the *New (Dutch) Catechism,* above, pp. 61–71; in particular, cf. the reference to George Tyrrell, footnote 85, above.

[4] See above, pp. 67–71; and the entire document of Feb. 22, 1967, "Petrum et Paulum Apostolos," above, pp. 164–170.

[5] *Pozo,* p. 41, quoting Vatican Council I, *DS* 3074.

[6] *Vatican II,* p. 380; Dogm. Const. on the Church, no. 25.

[7] *Vatican II,* p. 379; Dogm. Const. on the Church, no. 25. From the viewpoint of catechetical methodology, it should be noted that this is a doctrine that *witnesses* to Jesus Christ as the apostolic *kerygma* indefectibly proclaims Him to be. "Bishops who teach in communion with the Roman Pontiff are . . . *witnesses* of divine and Catholic truth." This is the reason why official catechisms should be used *rightly,* updated and not abandoned, for they contain the Creed itself, together with the initial simple explanations of the articles of faith professed by the Creed. See the *GCD,* nos. 116 and 119; and the conclusion above, pp. 253–259.

[8] *Pozo,* p. 42; see pp. 40–46, "Theological Evaluation of the Profession of Faith," summarized here, for a full explanation of the way Creeds receive "consequent infallibility," consequent namely upon acceptance by the Church. An earlier example is the Symbol "Quicumque."

[9] *Pozo,* p. 44.

[10] *Vatican II,* p. 363; Const. Dogm. on the Church, no. 12.

[11] See *CPG,* No. 7.

[12] See the text of this Allocution, above, pp. 190–194.

[13] *Pozo,* p. 46.

[14] *Pozo,* p. 46, text and footnotes.

[15] See above, p. 284, fn. 115.

[16] See *Vatican II,* pp. 905–906; Pastoral Constitution on the Church in the Modern World, no. 4, "The Situation of Man in the World Today": "Ours is a new age of history with critical and swift upheavals spreading gradually to all corners of the earth. They are the products of man's intelligence and creative activity, but they recoil upon him, upon his judgments and desires . . . Small wonder then that many of our contemporaries are prevented by this complex situation from recognizing permanent values and duly applying them to recent discoveries." Also see the Encyclical of Pope Paul VI *On The Development of the Peoples, Populorum Progressio,* (March 26, 1967). The permanent values of Christianity are expressions and applications of the abiding divine truth of the Catholic faith which the Creed summarizes and professes. This is the significance of the *Creed of the People of God:* it is the providential instrument for realizing the hope for authentic renewal of modern man and his culture which Vatican II intended.

[17] Cf. A. C. Cotter, S.J. *The Encyclical "Humani generis," with a Commentary.* Weston: Weston College Press, 1951. This helpful work presents the Latin and the English of the Encyclical on facing pages, followed by a detained commentary

giving the historical background and contemporary doctrinal necessity for each paragraph and sentence.

[18] Pope Paul VI, *Ecclesiam suam,* par. 26; and see the Papal Allocution of Jan. 19, 1972, above, p. 207; and the Opening Address to the 1967 Synod of Bishops.

[19] See above, p. 61. It is important for catechetical teaching that the new Flannery translation of the Documents of Vatican II has been published; it is a work of scholarship which puts an end to the transitory phase represented by the incompetent and biased Abbot-Gallagher. See the "Preface" by Cardinal John Wright in Flannery's volume, *Vatican II,* pp. xxiii–xxiv.

[20] Cf. *DS* 3020 and 3041, 3042, 3043; *Vatican I,* p. 48 and p. 51. *DS* 3020 cites the famous passage of Vincent of Lerins, *in eodem scilicet dogmate, eodem sensu eademque sententia:* "that is, with the same dogma, the same meaning, the same sense."

[21] Those who wish to omit the articles of the faith as the content of religious education, pursuing "creedlessness" as a policy in writing textbooks and constructing syllabi, are sometimes heard to say that the *Creed of the People of God* is "too cerebral." But, to indulge a moment of philosophical frankness, such attitudes reflect simplistic anti-intellectualism absorbed from a decadent cultural environment. The intelligence is the image of God upon the brow of a human child, the God-given power by which his whole person first knows the truth, then loves the values which the truth illumines for him. This paragraph stated so carefully by the Vicar of Christ is actually the "rationale of catechesis" in summary statement. It ought to be heard with an open mind, and its implications studied by careful and honest philosophical research. It is becoming increasingly clear that the renewal of Christian Philosophy, official in the Catholic Church throughout the past hundred years, has a catechetical importance which has become manifest only since the crisis of faith that has followed upon Vatican II.

[22] Cf. Cornelio Fabro, *Breve Introduzione al Tomismo.* Roma: Desclée, 1960; p. 73: ". . . that penetration of Modern Philosophy into the Seminaries which will assume the name of Modernism . . ."

[23] *Dossier,* p. 162.

[24] *Dossier,* p. 157.

[25] *Dossier,* pp. 157–164.

[26] The refusal to admit the existence of eternal truths implies that there is no Eternal Being; this leads directly to "process" philosophies and theologies, with their ideas of a finite and changing "god." All of this, to state the matter clearly, is atheism using traditional religious terminology as a disguise. Sound catechetical methodology unmasks such disguises when it encounters them in the teaching aids of religious education.

[27] Cf. Pope St. Pius X, *Pascendi* (Sept. 8, 1907): "We define . . . the whole system of the Modernists . . . as the synthesis of all heresies."

[28] *DS* 3020; *Vatican I,* p. 48.

[29] See above, p. 60.

[30] *Pozo,* P. 58. For a discussion of the matter summarized in this paragraph of the papal introduction to the *Creed,* see *Hardon,* "The Word of God," pp. 29–52; for practical guidance, see the *Roman Catechism,* pp. 1–13, on "The Necessity of Religious Instruction" and on "The Creed"; and the *GCD,* "Foreword" and Part One, nos. 1–9, "The Reality of the Problem."

[31] Par. no. 7 and no. 3 of the *Creed.*

[32] Address: The Editor, L'Osservatore Romano-English Edition, Vatican City, Rome, Italy. An air-mail subscription can be obtained, at the time of the present writing, for $24.00 per year.

[33] See above, Part Two, pp. 29–75.

[34] *DS* 3043; cf. footnote 20, above, p. 288.

[35] For the nature and role of "catechisms" in relationship to the Creed and its proper explanation, see the Conclusion above, pp. 253–259.

[36] Cf. Matt. 16, 13–20; for the bearing of this on the question of the infallibility of this *Creed of the People of God,* see footnote 8, above, p. 287.

[37] Cf. GCD, no. 119: "The greatest importance must be attached to catechisms published by ecclesiastical authority." See the conclusion below, pp. 253–259; *GCD,* no. 27, "clearly explaining the church's doctrine in its entirety"; and *GCD,* no. 38: "The goal of Catechesis is to present the entire content."

[38] Cf. *Vatican II,* p. 462; Decree on Ecumenism, no. 11: "Nothing is so foreign to the spirit of ecumenism as a false irenicism which harms the purity of Catholic doctrine and obscures its genuine and certain meaning." For the explicit rejection of "confusionism" see the Decree on Missionary Activity, no. 15: *seclusa omni . . . confusionismi . . . specie, AAS* (30 Nov. 1966) 964; cf. *Vatican II,* p. 830, where the word is translated into English less forcefully and significantly as "confusion."

[39] *Pozo,* p. 64, with reference to the *New (Dutch) Catechism* in illustration of these present dangers.

[40] *NDC,* p. 179.

[41] *NDC,* pp. 498–502.

[42] *Dossier,* p. 58; the passages which specifically concern the *New (Dutch) Catechism* are those cited in the two preceding notes. It has become characteristic of the Neo-Modernist approach in syllabi and textbooks for religious education not to give a sufficiently central importance to this mystery. Such an orientation inevitably turns out to be a man-centrism, violating *GCD,* nos. 40 and 41.

[43] *NDC,* p. 499.

[44] This tactic may be called the distinguishing characteristic and chief defect of the so-called "Green Bay Plan" and other similar approaches. In no. 166, discussing Catholic children up to the age of eleven, the authors of the *National Catechetical Directory, Second Consultation* (Washington: NCCB, 1975), write: ". . . teaching the truths of the faith can primarily be effective . . . to the degree that these truths are experienced concretely in his or her relationship to others . . . Aspects like Eucharist viewed as meal and as celebration can be presented effectively. More difficult concepts like Eucharist as redemptive sacrifice are best presented at a later stage." In other words, Catholic children are not to be taught the fact and the dogma of the Real Presence of Jesus Christ, their Divine Savior and Holy Redeemer, until they are eleven years old, or older. What this does to sacramental initiation is clear to see. It would take the present study too far afield to pursue this aberration and all its implications in detail. The gratuitous character of the horizontalism of this self-styled "experiential approach" would need analysis. The vertical dimension of a revealed Word of God descending by the ministry of His teaching Church to the spiritual power of insight and understanding with which the Creator has endowed human children is simply lacking. The endowment itself seems not to be understood. This failure in Christocentrism, *GCD* no. 40 and *passim,* needs study. Catechetical teaching cannot be too careful about the

unsound Christologies which have raised their heads so suddenly. See above, p. 284. Nothing is so calculated to place religious education quickly and directly into conflict with good Catholic homes and parishes as this approach which divides Christ, refusing to present Him to the young children in that fullness of His reality which the Creed professes. Cf. 1 John 2, 21–29; 1 John 4, 1–6; 2 John 7–11. Above all, the taproot of this methodological unsoundness needs careful research. The proponents seem to have the idea that Catholic doctrine is too "abstract," whereas its formulated teachings are simply the set of flagstones that take the mind to the most concrete of realities, Jesus Christ, God Incarnate. This taproot, as the light of dispassionate scientific study of the strange phenomenon proceeds, may well turn out to be that false philosophism in religion, the idea that God Himself is an abstract concept of the human mind, which the Catholic Church already has condemned in the most solemn manner possible. Cf. *DS* 3024, with no. 3001; *Vatican I*, p. 49: "If anyone should say . . . that God is a universal or indefinite being, which in determining itself constitutes the universe with its division into genera, species, and individuals, let him be anathema." Perhaps Pascal saw all this coming when he drew attention so forcefully to the difference between the wraith of the philosophers and the God of Revelation, the God of Abraham, Isaac and Jacob, whom Jesus Christ always called, in His own special way, "My Father."

[45] *GCD,* no. 38.

[46] *Pozo,* p. 61.

[47] Pope Paul VI, *Ecclesiam suam* (Aug. 6, 1964), par. 100.

[48] See *Pozo,* pp. 60–65, with the references; *Hardon,* "The Living God," pp. 53–67, and "Foundations of Orthodoxy," pp. 126–130; and see above, pp. 29–75.

[49] See the *Roman Catechism,* pp. 14–30, on the correct way of teaching the First Article of the Apostles' Creed, "I believe in God, the Father Almighty, Creator of Heaven and Earth," and the GCD, nos. 47–49. In earlier times the First Article of the Creed was largely taken for granted by catechists, due to the common consent of mankind with regard to the Supreme Being. Due to the rise and spread of contemporary philosophical atheism, with its applications in child-rearing and social customs, this is no longer possible, and careful attention must be given to the catechesis of the First Article. See the *GCD,* nos. 1–9, "The Reality of the Problem," and the Pastoral Constitution on the Church in the Modern World, nos. 19–21, on modern atheism, *Vatican II,* pp. 918–922.

[50] This is the meaning of the Constitution *Dei filius* as a whole; cf. *Vatican I,* pp. 37–52; and *Hardon,* Chapter II, "The Living God," pp. 53–67.

[51] Cf. *Vatican I,* pp. 40–41; DS 3002.

[52] *Pozo,* pp. 66–67.

[53] See above, pp. 9–10.

[54] *Pozo,* pp. 67–68.

[55] *NDC,* pp. 481–482. See *ibid.,* p. 110, on diabolical possession: "What powers are at work here we do not know;" and p. 242, for the subtly nuanced doubt in connection with the exorcism connected with the Sacrament of Baptism.

[56] See above, p. 65.

[57] *Dossier,* pp. 154–155, the eighth point on the agenda of the Gazzada Conference; see *ibid.,* pp. 211–217, for the record of the discussion with the theologians representing the Dutch hierarchy.

[58] *Dossier,* pp. 211–212.

59 See above, p. 184; and *Lawler,* "The Devil," pp. 86–88.
60 *Pozo,* pp. 68–69.
61 Cf. *Vatican II,* pp. 914–915; Pastoral Constitution on the Church in the Modern World, no. 14: *anima et corpore unus . . .*
62 *DS* 1440; for the English translation, Clarkson, p. 149.
63 *DS* 3896.
64 Pozo, p. 70, with reference to the *New (Dutch) Catechism.*
65 Cf. *NDC,* p. 382; and see the *Letter* of the Dutch Catholics to Pope Paul VI above, pp. 62–64.
66 *Dossier,* p. 155.
67 *Dossier,* pp. 217–218.
68 *Dossier,* pp. 218–220; see above, p. 184, for the final decision of the Commission of Cardinals, intended to guide the re-writing of the text of the *New (Dutch) Catechism,* a process which has never taken place.
69 Cf. *The Catechism of Christian Doctrine,* published by order of Pope St. Pius X. Middleburg, Notre Dame Institute Press, 1974; p. 115, "There is a special circumstance today . . ."; and his provision of help in the matter, "Basic Truths of the Christian Faith," the first 27 questions, pp. 1–3.
70 *Pozo,* p. 71.
71 Ryan, John K. (Transl.) *The Confessions of St. Augustine.* New York: Doubleday Image Books, 1960; p. 126 (Book V, no. 10). Perhaps the most helpful single source, apart from the Bible itself, for teaching the right concept of God is the series of Chapters in Book VII of *The Confessions.*
72 *Pozo,* p. 71, citing E. Power, S.J.
73 *Pozo,* p. 72. See *Vatican I,* pp. 40–41, for the teaching of the Council on the attributes of God, together with the commentary in *Hardon,* pp. 55–58; and *Lawler,* Chapter 2, "The Father of Our Lord Jesus Christ," pp. 41–54.
74 *GCD,* no. 47.
75 Cf. *DS* 800 and *DS* 3001.
76 *Pozo,* p. 74; for the English translation of the reference to the Constitution *Dei filius* in the Creed, see *Vatican I,* pp. 46–48.
77 *Pozo,* p. 75, citing the Council of Florence, *DS* 1330; the Fourth Lateran Council, *DS* 800 and 803–805; and the First Vatican Council, *DS* 3016, to show that the *Creed of the People of God* is faithful to what always has been the teaching of the Church on the mystery of God One and Three.
78 Cf. *Vatican II,* pp. 738–739.
79 *Pozo,* pp. 78–79.
80 For further study of the twentieth century problematic that seeks to separate "doctrine" and "life," cf. R. Garrigou-Lagrange, O.P. *The One God.* St. Louis; B. Herder, 1943; "Introduction," pp. 1–37; A. Zacchi, O.P. *Dio.* Roma: Ferrari, 1952; "Introduzione: cultura religiosa superiore," pp. 1–26; R. Spiazzi, O.P., "L'enciclica *Pascendi Dominici Gregis* di San Pio X e il problema di una 'Teologia Vitale'," *Divinitas* (1958) 25–50.
81 *Pozo,* p. 84.
82 Cf. Yves M.-J. Congar, O.P. *Tradition and Traditions.* New York: Macmillan, 1966, p. 21: "An adequate theory of revelation shows that all its weight bears on the vital covenant relationship that God wants to establish with men. This relationship is perfect and definitive in Jesus Christ, but we know Jesus Christ through the apostolic witness, and through that alone. The collection of

events, truths and realities, which constitute or form the basis of this relationship between men and God in Christ, has been given once and for all by the apostles, and no one can substantially add to it."

[83] *Pozo,* p. 85.

[84] Cf. *GCD,* no. 22, on the purpose of catechesis, which is "to help them deepen their conversion." This "conversion" is the orientation of human living to God in Christ: "Catechesis must necessarily be Christocentric." (no. 40).

[85] *Pozo,* p. 88, with reference to the *New (Dutch) Catechism* to illustrate the problem in contemporary religious education which the Supreme Pontiff has in mind.

[86] Cf. *NDC,* pp. 74 ff.

[87] *Dossier,* p. 165; for the full record of the discussion, cf. *ibid.,* pp. 164–168.

[88] *Pozo,* p. 88.

[89] See above, pp. 64–65.

[90] *Dossier,* p. 149.

[91] *Dossier,* pp. 164–165.

[92] For the text of the Commission on this point, see above, p. 184.

[93] *Pozo,* pp. 91–93.

[94] *GCD,* no. 83.

[95] *GCD,* no. 119. There is something tragic for Catholic children when the bias of the Neo-Modernist approach against the content, the articles of faith formulated in the Creed, prevents them from receiving the simple and objective kind of explanatory break-down given by the official catechisms, not as a mere memory-exercise, but according to the principles of sound catechetical methodology summarized in *GCD,* nos. 72–73.

[96] *GCD,* no. 83.

[97] *GCD,* no. 88; see nos. 83–97.

[98] Hence the *GCD,* no. 40, stresses: "Catechesis must necessarily be Christocentric." But since Jesus is God Incarnate, this fulfills the "Trinitarian Theocentrism of Catechesis" for which the *GCD* calls in no. 41. For specific guidelines and principles of method for teaching the truth of the Incarnation, cf. *GCD,* nos. 50–54. "Catechesis ought daily to defend and strengthen belief in the divinity of Christ, in order that he may be accepted not merely for his admirable human life, but that men might recognize him through his words and signs as God's only-begotten Son (cf. John 1, 18), 'God from God, light from light, true God from true God, consubstantial with the Father' (*DS* 150) . . ." (*GCD,* no. 53). This use of the Nicene Creed by the *General Catechetical Directory* illustrates aptly the relationship between Creed and Catechetics which is the object of the present study. The principles of catechetical methodology summarized here in connection with the teaching of the creedal article of faith in the Incarnation can be applied throughout the entire Creed, and need not be repeated unduly in this study. For assistance in preparing for catechetical teaching, whether that which is suitable for children, or the approaches which need to be implemented for adolescents and adults, one can do no better than to use the official *Roman Catechism,* pp. 31–87, a phrase-by-phrase discussion of the Second Article of the Apostles' Creed. And see *Hardon,* pp. 108–149, and *Lawler,* pp. 93–108, for helpful explanatory discussions which take the most recent documents of the Magisterium faithfully into account. For the most recent actions of the Magisterium in defense of the truth of the Incarnation of God, see above, pp. 209–213.

⁹⁹ Cf. Mt. 6, 9 ff.; Eph. 2, 1–21; Gal. 4, 1–7. One might say that the *General Catechetical Directory* is almost entirely devoted to the right kind of methodology in teaching about Jesus Christ in all the circumstances and levels of catechesis. This is what "The Ministry of the word," Part Two, nos. 10–35, is about; Part Three, "The Christian Message," nos. 36–69, gives methodological guidelines for keeping this Message centered upon Jesus Christ, so that it teaches who He is, and what kind of Religion He established. And *GCD,* nos. 50–54, treat specifically the correct methods of explaining the life and work of Jesus, on whatever level or circumstance of catechesis. Catechetical teachers can find basic resource material, linked with the Apostles' Creed, in the *Roman Catechism,* pp. 31–87. Also see *Hardon,* Chap. 4, "Jesus Christ," pp. 108–149; and *Lawler,* Chap. 5, "Fallen Man and the Faithfulness of God," pp. 78–92, chap. 6, "The Son of God Becomes our Brother," pp. 93–108, and chapters 8, 9, 10 on "The Public Life of Jesus," and His Redemption of Mankind, pp. 124–160.

¹⁰⁰ *Pozo,* pp. 97–98. As catechetical teachers know from experience, the teaching of Christian Morality is the great need and challenge of today. It must rest upon the foundation of the profession of faith which the Creed provides, for then Jesus Christ is Himself the rock upon which the house of youthful lives is built. For the basic guidelines of methodology in this teaching, cf. *GCD,* nos. 61, 62, 63 and 64. The classic and abiding resource for teachers of Christian Morality in their preparations is to be found in the *Roman Catechism,* Part III, pp. 357–475. For contemporary resource material in catechetical preparation that takes Vatican II and other recent documents of the Magisterium properly into account, see *Hardon,* Part Two, "Morality and the Spiritual Life," pp. 283–437; and *Lawler,* pp. 265–380.

¹⁰¹ *Pozo,* p. 101, again with a reference to the *New (Dutch) Catechism* to illustrate the Neo-Modernist problem which has grown up in contemporary religious education.

¹⁰² Cf. *NDC,* pp. 279–287.

¹⁰³ Cf. the *Letter* of Pope Paul VI to Cardinal Alfrink; above, pp. 64–65.

¹⁰⁴ *Dossier,* pp. 151–152.

¹⁰⁵ *Dossier,* p. 173.

¹⁰⁶ *Dossier,* p. 175.

¹⁰⁷ *Dossier,* p. 176.

¹⁰⁸ *Dossier,* p. 177.

¹⁰⁹ For the judgment of the Commission of Cardinals on this point of Catholic doctrine, see above, p. 185.

¹¹⁰ *Pozo,* pp. 104–105.

¹¹¹ *Pozo,* p. 105.

¹¹² *Pozo,* p. 108.

¹¹³ *Pozo,* p. 109.

¹¹⁴ *Pozo,* pp. 101–111; see the two Epistles of St. Peter, esp. 2 Pet. 1, 4.

¹¹⁵ Cf. *DS* 325.

¹¹⁶ *Pozo,* pp. 116–117. The *Creed of the People of God* in nos. 19–23 will profess in detail the Catholic faith in the work of the Holy Spirit in the Catholic Church as the religious institution founded by Jesus Christ. For assistance in preparing to teach about the Holy Spirit, cf. *GCD,* no. 47; the *Roman Catechism,* pp. 88–95 and 199–212; *Lawler,* chap. 11, "The Holy Spirit," pp. 161–173; and *Hardon,* chap. 6, "The Grace of God," pp. 172–205.

[117] *Pozo,* pp. 118–121. Again the *New (Dutch) Catechism* illustrates the problem of the Neo-Modernist approach in religious education and the reason why the Church professes more explicitly and with deeper understanding what always has been the Catholic faith regarding the Mother of Jesus Christ.

[118] *NDC,* p. 77.

[119] *Pozo,* p. 120.

[120] See above, pp. 62–64.

[121] *Dossier,* pp. 253–254.

[122] *NDC,* p. 540, repeating from p. 77 the same wording which gave the original offense.

[123] For the *Ineffabilis Deus* (Dec. 8, 1854), in which Pope Pius IX defined the dogma of the Immaculate Conception, cf. *DS* 2800–2804. The *Creed of the People of God* uses the actual words of this solemn definition

[124] *Pozo,* pp. 125–126.

[125] *Pozo,* pp. 127–129.

[126] Pozo, pp. 129–130; for the *Munificentissimus Deus* of Pope Pius XII, cf. *DS* 3900–3904.

[127] *Pozo,* pp. 131–132.

[128] *Pozo,* p. 133 (his emphasis).

[129] See the GCD, no. 68, "Mary, Mother of God Mother and Model of the Church"; the *Roman Catechism,* pp. 41–49; *Lawler,* chap. 15, "Mary, Mother and Model of the Church," pp. 234–246; *Hardon,* chap. 5, "Blessed Virgin Mary," pp. 150–171. The key to "formation" is contained in the concept that Mary is "the model of the Church." True education since classical antiquity always has been aware of the role of patterns, models and paradigms which make concrete the truths that are taught. Standing with the Mother of Jesus in this role are all the Saints of God, of whom she is the greatest of all, the Queen of the heavenly court. There is a special catechetical significance in the classical three-volume work of Werner Jaeger, *Paideia: The Ideals of Greek Culture.* Oxford: Blackwell, 1936, 1944, 1945, which clarifies in detail the role of models and paradigms in the educational processes of formative humanism.

[130] *Pozo,* pp. 137–139, again with reference to the *New (Dutch) Catechism* in illustration of the contemporary problem in religious education.

[131] Cf. *NDC,* pp. 263–267.

[132] Quoted by *Pozo,* p. 141.

[133] *Dossier,* pp. 168–169; for the larger context of philosophical evolutionism which the editors of *Dossier* use to defend the *New (Dutch) Catechism,* see *Dossier,* pp. 169–173.

[134] Cf. *NDC,* p. 263.

[135] *Dossier,* p. 150.

[136] Cf. *Dossier,* p. 168; for the judgment of the Commission of Cardinals, see above, p. 184.

[137] *Pozo,* pp. 139–141; cf. *NDC,* p. 262.

[138] *Pozo,* p. 135.

[139] *Pozo,* pp. 143–145; for this typical affirmation in the *New Catechism,* cf. *NDC,* p. 267.

[140] *GCD,* no. 54; cf. nos. 36–44 and 50–54; cf. the *Roman Catechism,* pp. 31–39. And see *Hardon,* pp. 91–102, and *Lawler,* chap. 5, "Fallen Man and the Faithfulness of God," pp. 78–92, where the references to more recent Documents

of the Magisterium, especially Vatican II, are given for use in preparation for catechetical teaching.

141 See par. no. 12 of the *Creed of the People of God.*

142 *Pozo,* p. 147.

143 *Roman Catechism,* pp. 50–52. In preparing for catechetical teaching, *Lawler* provides a detailed resource on "soteriology," the redeeming work of Christ and on its application in the sacramental life of the Church; cf. pp. 136–147, "By Dying He Destroyed our Death"; 148–160, "By Rising He Restored our Life"; Part III, pp. 265–517, "With Christ: Sharing the Life of God" is devoted to the application of the merits and fruits of the Redemption to souls; cf. esp. chapter 28, "The Sacraments of Initiation" and chapter 27, "The Eucharist: Center of Life." Also see the chapter, "Growth in Holiness," in Hardon, pp. 419–437, an excellent catechetical resource for teaching the personal component of the application, the *metanoia* and its practice of prayer.

144 *DS* 1600; cf. the canons on the Sacrament of Baptism, *DS* 1614–1627; for the English translation, *Clarkson,* pp. 262–263.

145 Cf. *DS* 1514; and *Pozo,* pp. 149–150.

146 *GCD,* nos. 54 and 55.

147 *GCD,* no. 56.

148 Cf. *GCD,* no. 57. In preparing for teaching the doctrine of the Redemption and the divinely-established sacramental system for the application of its fruits to souls, see the *Roman Catechism,* pp. 50–72, an explanation of the Apostles' Creed, and Part II, "The Sacraments," pp. 141–355; the discussion on "The Importance of Instruction on the Sacraments," pp. 141–160 is an example of catechetical methodology at its best. And see *Lawler* and *Hardon* as cited in note 143, above.

149 See the Nicene Creed, above, pp. 6–7.

150 *Pozo,* pp. 153–157.

151 For the doctrinal content in the preparation of teaching on "The Catholic Church," the primary resource is the Dogmatic Constitution on the Church, *Lumen gentium,* cited ten times in these paragraphs of the *Creed of the People of God;* cf. *Vatican II,* pp. 350–426. For the principles of methodology, cf. *GCD,* nos. 65–67, on how to catechize on "The Church, People of God and Saving Institution." See also the *Roman Catechism,* pp. 96–119, with the explanation of the importance of the Articles of the Apostles' Creed which profess faith "in the Holy Catholic Church, the Communion of Saints, the Forgiveness of Sins," p. 96 and p. 113. And *Lawler,* chapter 13, "The Catholic Church," pp. 186–210; *Hardon,* "The Church," pp. 206–253.

152 Pope Pius XII, Encyclical *Humani generis* (1950), par. 27: "Some think they are not bound by the doctrine, set forth in our Encyclical letter of a few years ago and based on the sources of revelation, according to which the Mystical Body of Christ and the Roman Catholic Church are one and the same." The reference is to *Mystici Corporis.* Cf. Jerome Hamer, O.P., *The Church is a Communion* (New York: Sheed and Ward), 1964.

153 *Pozo,* p. 159.

154 *Pozo,* pp. 159–161.

155 *Pozo,* pp. 162–163; for the reference, see *Vatican II,* pp. 754–755. The phrase, "fully by the Lord Jesus" is actually a rejection in the *Creed of the People of God* of the theory of "On-Going Revelation"; cf. *Vatican I,* p. 48 and 51; and

Pope Paul VI, *Allocution* of Jan. 19, 1972, *Oss. Rom. English,* (Jan. 27, 1972)
p. 1. See above on Popes John XXIII and Paul VI and the *eadem sententia* of
Vatican I, pp. 59–61.

156 Joseph P. Christopher (Transl.) *St. Augustine: The First Catechetical
Instruction.* Westminster, Maryland: The Newman Press, 1946; pp. 26–27. There
is a characteristic Neo-Modernist hostility toward the "Christian Era" of universal
history which begets a feeling of alienation toward the concrete Roman Catholic
Church of cultural and social history. When this is transferred to children and
young people, "The Ministry of the Word," defined and described in Part Two of
the *General Catechetical Directory,* nos. 10–35, is deprived of its authentic character
and is precluded from bearing its fruit. In fact, this alienation turns against Jesus
Christ, who lives and works in the concrete Roman Catholic Church of human
history. It begins to seek for and to build up a "Church-of-the-Future" which
teaches what it calls a "re-interpreted" Christian doctrine. This is the fundamental
distinction between authentic catechetical teaching and the approaches of unsound
types of religious education. Catechetical teachers can thread their way through the
pitfalls of the contemporary chaos and crisis in religious education by holding
firmly to the *Creed of the People of God* for catechetical content, and to the
General Catechetical Directory, especially Part Three, "The Christian Message,"
nos. 36–69, for catechetical methodology. The "Norms or Criteria" given in *GCD*
nos. 37–46 have been drawn up carefully by the Magisterium precisely to
guide catechetical teaching to health and soundness in the face of the Neo-
Modernist philosophical creedlessness. These norms constitute the positive position of the Catholic catechetical teacher. The *New (Dutch) Catechism* assists
negatively in helping to discern and evaluate the presence of "philosophical faith"
in religious education programs and textbooks which derive from it and continue to
embody its fundamental approach.

157 For the English translation of the Latin given in *DS* 3011, see *Vatican I,* p.
44. It is disregard for the "Ordinary and Universal Magisterium" which has introduced unsoundness regarding content into religious education programs and textbooks, and has resulted in much chaos and upset on the part of faithful Catholics.
For this "Ordinary and Universal Magisterium" is precisely the Apostolic Catechesis
which is the very life-blood of the Catholic Church, the dynamic factor which
constitutes her on-going Apostolicity. If catechetics is confined to nothing but
actions of the Extraordinary Magisterium, with the content of this "Ordinary and
Universal Magisterium" replaced by a new, philosophically-reinterpreted, doctrine
in the mode of the Neo-Modernist approach, a new teaching program must necessarily emerge, one that builds "The Church-of-the-Future" on the one hand, while
on the other hand it is allowing the historic Roman Catholic and Apostolic Church
to wither and, as it thinks, to die.

158 *Pozo,* pp. 165–166; see his note 42, p. 165, for the theological controversy
whether there is only one subject of infallible Magisterium in the Church, namely
the Pope, with the infallibility of the Episcopal College deriving from his; or
whether there are two subjects inadequately distinct, the Pope and the Episcopal
College. Both Vatican II and the *Creed of the People of God* prescind from this
discussion. Catechetical teaching can well follow this example of the Magisterium,
taking the matter as an instance of the difference between the catechesis of the
Catholic faith, and theological teaching and discussion.

159 *Vatican II,* pp. 379–380.

160 See the reference to the English Edition of *L'Osservatore Romano,* above, p. 289.

161 See *NDC,* p. 368.

162 *Dossier,* p. 156. For the record of the discussion, cf. pp. 236–243.

163 *Dossier,* pp. 237–238.

164 Cf. *Dossier,* pp. 238–240.

165 *Dossier,* p. 240.

166 *Dossier,* ibid., the final note of the editors who published the dossier.

167 See above, pp. 186–188.

168 For the Decree on Ecumenism, no. 2, cf. *Vatican II,* pp. 453–455.

169 Cf. the *Third Instruction on the Correct Application of the Constitution on the Sacred Liturgy from the Congregation for Divine Worship* (Sept. 30, 1970); English translation: Washington: NCCB, 1970.

170 *Pozo,* pp. 170–171.

171 *Pozo,* pp. 172–173.

172 The official English translation of the *Creed of the People of God* published by the United States Catholic Conference, Washington, D.C. fails to recognize and to translate the Latin word *revera;* we have amended the translation here with the phrase "in true reality." This may seem superficially to be a small point; but when the importance of the Latin of the Holy See is considered, many will agree that it is not small at all. At best, the omission indicates an unscholarly carelessness that ought not characterize any translating of documents of the Magisterium; at worst, such things manifest unsound doctrinal slants and contribute to a deception of the English-speaking reader. A Neo-Modernist symbolic thinker could not be expected to wax enthusiastic about the word *revera* at that particular point.

173 *Pozo,* pp. 176–177.

174 *Dossier,* pp. 153.

175 *Dossier,* pp. 188–190.

176 For the text of the judgment of the Commission of Cardinals, see above, pp. 185–186.

177 Cf. *NDC,* p. 340 and pp. 546–551 for the Supplement.

178 *NDC,* p. 551.

179 Again the *General Catechetical Directory* gives the guideline to sound teaching method in this matter, the use of words in such a way as to minister to the content of doctrine that is being taught. In its definition of the sacrament of Holy Orders, no. 57, the *Directory* mentions the "sacred power" which enables priests, "representing Christ's person, . . . (to) offer the Sacrifice of the Mass and preside at the Eucharistic banquet." This is the cure in catechetical methodology for all the unsoundness and irreverence which have been introduced by the "ordinary meal" approach.

180 *Pozo,* p. 178; for the passage in the Dutch Catechism, cf. *NDC,* p. 342.

181 *Clarkson,* p. 281; for the official Latin of the Council of Trent, cf. *DS* 1651: *vere, realiter et substantialiter* . . .

182 *Pozo,* pp. 179–180.

183 The Encyclical *Mysterium fidei* (Sept. 3, 1965), no. 39.

184 *Pozo,* p. 181.

185 *Clarkson,* p. 283 and p. 286; for the Canon, cf. *DS* 1652.

[186] See *Vatican I*, p. 48, for the solemn dogmatic definition which Pope Paul VI quotes in this passage; for the concern of Popes John XXIII and Paul VI to maintain this dogmatic definition of Vatican I, see above, pp. 60–61.

[187] Cf. *NDC*, p. 343.

[188] cf. *Pozo*, p. 182, with the reference to C. V. Héris, O.P., *L'Eucharistie: Mystère de Foi*. Paris: 1967.

[189] *Pozo*, pp. 183–185, again citing the *New (Dutch) Catechism* as the illustration of the problem which has raised its head in contemporary religious education.

[190] *Dossier*, p. 154; for the entire question of the teaching of the *Dutch Catechism* on the Holy Eucharist, see the record of the discussion at Gazzada, *Dossier*, pp. 196–211.

[191] *Dossier*, p. 197.

[192] *Dossier*, p. 205.

[193] *Dossier*, p. 209.

[194] Dossier, p. 209. For the judgment of the Commission of Cardinals, see above, pp. 185–186.

[195] *Clarkson*, p. 287.

[196] *NDC*, p. 346; repeated in the Supplement, p. 552.

[197] *Pozo*, p. 186. Where derivatives of the *Dutch Catechism's* approach are installed currently as religious education programs, the genuflection as an outward mark of reverence for the real presence, a bodily profession of faith, as it were, tends actually to disappear from entire parishes, and to be looked upon as a "strange action," a relic of an outmoded past. In this way creedlessness creates its own signs and symbols that reveal its presence.

[198] Cf. *NDC*, pp. 345–347; and again in the Supplement, pp. 551–552, which is something less than clear and complete.

[199] The Encyclical *Mysterium fidei* is the primary source for use in the preparation of catechetical teaching on the Holy Eucharist. For assistance in methodology, cf. the *GCD*, no. 58, on "The Eucharist: Center of the Entire Sacramental Life," and the *Roman Catechism*, pp. 213–260 on "The Sacrament of the Eucharist," pages which are official in their authority and unsurpassed in practical helpfulness, a classic blend of content and method. For catechetical resource material that takes recent documents of the Magisterium into account, see *Lawler*, Chap. 27, "The Eucharist—Center of Life," pp. 419–456, which contains with good logic a discussion of the Sacrament of Holy Order, pp. 438–456; and *Hardon*, pp. 457–481.

[200] *Vatican II*, p. 353.

[201] *Pozo*, p. 188; and see his accurate reference to Teilhard de Chardin, who represents a concept of Christian progress which differs fundamentally from that of the *Creed of the People of God:* for Teilhard conceives it in terms of this visible world with its civilization, science and merely natural human technology. See the note on contemporary aberrational Christology, above, pp. 284–285.

[202] *Vatican II*, p. 920; The Constitution on the Church in the Modern World, no. 20.

[203] *Pozo*, pp. 192–194, with the reference to the defective and superficial concept of love which characterizes the *New (Dutch) Catechism;* see, for example, *NDC*, p. 302, with its bow to contemporary confusionism: "Love is so divine that we can say not only 'God is love' but 'Love is God.' " The pansexual implications, however, are clear.

[204] Cf. *Vatican II*, pp. 388–396; and 766–798. See also the chapter in the

Dogmatic Constitution on the Church, "The Call to Holiness," pp. 396–402; "All Christians, in the conditions, duties and circumstances of their life and through all these, will sanctify themselves more and more if they receive all things with faith from the hand of the heavenly Father and cooperate with the divine will, thus showing forth in that temporal service the love with which God has loved the world." (p. 400).

205 For the Modernist approach to Christian doctrine, see the Encyclical *Pascendi* (Sept. 8, 1907) of Pope St. Pius X, "On the Doctrines of the Modernists." In par. 39, this document calls the Modernist approach "the synthesis of all the heresies." For the official recognition by the contemporary Holy See that the current Neo-Modernist approach has been re-born as the "Crisis of Faith" which has followed upon the Second Vatican Council, see *Ecclesiam suam*, the first Encyclical of Pope Paul VI (Aug. 6, 1964), "On the Paths of the Church," no. 26, a commentary on Romans 12, 2: "Do not be conformed to this world but be transformed by the renewal of your mind." In his *Allocution* of January 19, 1972, Pope Paul VI made the identification explicitly, and cited the basic documents of Pope St. Pius X: "This is how . . . our doctrine is separated from the errors which have circulated and still crop up . . . and which might ruin completely our Christian conception of life and history. Modernism was the characteristic expression of these errors, and it still exists today, under other names. See the Decree *Lamentabili* of St. Pius X, 1907, and his Encyclical *Pascendi*. So we can understand why the Catholic Church, in the past and today, has given and gives so much importance to the scrupulous preservation of the authentic revelation. She considers it an inviolable treasure, and is sternly aware of her fundamental duty to defend and transmit the doctrine of the faith in unequivocal terms. Orthodoxy is her first concern; the pastoral Magisterium her primary and providential function." And Pope Paul VI cites St. Paul, 1 Tim. 6, 20 and 2 Tim. 1, 14. (See the *Osservatore Romano-English Edition* (January 27, 1972), page one.) For the three historic moments of this doctrinal movement, see above, p. 261. In the contemporary "third moment" of this two-centuries-long doctrinal aberration, there is of course a new extensiveness of impact due to its skillful use of all the media of communication, its mastery of the techniques of cell-like networks of organization, and especially by its broad entry into the field of religious education.

206 Cf. Paul-Émile Langevin, S.J. *Jésus Seigneur et l'Eschatologie.* Paris: Desclée de Brouwer, 1967, esp. chapters 3 and 4; and A. Feuillet, "Parousie" in *Dictionnaire de la Bible.* Paris: Letouzey, 1960; Supplément, fasc. 35, col. 1331–1419.

207 *Pozo*, pp. 201–202; see par. 12 of the *Creed of the People of God.*

208 *Pozo*, pp. 202–203, citing the *New (Dutch) Catechism* once again as the illustration of the Neo-Modernist problem in contemporary religious education.

209 Cf. *NDC*, pp. 472–474 and 566–568.

210 *Dossier*, p. 155.

211 Cf. *Dossier*, pp. 221–226.

212 See above, p. 184; for the teaching of Vatican II, see the Dogmatic Constitution on the Church, nos. 49 and 51; *Vatican II*, pp. 409–413.

213 Cf. *DS* 72; 76; 648; 797; 801; 859; 1002.

214 *Pozo*, p. 206.

215 Cf. *NDC*, p. 474 and 478 ff.

216 *Pozo*, p. 209.

²¹⁷ The *Creed* refers to *Vatican II*, no. 49 of the Dogmatic Constitution on the Church. In the preparation of catechetical teaching, cf. the entire chapter, "The Pilgrim Church," *Vatican II*, pp. 407–413. For the principles that govern sound catechetical method regarding the Last Things, see the GCD, no. 69, "Final Communion with God." And the *Roman Catechism*, pp. 80–87, especially its characteristic helpful discussion of the importance of instruction regarding the Four Last Things, pp. 86–87; and pp. 120–140 on the Resurrection of the Body and Life Everlasting. These explanations on the right way of teaching these articles of the Apostles' Creed are an abiding resource for catechetical teaching, for they show how to blend content and method correctly in such a way that the light of instruction becomes a spiritual formation of the soul. See also *Lawler*, Part Four, "In Christ: Fulfillment of All," pp. 521–549; and *Hardon*, Chap. VIII, "Human Destiny," pp. 254–280.

²¹⁸ It is the great merit of the *Roman Catechism* that it continues in modern times the practice of the Catechumenate of the early Church in devoting instructional time to the *ex professo* teaching of prayer. See Part IV, "The Lord's Prayer," pp. 477–589. Even the method of the early Church is continued by this *official Catechism*. It is a masterly explanation of the components of the prayer taught by the Lord Jesus Himself when His disciples, noting His own habit and practice of prayer, came to Him and asked, "Lord, teach us how to pray." See also the chapter, "Growth in Holiness," in *Hardon*, pp. 419–437, a practical resource for catechetical teaching on this subject, in the context of the Second Vatican Council's "Universal Call to Sanctity."

Footnotes—Documents of the Magisterium Relating to the Creed of the People of God.

¹ I Tim. 2, 7. (Note: the footnotes of this Part Four are exclusively the references contained in the official texts of the Documents themselves; no additional comments have been volunteered. For the original Latin text, cf. *AAS* under the corresponding dates; for the English translations reprinted here, cf. the English Edition of *L'Osservatore Romano* at the corresponding dates.—E.K.)

² *I Epistula Clementis ad Corinthios*, V, 1–2; ed. Funk, I, p. 105.

³ Tacitus, *Annales*, XV, 44.

⁴ *I Epist. Clementis*, VI, 1; p. 107.

⁵ I Pet. 1, 4.

⁶ 8, 23.

⁷ 2 Cor. 1, 14.

⁸ Eph. 2, 20.

⁹ Cf. John 1, 14.

¹⁰ Cf. Matt. 16, 16–19.

¹¹ Cf. John 6, 68–69.

¹² Cf. Luke 22, 32.

¹³ Cf. Acts 2, 32–40.

¹⁴ I Pet. 5, 9.

¹⁵ Cf. Eph. 4, 4–16.

¹⁶ Cf. St. Aug. *De Civ. Dei*, 8, 4; P.L. 41, 228–29 and *Contra Faustum*, 20, 7; P.L. 42, 372.

¹⁷ Cf. Vincent Lerin. *Commonitorium* 1, 23; P.L. 50, 668; *DS* 3020.

18 Cf. Heb. 12, 2; Conc. Vat. I, Const. Dogm. *De Fide Catholica*, 3, *DS* 3008–20; Conc. Vat. II, *Lumen Gentium*, 5 etc.; Const. Dogm. *De Divina Revelatione*, 5, 8.

19 Heb. 11, 6.

20 Cf. Mark 16, 16; Eph. 2, 8; etc.

21 Ps. 45, 5.

22 Apostolic Exhortation *Postrema Sessio*, 4 November 1965, in *AAS* 57, 1965, p. 867.

23 Acts 20, 28.

24 *AAS* 56, 1964, pp. 609–659.

25 20 October 1962, *AAS* 54, 1962, p. 822.

26 82; *AAS* 58, 1966, pp. 1106–1107.

27 *Adversus Haereses* IV, 26; 2: 2; *PG* 7, 1053.

28 Cf. 2 Th. 2, 10.

29 Cf. Mt. 13, 52.

30 Cf. 2 Tim. 4, 1–4.

31 Dogmatic Constitution *Lumen Gentium*, 25; *AAS* 57, 1965, pp. 29–30.

32 *AAS* 54, 1962, p. 792.

33 Gal. 1, 8.

34 Heb. 4, 12; Rv. 1, 16; 2, 16.

35 Hans Urs Von Balthasar, *Das Ganze im Fragment*, Einsiedeln: Benzinger 1963, p. 296.

36 Eph. 3, 19.

37 Cf. *Relatio Commissionis in Synodo Episcoporum Constitutae*, Rome, October 1967, pp. 10–11.

38 *Declaration of the German Bishops*, Fulda, 27 December 1968, in *Herder Korrespondenz*, Freiburg im Breisgau, January 1969, p. 75.

39 Dogmatic Constitution *Dei verbum*, 24; *AAS* 58, 1966, p. 828.

40 2 Tim. 4, 1–5.

41 Dogmatic Constitution *Lumen Gentium*, 50; *AAS* 57, 1965, p. 56.

42 Lk. 11, 11.

43 Cf. 2 Jn. 7–9.

44 Acts 20, 30.

45 Mt. 7, 15–20.

46 Cf. Decree *Apostolicam Actuositatem*, 7, 13, 24; *AAS* 58, 1966, pp. 843–844, 849–850, 856–857.

47 *Enarratio in Psalmos*, 103; *Sermo*, 1, 19; PL 37, 1351.

48 Cf. Apostolic Exhortation *Postrema Sessio*, in *AAS* 57, 1965, p. 865.

49 Eph. 3, 20–21.

50 Cfr. Phil. 2, 6–8.

51 1 Cor. 8, 6.

52 Jn. 1, 1. 14 (cfr. 1, 18).

53 Cfr. Conc. Vat. I, Const. dogm. *Dei Filius*, c. 4; *Conc. Oec. Decr.*, Herder, 1962, p. 785; *DS* 3020.

54 *Missale Romanum*, ed. typica Typis Polyglottis Vaticanis 1970, p. 389; Dz.-Sch. 50. Cfr. also Conc. Nic. I: (*Expositio fidei*); *Conc. Oec. Decr.*, p. 4s.; *DS* 125 ss.

55 Cfr. Conc. Chalc. (*Definito*); *Conc. Oec. Decr.*, p. 62; *DS* 301.

56 Cfr. *ibid.*, *DS* 302.

302   Creed and Catechetics

57 Cfr. Conc. Lat. IV: Const. *Firmiter credimus; Conc. Oec. Decr.,* p. 206; *DS* 800f.

58 Cfr. Conc. Vat. II: *Const. dogm. Lumen Gentium,* nn. 3, 7, 52, 53; Const. dogm. *Dei Verbum,* nn. 2, 3; Const. past. *Gaudium et spes,* n. 22; Decr. *Unitatis redintegratio,* n. 12; Decr. *Christus Dominus,* n. 1; Decr. *Ad Gentes,* n. 3; cfr. also Pope Paul VI, *Solemnis professio fidei,* n. 11, AAS 60 (1968) 437.

59 Cfr. Conc. Flor.: Bulla *Laetentur caeli; Conc. Oec. Decr.,* p. 501 f; *DS* 1300.

60 2 Cor. 13, 14.

61 Cfr. Mt. 28, 19.

62 Jn. 15, 26.

63 Conc. Vat. II: Const. dogm. *Dei Verbum,* n. 10.

64 *Missale Romanum,* loc. cit.; *DS* 150.

65 Cfr. Conc. Lat. IV: Const. *Firmiter credimus; Conc. Oec. Decr.,* p. 206; *DS* 800.

66 *Ibid.*

67 Conc. Vat. I: Const. dogm. *Dei Filius,* c. 4, can. 3; *Conc. Oec. Decr.,* p. 787; *DS* 3043. See Pope John XXIII, *Alloc. in S. Conc. Vat. II inauguratione, AAS* 54 (1962) 792, and Conc. Vat. II: Const. past. *Gaudium et spes,* n. 62. Cfr. also Paul VI, *Solemnis professio fidei,* n. 4, *AAS* 60 (1968), 434.

68 Cfr. 1 Jn. 4, 9f.

69 Cfr. Conc. Vat. II: Const. dogm. *Dei Verbum,* n. 2; cfr. Eph. 2, 18; 2 Pet. 1, 4.

70 Cfr. Pope Paul VI, Apostolic Exhortation *Quinque iam anni,* in *AAS* 68 (1971), 99.

71 Cfr. 2 Tim. 4, 1–5. See Pope Paul VI, *ibid.,* p. 103f. See also *Synodus Episcoporum* (1967): *Relatio Commissionis Synodalis constitutae ad examen ulterius peragendum circa opiniones periculosas et atheismum,* II, 3: *De pastorali ratione agendi in exercitio magisterii,* Typis Polyglottis Vaticanis 1967, 10f (*Oss. Rom.* 30–31 Oct. 1967, p. 3).

72 Pope Paul VI, *ibid.,* p. 103.

73 Cfr. Pope Paul VI, *ibid.,* p. 100.

74 Cfr. Conc. Vat. II: Const. dogm. *Lumen Gentium,* nn. 12, 25; *Synodus Episcoporum* (1967): *Relatio Commissionis Synodalis . . . II,* 4: *De Theologorum opera et responsabilitate . . .* p. 11 (*Oss. Rom., loc. cit.*).

75 Conc. Vat. II: Const. dogm. *Dei Verbum,* n. 10.

76 Paul VI, Apostolic Exhortation *Quinque iam Anni, AAS* 63 (1971), p. 99.

77 Paul VI, Apostolic Constitution *Regiminis Ecclesiae Universae, AAS* 59 (1967), p. 897.

78 II Vatican Council: Dogmatic Constitution on the Church *Lumen Gentium,* 8; *Constitutiones Decreta Declarationes,* editio Secretariae Generalis, Typis Polyglottis Vaticanis, 1966, p. 104 ff.

83 II Vatican Council: Decree on Ecumenism *Unitatis Redintegratio,* 4; *Const. Decr. Decl.,* p. 250.

80 *Ibid.,* 4; *Const. Decr. Decl.,* p. 252.

81 II Vatican Council: Dogmatic Constitution on the Church *Lumen Gentium,* 8; *Const. Decr. Decl.,* p. 106.

82 *Ibid., Const. Decr. Decl.,* p. 105.

83 II Vatican Council: Decree on Ecumenism *Unitatis Redintegratio,* 4; *Const. Decr. Decl.,* p. 253.

84 Cf. *Ibid.,* 608; *Const. Decr. Decl.,* pp. 255–258.

85 Cf. *Ibid.,* 1; *Const. Decr. Decl.,* p. 243.

86 Cf. Paul VI, Encyclical Letter *Ecclesiam Suam, AAS* 56 (1964), p. 629.

87 II Vatican Council: Dogmatic Constitution on Divine Revelation *Dei Verbum,* 7; *Const. Decr. Decl.,* p. 428.

88 Cf. *Ibid.,* 10; *Const. Decr. Decl.,* p. 431.

89 Cf. *Ibid.,* 8; *Const. Decr. Decl.,* p. 430.

90 II Vatican Council: Dogmatic Constitution on the Church *Lumen Gentium,* 12; *Const. Decr. Decl.,* p. 113 ff.

91 *Ibid.; Const. Decr. Decl.,* p. 114.

92 Cf. *Ibid.,* 35; *Const. Decr. Decl.,* p. 157.

93 II Vatican Council: Dogmatic Constitution on Divine Revelation *Dei Verbum,* 8; *Const. Decr. Decl.,* p. 430.

94 Paul VI, Apostolic Exhortation *Quinque iam anni, AAS* 63 (1971), p. 99.

95 Cf. II Vatican Council: Dogmatic Constitution on the Church *Lumen Gentium,* 25; *Const. Decr. Decl.,* p. 138 ff.

96 II Vatican Council: *Ibid.,* 18; *Const. Decr. Decl.* p. 124 ff. Cf. I Vatican Council: Dogmatic Constitution *Pastor Aeternus,* Prologue; *Conciliorum oecumenicorum Decreta* (3), ed. *Instituto per le Scienze Religiose di Bologna,* Herder, 1973, p. 812 (*DS* 3051).

97 Paul VI, Apostolic Exhortation *Quinque iam Anni, AAS* 63 (1971), p. 100.

98 Decree of the Holy Office *Lamentabili* 5, *AAS* 40 (1907), p. 471 DS 3406). Cf. I Vatican Council: Dogmatic Constitution *Pastor Aeternus,* ch. 4; *Conc. Oec. Decr.* (3), p. 815 ff (*DS* 3009, 3074).

99 I Vatican Council; Dogmatic Constitution *Pastor Aeternus,* ch. 4; *Conc. Oec. Decr.* (3), p. 816 (DS 3070). Cf. II Vatican Council: Dogmatic Constitution on the Church *Lumen Gentium,* 25, and Dogmatic Constitution on Divine Revelation *Dei Verbum,* 4; *Const. Decr. Decl.,* p. 141 and 426.

100 Cf. II Vatican Council: Dogmatic Constitution on Divine Revelation *Dei Verbum,* 11; *Const. Decr. Decl.,* p. 434.

101 Cf. *Ibid.,* 9 ff.; *Const. Decr. Decl.,* p. 430–432.

102 Cf. II Vatican Council: Dogmatic Constitution on the Church *Lumen Gentium,* 25; *Const. Decr. Decl.* p. 139.

103 Cf. *Ibid.,* 25 and 22; *Const. Decr. Decl.,* p. 139 and 133.

104 I Vatican Council: Dogmatic Constitution *Pastor Aeternus,* ch. 4; *Conc. Oec. Decr.* (3), p. 816 (*DS* 3074). Cf. II Vatican Council: *Ibid.,* 25. *Const. Decr. Decl.,* pp. 139–141.

105 Cf. II Vatican Council: Dogmatic Constitution on the Church *Lumen Gentium,* 25; *Const. Decr. Decl.,* p. 139.

106 I Vatican Council: Dogmatic Constitution *Dei Filius,* ch. 3; *Conc. Oec. Decr.* (3), p. 807 (*DS* 3011). Cf. *C.I.C.,* can. 1323, par. 1 and can. 1325, par. 2.

107 Cf. Council of Trent, Sess. 6: Decree on Justification, ch. 6; *Conc. Oec. Decr.* (3), p. 672 (*DS* 1526); cf. also II Vatican Council: Dogmatic Constitution on Divine Revelation *Dei Verbum,* 5; *Const. Decr. Decl.,* p. 426.

108 Cf. I. Vatican Council: Constitution on the Catholic Faith *Dei Filius,* ch. 3; *Conc. Oec. Decr.* (3), p. 807 (*DS* 3008); cf. also II Vatican Council: Dogmatic Constitution on Divine Revelation *Dei Verbum,* 5; *Const. Decr. Decl.,* p. 426.

109 Cf. II Vatican Council: Decree on Ecumenism *Unitatis Redintegratio,* 11; *Const. Decr. Decl.,* p. 260.

[110] *Reflections and Suggestions Concerning Ecumenical Dialogue,* IV, 4 b, in *The Secretariat for Promoting Christian Unity: Information Service,* n. 12 (December 1970, IV), p. 8.

[111] I Vatican Council: Dogmatic Constitution *Dei Filius,* ch. 4; *Conc. Oec. Decr.* (3), p. 808 (*DS* 3016).

[112] Cf. Pius IX, Brief *Eximiam Tuam, ASS* 8 (1874–75), p. 447 (*DS* 2831); Paul VI, Encyclical Letter *Mysterium Fidei, AAS* 57 (1965), p. 757 ff. and *L'Oriente cristiano nella luce di immortali Concili in Insegnamenti di Paolo VI,* vol. 5, Vatican Polyglot Press, page 412 ff.

[113] Cf. I Vatican Council: Dogmatic Constitution *Dei Filius,* ch. 4; *Conc. Oec. Decr.* (3), p. 809 (*DS* 3020).

[114] *Ibid.*

[115] *Ibid.,* can 3; *Conc. Oec. Decr.* (3), p. 811 (*DS* 3043).

[116] John XXIII, *Alloc. in Concilii Vaticani inauguratione, AAS* 54 (1962), p. 792. Cf. II Vatican Council: Pastoral Constitution on the Church in the Modern World *Gaudium et Spes,* 62; *Const. Decr. Decl.,* p. 780.

[117] Paul VI, Apostolic Exhortation *Quinque iam Anni, AAS* 63 (1971), page 100 ff.

[118] II Vatican Council: Dogmatic Constitution on the Church *Lumen Gentium,* 10; Const. Decr. Decl., p. 110.

[119] *Ibid.,* 11; *Const. Decr. Decl.* p. 111.

[120] *Ibid.,* 10; *Const. Decr. Decl.,* p. 111.

[121] Cf. Pius XI, Encyclical Letter *Ad Catholici Sacerdotii, AAS* 28 (1936) page 10 (*DS* 3735). Cf. II Vatican Council: Dogmatic Constitution on the Church *Lumen Gentium,* 10, and Decree on the Priestly Life and Ministry *Presbyterorum Ordinis,* 2; *Const. Decr. Decl.,* p. 110 ff., 622 ff.

[122] Cf. II Vatican Council: Dogmatic Constitution on the Church *Lumen Gentium,* 28; *Const. Decr. Decl.,* p. 625.

[123] II Vatican Council: Decree on the Priestly Life and Ministry *Presbyterorum Ordinis,* 3; *Const. Decr. Decl.,* p. 625.

[124] Cf. II Vatican Council: Dogmatic Constitution *Lumen Gentium,* 24, 27 ff.; *Const. Decr. Decl.,* pp. 137, 143–149.

[125] II Vatican Council: Decree on the Priestly Life and Ministry, *Presbyterorum Ordinis,* 4; *Const. Decr. Decl.,* p. 627.

[126] Cf. Dogmatic Constitution on the Church *Lumen Gentium,* 11; *Const. Decr. Decl.,* p. 111 ff. also Council of Trent, Sess. 22; *Doctrina de Missae Sacrifico,* ch. 1 and 2; *Conc. Oec. Decr.* (3), pages 732–734 (*DS* 1739–1743).

[127] Cf. Paul VI, *Sollemnis Professio Fidei,* 24, *AAS* 60 (1968), p. 442.

[128] Council of Florence: *Bulla unionis Armenorum, Exsultate Deo; Conc. Oec. Decr.* (3), p. 546 (*DS* 1313).

[129] Council of Trent: Decree on the Sacraments, can 9 and Decree on the Sacrament of Order, ch. 4 and can. 4; *Conc. Oec. Decr* (3), pp. 685, 742, 744 (*DS* 1609, 1767, 1774).

[130] Cf. II Vatican Council: Dogmatic Constitution on the Church *Lumen Gentium,* 21 and Decree on the Priestly Life and Ministry *Presbyterorum Ordinis,* 2; *Const. Decr. Decl.,* pp. 133, 622 ff.

[131] Cf. Documents of the Synod of Bishops: I. *The Ministerial Priesthood,* part one, 5, *AAS* 63 (1971), p. 907.

[132] II Vatican Council: Dogmatic Constitution on the Church *Lumen Gentium,* 17; *Const. Decr. Decl.,* p. 123.

133 II Vatican Council: Decree on the Priestly Life and Ministry *Presbyterorum Ordinis,* 2; *Const. Decr. Decl.,* p. 621 ff. Cf. also: 1) Innocent III, Letter *Eius exemplo with Professio fidei Waldensis imposita,* PL, Vol. 215, col. 1510 (*DS* 794); 2) IV Lateran Council: Constitution I: *De Fide Catholica; Conc. Oec. Decr.* (3), p. 230 (DS 802); passage quoted on the Sacrament of the Altar to be read together with the following passage on the Sacrament of Baptism; 3) Council of Florence: *Bulla unionis Armenorum, Exultate Deo; Conc. Oec. Decr.* (3), p. 546 (*DS* 1321); passage quoted on the Minister of the Eucharist to be compared with nearby passages on the Minister of the other Sacraments; 4) Council of Trent, Sess 23: Decree on the Sacrament of Order, ch. 4; *Conc. Oec. Decr.* (3), p. 742 ff (*DS* 1767, 4469); 5) Pius XII Encyclical *Mediator Dei, AAS* 39 (1947), pp. 552–556 (*DS* 3849–3852).

134 Documents of the Synod of Bishops: I. *The Ministerial Priesthood,* part one, 4, *AAS* 63 (1971), p. 906.

135 Cf. Synod of Bishops (1967), *Relatio Commissionis Synodalis constitutae ad examen ulterius peragendum circa opiniones periculosas et atheismum,* II, 4: *De theologorum opera et responsabilitate,* Vatican Polyglot Press, 1967, p. 11 (*L'Osservatore Romano,* 30–31 October 1967, p. 3).

136 Cf. *AAS* 65 (1973), p. 323 f.

137 Cf. Second Vatican Council, Dogmatic Constitution *Lumen Gentium,* 3: *AAS* 57 (1965), p. 6.

138 Second Vatican Council, Pastoral Constitution *Gaudium et Spes,* 21: *AAS* 58 (1966), p. 1041.

139 Cf. Bull *Apostolorum Limina,* 23 March 1974: *AAS* 66 (1974), p. 306.

140 Saint Leo the Great, *Serm.* 26, 5: PL 54, 215.

141 Theodoret of Cyr, *Interpr. Epist. II ad Cor.:* PG 82, 411 A.

142 Second Vatican Council, Dogmatic Constitution *Lumen Gentium,* 7: *AAS* 57 (1965), p. 9.

143 Saint Augustine, *Serm.* 96, 7, 8: PL 38, 588.

144 Saint Jerome, *In Epist. ad Eph.* 1, 2: PL 26, 504.

145 Saint Ambrose, *In Luc.* 5, 58: PL 15, 1737.

146 Cf. Saint John Chrysostom, *In Matth.,* Homil. 15, 9: PG 57, 250; Saint Isidore of Pelusium, *Epist.* 4, 111: PG 78, 1178; Nicolas Cabasilas, *Explic. div. Liturg.* 26, 2: *Sourc. Chret.* 4 bis, p. 171.

147 Saint Cyril of Alexandria, *In Epist. II ad Cor.:* PG 74, 943 D.

148 Second Vatican Council, Dogmatic Constitution *Lumen Gentium,* 27: *AAS* 57 (1965), p. 32.

149 Cf. Second Vatican Council, Dogmatic Constitution *Lumen Gentium,* 11: *AAS* 57 (1965), p. 5.

150 Second Vatican Council, Dogmatic Constitution *Lumen Gentium,* 1: *AAS* 57 (1965), p. 5.

151 Second Vatican Council, Dogmatic Constitution *Lumen Gentium,* 4: *AAS* 57 (1965), p. 7.

152 Second Vatican Council, Pastoral Constitution *Gaudium et Spes,* 43: *AAS* 58 (1966), p. 1064.

153 Second Vatican Council, Decree *Unitatis Redintegratio,* 3: *AAS* 57 (1965), p. 92.

154 Second Vatican Council, Decree *Unitatis Redintegratio,* 2: *AAS* 57 (1965), p. 92.

306 Creed and Catechetics

155 Second Vatican Council, Dogmatic Constitution *Lumen Gentium*, 8: *AAS* 57 (1965), p. 11.
156 Second Vatican Council, Dogmatic Constitution *Lumen Gentium*, 8: *AAS* 57 (1965), p. 12.
157 Saint John Chrysostom, *In Epist. ad Coloss.*, Homil. 3, 5: PG 62, 324.
158 Cf. Second Vatican Council, Dogmatic Constitution *Dei Verbum*, 10: *AAS* 58 (1966), p. 822.
159 Second Vatican Council, Dogmatic Constitution *Lumen Gentium*, 23: *AAS* 57 (1965), p. 29.
160 Saint Augustine, *Epist.* 187, 11, 34: PL 33, 845.
161 Cf. Saint Ephrem the Syrian, *Comment, Evang. concord.* 1, 18: *Source chret.* 121, p. 52.
162 Second Vatican Council, Dogmatic Constitution *Dei Verbum*, 7: *AAS* 58 (1966), p. 820.
163 Second Vatican Council, Dogmatic Constitution *Dei Verbum*, 10: *AAS* 58 (1966), p. 822.
164 Second Vatican Council, Dogmatic Constitution *Dei Verbum*, 8: *AAS* 58 (1966), p. 820.
165 Cf. Second Vatican Council, Dogmatic Constitution *Lumen Gentium*, 9: *AAS* 57 (1965), p. 13.
166 Tertullian, *Apologeticum*, XXXIX, 7; *Corpus Christianorum*, Series Latina 1, 1, p. 151.
167 Saint Leo the Great, *Tract.* 84 bis; 2: *Corpus Christ.* 138 A, p. 530.
168 Saint Augustine, *In Io. Evang.*, 27, 5: PL 35, 1618.
169 Saint Leo the Great, *Serm.* 25, 3: PL 54, 214.
170 Saint Maximus of Turin, *Serm.* 37, 2: *Corpus Christ.* 23, p. 145.
171 Second Vatican Council, Dogmatic Constitution *Lumen Gentium*, 13: *AAS* 57 (1965), p. 17 f.
172 Cf. Saint Thomas, *Summa Theol.* II–II, p. 33, a. 4: *Opera Omnia*, Leonine ed., t. VIII, p. 266.
173 Cf. Saint Bonaventure, *In IV Sent.*, dist. 19, dub. 4: *Opera Omnia*, ad Claras Aquas, t. IV, p. 512.
174 Cf. Saint Jerome, *Contra Pelagian.*, 2, 11: PL 23, 546.
175 Second Vatican Council, Dogmatic Constitution *Lumen Gentium*, 11: *AAS* 57 (1965), p. 15.
176 *Ordo Paenitentiae*, Praenotanda, 7, Vatican Polyglot Press, 1974, p. 14.
177 Second Vatican Council, Dogmatic Constitution *Lumen Gentium*, 7: *AAS* 57 (1965), p. 10.
178 Saint Augustine, *Enarrat. in Ps.* 33, 19: PL 36, 318.
179 Cf. First Vatican Council, Dogmatic Constitution *Pastor Aeternus*, Introduction: *DS* 3050; Second Vatican Council, Dogmatic Constitution *Lumen Gentium*, 18: *AAS* 57 (1965), p. 22.
180 *Liturgia Horarum*, IV, Vatican Polyglot Press 1972, p. 513.
181 Cf. Second Vatican Council, Dogmatic Constitution *Lumen Gentium*, 21: *AAS* 57 (1965), p. 25.
182 Cf. Second Vatican Council, Dogmatic Constitution *Lumen Gentium*, 23: *AAS* 57 (1965), p. 27.
183 Second Vatican Council, Dogmatic Constitution *Lumen Gentium*, 8: *AAS* 57 (1965), p. 11.

[184] *Serm.* 138, 10: PL 38, 769.
[185] Second Vatican Council, Dogmatic Constitution *Lumen Gentium*, 65: *AAS* 57 (1965), p. 64.

Footnotes—Conclusion

[1] *GCD*, nos. 17–18. The important passage, "through the light of instruction," is quoted from the Vatican II Decree on the Pastoral Office of Bishops in the Church, no. 14: "Bishops should be especially concerned about catechetical instruction." Cf. Vatican II, p. 571. The Catholic Church understands this as a *bona fide* and true *instruction,* one which centers upon and explains the articles of faith professed by the Apostles' Creed. No other "instruction" could be a "light," because only these articles carry the whole person under instruction to Him who is the light of the world. In the Catholic approach this catechesis is not *merely* instruction, addressed abstractly to the intellect alone. It is practical and formative of the whole person, for it is interwoven with and followed up by instructional formation in personal prayer, in the social living of the Gospel morality, and in the sacramental life and worship of the Church. But the Catholic approach recognizes the dependence of these three areas upon the knowledge and the love of the articles of faith which profess Jesus Christ. The Neo-Modernist literature recognizes that these words of Vatican II, "through the light of instruction," contain a difficulty for the rationale of its approach. The litmus-test is always the attitude toward the articles of faith proposed and explained by the teaching authority of the Church. At best, and begrudgingly, this approach will admit the formulated doctrine of the faith only toward puberty. When it sees this doctrine present earlier in programs for children, it reacts vigorously. For it assumes, without reason or proof, that formulated doctrine, even this doctrine of the Catholic faith in Jesus Christ, makes the process of religious education abstract, unattractive to children and unfruitful. It can talk convincingly about its intentions, its plan to put the Christian way of life into practice, and its devotion to Christ. But the test is always the Creed, the presence or the absence of the articles of faith in catechetical programs. For this determines whether Jesus Christ is really and effectively the center of the teaching, or whether He is only vaguely and nominally present, in the context of naturalistic religiosity. See footnote no. 8, below.

[2] *GCD*, no. 25.

[3] *GCD*, no. 22.

[4] *GCD*, no. 40.

[5] Yves M.-J. Congar, O.P. *Tradition and Traditions.* New York: Macmillan, 1966; p. 21.

[6] Pope Paul VI, General Audience of Jan. 15, 1975. *L'Oss. Rom.-English Edition* (Jan. 23, 1975) p. 1.

[7] Pope Leo XIII, Encyclical *Testem benevolentiae* on False Americanism in Religion (Jan. 22, 1899); in John Tracy Ellis, (Ed.) *Documents of American Catholic History.* Milwaukee: Bruce, 1955; p. 554.

[8] Pope Leo XIII, *ibid.* Cf. George A. Kelly. *Who Should Run the Catholic Church? Social Scientists, Theologians or Bishops?* Huntington, Indiana: Our Sunday Visitor, 1976; p. 45: "The pressure on Catholicism to become another sect in the American pantheon is not a new one although the rival has become stronger. Pope Leo XIII once warned against what (when he said it in 1899)

certainly was a 'phantom' Americanism. His words may, however, have more significance today." Not least among the reasons for this greater significance is the sudden proliferation of defective programs and textbooks in religious education. It is a striking fact that they are defective by the very elements which Pope Leo XIII noted: omissions of creedal content, and the slanted re-interpretations inspired by what is called in certain circles "The New Hermeneutic." This is the reason why the term "Neo-Modernist" has been used in the present study to denote the approach in religious education which occasioned the *Creed of the People of God*. It is simply a matter of clear communication from the scholarly point of view. Much research is needed on the relationship between the phenomenon of "Modernism" in its three historic moments, and this "False Americanism in Religion" which seems to be approaching its maturity, not least in its application to religious education, in the present period after Vatican II.

⁹ Editorial, "La tentazione del 'Nuovo Cristianesimo,'" *La Civiltà Cattolica* (March 16, 1974); pp. 524–525 and 527; English translation in *Homiletic and Pastoral Review* (March, 1976) 133–144. The *Civiltà Cattolica* is the Jesuit periodical which has been published in Rome for over a century. It has been known through the years for an editorial staff that works in close communion with the Vicar of Christ.

¹⁰ *GCD*, no. 116.

¹¹ Cf. Jean-Claude Dhotel. *Les origines du catéchisme modern*. Paris: Aubier, 1967; "Les premières catéchismes Protestants," pp. 22–27. Luther pioneered in the production of booklets for children. The Catholic Church soon followed suit, in the work of St. Peter Canisius and others. Cf. *ibid.*, pp. 66–82, "L'oeuvre catéchétique de St. Pierre Canisius." But the Council of Trent in mandating the catechism now generally known as the *Roman Catechism*, held firmly to the tradition of oral catechesis. The *Roman Catechism* is not a brief question-and-answer booklet, but a comprehensive source book for a living adult catechist, the pastor of each Catholic parish, for his use in giving oral catechetical instructions to his people and their children. The contemporary works of Hardon and Lawler, for example, stand in this tradition.

¹² *GCD*, no. 119.

¹³ George A. Kelly, *Who Should Run the Catholic Church? Social Scientists, Theologians or Bishops?* Huntington: Our Sunday Visitor, 1976; p. 167.

¹⁴ Cf. the *GCD*, nos. 72 and 73, on "Inductive and Deductive Methods" and "Formulations." Catechisms accordingly are incorporated with pedagogical expertise into the so-called "religion textbooks," when they are qualitatively excellent in both content and method, as the substance of the doctrine of the Catholic faith which is to be handed on by the teaching. In an interview Cardinal John Wright has stated: "The *Catechetical Directory* which the Holy See put out is a great success, but not in the way it was intended; that is, as a guide for bishops and teachers from which to write their own catechisms. Even parents—parents who are probably unprepared to understand the technical directory—are ordering *Directories* by the dozens to be used as actual catechisms for instruction. The need, of course, is for catechisms." Cf. *The Michigan Catholic* (January 28, 1976), p. 1. There is a readily perceptible threat of national religious disaster in what Msgr. Kelly calls "the great decline of catechisms," in a failure to uphold the proper use of this printed tool, precisely because of the relationship between the Creed and catechetical teaching. The Italian Bishops' Conference saw to the updating of their national Catechism

immediately after Vatican II. The Bishops of England did likewise with their "Penny Catechism." Similar moves, very perceptive ones, have been made by certain episcopal conferences in Latin America.

[15] Cf. Joseph de Ghellinck, S.J. *Patristique et Moyen Age*. Paris: Desclée de Brouwer, 1946; Tome I, *Les recherches sur les origines du Symbole des Apôtres*, p. 23.

Bibliography and Abbreviations

AAS — *Acta Apostolicae Sedis* (Rome: 1909 ff.)

ACW — *Ancient Christian Writers,* ed. J. Quasten and J. C. Plumpe (Westminster, Maryland: 1956 ff.).

Badcock — F. J. Badcock, *The History of the Creeds* (London: 1938, 2nd ed.).

Bless — W. Bless, S.J. (ed.) *Report über den Holländischen Katechismus: Dokumente, Berichte, Kritik* (Freiburg: 1969).

Cerfaux — Lucien Cerfaux, *Christ in the Theology of St. Paul* (New York: 1959).

Clarkson — John F. Clarkson, S.J. (and others). *The Church Teaches: Documents of the Church in English Translation.* (St. Louis: 1955).

CPG — Pope Paul VI, *The Creed of the People of God* (Washington: 1968); "Solemnis Professio Fidei," *AAS* (10 Aug. 1968) 433–445.

DS — Denziger-Schönmetzer, *Enchiridion Symbolorum* (Freiburg: 1973; 35th Edition).

Dhanis — E. Dhanis, J. Visser and H. J. Fortmann, *Las Correcciones al Catecismo Holandés* (Madrid: 1969).

Dossier — Leo Alting von Geusau and Aldo Chiaruttini (Eds.) *Il Dossier del Catechismo Olandese* (Verona: 1968).

GCD — Sacred Congregation for the Clergy, *General Catechetical Directory* (Washington: 1971).

Garrido — Julio Garrido, *Catechismo para los hombres de ciencia religiosamente subdesarrollados* (Buenos Aires: 1969).

Garrone — Cardinal Garrone, *Le Credo lu dans l'histoire* (Paris: 1974).

Garrone — Cardinal Garrone, *La profession de foi de Paul VI: Introduction* (Paris: 1969).

Hardon — John A. Hardon, S.J. *The Catholic Catechism: A Contemporary Catechism of the Teachings of the Catholic Church* (New York: 1975).

JNDK — J. N. D. Kelly, *Early Christian Creeds* (London: 1972; third edition; first edition 1950).

311

Lawler — Ronald Lawler, O.F.M. Cap., Donald W. Wuerl and Thomas Comerford Lawler (Eds.). *The Teaching of Christ: A Catholic Catechism for Adults* (Huntington, Indiana, 1976).

LTK — *Lexikon für Theologie und Kirche* (Freiburg Br.: 1957 ff).

Lubac — Lubac, Henri de, S.J. *La foi chrétienne: Essai sur la structure du Symbole des Apôtres.* (Paris: 1972).

NDC — *A New Catechism: Catholic Faith for Adults, With Supplement* (New York: 1969).

PG — J. P. Migne, *Patrologia, Series Graeca.*

PL — J. P. Migne, *Patrologia, Series Latina.*

Pozo — Candido Pozo, S.J. *El Credo del Pueblo de Dios: Comentario Teológico* (Madrid: 1968).

Ratzinger — Joseph Ratzinger, *Introduction to Christianity* (New York: 1973).

Roman Catechism — John A. McHugh, O.P., and Charles J. Callan, O.P. (transl.) *Catechism of the Council of Trent for Parish Priests* (New York: 1923).

TDNT — Gerhard Kittel-Geoffrey W. Bromiley. *Theological Dictionary of the New Testament* (Grand Rapids, Michigan: 1964 ff.; Translation of Kittel, *Theologisches Wörterbuch zum Neuen Testament.* Stuttgart: 1933 ff.).

Vatican I — John F. Broderick, S.J. (Transl.). *Documents of Vatican Council I* (Collegeville, Minnesota: 1971).

Vatican II — Austin Flannery, O.P. (General Editor). *Vatican Council II: The Conciliar and Post Conciliar Documents* (New York: 1975).

Index

CREED AND CATECHETICS

Designed by Howard N. King
Composed by York Composition Co., Inc.
in 11 point Baskerville, 3 points leaded
with display lines in Baskerville
Printed letterpress from type by York Composition Company
on Glatfelter Offset, 60 pound basis
Bound by Maple-Vail Book Group
in Columbia Book Cloth
and stamped in All Purpose foil